The Secret Rose,
Stories by W. B. Yeats:
A Variorum Edition

The Secret Rose, Stories by W. B. Yeats: A Variorum Edition

EDITED BY

PHILLIP L. MARCUS,
WARWICK GOULD, *and*
MICHAEL J. SIDNELL

CORNELL UNIVERSITY PRESS

ITHACA AND LONDON

This book has been published with the aid of a grant from the
Hull Memorial Publication Fund of Cornell University.

First published 1981 by Cornell University Press.
Published in the United Kingdom by Cornell University Press Ltd.,
Ely House, 37 Dover Street, London W1X 4HQ

International Standard Book Number 0-8014-1194-7
Library of Congress Catalog Card Number 80-25824
Printed in the United States of America
*Librarians: Library of Congress cataloging information
appears on the last page of the book.*

Preface

Until recently, the literary reputation of W. B. Yeats depended primarily upon his poetry. The past few years have seen increasing interest in and praise for the plays, but the prose fiction continues to receive only minimal attention. Of course Yeats's stature as a prose writer is justly less than as a poet or dramatist; but his work in prose is better than has generally been recognized, and his stories deserve a wider audience. Furthermore, familiarity with the prose is essential for an accurate appreciation of his career. The development of Yeats was one of his major themes. He often directed attention to his earlier life and work in the later work, and it becomes ever clearer that our understanding of Yeats is impeded if we do not know the early work in its early forms and the transformations it underwent through revision. Thus, for example, 'The Wisdom of the King' is one of his earliest explorations of the wisdom-power antinomy that appears in 'Leda and the Swan,' 'Blood and the Moon,' and other poems; and the modifications of the passage about the King's 'wisdom' would have to be considered by anyone tracing Yeats's attitudes concerning this concept. On the other hand, though 'Proud Costello' was first published in 1896, it was not until 1925 that Yeats symbolized Costello's gyring life by making his hero mount a winding stair. This Variorum Edition of a major unit of the fiction will enable the reader to follow in all its complexity the evolution of the stories included. In addition, the information it contains about the history of the collected edition of Yeats's works undertaken in the 1930's has important implications for the editing of virtually all of Yeats's published texts.

Nearly a decade ago, we began working independently on editing projects involving the stories, then decided to combine our efforts; for the final product we share the responsibility equally. In work of this kind errors are almost inevitable, and this volume probably contains them; but we have done everything possible to make the edition complete, easy to use, and worthy of the author whose name it bears.

Preface

The preparation of this edition required the help of many individuals, and it was generously given. Our foremost debt is to Senator Michael B. Yeats and Miss Anne Yeats, both for aiding our research and for granting permission to print the published and unpublished materials by W. B. Yeats included in this edition. Michael Horniman of A. P. Watt, Ltd., T. M. Farmiloe of the Macmillan Press, Ltd., and Lydia Zelaya of Macmillan Publishing Co. were particularly helpful in our dealings with their firms. Among the many librarians who patiently provided information we are particularly grateful to Nora Niland of the Sligo County Library and Museum; Lola L. Szladits of the Berg Collection, New York Public Library; P. Baker of the Sterling Library, University of London; Ann Hyde of the Kenneth Spencer Research Library at the University of Kansas; N. Hyde of the Library, Royal Holloway College; and the staffs of the British Library, the Bodleian Library, the National Library of Ireland, the Library of Trinity College, Dublin, and the Manuscript Division of the New York Public Library. The staff of Cornell University Press offered invaluable assistance in the production of a very complex volume. Other individuals who have helped us in various ways include Barry B. Adams, Fredson Bowers, David R. Clark, Michael J. Colacurcio, R. Cooper, Douglas Cowling, Alan Denson, Rache Lovat Dickson, Donald D. Eddy, Paul Epril, David Farmer, Richard J. Finneran, Ian Fletcher, Joan Grundy, George M. Harper, the late T. R. Henn, Sarah J. Jaenike, Colton Johnson, Sydney Josephs, John V. Kelleher, John Kelly, Richard Londraville, W. W. Lyman, Alexander Macmillan, the Rt. Hon. Harold Macmillan, Mrs. Thomas Mark, William McCarthy, Daniel J. Murphy, William M. Murphy, Mary O'Connor, Roger Parisious, Susanne Schaup, Felicity, Michael G., and Anne Sidnell, Jane Solomon, Robert Stacey, Jon Stallworthy, Henry Summerfield, Stephen Tifft, Peter Timmerman, and Deirdre Toomey.

Financial support for research was provided by the University of Queensland Foundation; the University of London Central Research Fund; Trinity College, the University of Cambridge; Trinity College, the University of Toronto; the Social Sciences and Humanities Research Council of Canada; and Cornell University.

The texts from *Mythologies* (1932) are published with the permission of Senator Michael B. Yeats, Miss Anne Yeats, and the Macmillan Press, Ltd.

Other previously unpublished materials by W. B. Yeats are published with the permission of Senator Michael B. Yeats, Miss Anne Yeats, and the British Library.

Unpublished correspondence from the Macmillan Archive is quoted with the permission of the Macmillan Press, Ltd., and the British Library.

Preface

'A Very Pretty Little Story' is published with the permission of Mr. Colin Smythe and the Henry W. and Albert A. Berg Collection, the New York Public Library, Astor, Lenox and Tilden Foundations.

Published writings of W. B. Yeats are quoted by permission of Senator Michael B. Yeats, Miss Anne Yeats, the Macmillan Press, Ltd., and the Macmillan Publishing Co., Inc.

P.L.M.
Ithaca, New York

W.G.
London, England

M.J.S.
Toronto, Canada

Contents

Contents

Other Texts   175

Appendixes   237

Abbreviations
and Symbols

CB   *The Chap Book*
IR   *The Independent Review*
MM   *McClure's Magazine*
NO   *The National Observer*
NR   *The New Review*
P   *The Pageant*
S   represents variously *The Sketch, The Savoy,* and *The Speaker,* depending on the story in question; full details of periodical printings are given in the first note for each story.
WS   *The Weekly Sun Literary Supplement*
1897   *The Secret Rose* (London: Lawrence & Bullen, 1897; New York: Dodd, Mead & Co., 1897; Dublin: Maunsel, reissued 1905)
1897T   *The Tables of the Law. / The Adoration of the Magi.* (London: privately printed, 1897)
1904T   *The Tables of the Law and The Adoration of the Magi* (London: Elkin Mathews, 1904)
1905   *Stories of Red Hanrahan* (Dundrum: Dun Emer Press, 1904) [actually published 1905]
1908   *The Collected Works in Verse and Prose,* vols. 5 and 7 (Stratford-on-Avon: The Shakespeare Head Press, 1908)
1913   *Stories of Red Hanrahan: The Secret Rose: Rosa Alchemica* (London and Stratford-upon-Avon: A. H. Bullen, 1913)
1914   *Stories of Red Hanrahan / The Secret Rose / Rosa Alchemica* (New York: The Macmillan Company, 1914)
1914T   *The Tables of the Law; & The Adoration of the Magi* (Stratford-upon-Avon: The Shakespeare Head Press, 1914)
1925E   *Early Poems and Stories* (London: Macmillan & Co., 1925)
1925A   *Early Poems and Stories* (New York: The Macmillan Co., 1925)
1925   Both the above editions. [Where the two editions vary identically from the basic text the variant reading is identified as '1925.']
1927   *Stories of Red Hanrahan and The Secret Rose* (London: Macmillan and Co., 1927
        See also Appendix 5 (pp. 265–71).

Introduction

The stories by W. B. Yeats presented in this edition form a distinct and coherent unit within the body of his work. As the collective title for the Variorum Edition of these stories we have chosen *The Secret Rose*. This entire unit has never before been published in a single volume, under this or any other title. Yeats used *The Secret Rose* as the title of his 1897 collection containing most of the stories, and three other stories that belong to this unit were published separately. Yeats later arranged the stories in three groups, using 'The Secret Rose' as the title for only one of the groups. The three groups had no comprehensive title, though together they correspond to the collection Yeats had originally called *The Secret Rose*. We have used the title in a way the author himself had ceased to use it because it is the only Yeatsian title that has any claim to comprehensiveness and offers a traditional and convenient way to refer to *all* the related stories.

Despite his conviction that the revision of prose never culminated in the 'click of the box' that signaled the final form of verse, Yeats revised these stories as assiduously as he did his poems. The stories were frequently republished and Yeats made full use of the opportunities for modifying his texts. The revision of the prose for stylistic, symbolic, and thematic reasons was extensive and protracted; he also grouped and regrouped the stories in various ways and even dropped some stories and added one new one. Further complications in the evolution of the unit arose from conflict with a publisher's judgment and experimental collaboration with Lady Gregory in rewriting the Red Hanrahan stories.

In *The Wild Swans at Coole* (1919 edition), Yeats reintroduced into his work some of his fictional characters of the nineties and referred, in the poem 'The Phases of the Moon,' to 'that extravagant style . . . learnt from Pater' of the stories in which these characters had earlier appeared. The reference to the Paterian style loses much of its point if the stories are remembered only in their later versions, for Yeats had been at some

Introduction

pains to subdue that Paterian extravagance through revision. The stylistic revision of the stories was one aspect of a continuing and comprehensive attempt to bring all his work to a symbolic and thematic unity. Revision of early productions was not, however, the only means by which Yeats attempted to unify his work. By 1919, he was also beginning to derive a new synthesis from the contrast between the earlier and later work and selves. The new synthesis depended on the perception of distinctions between early and late work which revision tended to blur. To appreciate these contrary aspects of Yeats's struggle for unity we need to know the early work in its early forms and the process of the revision as well as the 'final' versions (where they survive) of his texts. That is to say we must come to terms with the reality of Yeats's 'multiple texts.' This edition is designed to conform to that reality and to stimulate appreciation of the struggle for unity embodied in them.

Given the peculiar character of the texts of the stories, we have concerned ourselves only in part with Yeats's 'final intentions.' His texts have been transmitted (with few exceptions) in a way quite different from those of most modern and nearly all earlier authors. There were many printings of the stories and few over which Yeats did not exercise close supervision.[1] Each new printing was an opportunity for revision and rewriting as well as correction. New versions were built on old ones—often, quite literally, on printed copy. Since authorial revision is so extensive from printing to printing, the nonauthorial elements become scarcely discernible. Textual errors may disappear not because they are corrected but because the passages in which they occur are extensively revised for literary reasons, or even expurgated. On the other hand, an editor's punctuation or even an error may be adopted after the fact, in the context of a careful revision, and become Yeats's new intention. In this situation, the texts that were actually printed at each stage have the highest importance as the substantial embodiments of

---

[1] The evidence of Yeats's supervision of the production of most of the editions concerned is found in published and unpublished correspondence and in extant proof materials. In three instances it is difficult to be certain that Yeats exercised supervision of the texts, though even with these editions there is some indication of Yeats's involvement in publication. One of them is *Stories of Red Hanrahan: The Secret Rose: Rosa Alchemica*, published in 1913; a letter of the same year (*Letters of W. B. Yeats*, ed. Allan Wade [London: Rupert Hart-Davis, 1954], 575–77) shows Yeats concerned that Bullen should keep the various parts of the *Collected Works* available in satisfactory versions. Another of the three editions contains twelve slight variants. This is *The Tables of the Law; & The Adoration of the Magi*, which appeared in the same year, 1914, as the heavily revised *Stories of Red Hanrahan: The Secret Rose: Rosa Alchemica*. *Stories of Red Hanrahan and The Secret Rose* (1927) was planned by Yeats (in collaboration with Norah McGuinness) as a talismanic book, though in this case there is no evidence of any renewed concern for the text, which he had recently revised for *Early Poems and Stories* (1925).

Yeats's intentions of the moment and (even where they are in small particulars deficient in that respect) as the bases of subsequent versions. The chief interest of the printed texts lies in their relationship with one another, not in their bearing on Yeats's 'final' intentions; consequently this edition is designed to display *not* a 'best' text and the means (elimination of nonauthorial elements, adjudication among authorial readings, and so on) by which a 'best' text is produced—not this, but the full relationship among the texts. In this edition, all the texts printed in Yeats's lifetime can be reconstructed in their entirety from the collations, and the evolution of each story traced through successive printings.

Canon and Order of the Stories

Yeats published twenty-three stories.[2] One of these, 'Dhoya,' appeared with the short novel, 'John Sherman,' as a separate volume.[3] Two others ('Michael Clancy, the Great Dhoul and Death' and 'The Cradles of Gold') were published in periodicals in the nineties but, like 'Dhoya,' never formed part of the Secret Rose unit.[4] In the collection published as *The Secret Rose* in 1897 there were seventeen stories, in the following order:

The Binding of the Hair
The Wisdom of the King
Where there is Nothing, there is God
The Crucifixion of the Outcast
Out of the Rose
The Curse of the Fires and of the Shadows
The Heart of the Spring
Of Costello the Proud, of Oona the Daughter of Dermott and of the
    Bitter Tongue
The Book of the Great Dhoul and Hanrahan the Red
The Twisting of the Rope and Hanrahan the Red
Kathleen the Daughter of Houlihan and Hanrahan the Red
The Curse of Hanrahan the Red
The Vision of Hanrahan the Red
The Death of Hanrahan the Red
The Rose of Shadow

---

[2]This tally does not include *John Sherman,* the stories in *The Celtic Twilight, Stories of Michael Robartes and His Friends,* or the posthumously published *The Speckled Bird.*

[3]*John Sherman and Dhoya* by 'Ganconagh' was originally published, in 1891, in Unwin's Pseudonym Library. The volume has been edited by Richard J. Finneran (Detroit: Wayne State University Press, 1969).

[4]These stories appear in *Uncollected Prose by W. B. Yeats,* Vol. I, collected and edited by John P. Frayne (London: Macmillan, 1970).

Introduction

The Old Men of the Twilight
Rosa Alchemica

Also in 1897, a small volume containing two other stories, 'The Tables of the Law' and 'The Adoration of the Magi,' was published 'privately,' though with the fleuron of Lawrence and Bullen (the publishers of *The Secret Rose*) on the title page. Yeats himself must have been responsible for an unsigned note in this book informing readers that 'these stories were originally intended to follow "Rosa Alchemica" in "The Secret Rose."'[5] Yeats elaborated the note in *Early Poems and Stories* (1925), in which he declared that the two stories 'were intended to be part of "The Secret Rose", but the publisher, A. H. Bullen, took a distaste to them and asked me to leave them out, and then after the book was published liked them and put them into a little volume by themselves.'[6] Elsewhere Yeats was even more emphatic, saying Bullen 'made me leave them out.'[7] In the *Collected Works* of 1908 the two stories were reunited with 'Rosa Alchemica' but in the 1913 and 1914 editions of *The Secret Rose* they were omitted once again. In 1914, the two stories were published as a separate volume again. *Early Poems and Stories* (1925) reassociated 'The Tables of the Law' and 'The Adoration of the Magi' with 'Rosa Alchemica' as the triptych Yeats had first intended, and the *Mythologies* proofs of 1931-32 preserve this arrangement.

In 1897, then, nineteen stories constituted the unit in Yeats's intention. In 1905, the separate publication of the 'Hanrahan' stories, redone with Lady Gregory's help to bring them 'closer to the life of the people,'[8] rearranged the overall pattern of the unit. In the 1897 volume, the Hanrahan stories had not been presented as a distinct group, though they did form a connected set within the collection; from 1905, the stories of Hanrahan were treated as a group distinct from the Secret Rose stories. Moreover, 'The Book of the Great Dhoul and Hanrahan the Red,' the first story in the set as published in *The Secret Rose*, was replaced by an entirely new story, 'Red Hanrahan,' in the separately published set.

In 1908, Yeats abandoned 'The Binding of the Hair' and 'The Rose of Shadow.' 'Where there is Nothing, there is God' survived into the 1908 volume but thereafter Yeats vacillated. He revised the story extensively for the 1914 volume, omitted it from the editions of 1925 and 1927, then

---

[5] The note appears on page 4.
[6] *Early Poems and Stories* (1925), p. 528.
[7] See pp. 262-63 for the full statement from which this phrase is taken.
[8] *Early Poems and Stories* (1925), p. 528. See also Wade, *Letters*, p. 361.

restored it to the collection in 1931 when he began to prepare the *Mythologies* text.

The *Mythologies* text of 1931-32 includes seventeen stories arranged in three groups: 'The Secret Rose' (eight stories); 'Stories of Red Hanrahan' (six stories); 'Rosa Alchemica,' 'The Tables of the Law,' and 'The Adoration of the Magi.' The present edition comprises the seventeen stories that appear in *Mythologies,* and the three stories (including 'The Book of the Great Dhoul...') that were abandoned after their appearance in *The Secret Rose*—in all their printed forms. The scope of this edition, that is to say, is determined by the most inclusive possible conception of the unit.

The stories of *The Secret Rose* and *The Tables of the Law & The Adoration of the Magi* were arranged as a sequence of spiritual events through history, from the Heroic Age to the present.[9] In subsequent editions this order was altered by omission and rearrangement and its attractive thematic implications lost. The arrangement in this edition, respecting the conscious evolution of Yeats's intentions, follows that of *Mythologies.* Abandoned texts are placed in a separate section.

The Basic Texts

The basic text for most of the stories is that of the page proofs of *Mythologies,* set in 1931 for Macmillan of London, corrected by Yeats in 1932, and never published. This text differs in numerous details from the posthumous *Mythologies* published by Macmillan in 1959. For 'The Binding of the Hair' and 'The Rose of Shadow,' abandoned after their appearance in *The Secret Rose* (1897), the 1897 volume is the source of the basic text. Between the periodical and 1897 versions of the Red Hanrahan stories and the versions published in 1905 and after the differences are so great that they cannot be presented through variant readings: thus in this edition the 1897 texts of the stories are printed separately as a basic text, with variants from the periodical versions that preceded them; while the 1905 and later versions are collated against the basic text of the *Mythologies* proofs.

The Origins of the Mythologies *Text of 1931-32*

The *Mythologies* page proofs (now in the collection of Senator Michael B. Yeats) were prepared as Volume II of a projected 'Edition de Luxe' of

[9]See Phillip L. Marcus, *Yeats and the Beginning of the Irish Renaissance* (Ithaca, N.Y.: Cornell University Press, 1970), pp. 49-50.

the works of Yeats. (Proofs of other volumes are in the Macmillan Archive and the British Library.[10]) The surviving fragments of the edition and the correspondence concerning its preparation provide crucial information about Yeats's last version of the Secret Rose stories and a rationale for the choice of a basic text.

On December 23, 1920, Yeats wrote to Macmillan from Oxford: 'I don't think it likely with book producing at its present expensiveness that you are anxious to publish the six volume edition of my collected work, which you will find in our original agreement. I wonder if you might not do something short of it with profit.'[11] There follow Yeats's plans for what became in fact the uniform edition that Macmillan issued from 1922 onward. But the question of an Edition de Luxe, as the project was termed until after Yeats's death (when it was named the Coole Edition by Mrs. W. B. Yeats), remained open. Yeats's first extant reference to it after the appearance of the uniform edition of the 1920s came in a letter to Olivia Shakespear on December 27, 1930: 'Macmillan are going to bring out an *Edition de Luxe* of all my work published and unpublished. The unpublished to include *A Vision* (rewritten of course), my *Wheels and Butterflies* (a book of plays and essays almost finished) and *Byzantium* (the new book of verse). The new stories of Hanrahan and those Cuala diaries and the Sophocles versions. I am to be ready next autumn at latest. Months of rewriting. What happiness!'[12] The question of the contents was settled in London toward the end of May 1931, at a meeting between Yeats and Harold Macmillan.[13] A letter from Yeats to Sir Frederick Macmillan written on May 7, 1931, indicates that seven volumes were planned.[14]

In an undated letter of late 1930 to Sir Frederick Macmillan, Yeats added, in a postscript, 'You have the best reader for the press I have ever come across.'[15] It is quite clear that a special relationship developed between Yeats and Thomas Mark, the Macmillan editor who helped him to prepare his works for the press. Charles Morgan has given some idea of the responsibility which Yeats entrusted to Mark: 'When a complete edition was projected, his whole works were elaborately studied on his behalf, phrase by phrase and comma by comma, before being submitted

---

[10]For accounts of the Macmillan Archive, see W. E. Fredeman, 'The Significance of a Publisher's Archive: The Macmillan Papers,' in *Studies in Bibliography*, 23 (1970), 183-91; and Philip V. Blake-Hill, 'The Macmillan Archive,' *British Museum Quarterly*, 36 (Autumn 1972), 74-80.
[11]B.L. Add. MS. 55003, f. 64.
[12]*Letters*, p. 780.
[13]Letter from Michael Horniman to Warwick Gould, July 11, 1973.
[14]B.L. Add. MS. 55003, f. 121.
[15]B.L. Add. MS. 55003, f. 119.

to his personal care. The edition has been delayed by the war, but all of it was seen and revised by Yeats. He attended to every point that was raised, explaining his meaning where he thought it might have been missed, and writing: "For the first time there will be a satisfactory text of my work, thanks to your watchfulness and patience.'"[16] Morgan accurately states Yeats's interest in the work but exaggerates his carefulness. Yeats did not in fact comment upon *every* point that was raised, but his silence is usually explained by some general delegation of responsibility to Mark. And the *final* text of the entire edition was *not* seen and approved by Yeats: when published as the Uniform Edition in the 1950s and 1960s, it was seen through the press by Thomas Mark, with the advice and guidance of Mrs. Yeats.

The extent of Mark's responsibilities and Yeats's trust in him increased as work on the edition advanced. Yeats wrote to Harold Macmillan on September 8, 1932: 'I would be very much obliged if you would give the enclosed letter to the admirable scholar who is assisting in the correction of the proofs of my new collected edition. It is partly a letter of thanks and partly an explanation of certain metrical tricks of mine which have puzzled him.'[17] The 'enclosed letter' is not in the Archive, but has been quoted from by Jon Stallworthy: 'Again, as late as 1932 he wrote to his publisher: "I have never been able to punctuate properly. I do not think I have ever differed from a correction of yours in punctuation. I suggest that in the remaining volumes you do not query your own corrections."'[18] That this was the letter in question seems likely in light of a letter from Mark to Yeats, dated September 16, 1932, in which Mark refers to the 'metrical tricks' and thanks Yeats for having offered him 'a free hand with the punctuation.'[19]

The first volume of the seven was to have contained the poems;[20] the second, *Mythologies,* was to contain *The Celtic Twilight*; the 'Secret Rose' and 'Hanrahan' groups of stories, 'Rosa Alchemica,' 'The Tables of the Law,' 'The Adoration of the Magi'; and *The Irish Dramatic Movement.* The *Mythologies* proofs bear printer's date stamps of various dates between September 30, 1931, and October 26, 1931. Anxious to plan his summer's work, Yeats wrote to Harold Macmillan on May 15, 1932, asking

[16]Charles Morgan, *The House of Macmillan (1843–1943)* (London: Macmillan, 1943), p. 223.
[17]B.L. Add. MS. 55003, f. 136.
[18]Jon Stallworthy, *Between the Lines: Yeats's Poetry in the Making* (Oxford: The Clarendon Press, 1963), p. 12.
[19]*Letters to W. B. Yeats,* ed. Richard J. Finneran, George M. Harper, and William M. Murphy, 2 vols. (New York: Columbia University Press, 1977), II, 543-44.
[20]Proof materials for the volume of poems can be found in the collection of Senator Yeats and in the National Library of Ireland.

for proofs,[21] and the proofs were promised in 'about a fortnight's time.'[22] Some delays were caused by Thomas Mark's thoughful reading of the proofs and there were other interruptions; in a letter of June 3, 1932, Yeats asked the publishers to advise him separately when sending proofs, saying that the De Valera government had 'reduced our Custom House to chaos.'[23] On June 17, 1932, in reply to another impatient letter asking for proofs of the Edition de Luxe, Harold Macmillan took the opportunity to chide Yeats gently for failing to supply copy:

> Your letter reached us this morning, and I write to say that we are sending, by registered post, a complete marked set of proofs of Volume I (Poems) of the Edition de Luxe of your works, together with the printed pages and other material with which you supplied us for use as 'copy'. We expect to be able to forward Volume II on Monday.
>
> Perhaps you could let us have an idea of when you are likely to go to the United States, as we could then do our best to let you have the bulk of the proofs before you leave. No doubt you remember that we have not yet received any material for Volume VII (Discoveries), and that you are going to supply us with additional essays for Volume V. You were also thinking of substituting a new version of the opening essays in Volume IV (the second volume of Plays) for the one now in type, and if you could let me have this 'copy' we could set it up and need not trouble you with the proofs except in this revised form.[24]

The proofs for Volume II (*Mythologies*) were forwarded as promised on June 22, 1932, together with the printed copy from which they had been set up.[25]

Yeats went over the proofs himself and returned them to Harold Macmillan on July 5, 1932: 'I return the proof sheets of two volumes of the new collected edition. The volume called 'Mythologies' I need not see again. Your reader can complete the revision better than I could. I want however a "revise" of the whole of the volume of poems. It is I think the only troublesome volume owing to the fact that I have written a great deal since I sent you the typed copy.'[26] The prose volume was easier to prepare than the volume of poetry, not because the correction of prose was intrinsically less arduous, but because the volume of poetry contained so much recent work. Yeats certainly felt that the prose was

---

[21]B.L. Add. MS. 55003, f. 124.
[22]B.L. Add. MS. 55728, f. 397.
[23]B.L. Add. MS. 55003, f. 126.
[24]B.L. Add. MS. 55003, f. 128. Harold Macmillan's reply is quoted from B.L. Add. MS. 55729, ff. 477–78.
[25]B.L. Add. MS. 55729, f. 605.
[26]B.L. Add. MS. 55003, f. 129.

being given the same careful treatment as the poetry. Correction where there had not been substantive revision he could confidently trust to the conscientious and precise mind of Thomas Mark.

The next problem with the Edition de Luxe project was precipitated by Yeats himself. About the time he was correcting proofs of the third volume (the first volume of plays), he wrote to Macmillan from Riversdale to say that he was publishing 'a sheaf of lyrics' (*Words for Music Perhaps and Other Poems*) with the Cuala Press.[27] He was violating the spirit of the agreement he had entered into for the Edition de Luxe, which was to contain any new work, and was also running the risk of losing his copyright in America if he did not publish the new poems there within six months. He preferred to secure the copyright in America after publishing the new lyrics in the Edition de Luxe, and thus in effect he was asking Macmillan whether there was any chance of it appearing within six months.

Harold Macmillan's reply cast the shadow of the Depression over the immediate future of the whole edition:

> I do not think we could have any objection to this [Cuala volume] in spite of our agreement, because I am afraid we have taken a long time to produce the Edition de Luxe. The fact is that the work has taken us rather longer than we expected, and also, to be quite frank with you, conditions are so bad at the present time that I am not particularly anxious to hurry on the production, as I think it would hardly be in our interest to do so. . . .
>
> I am very glad to hear that you can let us have the rest of the contents of the seven volumes before you leave for America in October. I will look very carefully into the whole situation again and write in a week or ten days' time. My own feeling is that we ought to wait now and see whether this Autumn may bring rather better times for the world in general and the book trade in particular, with a view to announcing and subscribing the Edition de Luxe early next spring. This is only my own present idea, and circumstances might arise which might alter it.
>
> I am very much obliged to you for writing to me so frankly on the whole matter.[28]

Yeats was 'relieved' to get this reply, but his relief was due to the fact that the firm had not remonstrated with him concerning the 'spirit of the agreement'; impending delay held no advantages for him.[29] He asked on August 13, 1932, for the revise of Volume I to be sent.[30] This was soon

---

[27]B.L. Add. MS. 55003, ff. 131–32; the proofs of this volume of plays were sent on July 25, 1932 (B.L. Add. MS. 55731, f. 85).

[28]B.L. Add. MS. 55731, ff. 405–7 (August 11, 1932).

[29]B.L. Add. MS. 55003, f. 135.

[30]B.L. Add. MS. 55003, f. 135.

done, and Macmillan's note at the time read 'This revise, which is accompanied by your own marked proofs, has been checked, but will be read through carefully once more before it is passed for press.'[31] It appears that the firm hoped, even though the project was for the moment under a cloud, to finish preparatory work on Volume I quickly.

At the same time, proofs of Volume VI, *Autobiographies,* together with the copy from which it was set up, were sent to Yeats.[32] Proofs of Volume IV began to be sent on August 29, 1932,[33] but the printers could go no farther than page 288 until Yeats supplied the Introduction to *Wheels and Butterflies,* which was sent shortly afterward.[34]

Yeats had determined to leave for the United States, via England, on October 6, 1932.[35] At that time he was still working on the revise of Volume I.[36] He had considered himself done with the marked first proof of Volume II (*Mythologies*) on July 5.[37] He had in his possession proofs of Volume III and the first 288 pages of Volume IV (both volumes of plays).[38] He had promised extra material for Volume V,[39] which was to have been a volume of essays; still had the proofs of Volume VI (*Autobiographies*); and had not, as far as can be determined, submitted copy for Volume VII, which was to have been called *Discoveries,* and would perhaps have contained *Per Amica Silentia Lunae* and *A Vision* in a revised version. The project was well in hand by autumn 1932, but hopelessly behind the schedule Yeats had happily planned as 'months of re-writing' in the letter to Olivia Shakespear written December 27, 1930, when he was to have been ready 'next autumn at latest.'

From this point on, the Edition de Luxe remained in abeyance until Yeats's death in early 1939. Yet it was in 'active' abeyance, delayed but by no means abandoned. Throughout the intervening years, Yeats and Harold Macmillan corresponded about the edition, and Thomas Mark's help was frequently acknowledged. Two separate factors combined to ensure that the delay caused by 'hard times' would last until Yeats's death. In the first place, Yeats was writing much new work and wished to have it published in the usual way. Then there was a proposal that came originally from George P. Brett of Macmillan in New York, suggesting

[31]B.L. Add. MS. 55731, f. 569 (August 23, 1932). Pages 1–384 only were sent on this date.
[32]B.L. Add. MS. 55731, f. 569.
[33]B.L. Add. MS. 55732, f. 42.
[34]B.L. Add. MS. 55732, f. 122.
[35]B.L. Add. MS. 55003, f. 137.
[36]B.L. Add. MS. 55732, f. 366.
[37]B.L. Add. MS. 55003, f. 129.
[38]B.L. Add. MS. 55731, f. 85, and B.L. Add. MS. 55732, f. 42.
[39]B.L. Add. MS. 55003, f. 137.

that his firm, in collaboration with Charles Scribner's Sons, should bring out a subscription set of Yeats's work.[40]

In any event, Macmillan would have been hard pressed to sell the Edition de Luxe in the thirties. Even in 1936, when Harold Macmillan judged that the book trade had recovered from the slump, he felt that the recovery had not extended to the collectors' market at which *de luxe* editions were to be aimed.[41] Apparently Yeats and Macmillan thought that the addition of new work to the Edition de Luxe when it was ready to be published would be a simple matter of adding material to the end of each volume.[42] Yeats, writing *Dramatis Personae* and revising *A Vision,* did not seem to be worried about the outcome.

When Yeats advised Harold Macmillan of the offer from New York, proposed by Macmillan of New York and Scribner, Harold Macmillan wrote to H. Watt immediately:

> At the same time, you and he [Yeats] will realise that the publication of our edition, a great deal of which is now in type, had better be postponed until we judge that the general situation will justify the publication of another collected edition. Although I do not suppose that many of the American sets will reach this country, some of them will; and it is therefore important that we should be allowed to judge as to the moment when it may be possible to produce our edition. Since, however, we have, quite frankly, found difficulty in pursuing our edition with any vigour, in the present state of the market, I am very glad that this American proposal has come along, which will give Mr. Yeats a substantial profit and will not impede the publication of an English edition.
>
> By the way, I shall be glad if a condition can be made that we shall have a set of the American edition. It will be useful to us for many purposes.[43]

In November 1936, Macmillan again wrote to Watt, saying:

> On the whole I think it would be judicious for us to hold over our edition for the time being, as we want to make it a very fine piece of work and to see that it has the special features that makes [*sic*] so much difference to the success of such an edition. In the circumstances, if Mr. Yeats does not mind, we should prefer not to let Scribners have the sheets or corrected proofs of our own edition. For one thing, we want to put the revises of two or three of the volumes in hand, now that we have the further instructions Mr. Yeats has given on our lists, and for another, I think that the more divergence there could be between our edition and Scribners, the better it would be in

---

[40]B.L. Add. MS. 55003, f. 193 (November 18, 1935).
[41]B.L. Add. MS. 55779, ff. 151-54 (March 31, 1936).
[42]B.L. Add. MS. 55003, f. 145; B.L. Add. MS. 55743, ff. 194-95.
[43]B.L. Add. MS. 55774, ff. 153-54 (November 27, 1935).

the interests of the former. My own suggestion would be that Scribners should be told to follow the text of our two volumes of Collected Plays and Collected Poems for those works—it is, after all, the latest text in both cases—and that of our Uniform (10/6d.) Edition for the prose works; but we should not wish to oppose Mr. Yeats' own wishes in this matter. Perhaps you will kindly put these observations before him. . . .[44]

Watt agreed with these observations. Yeats eventually provided copy for the various volumes, but the project was abandoned before reaching proof.[45]

The further progress of the Edition de Luxe in the years before Yeats's death is easy to chronicle. From time to time Thomas Mark would order revises of various volumes or new copy, suggesting that the firm wanted to be ready to publish quickly when they felt the time was right. There are no letters in the Archive from Yeats to his publisher from November 11, 1937, to January 9, 1939.[46] Yeats's death at the end of January acted as a spur toward publication. A flurry of activity is evident between that date and the event which killed the edition—the outbreak of the war. Harold Macmillan wrote to Mrs. Yeats concerning the projected date and possible name for the edition: 'The edition is, as

[44]B.L. Add. MS. 55787, ff. 444-45. The lists referred to were new revised lists of contents for the Edition de Luxe, which was expanding rapidly under the pressure of Yeats's newly written work. They have not come to light. See B.L. Add. MS. 54903, f. 133 (October 23, 1936); Add. MS. 55786, f. 497; Add. MS. 54903, f. 136; Add. MS. 55787, f. 362 (November 12, 1936).

[45]B.L. Add. MS. 54903, f. 151 (November 16, 1936). On the Scribner project, see Edward Callan, *Yeats on Yeats* (Dublin: Dolmen Press, forthcoming 1981). In the library of Miss Anne Yeats are several volumes of Yeats's works annotated or corrected by Yeats or his wife. These volumes were sometimes used as copy for new editions, sometimes as author's file copies of corrected copy sent to publishers. Among these volumes are some that seem to have been used for the Scribner edition. One volume, *Essays* (London, 1924), with an inscription in Yeats's hand, has on the front cover a paper label marked 'B.' Also labeled 'B' is a copy of *Plays and Controversies* (New York, 1924). In the latter there are slight corrections in Yeats's hand; the former has many changes in Mrs. Yeats's hand, and some by Yeats. Yeats canceled the dedication to Lennox Robinson by writing a deletion sign and adding 'for Scribner.' If these volumes were involved in the preparation of the Scribner edition, then the copy of *Early Poems and Stories* (New York, 1925) with a paper label marked 'C' may well have been copy for Scribner or a corresponding file volume. There are no corrections to any prose works in the volume; in blue ink Yeats corrected one misprint in the poems and added but then canceled a direction concerning the text of 'Fergus and the Druid.' The passage in the 'Notes' dealing with the prose works in the collection has been deleted in pencil, raising the question of whether this particular book was submitted as copy for part of the volume of poems and another copy used for the Scribner volume of stories. That such is not the case is indicated by the fact that the stories themselves were not canceled and by Yeats's express desire (in a 1935 letter quoted by Callan) that Scribner should use *Collected Poems* (1933) as copy for the poems. The explanation may well be that the book Yeats used for Scribner had previously been marked for some other purpose.

[46]B.L. Add. MS. 55003, ff. 230-31.

you know, intended to be a definitive and complete edition of Mr. Yeats's works in prose and verse. We have now planned it as eleven volumes, provisionally arranged as shown on the list I enclose. We should like to publish it in September.... I think that the edition ought, if possible, to be given some appropriate name (like the Sussex Edition of Kipling's works), and I wonder if you have any ideas on that point.' The new plan called for two volumes of poems, three of plays, Volumes VI and VII for *Autobiographies*, *Mythologies* as Volume VIII, *Discoveries* (including *A Vision*) as Volume IX, and two volumes of *Essays*. Macmillan had decided to remove *The Irish Dramatic Movement* from *Mythologies* and replace it with *Per Amica Silentia Lunae*.[47]

At the same time, Thomas Mark wrote to Mrs. Yeats on more technical matters:

> There were some queries I was going to submit to Mr Yeats when I went through the revised proofs, and I should be glad to have your advice on some points if it would not be troubling you too much. The most important problem relates to some quotations from Blake.... Please let me know if you would rather let questions like this be decided here. I need scarcely say that it will give me great pleasure to do anything I can with regard to the existing volumes, the new material you have ready, and the volume that has still to be edited, as I have always taken great pride in the work that has been entrusted to me in connection with Mr. Yeats' writings.[48]

It must have been at this time that Mrs. Yeats suggested the name 'Coole Edition' for the Edition de Luxe.[49] There is no indication of whether the title originated with Yeats himself. The publishers accepted the suggestion, and a sample prospectus was sent in proof to Mrs. Yeats for her comments.[50]

Other letters from Thomas Mark to Mrs. Yeats show the extent of their roles in the preparation of the edition after the death of Yeats. In one Mark wrote:

> We have sent the printers the two corrections for the Collected Poems, and I have marked them in the proofs of The Coole Edition. I had marked

[47]B.L. Add. MS. 55820, ff. 203-5 (February 28, 1939). The list is not present, but its contents can be inferred from a contemporary prospectus prepared by Macmillan; see B.L. Add. MS. 55890, f. 1.

[48]B.L. Add. MS. 55822, ff. 342-44 (April 14, 1939). The volume still to be edited was one which Mrs. Yeats suggested could be called *Essays and Autobiographical Fragments*, and which she wanted to follow the publication of the Coole Edition at some later date; see B.L. Add. MS. 54904, f. 171 (April 17, 1939).

[49]See B.L. Add. MS. 54904, f. 171; B.L. Add. MS. 55822, f. 452 (April 19, 1939).

[50]B.L. Add. MS. 55822, f. 452; B.L. Add. MS. 55822, f. 550 (April 21, 1939).

'Pallas Athena' in the prose-works, as I thought 'Athene' might be preferable, and I meant to query it to Mr. Yeats. You will see the proofs in which it occurs, and no doubt the alteration should be made, as it has now been authorised for the poems. No alteration will be made, of course, in words and phrases that have been deliberately repeated, but I will draw your attention to anything that appears purely accidental in the prose. I shall feel much more satisfied if I can refer matters of this kind to you.[51]

In another he solicited further assistance: 'I should feel more at ease if you would let me send you my marked proofs of all the volumes before they go to press, as there are always one or two points on which I should like your advice.'[52] As time went on, Mark naturally became less sure about just what Yeats had wanted, and his uncertainty was increased by the fact, evidenced by the *Mythologies* proofs, that Yeats himself corrected proof with an eye to a particular correction in a particular context rather than to any principle of uniformity. Mark wrote to Mrs. Yeats: 'As regards the Gaelic names, I should be grateful if you would check them. I made a kind of index of them as I went along to see that they were uniform. As the aitch in Uladh and other names had been dropped in the first volume—I think Mr. Yeats took them out—they were altered in the other volumes, but it is quite simple to correct them.'[53] A few days later he wrote to her again:

Thank you for your letter of June 22nd with your comments on my notes. I will make the Gaelic spellings uniform when I have the proofs of the plays.

I am glad that you can deal with the proofs in the next three weeks, as I hope to go away myself on July 15th. Your notes and comments are being most valuable. I am sending you to-day the proofs of Volumes VIII, IX and X, 'Mythologies', 'Discoveries', and 'Essays', with the marked proofs of Volume VIII. The other two volumes were not read by Mr. Yeats.

The marked proof of the old Volume II of the Edition de Luxe was thus sent at this point, to be used by Mrs. Yeats when she was looking over proof of Volume VIII of the Coole Edition. The new proof must have been a marked set of the 'revise' of the 1931–32 proofs prepared at Mark's request after Yeats had returned them.[54] There is no evidence that Yeats had ever seen the 'revise,' and his instruction that 'The volume called "Mythologies" I need not see again' is strong evidence to the contrary.

[51]B.L. Add. MS. 55822, ff. 551–52.

[52]B.L. Add. MS. 55825, ff. 217–18 (June 12, 1939).

[53]B.L. Add. MS. 55825, ff. 532–33 (June 20, 1939).

[54]B.L. Add. MS. 55826, f. 50; Birch Grove House, 'Printers and Authors' Records, Vol. 32, f. 9. R. & R. Clark's records show that no further revises were printed. The new proofs have not been located.

The new proofs of *Mythologies* were returned by July 11, 1939,[55] but Mrs. Yeats did not return the marked first proof of *Mythologies* from 1932; so that in the 1950s, when Mark was preparing *Mythologies* for the press, he did not have Yeats's own proof comments with him; and his access to Mrs. Yeats's advice was severely restricted.

The war ended all plans for publication of the Coole Edition, despite the hopes of Macmillan. 'The Coole Edition has to wait for better times,' wrote Mark to Mrs. Yeats on October 19, 1939.[56] In the case of *Mythologies*, those times were not to come for twenty years.[57]

The Page Proofs of 1931–32

The page proofs of *Mythologies* (1931–32) consist of thirty sheets, each of sixteen pages, folded and cut. These are numbered (with the first page of each sheet given after the sheet number) B (Half title), C 17, D 33, E 49, F 65, G 81, H 97, I 113, K 129, L 145, M 161, N 177, O 193, P 209, Q 225, R 241, S 257, T 273, U 289, X 305, Y 321, Z 337, 2A 353, 2B 379, 2C 385, 2D 401, 2E 417, 2F 433, 2G 449, 2H 465.

These sheets were printed on various dates in late 1931. The first page of each sheet has the printer's stamp of R & R Clark, Ltd., usually in the bottom left-hand corner of the page. The first sheet is dated '30 Sept 1931,' the last, '26 Oct 1931.' The sheets are also stamped 'First Proof.' The pages are larger than the pages in the Uniform Edition, and although the type face is the same, and the number of lines of type on each page is the same, the whole has been set with more generous use of space between lines and between words. The texts of the Secret Rose unit are on pages 127–299.

It is clear that the Secret Rose and Hanrahan groups, 'Rosa Alchemica,' 'The Tables of the Law,' and 'The Adoration of the Magi' were set up from a printed copy of the English edition of *Early Poems and Stories* (1925). Where the English and American editions of 1925 differ, 1931 nearly always has the same reading as the English version. In one of the two exceptions, 'then' for 'them' in 'Red Hanrahan's Curse,' line 33, the printer merely corrected a typographical error in the English edition; the other, 'toward' for 'towards' in 'Proud Costello . . . ,' line 288, could have been either a slip or another intentional change by the printer. The volume *Stories of Red Hanrahan and The Secret Rose*, published in 1927, had virtually the same text as the 1925 English edition, but was an unlikely choice as copy for 1931 as it did not contain 'Rosa

---

[55]B.L. Add. MS. 55826, f. 436.
[56]B.L. Add. MS. 55830, f. 334.
[57]The treatment of the Edition de Luxe project in this edition is of necessity a brief one. A full account is currently being prepared by Warwick Gould.

Introduction

Alchemica,' 'The Tables of the Law,' and 'The Adoration of the Magi.' In three instances ('The Twisting of the Rope,' lines 195, 196, 202) in which 1927 and the English version of 1925 differ, 1931 shows the same reading as 1927; all of these involve only the placement of a comma or period inside rather than outside a final quotation mark, and provide no evidence that 1927 was being 'followed.'

The 1931 page proofs included one story, 'Where there is Nothing, there is God,' that had not been included in 1927 or in either the English or the American versions of 1925. This story was set up from either the 1908 or the 1913 volume. (See the headnote to the collation of 'Where there is Nothing, there is God.')

There is no evidence that Yeats revised the text of the stories before they were set up in page proof in 1931. The brief section 'Notes' was changed substantively because it included a comment on the poetry section of the 1925 volume; the 1931 version of 'Notes' omitted this and included instead a paragraph on *The Irish Dramatic Movement,* which was put in *Mythologies* in the 1931 proofs but replaced by *Per Amica Silentia Lunae* in the 1959 volume. However, in the texts of the stories themselves, all differences between the copy text and the uncorrected 1931 proofs are slight, and almost certainly attributable to the printer. Thus in line 71 of 'The Tables of the Law,' the diphthong of 'mediævalism' was separated, and in 'Rosa Alchemica,' line 542, a period was placed outside a final quotation mark. In at least one instance, the printer corrected a substantive error in his copy, having observed that for reasons of consistency 'Aodh' in line 131 of 'Where there is Nothing, . . .' should have been 'Olioll.'[58] On several other occasions he introduced new errors, some of them not caught in proofreading. The most serious example of this occurred in line 160 of 'The Tables of the Law,' in which the change from 'are' to 'and' distorts the syntax. In the same story, line 366, 'faint' was dropped from 'a faint voice' and never restored. When preparing copy for his 1925 collected edition, Yeats *had* subjected the stories to substantive revision; but by 1931 he was generally satisfied with them, and could leave minor problems involving accidentals and consistency to be taken care of in correcting the page proofs.

The 1931 page proofs had been read very carefully by Thomas Mark, who made many corrections and queries to Yeats in light blue ink. (Occasionally they are written over pencil, perhaps indicating that he had skimmed the proofs and noted a few points before undertaking full-scale correction.) Yeats's responses and comments are in dark blue or blue-black ink. In addition, there are throughout the proofs a consider-

[58]'Aodh' was a vestigial reading from the earliest version of the story.

able number of queries and a few unqueried changes in pencil. The half-title page of the proofs bears the note 'Marked by Sutherland,' and it may have been this (unidentified) reader who was responsible for the penciled notes. It is possible that a few of the penciled notes were also made by Mark; but, while Yeats responded to almost all of Mark's queries in ink, there are no certain responses in Yeats's hand to the queries in pencil—a fact which may indicate that the latter group, whether by Sutherland, Mark, or someone else, were added after Yeats had returned the proofs with his own responses.[59]

It is clear from Yeats's correspondence that he was satisfied with the corrected page proofs and content to leave any further changes in the hands of Mark, who could 'complete the revision better than I could.' However, when the *Mythologies* text was finally published over a quarter of a century later, in 1959, it contained many changes that Yeats had not specifically authorized, and some actually at variance with principles agreed upon between Yeats and Mark—as well as a few typographical errors. The differences between 1932 and 1959 are listed in Appendix 1. Some of them resulted from changes suggested after Yeats's death by Mrs. Yeats, others from the fact that when the idea of a collected edition was revived in the 1950s, Mark did not feel bound by the 1932 text and made some decisions different from those he and Yeats had made long before. In other words, what Mark would have sent to press as the 'final' text in the early 1930s was not what he did send in the late fifties. Yeats *had* carefully checked the 1931–32 proofs, which must thus, in their corrected state, be considered the most appropriate choice for the primary basic text for the Variorum Edition. (See also pp. 3–4.)

The Collations

Certain purely typographical features have not been treated as variants. In this edition single quotation marks are basic and double quotation marks are used for quotation-within-quotation. All readings from the printed texts are regularized to this form. Capitalization of the entire first word or the first line of a story (common in the periodical versions) is disregarded; as is the nonidentation of the first line of the opening paragraph.

Apart from the purely typographical features we have recorded all instances in which the earlier printings differ from the basic text, including apparently trivial differences of spelling and punctuation. Yeats

[59] 'The Old Men . . . ,' line 12, may be an exception, but the cancellation line is not certainly Yeats's. Mrs. Thomas Mark very kindly examined the penciled notes, but could not say conclusively that any of them had been made by her husband.

permitted others to correct spelling and punctuation for him but he was far from indifferent to the final result. The 1931–32 page proofs for *Mythologies* show that Yeats paid close attention to the suggestions made by his editor.

The following editorial conventions are used in recording the variants:

1. The lines of each story have been numbered; the lineation in this edition does not correspond to previous printings of the basic texts.

2. In addition to line numbers, contextual key-words are used to locate the variant readings in relation to the basic text. Thus, in the entry for lines 25–26 of 'The Crucifixion . . . ,'

> *had* often looked upon a cross ere now. But presently the fit passed, and he hurried on. *He* . . . NO.

the words 'had' and 'He' appear in the basic text as well as in the *National Observer* text and are the contextual key-words. The matter between these words is the variant reading appearing in the *National Observer*. The line numbers refer to the contextual key-words. Where ambiguity would otherwise be possible, more than one key-word on either side of the variant may be given.

3. Contextual key-words are used also to relate variants in punctuation to the basic text. Thus in 'The Crucifixion . . . ,' lines 38–39, the two earliest printings place a comma between 'turf' and 'that' and the variant is entered as:

> *turf, that* . . . NO, 1897.

The two contextual key-words fall in different lines in the basic text; hence the reference to lines 38 and 39.

4. In the case of variant spellings, only the variant word is entered in the collation, thus:

> *blessed* . . . NO to 1908.

Here ('The Crucifixion . . . ,' line 106), the word appears as 'Blessed' in the basic text but with the lower case initial in the printings up to and including that of 1908.

Several stories were subject to the consistent revision of spellings in one or more printings, and in these cases the variant spellings, keyed to the printings, may be listed at the beginning of the collations. Variant spellings appearing in these lists are not specifically recorded again in the line-by-line collation, though every entry reproduces the spelling actually found in it.

5. Contextual key-words are printed in italics to distinguish them from variant words, which are printed in roman type. This procedure serves also to distinguish verbal variants from those involving punctuation only (as in the contrasting examples given in 2 and 3 above). No effort has been made to differentiate by typeface between variant and nonvariant punctuation, which may be either in roman or in italic, depending upon the typeface used in the contiguous words. For variants involving only spelling, the type used is italic as for contextual key-words. An asterisk (*) following a variant printed entirely in italics indicates that the variant involves the addition of one or more words in the basic text.

6. The suspension points (. . .) preceding the abbreviated identification of the printing(s) in which the variant occurs indicate that the text now becomes identical with the basic text and continues so until the next recorded variant.

7a. In general, each entry gives all variants from a particular portion of the basic text: the less frequent form of the variant (or, in cases of equal frequency, the later form) is contained in square brackets within the more common (or earlier) form. Occasionally the resultant entry would be too complex, and separate entries are given. The combined form is illustrated in the following example:

> *leaves,* had soon a leaping blaze that cast its flickering light over the knight [cast a flicker over the face of the knight 1897] and over the piled-up heads of the wood-thieves. *Then . . .* NO, 1897.

In the *National Observer* the passage appeared as above, except the matter within square brackets; in 1897 (*The Secret Rose*), the 'cast . . . knight' section, only, was changed in the manner indicated by the reading within the square brackets. After 1897 the passage was reduced to the form in which it appears in the basic text:

> leaves, made a very good blaze. Then . . .

This example from 'Out of the Rose' (line 108) is typical of the many entries in the collations that show a passage being at first slightly, and then more extremely, revised by Yeats.

b. Where the variant of a variant is punctuational, the tilde (~) is substituted for the word preceding the variant punctuation mark, and is followed by the punctuation mark or, where the variant is absence of

Introduction

punctuation, by a caret (∧); as in 'Out of the Rose,' line 154:

> *shining* out upon the world to keep it alive, [~ ∧ NO] with a less clear *lustre* . . . NO to 1913.

In this instance, the *National Observer* printing omitted the comma after 'alive' but was in other respects identical (in this portion of the text) with all printings up to 1913. In 1914 a further slight change occurred and, not to make the single entry too complex, this further variant is added after a semicolon, so that the full entry reads:

> *shining* out upon the world to keep it alive, [~ ∧ NO] with a less clear *lustre* . . . NO to 1913; *shining* out upon the world to keep the world alive, with a less clear *lustre* . . . 1914.

In keeping with this example, the variants from a particular portion of the basic text are either compressed or arranged in chronological sequence as clarity demands and permits.

  c. Where variants are related to each other but do not begin or end at precisely the same point (in relation to the basic text) contextual words may be added to one variant in order to highlight the relationship.

  8. In the example under 7b above, 'NO to 1913' indicates that the particular variant is found in the two printings so indicated and in all the printings falling chronologically between them. All variants which occur in an unbroken sequence of three or more printings are identified in this way. A list of all printings is given at the head of the collation for each story.

  9. Word division is treated as follows:

  a. When a compound word in the basic text has appeared in a different form (i.e. as two words, hyphenated, or unhyphenated) in the earlier printings, a variant is recorded; as also are instances in which two words in the basic text have appeared hyphenated or joined in earlier printings. Thus:

> *birthplace* 1925, 1927; *birth-place* NO to 1914.

In this example ('The Crucifixion . . . ,' line 7), the variant is keyed to the basic text by repetition of the form used in the basic text; this is followed by a list of all the printings (in chronological order) which use the *same* form as the basic text; then, following a semicolon, the variant forms are given in chronological order. In the present example, 'birthplace' appears in the basic text and was first printed in 1925. The form 'birth-place' appeared first in the *National Observer* and was repeated in all printings up to and including that of 1914.

b. Where, in one or more printings, word division occurs at the end of a line a slash indicates the feature, thus (from 'The Old Men of the Twilight,' lines 23–24):

shot-gun   WS, 1897 to 1913, 1925, 1927; *shotgun*   CB; *shot- / gun*   1914.

c. Where a word is hyphenated at line-end in one or more printings and is consistently joined or consistently hyphenated within the line in all other printings and is thus (and in itself) unambiguous, no variant is recorded. (See also Appendix 2.)

d. In the following example there are variant forms of word division for which there are no corresponding forms in the basic text:

it, the Rose shone a deep blood colour in the fire-light, and, ever as he spake the *lad* ... NO; *it, the* Rose shone a deep blood-colour in the fire- / light [fire-light 1897; firelight 1914], and the *lad* ... 1897 to 1914.

These variants correspond to a part of the basic text ('Out of the Rose,' line 140) which reads simply 'it, the lad,' all reference to rose and fire having been omitted. Thus 'blood-colour' and 'fire-light' are not specifically relatable to the basic text. There is, however, a relation between the variants themselves. Unremarkably, 'blood-colour' is hyphenated in 1897 and for as long thereafter as the word was retained at all. In the *National Observer* it had been printed as two words. The word 'fire-light' has likewise no existence in the basic text but a more interesting one amongst the variant versions. The word appeared within the line and hyphenated in 1897; subsequently (in 1908) it was hyphenated at line-end and continued thus until, in 1914, it appeared as an unhyphenated word. Thereafter the word disappeared along with the passage of which it was a part. As in this example, so throughout the collations variations in word division are presented (where there is no corresponding element in the basic text) in the regular forms for the sequential or combined entries of variants.

e. Because the basic texts have been newly set for this edition, there are variations in line-end hyphenation between the 1932 and 1897 texts and the text of the Variorum. The original readings can be reconstructed as follows: if a word hyphenated at line-end in the original of the basic text does not fall at line-end in this edition, (1) it will be hyphenated and will be listed in Appendix 2 (words hyphenated at line-end in the originals of the basic texts and also hyphenated in earlier printings when they appeared within the line); or (2) it will be joined, its proper form as determined by consistency in earlier printings; or (3) it will be hyphenated in the text but printed with a slash in the collations (e.g., 'Glen- / Car') and its full history included as a variant. If a word *not* hyphenated at line-end in the original of the basic text is hyphenated at line-end in this edition, its normal form is joined. In a few instances, words hyphenated within the line in the originals of the basic texts fall at line-end in this edition; such instances are indicated by a hyphen symbol (=).

The Secret Rose:
Texts and Variants

Texts from
Mythologies (1932)

The basic text for stories in this section is that of the 1931–32 page proofs in their corrected form. Queried changes where the query mark has been canceled have been incorporated, as have changes made in ink without query. Unqueried changes in pencil have not been incorporated, as their authority is doubtful; such changes in line 24 of 'The Heart of the Spring' and line 134 of 'Proud Costello...' resulted in readings accepted as emendations for other reasons, as explained below. (Of seven other unqueried changes in pencil, three were adopted in 1959.)

On the half-title page of the proofs Thomas Mark observed to Yeats that 'S. is used for Saint in the beginning of Vol. I and elsewhere. St. is used in Vol. II' and queried 'Which form should be followed throughout this edition?' Yeats replied 'use S.' In several instances (listed in Appendix 1), the change was not actually made, and we have emended the basic text to read 'S.'

In a second note, Mark raised another general problem:

> 'He said' etc., before quoted speech, are followed by either a comma or a colon in the text of this volume. Is it worth while to aim at any uniformity in this detail, as suggested in the margins?

Yeats replied:

> I leave this to Macmillan s reader. I have accepted his suggestions ~~where eve~~ where ever he has made the correction but I am a babe in such things. ~~Bullen~~ Some printer s reader put in those colons[.]

Most but not all such colons were changed to commas. In the absence of a definite statement of preference on Yeats's part, no emendation has been made in this edition in the remaining instances. In setting the 1931 proofs, the printer erroneously used a double quotation mark instead of a single one in line 24 of 'The Heart of the Spring'; in line 134 of 'Proud Costello . . .'; and in line 68 of 'Red Hanrahan.' In each case the basic text of this edition incorporates the correct form.

At the same time, the printer introduced three substantive variations from copy that might have been errors. In 'The Crucifixion of the Outcast,' lines 156–57, the clause 'I said what I could for you' became 'I said what I could do for you.' In 'The Tables of the Law,' lines 160–61, 'and those two last, that are fire and gold, are devoted to the satirists . . .' became 'and those two last, that are fire and gold, and devoted to the satirists. . . .' In the same story, at line 366, the phrase 'a faint voice' became 'a voice.' None of these was corrected, though in the case of the first the 'other' reader queried the deletion of 'do' and the correction was actually made in the 1959 text. The reading 'and devoted' is particularly likely to have been an error, as it destroys the parallelism of construction maintained through all the other parts of the sentence. Apparently Yeats noticed none of these problems and if it was Mark who deleted 'do' he did so only after the 1931–32 proofs had been abandoned. To emend now would be to take the same sort of liberty as Mark and Mrs. Yeats did after Yeats himself was dead, and thus in effect to sanction the posthumous 1959 text. Consequently the 1931–32 readings are retained.

A complete list of variants between the copy text and the text of *Mythologies* (1959) is given in Appendix 1.

THE SECRET ROSE

(1897)

'As for living, our servants will do that for us.'—VILLIERS DE L'ISLE
ADAM
'Helen, when she looked in her mirror, and saw there the wrinkles of old
age, wept, and wondered that she had twice been carried away.'—A quota-
5   tion from Ovid in one of LEONARDO DA VINCI'S note-books

To the Secret Rose

Far-off, most secret, and inviolate Rose,
Enfold me in my hour of hours; where those

Section title. Printings: 1908; 1913; 1914; 1925; 1927.
Text from 1932.
[date lacking: 1908 to 1927]
Epigraphs. Printings: 1897; 1908; 1913; 1914; 1925; 1927.
Text from 1932.
[In all texts prior to 1932, the quotations are in roman, the sources in italics; the quotations
are not set off by quotation marks; there are periods following the sources.]
1   us. *Villiers* . . . 1897.
1–2   *l'Isle Adam.* 1897; *L'Isle Adam.* 1908 to 1927.
3   *mirror,* seeing *the* . . . 1897 to 1914.
3–4   *the* withered wrinkles made in her face by old *age* . . . 1897 to 1914.
4   *wondered* why *she* . . . 1897 to 1914.
4–5   *away. Leonardo* . . . 1897; *away.—Leonardo* . . . 1908, 1913; *away.—From*
Leonardo . . . 1914 to 1927.*
5   *Vinci.* 1897 to 1913; *Vinci's note books.* 1914 to 1927.*
5   *note-books; note books* 1914 to 1927.

To the Secret Rose. Printings [in editions of the stories]: 1897; 1908; 1913; 1914; 1925;
1927; 1932.
Text from 1932.
[For collation of this poem, see *The Variorum Edition of the Poems of W. B. Yeats*, ed. Peter Allt
and Russell K. Alspach (1957; rpt. New York: Macmillan, 1973), pp. 169–70.]

Who sought thee in the Holy Sepulchre,
Or in the wine-vat, dwell beyond the stir
5 *And tumult of defeated dreams; and deep*
Among pale eyelids, heavy with the sleep
Men have named beauty. Thy great leaves enfold
The ancient beards, the helms of ruby and gold
Of the crowned Magi; and the king whose eyes
10 *Saw the Pierced Hands and Rood of elder rise*
In Druid vapour and make the torches dim;
Till vain frenzy awoke and he died; and him
Who met Fand walking among flaming dew
By a grey shore where the wind never blew,
15 *And lost the world and Emer for a kiss;*
And him who drove the Gods out of their liss
And till a hundred morns had flowered red
Feasted, and wept the barrows of his dead;
And the proud dreaming king who flung the crown
20 *And sorrow away, and calling bard and clown*
Dwelt among wine-stained wanderers in deep woods;
And him who sold tillage, and house, and goods,
And sought through lands and islands numberless years,
Until he found, with laughter and with tears,
25 *A woman of so shining loveliness*
That men threshed corn at midnight by a tress,
A little stolen tress. I, too, await
The hour of thy great wind of love and hate.
When shall the stars be blown about the sky,
30 *Like the sparks blown out of a smithy, and die?*
Surely thine hour has come, thy great wind blows,
Far-off, most secret, and inviolate Rose?

THE CRUCIFIXION OF THE OUTCAST

A man, with thin brown hair and a pale face, half ran, half walked, along the road that wound from the south to the town of Sligo. Many called him Cumhal, the son of Cormac, and many

Printings: *The National Observer,* March 24, 1894; 1897; 1908; 1913; 1914; 1925; 1927.
Text from 1932.
Title: A CRUCIFIXION NO; ... OUTCAST. 1913.
2–4 *south* out the town of Sligech. Lua Ech Ella was his name, *and he was* ... NO.
2–3 *to the Town of* the Shelly River. *Many* ... 1897.

called him the Swift Wild Horse; and he was a gleeman, and he
wore a short parti-coloured doublet, and had pointed shoes, and a
bulging wallet. Also he was of the blood of the Ernaans, and his
birthplace was the Field of Gold; but his eating and sleeping places
were in the five kingdoms of Eri, and his abiding place was not
upon the ridge of the earth. His eyes strayed from the tower of
what was later the Abbey of the White Friars to a row of crosses
which stood out against the sky upon a hill a little to the eastward of
the town, and he clenched his fist, and shook it at the crosses. He
knew they were not empty, for the birds were fluttering about
them; and he thought how, as like as not, just such another vagabond as himself had been mounted on one of them; and he muttered: 'If it were hanging or bow-stringing, or stoning or behead-
ing, it would be bad enough. But to have the birds pecking your
eyes and the wolves eating your feet! I would that the red wind of
the Druids had withered in his cradle the soldier of Dathi, who
brought the tree of death out of barbarous lands, or that the lightning, when it smote Dathi at the foot of the mountain, had smitten
him also, or that his grave had been dug by the green-haired and
green-toothed merrows deep at the roots of the deep sea.'

While he spoke, he shivered from head to foot, and the sweat
came out upon his face, and he knew not why, for he had looked
upon many crosses. He passed over two hills and under the
battlemented gate, and then round by a left-hand way to the door
of the Abbey. It was studded with great nails, and when he knocked

---

4 *Swift, Wild* ... 1897 to 1927.
4–6 *gleeman,* as was denoted by his short particoloured doublet, his pointed shoes, his *bulging* ... NO.
6 *of Ernaans* ... NO.*
7 *birthplace* 1925, 1927; *birth-place* NO to 1914.
7 *was* Gort-an-oir; *but* ... NO.
7 *eating and sleeping places* 1897 to 1927; *eating- and sleeping- / places* NO.
7–8 *places were in* [*places* where *in* 1913] *the* four provinces *of* ... NO to 1914.
9–10 *from the* Abbey tower of the White Friars and the town battlements *to* ... NO to 1914.
14 *how, like as not* ... NO.*
14–15 *another* a *vagabond* ... NO.
15 *himself* was hanged *on* ... NO to 1914.
15–16 *them.* ¶ *'If* ... NO.*
15–16 *muttered; 'If* ... 1897.
16 *bow-stringing* 1925A, 1927; *bowstringing* NO, 1908 to 1914; *bow- / stringing* 1897, 1925E.
17 *enough,'* he muttered. *'But* ... NO.
23–24 *sea. 'While* ... NO.
24 *he* spake, *he* ... NO.
25–26 *had* often looked upon a cross ere now. But presently the fit passed, and he hurried on. *He* ... NO.

30   at it he roused the lay brother who was the porter, and of him he
asked a place in the guest-house. Then the lay brother took a glowing turf on a shovel, and led the way to a big and naked outhouse
strewn with very dirty rushes; and lighted a rush-candle fixed between two of the stones of the wall, and set the glowing turf upon
the hearth and gave him two unlighted sods and a wisp of straw,
35   and showed him a blanket hanging from a nail, and a shelf with a
loaf of bread and a jug of water, and a tub in a far corner. Then the
lay brother left him and went back to his place by the door. And
Cumhal the son of Cormac began to blow upon the glowing turf
that he might light the two sods and the wisp of straw; but the sods
40   and the straw would not light, for they were damp. So he took off
his pointed shoes, and drew the tub out of the corner with the
thought of washing the dust of the highway from his feet; but the
water was so dirty that he could not see the bottom. He was very
hungry, for he had not eaten all that day, so he did not waste much
45   anger upon the tub, but took up the black loaf, and bit into it, and
then spat out the bite, for the bread was hard and mouldy. Still he
did not give way to his anger, for he had not drunken these many
hours; having a hope of heath beer or wine at his day's end, he had
left the brooks untasted, to make his supper the more delightful.
50   Now he put the jug to his lips, but he flung it from him straightway,
for the water was bitter and ill-smelling. Then he gave the jug a
kick, so that it broke against the opposite wall, and he took down
the blanket to wrap it about him for the night. But no sooner did he
touch it than it was alive with skipping fleas. At this, beside himself
55   with anger, he rushed to the door of the guest-house, but the lay
brother, being well accustomed to such outcries, had locked it on

---

29   *it, he roused* . . . NO to 1914.
30   *guest-house. So the* . . . NO.
31   *big, naked* . . . NO.*
32   *and* when he had *lighted* . . . NO.
33   *wall, he set* . . . NO.
34   *hearth,* gave the man *two* . . . NO.
35   *nail, a shelf* . . . NO.*
36   *tub, in* . . . NO.
36–38   *Then* he left the man, and returned to his watch. And Lua Ech Ella *began* . . . NO.
38–39   *turf, that* . . . NO, 1897.
39–40   *but* his blowing profited him nothing, for the sods and the straw *were* . . . NO, 1897.
44   *day; so* . . . NO to 1914.
47   *his* wrath, *for* . . . NO, 1897.
48   *hours: having* . . . NO.
49   *untasted to* . . . NO.
54   *it than it* seemed *alive* . . . NO.
55   *to the* guest-house door, *but* . . . NO.
56   *such* outbursts, *had* . . . NO.

8

the outside; so he emptied the tub and began to beat the door with it, till the lay brother came to the door and asked what ailed him, and why he woke him out of sleep. 'What ails me!' shouted Cumhal;
60 'are not the sods as wet as the sands of the Three Rosses? and are not the fleas in the blanket as many as the waves of the sea and as lively? and is not the bread as hard as the heart of a lay brother who has fogotten God? and is not the water in the jug as bitter and as ill-smelling as his soul? and is not the foot-water the colour that
65 shall be upon him when he has been charred in the Undying Fires?' The lay brother saw that the lock was fast, and went back to his niche, for he was too sleepy to talk with comfort. And Cumhal went on beating at the door, and presently he heard the lay brother's foot once more, and cried out at him, 'O cowardly and tyrannous
70 race of monks, persecutors of the bard and the gleeman, haters of life and joy! O race that does not draw the sword and tell the truth! O race that melts the bones of the people with cowardice and with deceit!'

'Gleeman,' said the lay brother, 'I also make rhymes; I make
75 many while I sit in my niche by the door, and I sorrow to hear the bards railing upon the monks. Brother, I would sleep, and therefore I make known to you that it is the head of the monastery, our gracious abbot, who orders all things concerning the lodging of travellers.'
80 'You may sleep,' said Cumhal. 'I will sing a bard's curse on the abbot.' And he set the tub upside down under the window, and stood upon it, and began to sing in a very loud voice. The singing

---

57   *so* the man *emptied . . .* NO; *so* Cumhal *emptied . . .* 1897.
58   *it: till . . .* NO.
58   *door, and . . .* NO, 1897.
58   *asked* the man *what . . .* NO.
59–60   *shouted* Ech Ella, *'are not . . .* NO.
59–60   *Cumhal, 'are not . . .* 1897 to 1914.
60   *of* Rosses? *and . . .* NO.
60   *Three* Headlands? *and . . .* 1897.
64   *foot-water* 1897 to 1927; *foot water* NO.
67   *And* Ech Ella *went . . .* NO.
69   *foot,* and once more, *'O . . .* NO.
70   *of* friars,' he cried out at him, *'persecutors . . .* NO; *of* friars, *persecutors . . .* 1897 to 1914.
71   *that* doth *not . . .* NO.
72   *that* melteth *the bones . . .* NO.
76   *the* friars. *Brother . . .* NO to 1914.
77   *of* this *monastery . . .* NO.
78   *gracious* Coarb, *who . . .* NO, 1897.
80   *said* Ech Ella, *'I . . .* NO.
80   *Cumhal, 'I . . .* 1897 to 1927.
80–81   *curse* upon the Coarb.' *And . . .* NO.
80–81   *the* Coarb.' *And . . .* 1897.

awoke the abbot, so that he sat up in bed and blew a silver whistle
until the lay brother came to him. 'I cannot get a wink of sleep with
85 that noise,' said the abbot. 'What is happening?'

'It is a gleeman,' said the lay brother, 'who complains of the sods,
of the bread, of the water in the jug, of the foot-water, and of the
blanket. And now he is singing a bard's curse upon you, O brother
abbot, and upon your father and your mother, and your
90 grandfather and your grandmother, and upon all your relations.'

'Is he cursing in rhyme?'

'He is cursing in rhyme, and with two assonances in every line of
his curse.'

The abbot pulled his night-cap off and crumpled it in his hands,
95 and the circular grey patch of hair in the middle of his bald head
looked like the cairn upon Knocknarea, for in Connaught they had
not yet abandoned the ancient tonsure. 'Unless we do somewhat,'
he said, 'he will teach his curses to the children in the street, and the
girls spinning at the doors, and to the robbers upon Ben Bulben.'
100 'Shall I go, then,' said the other, 'and give him dry sods, a fresh
loaf, clean water in a jug, clean foot-water, and a new blanket, and
make him swear by the blessed S. Benignus, and by the sun and
moon, that no bond be lacking, not to tell his rhymes to the children in the street, and the girls spinning at the doors, and the
105 robbers upon Ben Bulben?'

'Neither our Blessed Patron nor the sun and moon would avail at
all,' said the abbot; 'for to-morrow or the next day the mood to
curse would come upon him, or a pride in those rhymes would

---

83   *the* Coarb, *so* . . . NO, 1897.
85   *the* Coarb. '*What* . . . NO, 1897.
87   *foot-water* 1897 to 1927; *foot water* NO.
88–89   *brother* Coarb, *and upon* . . . NO, 1897.
94   *The* Coarb *pulled* . . . NO, 1897.
95   *circular* brown *patch* . . . NO to 1914.
96   *like* an island in the midst of a pond, *for* . . . NO to 1914.
97   *tonsure* for the style then coming into use. 'If we [use. 'Unless we 1914] do not
somewhat . . . NO to 1914.
98   *and* to *the* . . . NO.
99–100   *robbers* on *Ben Bulben?'* ¶'*Shall* . . . NO; *robbers* on the mountain of Gulben.'
¶'*Shall* . . . 1897.
100   *go then* . . . NO, 1897.
102   *St.* . . . NO, 1897; *Saint* . . . 1908 to 1927.
104   *spinning* in *the doors* . . . NO.
105–6   *robbers* on *Ben Bulben?'* ¶'*Neither* . . . NO; *robbers* on the mountain of Gulben?'
¶'*Neither* . . . 1897.
106   *blessed* . . . NO to 1908.
106   *and the* moon . . . NO, 1897.
107   *the* Coarb: '*for* . . . NO, 1897.

move him, and he would teach his lines to the children, and the
110 girls, and the robbers. Or else he would tell another of his craft how
he fared in the guest-house, and he in his turn would begin to
curse, and my name would wither. For learn there is no steadfast-
ness of purpose upon the roads, but only under roofs and between
four walls. Therefore I bid you go and awaken Brother Kevin,
115 Brother Dove, Brother Little Wolf, Brother Bald Patrick, Brother
Bald Brandon, Brother James, and Brother Peter. And they shall
take the man, and bind him with ropes, and dip him in the river
that he shall cease to sing. And in the morning, lest this but make
him curse the louder, we will crucify him.'
120 'The crosses are all full,' said the lay brother.
'Then we must make another cross. If we do not make an end of
him another will, for who can eat and sleep in peace while men like
him are going about the world? We would stand shamed indeed
before blessed S. Benignus, and sour would be his face when he
125 comes to judge us at the Last Day, were we to spare an enemy of his
when we had him under our thumb! Brother, there is not one of
these bards and gleemen who has not scattered his bastards
through the five kingdoms, and if they slit a purse or a throat, and
it is always one or the other, it never comes into their heads to
130 confess and do penance. Can you name one that is not heathen in
his heart, always longing after the Son of Lir, and Aengus, and
Bridget, and the Dagda, and Dana the Mother, and all the false
gods of the old days; always making poems in praise of those kings
and queens of the demons, Finvaragh, whose home is under

---

113 *the* rounds, *but* . . . NO.
113 *only roofs, and* . . . NO.*
113 *roofs, and* . . . 1897, 1908.
114-16 *Brother* Gilla Kevin, Brother Gilla Collum, Brother Maol Patrick, Brother Maol
Brandon . . . NO.
116 *James and* . . . NO to 1914.
118 *he* may *cease* . . . NO to 1908.
123-24 *world? Ill should we stand before* . . . NO to 1914.
124 *St.* . . . NO, 1897; *Saint* . . . 1908 to 1927.
126-30 *Brother, the bards and the gleemen are an evil race, ever cursing and ever stirring*
up the people, and immoral and immoderate in all things, and *heathen* . . . NO to 1914.
130-31 *in their hearts, ever longing* . . . NO.
130-31 *in their hearts, always* . . . 1897 to 1914.
131-32 *after M'Lir and Angus and Brigit and Dean Ceact and Danaan the Mother* . . . NO.
131 *Angus* . . . 1897.
133 *days; ever making* . . . NO.
134-36 *demons,* Finvana of Knockmar, and Ard-Roe of Mullin-a- / Shee, and Clena of Ton
Clena, and Eiveen of Craglea, *and him* . . . NO.
134-36 *demons,* Finvaragh of the Hill in the Plain, and Red Aodh of the Hill of the Shee,
and Cleena of the Wave, and Eiveen *of the Grey* . . . 1897.

135 Cruachmaa, and Red Aodh of Cnocna-Sidhe, and Cleena of the
Wave, and Aoibhell of the Grey Rock, and him they call Donn of
the Vats of the Sea; and railing against God and Christ and the
blessed Saints.' While he was speaking he crossed himself, and
when he had finished he drew the night-cap over his ears to shut
140 out the noise, and closed his eyes and composed himself to sleep.
   The lay brother found Brother Kevin, Brother Dove, Brother
Little Wolf, Brother Bald Patrick, Brother Bald Brandon, Brother
James, and Brother Peter sitting up in bed, and he made them get
up. Then they bound Cumhal, and they dragged him to the river,
145 and they dipped him in it at the place which was afterwards called
Buckley's Ford.
   'Gleeman,' said the lay brother, as they led him back to the
guest-house, 'why do you ever use the wit which God has given you
to make blasphemous and immoral tales and verses? For such is the
150 way of your craft. I have, indeed, many such tales and verses
wellnigh by rote, and so I know that I speak true! And why do you
praise with rhyme those demons, Finvaragh, Red Aodh, Cleena,
Aoibhell and Donn? I, too, am a man of great wit and learning, but
I ever glorify our gracious abbot, and Benignus our Patron, and
155 the princes of the province. My soul is decent and orderly, but
yours is like the wind among the salley gardens. I said what I could
do for you, being also a man of many thoughts, but who could help
such a one as you?'
   'Friend,' answered the gleeman, 'my soul is indeed like the wind,
160 and it blows me to and fro, and up and down, and puts many things

---

135 *Cnocna-Sidhe* 1914, 1927; *Cnoc- / na-Sidhe* 1908, 1913; *Cnocna- / Sidhe* 1925.
136 *Don* . . . NO, 1897.
138 *Saints.' ¶While* . . . NO.
138 *speaking he* still signed *himself* . . . NO.
139 *night-cap* 1914, 1927; *nightcap* NO to 1913; *night- / cap* 1925.
139 *ears, to* . . . NO to 1914.
140 *eyes, and* . . . NO to 1914.
140–43 *sleep.* As for the lay brother, he found the friars denoted *sitting* . . . NO.
143 *James and Brother* . . . 1897 to 1914.
144 *up. So then* . . . NO.
144 *bound* Ech Ella, *and* . . . NO.
151 *wellnigh* 1925, 1927; *well nigh* NO to 1914.
152–53 *demons,* Finvana, Ard-Roe, Clena and Eiveen *and Don?* . . . NO.
152–53 *Cleena,* Eiveen *and Don?* . . . 1897.
154 *gracious* Coarb, *and Benignus* . . . NO, 1897.
156–57 *could for* . . . NO to 1925.*
158–59 *you?' ¶'My soul, friend,' answered* . . . NO, 1897.
159 *gleeman, 'is* . . . NO, 1897.*
160 *fro, up* . . . NO.*

into my mind and out of my mind, and therefore am I called the Swift Wild Horse.' And he spoke no more that night, for his teeth were chattering with the cold.

165 The abbot and the monks came to him in the morning, and bade him get ready to be crucified, and led him out of the guest-house. And while he still stood upon the step a flock of great grass=barnacles passed high above him with clanking cries. He lifted his arms to them and said, 'O great grass-barnacles, tarry a little, and mayhap my soul will travel with you to the waste places of the shore 170 and to the ungovernable sea!' At the gate a crowd of beggars gathered about them, being come there to beg from any traveller or pilgrim who might have spent the night in the guest-house. The abbot and the monks led the gleeman to a place in the woods at some distance, where many straight young trees were growing, and 175 they made him cut one down and fashion it to the right length, while the beggars stood round them in a ring, talking and gesticulating. The abbot then bade him cut off another and shorter piece of wood, and nail it upon the first. So there was his cross for him; and they put it upon his shoulder, for his crucifixion was to be 180 on the top of the hill where the others were. A half-mile on the way he asked them to stop and see him juggle for them; for he knew, he said, all the tricks of Aengus the Subtle-hearted. The old monks were for pressing on, but the young monks would see him: so he did many wonders for them, even to the drawing of live frogs out 185 of his ears. But after a while they turned on him, and said his tricks were dull and a little unholy, and set the cross on his shoulders

---

161–62   *called* Lua Ech Ella, *the swift, wild horse.' And* ... NO.
162   *Swift, Wild* ... 1897 to 1927.
163–64   *cold.* ¶So the Coarb [*cold.* ¶*The* Coarb 1897] and the friars *came* ... NO, 1897.
164   *the* friars *came* ... 1908 to 1914.
168   *said 'O* ... NO.
168   *great* grass-barnacle, *tarry* ... NO.
170   *and the ungovernable* ... NO.*
170–73   *beggars,* who had come to beg from any traveller or pilgrim who might have spent the night in the guest- / house, gathered about them. So the Coarb and the friars *led* ... NO.
172–73   *The* Coarb and the friars *led* ... 1897.
173   *the* friars *led* ... 1908 to 1914.
177   *The* Coarb *then* ... NO, 1897.
181   *for them: for* ... NO, 1897.
182   *Angus* ... NO, 1897.
182   *Subtle-Hearted* ... NO, 1897.
182   *old* friars *were* ... NO to 1914.
183   *young* friars wanted *to see* ... NO.
183   *young* friars *would* ... 1897 to 1914.
186   *a* shade *unholy* ... NO to 1914.

again. Another half-mile on the way and he asked them to stop and
hear him jest for them, for he knew, he said, all the jests of Conan
the Bald, upon whose back a sheep's wool grew. And the young
190 monks, when they had heard his merry tales, again bade him take
up his cross, for it ill became them to listen to such follies. Another
half-mile on the way, he asked them to stop and hear him sing the
story of White-breasted Deirdre, and how she endured many sorrows, and how the sons of Usna died to serve her. And the young
195 monks were mad to hear him, but when he had ended they grew
angry, and beat him for waking forgotten longings in their hearts.
So they set the cross upon his back and hurried him to the hill.

When he was come to the top, they took the cross from him, and
began to dig a hole for it to stand in, while the beggars gathered
200 round, and talked among themselves. 'I ask a favour before I die,'
says Cumhal.

'We will grant you no more delays,' says the abbot.

'I ask no more delays, for I have drawn the sword, and told the
truth, and lived my dream, and am content.'
205 'Would you, then, confess?'

'By sun and moon, not I; I ask but to be let eat the food I carry in
my wallet. I carry food in my wallet whenever I go upon a journey,
but I do not taste of it unless I am wellnigh starved. I have not eaten
now these two days.'
210 'You may eat, then,' says the abbot, and he turned to help the
monks dig the hole.

---

187 *half-mile, and he . . .* NO.*
187 *way, and he . . .* 1897 to 1914.
189-90 *young* friars, *when . . .* NO to 1914.
192 *half-mile,* and again *he . . .* NO.
193 *White-Breasted . . .* NO, 1897.
194-95 *young* friars *were . . .* NO to 1914.
195 *ended, they . . .* NO, 1897.
197 *back, and . . .* NO to 1908.
199 *hole* to stand it *in . . .* NO to 1914.
200 *themselves. I ask . . .* NO.
201-2 *says* Ech Ella. ¶*'We . . .* NO.
202-3 *the* Coarb. ¶*'I ask . . .* NO, 1897.
204 *my* vision, *and . . .* NO to 1914.
205 *you then confess . . .* NO, 1897.
206 *I! I ask . . .* NO.
207 *carry* some *whenever . . .* NO.
208 *but* never touch it until upon the point of starvation. *I have . . .* NO.
208 *wellnigh* 1925, 1927; *well-nigh* 1897, 1914; *well- / nigh* 1908, 1913.
210 *the* Coarb, *and . . .* NO, 1897.
210-11 *help the* friars *dig . . .* NO to 1914.

The gleeman took a loaf and some strips of cold fried bacon out of his wallet and laid them upon the ground. 'I will give a tithe to the poor,' says he, and he cut a tenth part from the loaf and the
215 bacon. 'Who among you is the poorest?' And thereupon was a great clamour, for the beggars began the history of their sorrows and their poverty, and their yellow faces swayed like Gara Lough when the floods have filled it with water from the bogs.

He listened for a little, and, says he, 'I am myself the poorest, for
220 I have travelled the bare road, and by the edges of the sea; and the tattered doublet of parti-coloured cloth upon my back and the torn pointed shoes upon my feet have ever irked me, because of the towered city full of noble raiment which was in my heart. And I have been the more alone upon the roads and by the sea because I
225 heard in my heart the rustling of the rose-bordered dress of her who is more subtle than Aengus the Subtle-hearted, and more full of the beauty of laughter than Conan the Bald, and more full of the wisdom of tears than White-breasted Deirdre, and more lovely than a bursting dawn to them that are lost in the darkness. There-
230 fore, I award the tithe to myself; but yet, because I am done with all things, I give it unto you.'

So he flung the bread and the strips of bacon among the beggars, and they fought with many cries until the last scrap was eaten. But meanwhile the monks nailed the gleeman to his cross, and set it
235 upright in the hole, and shovelled the earth into the hole, and trampled it level and hard. So then they went away, but the beggars stayed on, sitting round the cross. But when the sun was sinking, they also got up to go, for the air was getting chilly. And as soon as they had gone a little way, the wolves, who had been showing them-
240 selves on the edge of a neighbouring coppice, came nearer, and the

---

217 *poverty,* their yellow faces swaying about in their excitement *like* ... NO.
217 *like* the Garovogue *when* ... NO; *like* the Shelly River *when* ... 1897.
220 *by the* glittering footsteps *of* ... NO, 1897.
221 *parti- / coloured; particoloured* NO to 1913; *parti-coloured* 1914 to 1927.
224 *sea, because* ... NO, 1897.
225 *rose- / bordered* 1927; *rose-bordered* NO to 1925.
226 *Angus, the* ... NO, 1897; *Aengus, the* ... 1908 to 1914.
226 *Subtle-Hearted* ... NO, 1897.
228 *White-Breasted* ... NO, 1897.
228 *Deidre* ... NO.
230 [In NO, the comma after 'yet' is erroneously printed above the line.]
234 *the* friars *nailed* ... NO to 1914.
235 *earth* in at the foot, *and* ... NO to 1914.
236-37 *beggars* stared *on* ... NO to 1913.

birds wheeled closer and closer. 'Stay, outcasts, yet a little while,' the crucified one called in a weak voice to the beggars, 'and keep the beasts and the birds from me.' But the beggars were angry because he had called them outcasts, so they threw stones and mud at him,
245 and one that had a child held it up before his eyes and said that he was its father, and cursed him, and thereupon they left him. Then the wolves gathered at the foot of the cross, and the birds flew lower and lower. And presently the birds lighted all at once upon his head and arms and shoulders, and began to peck at him, and
250 the wolves began to eat his feet. 'Outcasts,' he moaned, 'have you all turned against the outcast?'

OUT OF THE ROSE

One winter evening an old knight in rusted chain-armour rode slowly along the woody southern slope of Ben Bulben, watching the sun go down in crimson clouds over the sea. His horse was tired, as after a long journey, and he had upon his helmet the crest of no
5 neighbouring lord or king, but a small rose made of rubies that glimmered every moment to a deeper crimson. His white hair fell in thin curls upon his shoulders, and its disorder added to the

---

241   *wheeled* close and closer yet. '*Stay* . . . NO.
244-46   *him, and* went their way. *Then* . . . NO to 1914.
250-51   *you* also *turned* . . . NO to 1914.
[In NO, the story is signed W. B. Yeats., and is followed by a note in brackets: '*Note.*—This story was suggested by the opening incidents of the eleventh century poem, *The Vision of Maconglinne.*']

Printings: *The National Observer,* May 27, 1893; 1897; 1908; 1913; 1914; 1925; 1927. Text from 1932.
Title: . . . ROSE. 1913.
1   chain- / armour 1927; chain armour NO; chain-armour 1897 to 1925.
2   *of* the mountain of Gulben, *watching* . . . 1897.
3   *sun* set *in* . . . NO.
3   *clouds* upon the western *sea* . . . NO.
3-6   *sea.* A small rose, made of rubies, was set on the curved top of his helmet, and glowed in the level rays. He kept no watch upon the woods, so often a hiding-place for the native soldiers, perhaps because he was aware of the truce between De Courcey and Fitzgerald—it was late . . . late . . . in the fourteenth century—though this seemed scarce likely, for he bore the arms of no neighbouring lord or prince, and his horse was tired, as with a long journeying. *His* . . . NO [The suspension points in 'late . . . late . . .' are in Yeats's text.].
4   *helmet, the* . . . 1897.
7   *and* seemed by *its* . . . NO.
7   *disorder* to add *to* . . . NO.
7-8   *the* inexplicable *melancholy* . . . NO.

16

melancholy of his face, which was the face of one of those who have
come but seldom into the world, and always for its trouble, the
10 dreamers who must do what they dream, the doers who must
dream what they do.

After gazing a while towards the sun, he let the reins fall upon
the neck of his horse, and, stretching out both arms towards the
west, he said, 'O Divine Rose of Intellectual Flame, let the gates of
15 thy peace be opened to me at last!' And suddenly a loud squealing
began in the woods some hundreds of yards farther up the
mountain-side. He stopped his horse to listen, and heard behind
him a sound of feet and of voices. 'They are beating them to make
them go into the narrow path by the gorge,' said some one, and in
20 another moment a dozen peasants armed with short spears had
come up with the knight, and stood a little apart from him, their
blue caps in their hands.

'Where do you go with the spears?' he asked; and one who
seemed the leader answered: 'A troop of wood-thieves came down
25 from the hills a while ago and carried off the pigs belonging to an
old man who lives by Glen-Car Lough, and we turned out to go
after them. Now that we know they are four times more than we
are, we follow to find the way they have taken; and will presently

---

8-9 *his* finely-cut face and dreaming eyes. He seemed to be that strange being who
appears *but* ... NO.
9 *seldom* in *the world* ... NO.
9-12 *and,* when he does, binds the hearts of men with his look of mystery—doer and
dreamer in one. ¶*After* ... NO.
9 *trouble,* and to bind the hearts of men as within a leash of mystery; *the* ... 1897.
14 *he* spoke aloud, '*O* ... NO.
16 *yards* further *up* ... NO to 1914.
17 *mountain-side* 1925, 1927; *mountain side* NO to 1914.
19-20 *said* a voice with the deep chest utterance of the native Irish. 'What a noise two pigs
can make,' said another. 'As much as if they were two fat friars caught by the little old one
when almost through the gates.' 'May the holy frogs sit upon all friars,' replied the first
voice. *In another* ... NO; *said* one voice; 'what a noise two pigs can make!' said another; 'as
much as if they were two fat friars caught by the little old one almost through the gates.'
'May the holy frogs spit upon all friars!' replied the first voice. *In another* ... 1897.
19 *some one* NO, 1897, 1925, 1927; *someone* 1908 to 1914.
23 *Where* go ye *with* ... NO.
23-24 *who* looked *the* ... NO.
26 *man* at Drum- / sligo, *and* ... NO.
26 *by* the Lough of the Weir, *and* ... 1897.
26 *Glen-* / *Car; Glen Car* 1908 to 1927.
27 *them.* But now *that* ... NO.
27 *we* find them to be fully *four* ... NO.
27-29 *than* ourselves, we will go home again when we have seen the way they take, and
report whither they have gone *to De* ... NO.

30 tell our story to De Courcey, and if he will not help us, to Fitzgerald; for De Courcey and Fitzgerald have lately made a peace, and we do not know to whom we belong.'

'But by that time,' said the knight, 'the pigs will have been eaten.'

'A dozen men cannot do more, and it was not reasonable that the whole valley should turn out and risk their lives for two, or for two
35 dozen pigs.'

'Can you tell me,' said the knight, 'if the old man to whom the pigs belong is pious and true of heart?'

'He is as true as another and more pious than any, for he says a prayer to a saint every morning before his breakfast.'

40 'Then it were well to fight in his cause,' said the knight, 'and if you will fight against the wood-thieves I will take the main brunt of the battle, and you know well that a man in armour is worth many like these wood-thieves, clad in wool and leather.'

And the leader turned to his fellows and asked if they would take
45 the chance; but they seemed anxious to get back to their cabins.

'Are the wood-thieves treacherous and impious?'

'They are treacherous in all their dealings,' said a peasant, 'and no man has known them to pray.'

'Then,' said the knight, 'I will give five crowns for the head of
50 every wood-thief killed by us in the fighting'; and he bid the leader show the way, and they all went on together. After a time they came to where a beaten track wound into the woods, and, taking this,

---

29-31 *help* we will to Fitzgerald with our tale, for *we do* ... NO.
31 *not* well *know* ... NO.
33 *reasonable* to think *that* ... NO.
33-34 *the* entire *valley* ... NO.
34 *two*, aye, *or* ... NO.
36 *Can* ye *tell* ... NO.
37 *belong* be *pious* ... NO.
40-41 *if* ye *will fight* ... NO.
42 *and* ye *know* ... NO.
42 *that* one *man* ... NO.
42-43 *many* who, *like* ... NO.
43 *wood-thieves*, are clad but *in* ... NO.
44-45 *take* their *chance* ... NO.
46 *wood-thieves* men false of heart, and are they *impious* ... NO; *wood-thieves* false of heart, and are they *impious* ... 1897.
47 *are* false and *treacherous* ... NO, 1897.
49 *Then I* ... NO.*
50 *the* fight.' ¶Then, all doubts disappeared, and the knight, having *bid* ... NO.
50 *fighting;'* and ... 1897.
51 *way*, the troop moved rapidly on. *After* ... NO.
52 *track* entered *the* ... NO.

they doubled back upon their previous course, and began to ascend the wooded slope of the mountain. In a little while the path grew
55 very straight and steep, and the knight was forced to dismount and leave his horse tied to a tree-stem. They knew they were on the right track, for they could see the marks of pointed shoes in the soft clay and mingled with them the cloven footprints of the pigs. Presently the path became still more abrupt, and they knew by the
60 ending of the cloven footprints that the thieves were carrying the pigs. Now and then a long mark in the clay showed that a pig had slipped down, and been dragged along for a little way. They had journeyed thus for about twenty minutes, when a confused sound of voices told them that they were coming up with the thieves. And
65 then the voices ceased, and they understood that they had been overheard in their turn. They pressed on rapidly and cautiously, and in about five minutes one of them caught sight of a leather jerkin half hidden by a hazel-bush. An arrow struck the knight's chain-armour, but glanced off, and then a flight of arrows swept
70 over their heads. They ran and climbed, and climbed and ran towards the thieves, who were now all visible standing up among the bushes with their still quivering bows in their hands: for they had only their spears and they must at once come hand to hand. The knight was in the front and struck down first one and then
75 another of the wood-thieves. The peasants shouted, and, pressing on, drove the wood-thieves before them until they came out on the

---

54   *of the* mountains. *In* . . . NO to 1914.
54   *a short time the* . . . NO.
55   *strait* . . . NO, 1897.
57   *track: for* . . . NO to 1914, 1925A.
58-59   *Presently, the path* . . . NO, 1897.
59-60   *by the* ceasing *of* . . . NO.
63   *thus, for* . . . NO, 1897.
67   *one caught* . . . NO.*
68   *hazel-bush* 1897 to 1927; *hazel bush* NO.
68-69   *the* chain knight's *armour* . . . NO.
69   *off* harmlessly, *and* . . . NO to 1914.
69-70   *flight* swept by them with the buzzing sound of great bees. *They* . . . NO.
69-70   *swept* by them with the buzzing sound of great bees. *They* . . . 1897 to 1914.
73   *spears, and* . . . NO to 1908.
74   *front, and struck* . . . NO to 1908.
74   *and* smote *down* . . . NO to 1913.
75   *shouted* aloud, *and* . . . NO, 1897.
76   *on, they* drove . . . NO, 1897.
76   *wood-thieves* NO, 1897, 1914 to 1927; *wood- / thieves* 1908, 1913.

flat top of the mountain, and there they saw the two pigs quietly grubbing in the short grass, so they ran about them in a circle, and began to move back again towards the narrow path: the old knight
80 coming now the last of all, and striking down thief after thief. The peasants had got no very serious hurts among them, for he had drawn the brunt of the battle upon himself, as could well be seen from the bloody rents in his armour; and when they came to the entrance of the narrow path he told them to drive the pigs down
85 into the valley, while he stood there to guard the way behind them. So in a moment he was alone, and, being weak with loss of blood, might have been ended there and then by the wood-thieves had fear not made them begone out of sight in a great hurry.

An hour passed, and they did not return; and now the knight
90 could stand on guard no longer, but had to lie down upon the grass. A half-hour more went by, and then a young lad with what appeared to be a number of cock's feathers stuck round his hat came out of the path behind him, and began to move about among the dead thieves, cutting their heads off. Then he laid the heads in
95 a heap before the knight, and said, 'O great knight, I have been bid come and ask you for the crowns you promised for the heads: five crowns a head. They told me to tell you that they have prayed to God and His Mother to give you a long life, but that they are poor peasants, and that they would have the money before you die. They
100 told me this over and over for fear I might forget it, and promised to beat me if I did.'

The knight raised himself upon his elbow, and, opening a bag

---

78 *they* stood *about* ... NO, 1897.
79 *narrow* paths: *the* ... NO.
84 *he* bade them *drive* ... NO to 1913.
87 *wood-thieves* he had beaten off, *had* ... NO to 1913.
88 *begone* 1914 to 1927; *be gone* NO, 1897; *be- / gone* 1908, 1913.
90 *stand* and pace *on* ... NO.
91 *lad, with* ... NO to 1908.
92–93 *hat, came* ... NO to 1927.
94 *heads* of. *Then* ... 1897.
94 *off, Then* ... 1913.
94 *off.* Next *he* ... NO.
95 *and* spake thus: *'O* ... NO.
95 *said: 'O* ... 1897 to 1927.
96 *heads—five* ... NO.
97 *They* bid me *tell* ... NO to 1913.
102 *and opening* ... NO to 1927.

that hung to his belt, counted out the five crowns for each head. There were thirty heads in all.

105 'O great knight,' said the lad, 'they have also bid me take all care of you, and light a fire, and put this ointment upon your wounds.' And he gathered sticks and leaves together, and, flashing his flint and steel under a mass of dry leaves, made a very good blaze. Then, drawing off the coat of mail, he began to anoint the wounds: but he
110 did it clumsily, like one who does by rote what he has been told. The knight motioned him to stop, and said, 'You seem a good lad.'

'I would ask something of you for myself.'

'There are still a few crowns,' said the knight; 'shall I give them to you?'

115 'O no,' said the lad. 'They would be no good to me. There is only one thing that I care about doing, and I have no need of money to do it. I go from village to village and from hill to hill, and whenever I come across a good cock I steal him and take him into the woods, and I keep him there under a basket until I get another good cock,
120 and then I set them to fight. The people say I am an innocent, and do not do me any harm, and never ask me to do any work but go a message now and then. It is because I am an innocent that they send me to get the crowns: any one else would steal them; and they dare not come back themselves, for now that you are not with them
125 they are afraid of the wood-thieves. Did you ever hear how, when

---

104   *thirty in* ... NO.*
104-5   *all.* ¶'They have also bid me, O great knight,' continued the lad, *'take* ... NO.
106-7   *your* wound.' *And* ... NO.
107   *together and* ... NO.
108   *leaves,* had soon a leaping blaze that cast its flickering light over the knight [cast a flicker over the face of the knight 1897] and over the piled-up heads of the wood-thieves. *Then* ... NO, 1897.
108   *leaves,* had *made* ... 1908 to 1914.
109   *off, the coat* ... NO.
109   *mail he began* ... NO.
110   *did so clumsily* ... NO.
110   *who* repeated mechanically *what* ... NO.
110   *he* had *been* ... NO to 1914.
111   *and he said* ... NO.
111   *said: 'You* ... NO to 1927.
113   *knight; 'will I* ... NO.
119   *basket, until* ... NO to 1908.
120   *am* a bit *innocent* ... NO, 1897.
122   *am* a bit *innocent* ... NO, 1897.
123   *any one* NO, 1897, 1925, 1927; *anyone* 1908 to 1914.
124-25 *them* the fear of the wood-thieves is upon them. *Did* ... NO, 1897.

the wood-thieves are. christened, the wolves are made their god-
fathers, and their right arms are not christened at all?'

'If you will not take these crowns, my good lad, I have nothing
for you, I fear, unless you would have that old coat of mail which I
130 shall soon need no more.'

'There was something I wanted: yes, I remember now,' said the
lad. 'I want you to tell me why you fought like the champions and
giants in the stories and for so little a thing. Are you indeed a man
like us? Are you not rather an old wizard who lives among these
135 hills, and will not a wind arise presently and crumble you into dust?'

'I will tell you of myself,' replied the knight, 'for now that I am
the last of the fellowship, I may tell all and witness for God. Look at
the Rose of Rubies on my helmet, and see the symbol of my life and
of my hope.' And then he told the lad this story, but with always
140 more frequent pauses; and, while he told it, the lad stuck the cock's
feathers in the earth in front of him, and moved them about as
though he made them actors in the play.

'I live in a land far from this, and was one of the Knights of S.
John,' said the old man; 'but I was one of those in the Order who
145 always longed for more arduous labours in the service of the truth
that can only be understood within the heart. At last there came to
us a knight of Palestine, to whom the truth of truths had been
revealed by God Himself. He had seen a great Rose of Fire, and a

---

126-27   *godfathers* 1925E, 1927; *god-fathers* NO, 1897, 1914, 1925A; *god- / fathers* 1908, 1913.
126-27   *god-fathers and* ... 1925A.
127-28   *all?* ¶'*If* ... NO.
131   *wanted—yes* ... NO.
132-33   *the* gods and giants and heroes *in* ... NO, 1897.
133   *stories* I love *for* ... NO.
134   *rather* some *old* ... NO.
134   *who* dwells, unknown to us all, *among* ... NO.
135   *presently, and* ... NO, 1897.
135   *into* a fine *dust* ... NO.
137   *fellowship I* ... NO, 1897.
139   *And* he then *told* ... NO.
139-40   *with* ever *more* ... NO.
140   *it, the* Rose shone a deep blood colour in the fire-light, and, ever as he spake the *lad* ... NO; *it, the* Rose shone a deep blood-colour in the fire- / light [fire-light 1897; firelight 1914], and the *lad* ... 1897 to 1914.
143   *I* dwelt *in* ... NO.
143   *St.* ... NO, 1897, 1913 to 1927; *Saint* ... 1908.
144-45   *who* ever *longed* ... NO.
145-46   *of the* Most High. *At.* ... NO to 1913.

Voice out of the Rose had told him how men would turn from the
150 light of their own hearts, and bow down before outer order and
outer fixity, and that then the light would cease, and none escape
the curse except the foolish good man who could not think, and the
passionate wicked man who would not. Already, the Voice told
him, the light of the heart was shining with less lustre, and, as it
155 paled, an infection was touching the world with corruption; and
none of those who had seen clearly the truth could enter into the
Kingdom of God, which is in the Heart of the Rose, if they stayed
on willingly in the corrupted world; and so they must prove their
anger against the Powers of Corruption by dying in the service of
160 the Rose. While the knight of Palestine was telling us these things
the air was filled with fragrance of the Rose. By this we knew that it
was the very Voice of God which spoke to us by the knight, and we
told him to direct us in all things, and teach us how to obey the
Voice. So he bound us with an oath, and gave us signs and words
165 whereby we might know each other even after many years, and he
appointed places of meeting, and he sent us out in troops into the
world to seek good causes, and die in doing battle for them. At first
we thought to die more readily by fasting to death in honour of
some saint; but this he told us was evil, for we did it for the sake of
170 death, and thus took out of the hands of God the choice of the time
and manner of our death, and by so doing made His power the less.

---

150 *before* mere external [*before* external 1897] *order* ... NO, 1897.
152 *not, and* ... NO to 1914.*
153 *not,* think. *Already* ... NO to 1914.
154 *the* wayward *light* ... NO to 1914.
154 *shining* out upon the world to keep it alive, [∼ ∧ NO] with a less clear *lustre* ... NO to
1913; *shining* out upon the world to keep the world alive, with a less clear *lustre* ... 1914.
154 *and* that, *as* ... NO to 1927.
155 *paled,* a strange *infection* ... NO to 1914.
155 *the* stars and the hills and the grass and the trees *with* ... NO to 1914.
155–56 *corruption, and* that *none* ... NO to 1927.
156 *truth* and the ancient way [∼, NO, 1897] *could* ... NO to 1914.
158 *the* infected world, and *they* ... NO; *the* infected *world; and so they* ... 1897.
160 *Rose* of God. *While* ... NO to 1914.
160 *Knight* ... 1913, 1914, 1925A.
160–61 *things* we seemed to see in a vision a crimson [a great crimson NO] Rose
spreading itself about him, so that he seemed to speak out of its heart, and the air was filled
[air seemed filled NO] with fragrance. *By* ... NO to 1914.
162 *voice* ... NO.
162–63 *we* gathered about him and bade him *direct* ... NO to 1913.
168 *fasting* unto *death* ... NO, 1897.
169 *he* bade us know *was* ... NO, 1897.

We must choose our service for its excellence, and for this alone, and leave it to God to reward us at His own time and in His own manner. And after this he compelled us to eat always two at a table
175 and watch each other lest we fasted unduly. And the years passed, and one by one my fellows died in the Holy Land, or in warring upon the evil princes of the earth, or in clearing the roads of robbers; and among them died the knight of Palestine, and at last I was alone. I fought in every cause where the few contended against
180 the many, and my hair grew white, and a terrible fear lest I had fallen under the displeasure of God came upon me. But, hearing at last how this western isle was fuller of wars and rapine than any other land, I came hither, and I have found the thing I sought, and, behold! I am filled with a great joy.'
185   Thereat he began to sing in Latin, and, while he sang, his voice faltered and grew faint. Then his eyes closed, and his lips fell apart, and the lad knew he was dead. 'He has told me a good tale,' said the lad, 'for there was fighting in it, but I did not understand much of it, and it is hard to remember so long a story.'
190   And, taking the knight's sword, he began to dig a grave in the soft clay. He dug hard, and he had almost done his work when a cock crowed in the valley below. 'Ah,' he said, 'I must have that bird'; and he ran down the narrow path to the valley.

---

173   *reward at* . . . NO.*
174   *to* dine *always* . . . NO.
174-75   *table* [~, NO] to *watch* . . . NO to 1914.
175   *unduly,* for there were some among us who still contended that if you fasted out of a sheer love to the holiness of saints and then died, the death would be acceptable.
And . . . NO; *unduly,* for some among us said that if one fasted for a love of the holiness of saints and then died, the death would be acceptable. *And* . . . 1897 to 1913.
176   *fellows* fell *in the* . . . NO.
184   *and behold* . . . NO, 1897.
184   *filled* of *a* . . . NO.
185   *sing* a Latin hymn, *and* . . . NO, 1897.
185-86   *voice* grew exceeding *faint. Then* . . . NO; *voice* grew fainter and fainter.
Then . . . 1897 to 1913.
186-87   *closed, and* fell apart *and* . . . NO.*
187-88   *tale,'* he said, *'for* . . . NO to 1914.
191   *dug* with great energy, a faint light of dawn touching his hair, and *had* . . . NO.
191   *hard, and* a faint light of dawn had touched his hair and *he* . . . 1897 to 1914.
193   *bird.' And* therewith disappeared *down* . . . NO.
[In NO, the story is signed W. B. Yeats.]

THE WISDOM OF THE KING

The High Queen of Ireland had died in childbirth, and her child
was put to nurse with a woman who lived in a little house within the
border of the wood. One night the woman sat rocking the cradle,
and meditating upon the beauty of the child, and praying that the
gods might grant him wisdom equal to his beauty. There came a
knock at the door, and she got up wondering, for the nearest
neighbours were in the High King's house a mile away and the
night was now late. 'Who is knocking?' she cried, and a thin voice
answered, 'Open! for I am a crone of the grey hawk, and I come
from the darkness of the great wood.' In terror she drew back the
bolt, and a grey-clad woman, of a great age, and of a height more
than human, came in and stood by the head of the cradle. The
nurse shrank back against the wall, unable to take her eyes from the
woman, for she saw by the gleaming of the firelight that the feathers of the grey hawk were upon her head instead of hair. 'Open!'
cried another voice, 'for I am a crone of the grey hawk, and I watch
over his nest in the darkness of the great wood.' The nurse opened
the door again, though her fingers could scarce hold the bolts for

Printings: *The New Review*, September, 1895; 1897; 1908; 1913; 1914; 1925; 1927.
Text from 1932.
Title: WISDOM NR; ... KING. 1913.
1   *The* Queen of Eri *had* ... NR.
1   *High Queen; High-Queen* 1897 to 1927.
1   *of* the Island of Woods *had* ... 1897 to 1913.
1   *died, in* ... NR.
1   *childbirth* 1908 to 1927; *child-birth* NO, 1897.
2   *nurse, with* ... 1897.
2   *in a* hut of mud and wicker [of mud-plastered wicker NR], *within* ... NR to 1913.
2   *house, within* ... 1914.
3   *the* forest. *One* ... NR.
4   *and* pondering over *the beauty* ... NR to 1913.
5   *grant* it *wisdom* ... NR.
6   *up,* not a little *wondering* ... NR to 1914.
7   *the* royal dun *a* ... NR; *the* dun of the High-King *a* ... 1897 to 1913.
7   *High King's; High-King* 1897 to 1913; *High-King's* 1914 to 1927.
7-8 *away, and* who would come from there so late at night? '*Who* ... NR.
7   *away; and* ... 1897 to 1914.
8-9 *voice* replied, '*Open* ... NR.
10   *of the* forest.' *In* ... NR.
11   *of* enormous *age and* ... NR.
12   *than* mortal, *came* ... NR.
15   *hair.* But the child slept, and the fire danced, for the one was too ignorant and the
other too full of gaiety to know what a dreadful being stood there. '*Open* ... NR to 1914.
17   *of the* forest.' *The* ... NR.

trembling, and another grey woman, not less old than the other,
20 and with like feathers instead of hair, came in and stood by the
first. In a little, came a third grey woman, and after her a fourth,
and then another and another and another, until the hut was full
of their immense bodies. They stood silent for a long time, but at
last one muttered in a low thin voice: 'Sisters, I knew him far away
25 by the redness of his heart under his silver skin'; and then another
spoke: 'Sisters, I knew him because his heart fluttered like a bird
under a net of silver cords'; and then another took up the word:
'Sisters, I knew him because his heart sang like a bird that is happy
in a silver cage.' And after that they sang together, those who were
30 nearest rocking the cradle with long wrinkled fingers; and their
voices were now tender and caressing, now like the wind blowing in
the great wood, and this was their song:

Out of sight is out of mind:
Long have man and woman-kind,
35   Heavy of will and light of mood,
Taken away our wheaten food,
Taken away our Altar stone;
Hail and rain and thunder alone,
And red hearts we turn to grey,
40   Are true till Time gutter away.

When the song had died out, the crone who had first spoken,
said: 'We have nothing more to do but to mix a drop of our blood
into his blood.' And she scratched her arm with the sharp point of a
spindle, which she had made the nurse bring to her, and let a drop
45 of blood, grey as the mist, fall upon the lips of the child; and passed
out into the darkness.

19-20 *the* first, *and with* . . . NR.
21 *little* while, and in like manner, *came* . . . NR.
22 *another, and another, and another* . . . NR.
22-23 *immense* forms. *They* . . . NR, 1897.
23 *stood* a long time in perfect silence and stillness, for they were of those whom the dropping of the sand has never troubled, *but at* [troubled. *But at* NR] . . . NR to 1914.
28-29 *that* had forgotten the silver cords.' *And* . . . NR, 1897.
30 *fingers. And their* . . . NR.
31-33 *in the* forest: ¶*Out* . . . NR.
34 *woman-kind* 1897 to 1927; *woman kind* NR.
42-43 *said,* 'Nothing now remains but that a drop of our blood be mixed *into* . . . NR, 1897.
44 *spindle* she had bade *the* . . . NR.
46-47 *darkness.* Then the others passed out in silence; and all the while the child had not opened its pink lids or the fire ceased to dance, for the one was too ignorant, and the other too full of gaiety to know. And *when the crones* . . . NR; *darkness.* Then the others passed out

When the crones were gone, the nurse came to her courage again, and hurried to the High-King's house, and cried out in the midst of the assembly hall that the Sidhe had bent over the child
50 that night; and the king and his poets and men of law went with her to the hut and gathered about the cradle, and were as noisy as magpies, and the child sat up and looked at them.

Two years passed over, and the king died; and the poets and the men of law ruled in the name of the child, but looked to see him
55 become the master himself before long, for no one had seen so wise a child, and everything had been well but for a miracle that began to trouble all men; and all women, who, indeed, talked of it without ceasing. The feathers of the grey hawk had begun to grow in the child's hair, and though his nurse cut them continually, in but a
60 little while they would be more numerous than ever. This had not been a matter of great importance, for miracles were a little thing in those days, but for an ancient law of Ireland that none who had

---

in silence one by one; and all the while the child had not opened his pink eyelids or the fire ceased to dance, for the one was too ignorant, and the other too full of gaiety to know how great the beings were that had bent over a cradle. ¶ *When the crones* . . . 1897; *darkness.* Then the others passed out in silence one by one; and all the while the child had not opened his pink eyelids or the fire ceased to dance, for the one was too ignorant and the other too full of gaiety to know what great beings had bent over the cradle. ¶ *When the crones* . . . 1908 to 1914.
47-48 *courage, and hurried* . . . NR.*
48 *the* king's dun, *and* . . . NR; *the* dun of the High-King, *and* . . . 1897 to 1913.
49 *the* banqueting *hall* . . . NR.
49 *Shee,* whether for good or evil, *had* . . . NR; *Sidhe* [*Shee* 1897], whether for good or evil she knew not, *had* . . . 1897 to 1914.
50 *king, and his* . . . NR.
50 *poets and* ollaves, and his huntsman, and his cook, and his chief warrior *went* . . . NR.
50 *law,* and his huntsmen [hunstmen 1914], and his cooks [cook 1897], and his chief warriors *went* . . . 1897 to 1914.
51-52 *cradle, and the* . . . NR.*
53 *king* fell fighting against the Ossorians; *and the poets* . . . NR; *king died* fighting against the Fer Bolg; *and the poets* [the People of the Bag; *and the poets* 1897] . . . 1897 to 1914.
53-54 *poets and the* ollaves *ruled* . . . NR.
56 *child, and* tales of his endless questions about the household of the gods and the making of the world went hither and thither among the wicker houses of [wicker homes of NR] the poor. *Everything had* . . . NR to 1913; *child, and* tales of his endless questions about the world and the gods went hither and thither among the houses of the poor. *Everything had* . . . 1914.
56 *well, but* . . . 1897.
57 *and* especially *all* . . . NR.
59 *continually,* it needed *but* . . . NR, 1897.
60 *while* and they were *more* . . . NR, 1897.
61 *great* moment, *for* . . . NR to 1913.
61-62 *were* not uncommon *in* . . . NR.
62 *of* Eri [~: NR] *that* . . . NR to 1913.

any blemish of body could sit upon the throne; and as a grey hawk is a brute thing of the air, it was not possible to think of one in
65 whose hair its feathers grew as other than marred and blasted; nor could the people separate from their admiration of the wisdom that grew in him a horror as at one of unhuman blood. Yet all were resolved that he should reign, for they had suffered much from foolish kings and their own disorders; and no one had any other
70 fear but that his great wisdom might bid him obey the law, and call some other to reign in his stead.

When the child was seven years old the poets and the men of law were called together by the chief poet, and all these matters weighed and considered. The child had already seen that those
75 about him had hair only, and, though they had told him that they too had had feathers but had lost them because of a sin committed by their forefathers, they knew that he would learn the truth when he began to wander into the country round about. After much consideration they made a new law commanding every one upon
80 pain of death to mingle artificially the feathers of the grey hawk into his hair; and they sent men with nets and slings and bows into the countries round about to gather a sufficiency of feathers. They

---

63-64   *hawk* was a wild thing of the air [~, NR] which had never sat at the board, or listened to the songs of the poets in the light of the fire, *it* [in the firelight, *it* NR] ... NR to 1913; *hawk* was a wild thing of the air which had never sat at the board, or listened to the songs of the poets, *it* ... 1914.
66-67   *admiration a* ... NR.*
69   *disorders, and* desired, besides, to behold the spectacle of his days to the full. And *no* ... NR; *disorders, and* moreover they desired to watch out the spectacle of his days; and *no* ... 1897 to 1914.
69-70   *any fear* ... NR.*
70-71   *call* Eocha of Olnemachia, who [of the Plain of Towers, who 1897] had but a common mind, *to* ... NR, 1897; *call some other,* who had but a common mind, *to* ... 1908 to 1914.
72-73   *old, the* ollaves and poets were summoned *by* ... NR.
73-74   *poet. The* ... NR.*
74   *already* noticed *that* ... NR.
75-77   *though* his mind was laid at rest by the explanation that they had torn out the feathers in sorrow for the slaying of the king, he *knew* ... NR.
78-79   *the* surrounding country. But, after a long deliberation, it was decided to decree a *law* ... NR.
79   *they* decreed *a* ... 1897 to 1913.
79   *every one* NR to 1913, 1925, 1927; *everyone* 1914.
80   *mingle* by a subtlety of art *the feathers* ... NR, 1897.
81-83   *and* men with nets and slings, for as yet the bow was not invented, were sent into surrounding countries to gather feathers. And it was also decreed *that* ... NR.
81   *slings,* for as yet the bow was not invented, *into* ... 1897.

decreed also that any who told the truth to the child should be put to death.

85   The years passed, and the child grew from childhood into boyhood and from boyhood into manhood, and became busy with strange and subtle thought, distinctions between things long held the same, resemblance of things long held different. Multitudes came from other lands to see him and to question him, but there

90 were guards set at the frontiers, who compelled all to wear the feathers of the grey hawk in their hair. While they listened to him his words seemed to make all darkness light and filled their hearts like music; but when they returned to their own lands his words seemed far off, and what they could remember too strange and

95 subtle to help them in their lives. A number indeed did live differently afterwards, but their new life was less excellent than the old: some among them had long served a good cause, but when they heard him praise it, they returned to their own lands to find what they had loved less lovable, for he had taught them how little

100 divides the false and true; others, again, who had served no cause, but had sought in peace the welfare of their own households,

---

83–85 *be* flung from a cliff into the sea. ¶*The* . . . NR to 1914.
85 *and he grew* . . . NR.
86 *manhood; and,* instead of being curious about all things, he had long been *busy* . . . NR; *manhood, and* from being curious about all things he *became busy* . . . 1897 to 1914.
87 *subtle* thoughts which came to him in dreams, and with *distinctions* . . . NR to 1914.
88 *same* and with the *resemblance* . . . NR to 1914.
88 *held* diverse. *Multitudes* . . . NR.
89–90 *from* all lands to look upon him and to ask his counsel, but all who came were forced by the guards set at the frontiers *to* . . . NR.
89–90 *and to* ask his counsel, but there were guards set at the frontiers, who compelled all that came *to* [*came, to* 1897] . . . 1897 to 1914.
91–92 *him, his* . . . NR.
93 *but,* alas, *when* . . . NR to 1913.
94 *remember* were *too* . . . NR.
95 *them* to live [*them* live NR] out their hasty days. *A* . . . NR to 1913.
95 *number, indeed, did* . . . NR.
95–96 *differently, but* . . . NR.*
97 *old. Some* . . . NR.
98 *it* and their labour, *they* . . . NR to 1913.
99 *lovable* and their arm lighter in the battle, [~; NR] *for* . . . NR to 1913.
99–100 *little* a hair *divides* . . . NR to 1914.
100 *true. Others again* . . . NR.
100 *others again* . . . 1897.
101 *but* wrought *in* . . . 1897 to 1913; *but* built up *in* . . . 1914.
101 *had* wrought *in* . . . NR.
101–2 *households,* when he had expounded their purpose *found* . . . NR; *households,* when he had expounded the meaning of their purpose, [~ ʌ 1897] *found* . . . 1897 to 1913.

found their bones softer and less ready for toil, for he had shown them greater purposes; and numbers of the young, when they had heard him upon all these things, remembered certain strange
105 words that made ordinary joys nothing, and sought impossible joys and grew unhappy.

Among those who came to look at him and to listen to him was the daughter of a little king who lived a great way off; and when he saw her he loved, for she was beautiful, with a beauty unlike that of
110 other women; but her heart was like that of other women, and

---

102 *and* their will *less* ... NR to 1914.
102 *toil; for* ... NR.
103 *them* mightier purposes. And great *numbers* ... NR.
104-7 *upon* the making of the world and the building of mankind, remembered words and sentences that became like a fire in their hearts, and made all kindly joys and traffic between man and man as nothing, and went different ways, but all into vague regret. And when any asked him concerning the common things of life—disputes about a merring, or about cattle, or about an eric—he would turn to those nearest him for advice; but this was held to be from courtesy, for none knew that these matters were hidden from him, by thoughts and dreams that filled his mind like the marching and counter-marching of armies. Far less could any know that his heart wandered, lost and futile, amid throngs of masterful thoughts and dreams, shuddering at its own consuming solitude. ¶Now, *among* ... NR.
104-7 *certain* words that became like a fire in their hearts, and made all kindly joys and traffic between man and man as nothing, and went different ways, but all into vague regret. ¶When any asked him concerning the common things of life; disputes about the mear of a territory, or about the straying of cattle, or about the penalty of blood; he would turn to those nearest him for advice; but this was held to be from courtesy, for none knew that these matters were hidden from him [~, 1897] by thoughts and dreams that filled his mind like the marching and counter-marching of armies. Far less could any know that his heart wandered lost amid throngs of overcoming thoughts and dreams, shuddering at its own consuming solitude. ¶*Among* ... 1897 to 1913.
105-7 *made* all kindly joys and traffic between man and man as nothing, and went different ways, but all into vague regret. ¶When any asked him about the common things of life; disputes about the mearing of a territory, or about the straying of cattle, or about the penalty of blood; he would turn to those nearest him for advice; but this was held to be from courtesy, for none knew that these matters were hidden from him by thoughts and dreams that filled his mind like the marching and counter-marching of armies. Far less could any know that his heart wandered lost amid throngs of overcoming thoughts and dreams, shuddering at its own solitude. ¶*Among* ... 1914.
107 *and listen* ... NR.*
108 *a* poor chief *who* ... NR.
109 *her, he* ... NR.
109-10 *a* strange and pale [strange pale NR] beauty unlike the women of his land; but [land. But NR] Dana, the great mother, had decreed her a heart that was but as the heart of others, *and* ... NR to 1913.
109-10 *unlike* the women of his land; but Dana, the great mother, had decreed her a heart that was but as the heart of others, *and* ... 1914.

when she thought of the mystery of the hawk feathers she was afraid. Overwhelmed with his greatness, she half accepted, and yet half refused his love, and day by day the king gave her gifts the merchants had carried from India or maybe from China itself; and
115 still she was ever between a smile and a frown; between yielding and withholding. He laid all his wisdom at her feet, and told a multitude

---

111 *she* considered *the mystery* . . . NR to 1913.
111 *the* hawk's *feathers* . . . NR.
111-12 *was* full of horror. He called her to him when the assembly was over and talked of her great beauty, and praised her simply and frankly as though she were a fable of the bards, and asked her humbly to give him her love, for he was only subtle in his dreams. *Overwhelmed* . . . NR; *was* troubled with a great horror. He called her to him when the assembly was over and told her of her beauty, and praised her simply and frankly as though she were a fable of the bards; and he asked her humbly to give him her love, for he was only subtle in his dreams. *Overwhelmed* . . . 1897 to 1913; *was afraid.* He called her to him when the assembly was over and told her of her beauty, and praised her simply and frankly, and humbly asked her to give him her love, for he was only subtle in his dreams. *Overwhelmed* . . . 1914.
112 *half* consented, *and* . . . NR.
113 *refused,* for she longed to marry some warrior who [some man who 1914] could carry her over a mountain in his arms. *Day by* . . . NR to 1914.
113-15 *her* presents: cups with ears of gold, and findrinny wrought by the craftsmen of distant lands; cloth from over sea, woven with curious figures, but to her less beautiful than the bright cloth of Cathair. *And still* . . . NR; *her gifts;* cups with ears of gold and findrinny wrought by the craftsmen of distant lands; cloth from over sea, which, though woven with curious figures, seemed to her less beautiful than the bright cloth of her own country; *and* [cloth woven in the Island of Woods; *and* 1897] *still* . . . 1897 to 1913.
113 *her gifts;* gold enamelled cups and cloths *the* . . . 1914.
116 *He* poured *his* . . . NR; *He laid* down *his* . . . 1897 to 1914.
116-19 *told* how the heroes, when they die, return to the world and begin their labour anew; how the kind and mirthful Tuatha de Danaan drove out the gigantic, gloomy, and misshapen gods of old times; and of the great Moods, which are alone immortal, and the creators of mortal things; and how every Mood is a being that wears, to mortal eyes, the shape of Fintain, who dwells, disguised as a salmon, in the floods; or of the Dagda, whose cauldron is never empty; or of Lir, whose children wail upon the waters; or of Angus, whose kisses were changed into birds; or of Len, the goldsmith, from whose furnace rainbows break. And still she half refused, and still he hoped, for he could not believe that a beauty so like to wisdom could hide a common heart. ¶*There* . . . NR; *told* how the heroes when they die return to the world and begin their labour anew; how the kind and mirthful Children of Dana drove out the huge and gloomy and misshapen People from under the Sea; and how the great Moods are alone immortal, and the creators of mortal things; and how every Mood is a being that wears, to mortal eyes, the shape of Fair-brows, who dwells, as a salmon, in the floods; or of the Dagda, whose cauldron is never empty; or of Lir, whose children wail upon the waters; or of Angus, whose kisses were changed into birds; or of Len, the goldsmith, from whose furnace break rainbows and fiery dew; or of some other of the children of Dana: and still she half refused, and still he hoped, for he could not believe that a beauty so much like wisdom could hide a common heart. ¶*There* . . . 1897; *told* how the heroes when they die return to the world and begin their labour anew; how the kind and mirthful Men of Dea drove out the huge and gloomy and misshapen People from Under the Sea; and a multitude of things that even the Sidhe have forgotten, either

of things that even the Sidhe have forgotten, and he thought she understood because her beauty was like wisdom.

There was a tall young man in the house who had yellow hair,
120 and was skilled in wrestling; and one day the king heard his voice among the salley bushes. 'My dear,' it said, 'I hate them for making you weave these dingy feathers into your beautiful hair, and all that the bird of prey upon the throne may sleep easy o' nights'; and then the low, musical voice he loved answered: 'My hair is not beautiful
125 like yours; and now that I have plucked the feathers out of your hair I will put my hands through it, thus, and thus, and thus; for it does not make me afraid.' Then the king remembered many things that he had forgotten without understanding them, chance words of his poets and his men of law, doubts that he had reasoned away;
130 and he called to the lovers in a trembling voice. They came from among the salley bushes and threw themselves at his feet and

---

because they happened so long ago or because they have not time to think of them; and still she half refused, and still he hoped, because he could not believe that a beauty so much like wisdom could hide a common heart. ¶*There* . . . 1908, 1913; *told* how the heroes when they die return to the world and begin their labour anew; and a multitude of things that even the Sidhe have forgotten, either because they happened so long ago or because the Sidhe have not time to think of them; and still she half refused, and still he hoped, because he could not believe that a beauty so much like wisdom could hide a common heart. ¶*There* . . . 1914.
119 *a* broad-shouldered boy in the dun, who had long *yellow* . . . NR.
119 *the* dun *who* . . . 1897 to 1913.
120 *in wrestling* and [*in* boxing and NR] in the training of horses; *and* . . . NR to 1913.
120 *day* when the king walked in the orchard, which was between the foss and the forest, he *heard* . . . NR to 1914.
121 *bushes* which hid the waters of the foss. 'My blossom,' *it* . . . NR to 1913.
121 *bushes* which hid the waters of the foss. '*My* . . . 1914.
123 *prey* who sits *upon* . . . NR.
125 *yours*, that is heavy as a shower of gold thread woven by the merchants of Cathair; *and* . . . NR.
125-26 *plucked* away the feathers *I* . . . NR, 1897.
126 *it—thus—and thus—and thus; for* . . . NR.
126-27 *for it* casts no shadow of terror and darkness upon my heart.' Then did the king remember *many* . . . NR.
126-27 *for it* casts no shadow of terror and darkness upon my heart.' *Then* . . . 1897 to 1913.
128-29 *that* had puzzled him: evasions and equivocations of his ollaves and poets, *doubts* . . . NR.
128 *them*, doubtful *words* . . . 1897 to 1914.
129-30 *away*, his own continuous feeling of solitude. And he [own continual solitude; and he 1897] called the lovers to him *in* . . . NR, 1897.
129-30 *away*, his own continual solitude; *and* . . . 1908, 1913.
131 *bushes, and threw* . . . NR.
131 *feet, and* . . . NR.

prayed for pardon. He stooped down and plucked the feathers out
of the hair of the woman and turned away without a word. He went
to the hall of assembly, and having gathered his poets and his men
135 of law about him, stood upon the daïs and spoke in a loud, clear
voice: 'Men of law, why did you make me sin against the laws? Men
of verse, why did you make me sin against the secrecy of wisdom,
for law was made by man for the welfare of man, but wisdom the
gods have made, and no man shall live by its light, for it and the hail
140 and the rain and the thunder follow a way that is deadly to mortal
things? Men of law and men of verse, live according to your kind,
and call Eochaid of the Hasty Mind to reign over you, for I set out
to find my kindred.' He then came down among them, and drew
out of the hair of first one and then another the feathers of the
145 grey hawk, and, having scattered them over the rushes upon the
floor, passed out, and none dared to follow him, for his eyes
gleamed like the eyes of the birds of prey; and no man saw him
again or heard his voice.

---

132 *pardon*, [~; NR] and *he stooped* . . . NR to 1914.
133-34 *of the* girl's hair, and then turned away towards the dun. He strode into the great
hall, *and having* . . . NR.
133-34 *and* then turned away towards the dun without a word. He strode into
the . . . 1897 to 1913.
134-35 *his ollaves* and poets about him, mounted *upon* . . . NR.
135 *daïs, and* . . . NR.
136 *laws* of Eri? *Men* . . . NR to 1913.
137-38 *wisdom? For law* . . . NR; *wisdom? for law* . . . 1925A.
141 *things. Men* . . . NR, 1897, 1925A.
142 *call Eocha of* Olnemachia *to* [*of the* Plain of Towers *to* 1897] . . . NR, 1897.
142 *Eocha* . . . 1908 to 1927.
142-43 *I go to* . . . NR.
143 *kindred.'* So he went round *among* . . . NR.
143-45 *drew* the grey hawk's feathers out of the hair of first one and then another,
and . . . NR.
147 *prey. And* . . . NR.
147 *Man* ever beheld *him* . . . NR.
148 *voice.* Some [*voice.* But some NR] believed that he found his eternal abode among
the demons, and some [demons; some NR] that he dwelt henceforth with the dark and
dreadful goddesses, who sit all night about the pools in the forest [~, NR] watching the
constellations rising and setting in [constellations rise and set in NR] those desolate
mirrors. NR to 1914.
[In NR, the story is signed W. B. YEATS.]

THE HEART
OF THE SPRING

A very old man, whose face was almost as fleshless as the foot of a
bird, sat meditating upon the rocky shore of the flat and hazel=
covered isle which fills the widest part of Lough Gill. A russet-faced
boy of seventeen years sat by his side, watching the swallows dip-
5   ping for flies in the still water. The old man was dressed in threadbare blue velvet and the boy wore a frieze coat and had a rosary
about his neck. Behind the two, and half hidden by trees, was a
little monastery. It had been burned down a long while before by
sacrilegious men of the Queen's party, but had been roofed anew
10 with rushes by the boy, that the old man might find shelter in his
last days. He had not set his spade, however, into the garden about
it, and the lilies and the roses of the monks had spread out until
their confused luxuriance met and mingled with the narrowing
circle of the fern. Beyond the lilies and the roses the ferns were so
15 deep that a child walking among them would be hidden from sight,
even though he stood upon his toes; and beyond the fern rose
many hazels and small oak-trees.

'Master,' said the boy, 'this long fasting, and the labour of beckoning after nightfall to the beings who dwell in the waters and

Printings: *The National Observer*, April 15, 1893; 1897; 1908; 1913; 1914; 1925; 1927.
Text from 1932.
Title: . . . SPRING. 1913.
1 *was* fleshless well-nigh *as the* . . . NO.
2 *sat* plunged in thought *upon* . . . NO.
3 *of* the Lough of the Brightness. *A* . . . 1897.
3 *of* the *Lough* . . . 1908, 1913.
3-4 *russet-faced* lad of twenty *sat* . . . NO.
6 *velvet, and the* . . . NO to 1913.
6 *the* lad *wore* . . . NO.
6-7 *wore* the frieze cloak and blue cap of the Irish commonalty in [Irish peasantry
in 1897] the seventeenth century, and had about his neck a rosary of blue beads.
Behind . . . NO, 1897.
6-7 *coat and* a blue cap, and had about his neck a rosary of blue beads. *Behind* . . . 1908,
1913.
10 *the* lad, *that* . . . NO.
13 *confused* luxuriancy *met* . . . NO to 1913.
15 *that* the child who walked *among* . . . NO.
17 *oak-trees* 1897, 1925, 1927; *oak trees* NO, 1908 to 1914.
18-19 *labour* too, perhaps, of calling o' nights *the beings* . . . NO; *labour* too, perhaps, of
calling and beckoning with your rod of quicken wood o' nights *the beings* . . . 1897.
19 *nightfall* with your rod of quicken wood *to* . . . 1908, 1913.

20   among the hazels and oak-trees, is too much for your strength. Rest
from all this labour for a little, for your hand this day seemed more
heavy upon my shoulder and your feet less steady than I have
known them. Men say that you are older than the eagles, and yet
you will not seek the rest that belongs to age.' He spoke eagerly, as
25   though his heart were in the words; and the old man answered
slowly and deliberately, as though his heart were in distant days
and events.

     'I will tell you why I have not been able to rest,' he said. 'It is right
that you should know, for you have served me faithfully these five
30   years, and even with affection, taking away thereby a little of the
doom of loneliness which always falls upon the wise. Now, too, that
the end of my labour and the triumph of my hopes is at hand, it is
more needful for you to have this knowledge.'

     'Master, do not think that I would question you. It is my life to
35   keep the fire alight, and the thatch close that the rain may not come
in, and strong, that the wind may not blow it among the trees; and
to take down the heavy books from the shelves, and to possess an
incurious and reverent heart. God has made out of His abundance
a separate wisdom for everything which lives, and to do these
40   things is my wisdom.'

     'You are afraid,' said the old man, and his eyes shone with a
momentary anger.

---

20   *oak trees,* and of watching to beckon them to you with your rod of peeled quicken
wood, *is* . . . NO.
20   *oak-trees* 1897 to 1927; *oak trees* NO.
21   *little* to-day *for* . . .1914; *little for* . . . 1925A.
21   *hand seemed* . . . NO to 1914.*
22   *steady* under you to-day *than* . . . NO to 1913.
24   *spoke* in an eager, impulsive way, *as* . . . NO to 1913.
25   *words* and thoughts of the moment; *and* . . . NO to 1913.
26   *heart* was *in* . . . NO.
27-28   *and* distant deeds. ¶*'I will* . . . NO to 1913.
30   *years* and more, *and* . . . NO to 1913.
31   *which* ever *falls* . . . NO.
32-33   *it is* the *more* . . . NO to 1914.
34   *is* for me *to* . . . NO to 1914.
35-36   *close* against the rain, and strong, lest the wind *blow* . . . NO to 1913.
36-37   *and* it is for me to take *the heavy* . . . NO to 1913.
37   *shelves, and to* lift from its corner the great gilded and painted roll that holds the names
of all in the Ten Races of the Spirits, and to possess the while *an* . . . NO; *shelves, and to* lift
from its corner the great painted roll with the names of the Sidhe [Shee 1897], and to
possess the while *an* . . . 1897 to 1913; *shelves,* possessing the while *an* . . . 1914.
38   *heart,* for right well I know that *God* . . . NO to 1913; *heart,* for *God* . . . 1914.
39   *and* that *to* . . . NO.
41   *afraid,* Maurteen'; *and* . . . NO.
41-42   *a* moment of *anger* . . . NO.

'Sometimes at night,' said the boy, 'when you are reading, with a stick of mountain ash in your hand, I look out of the door and see,
45 now a great grey man driving swine among the hazels, and now many little people in red caps who come out of the lake driving little white cows before them. I do not fear these little people so much as the grey man; for, when they come near the house, they milk the cows, and they drink the frothing milk, and begin to
50 dance; and I know there is good in the heart that loves dancing; but I fear them for all that. And I fear the tall white-armed ladies who come out of the air, and move slowly hither and thither, crowning themselves with the roses or with the lilies, and shaking about them their living hair, which moves, for so I have heard them tell the
55 little people, with the motion of their thoughts, now spreading out and now gathering close to their heads. They have mild, beautiful faces, but I am afraid of the Sidhe, and afraid of the art which draws them about us.'

'Why,' said the old man, 'do you fear the ancient gods who made
60 the spears of your father's fathers to be stout in battle, and the little people who came at night from the depth of the lakes and sang among the crickets upon their hearths? And in our evil day they still watch over the loveliness of the earth. But I must tell you why I have fasted and laboured when others would sink into the sleep of
65 age, for without your help once more I shall have fasted and laboured to no good end. When you have done for me this last thing, you may go and build your cottage and till your fields, and take some girl to wife, and forget the ancient gods, for I shall leave

---

43   *the* lad, *'when* ... NO.
43-44   *with* the rod of quicken [of peeled quicken NO] wood *in* ... NO to 1914.
53-54   *about their* ... NO to 1913.*
54   *moves—for* ... NO.
54-55   *tell* each other, [~— NO] *with* ... NO to 1914.
57   *faces,* Aengus, son of Forbis, *but* ... 1914.
57   *but,* Angus Mac Forbis, I fear all these beings—I fear the Ten Races of the Spirits, and I fear *the art* ... NO; *but,* Aengus [Angus 1897], son of Forbis, I fear all these beings, I fear the people of the Sidhe [Shee 1897; of Sidhe 1913], and I fear *the art* ... 1897 to 1913.
59   *'Why,'* asked the other, *'do* ... NO.
61   *the* depths *of* ... NO.
63   *earth!* Willy-nilly *I must* ... NO.
66-67   *done* me this last service, *you* ... NO.
68   *Ancient Gods* ... 1925A.
68-69   *gods.* I have saved all the gold and silver pieces that were given to me by earls and knights and squires for keeping them from the evil eye and from the love-weaving enchantments of witches, and by earls' and knights' and squires' ladies for keeping the [for saving the NO] people of the Sidhe [Shee NO, 1897] from making the udders of their cattle fall dry, and taking the butter from their churns. I have saved it all for the day when

70 behind me in this little house money to make strong the roof-tree
of your cottage and to keep cellar and larder full. I have sought
through all my life to find the secret of life. I was not happy in my
youth, for I knew that it would pass; and I was not happy in my
manhood, for I knew that age was coming; and so I gave myself, in
youth and manhood and age, to the search for the Great Secret. I
75 longed for a life whose abundance would fill centuries, I scorned
the life of fourscore winters. I would be—no, I *will* be!—like the
Ancient Gods of the land. I read in my youth, in a Hebrew manuscript I found in a Spanish monastery, that there is a moment after
the Sun has entered the Ram and before he has passed the Lion,
80 which trembles with the Song of the Immortal Powers, and that
whosoever finds this moment and listens to the Song shall become
like the Immortal Powers themselves; I came back to Ireland and
asked the faery men, and the cow-doctors, if they knew when this
moment was; but though all had heard of it, there was none could
85 find the moment upon the hour-glass. So I gave myself to magic,
and spent my life in fasting and in labour that I might bring the
Gods and the Men of Faery to my side; and now at last one of the
Men of Faery has told me that the moment is at hand. One, who
wore a red cap and whose lips were white with the froth of the new
90 milk, whispered it into my ear. To-morrow, a little before the close
of the first hour after dawn, I shall find the moment, and then I
will go away to a southern land and build myself a palace of white
marble amid orange trees, and gather the brave and the beautiful
about me, and enter into the eternal kingdom of my youth. But,
95 that I may hear the whole Song, I was told by the little fellow with
the froth of the new milk on his lips that you must bring great

---

my work should be at an end, and now that the end is at hand you shall not lack for gold
and silver pieces enough *to* [lack for *money to* 1914] . . . NO to 1914.
69 *roof-tree* 1897 to 1927; *rooftree* NO.
71 *life,* Maurteen, *to* . . . NO.
76 *be*—nay, *I* . . . NO to 1913.
78 *moment, after* . . . 1897.
83 *fairy* . . . NO to 1914.
83 *and* even the wisest of *the* . . . NO.
84 *heard* the tradition, there were *none* . . . NO.
86–87 *the Gods and* the Fairies *to* . . . NO to 1913.
87–88 *one of the* Fairies *has* . . . NO to 1913.
88 *told that* . . . NO.*
95 *Song,* you must bring, said *the* . . . NO.
95 *Song,* you must bring, *I* . . . 1897.
96 *lips, great* . . . NO, 1897.*
96 *lips, that* . . . 1908 to 1927.

masses of green boughs and pile them about the door and the
window of my room; and you must put fresh green rushes upon
the floor, and cover the table and the rushes with the roses and the
100 lilies of the monks. You must do this to-night, and in the morning
at the end of the first hour after dawn, you must come and find
me.'

'Will you be quite young then?' said the boy.

'I will be as young then as you are, but now I am still old and
105 tired, and you must help me to my chair and to my books.'

When the boy had left the wizard in his room, and had lighted
the lamp which, by some contrivance, gave forth a sweet odour as
of strange flowers, he went into the wood and began cutting green
boughs from the hazels, and great bundles of rushes from the
110 western border of the isle, where the small rocks gave place to
gently sloping sand and clay. It was nightfall before he had cut
enough for his purpose, and wellnigh midnight before he had carried the last bundle to its place, and gone back for the roses and the
lilies. It was one of those warm, beautiful nights when everything
115 seems carved of precious stones. Sleuth Wood away to the south
looked as though cut out of green beryl, and the waters that mirrored it shone like pale opal. The roses he was gathering were like
glowing rubies, and the lilies had the dull lustre of pearl. Everything had taken upon itself the look of something imperishable,
120 except a glow-worm, whose faint flame burnt on steadily among
the shadows, moving slowly hither and thither, the only thing that
seemed alive, the only thing that seemed perishable as mortal hope.
The boy gathered a great armful of roses and lilies, and thrusting
the glow-worm among their pearl and ruby, carried them into the

---

99   *floor and cover* . . . NO.
103-4   *the* lad. ¶*'I will* . . . NO.
104   *are,* Maurteen; *but* . . . NO.
106   *the* lad had left Angus Mac Forbis *in* . . . NO.
106   *left* Aengus [Angus 1897] son of Forbis *in* . . . 1897 to 1914.
106   *and lighted* . . . NO.*
107   *contrivance* of the wizard's, *gave* . . . NO to 1914.
109   *hazels, great* . . . NO.*
111   *nightfall* 1908 to 1927; *night-fall* NO, 1897.
112   *wellnigh; well-nigh* NO, 1908 to 1927; *well- / nigh* 1897.
115   *stones.* The woods of Slish *away* . . . NO; *stones.* The woods of the Sleuth Hound
away . . . 1897.
116-17   *mirrored* them *shone* . . . NO to 1913.
118   *dull* lustrousness *of* . . . NO.
122-23   *hope.* He *gathered* . . . NO.
124   *the* glow-worms *among* . . . NO.

125 room, where the old man sat in a half-slumber. He laid armful after
armful upon the floor and above the table, and then, gently closing
the door, threw himself upon his bed of rushes, to dream of a
peaceful manhood with a desirable wife and laughing children. At
dawn he got up, and went down to the edge of the lake, taking the
130 hour-glass with him. He put some bread and wine into the boat,
that his master might not lack food at the outset of his journey, and
then sat down to wait the close of the first hour after dawn.
Gradually the birds began to sing, and when the last grains of sand
were falling, everything suddenly seemed to overflow with their
135 music. It was the most beautiful and living moment of the year; one
could listen to the spring's heart beating in it. He got up and went
to find his master. The green boughs filled the door, and he had to
make a way through them. When he entered the room the sunlight
was falling in flickering circles on floor and walls and table, and
140 everything was full of soft green shadows. But the old man sat
clasping a mass of roses and lilies in his arms, and with his head
sunk upon his breast. On the table, at his left hand, was a leather
wallet full of gold and silver pieces, as for a journey, and at his right
hand was a long staff. The boy touched him and he did not move.
145 He lifted the hands, but they were quite cold, and they fell heavily.
'It were better for him,' said the lad, 'to have said his prayers and
kissed his beads!' He looked at the threadbare blue velvet, and he
saw it was covered with the pollen of the flowers, and while he was

---

128 *with* his chosen wife at his side, and the laughter of children in his ears. *At* . . . NO to
1913.
128 *wife, and* . . . 1914, 1925A.
129 *he* rose, *and* . . . NO to 1913.
130 *and* a flask of wine in *the* . . . NO to 1913.
132-33 *wait* until the hour from dawn had gone by. *Gradually* . . . NO to 1914.
134 *falling* all nature *suddenly* . . . NO.
138-39 *room* he saw the sunlight *falling* . . . NO.
139 *on* the *floor* . . . 1925A.
139-40 *table, and* found everything *full* . . . NO.
142 *table,* as for a journey, to the left of him, *was* . . . NO.
142 *hand was* . . . 1897.
142 *leathern* . . . NO to 1913.
143 *pieces, and* . . . NO.*
144 *The* lad *touched* . . . NO.
145-46 *He* tried to lift the clasped hands, but they fell heavily. Angus Mac Forbis was
dead. ¶*'It* . . . NO.
145 *hands but* . . . 1897 to 1927.
146 *have* told his beads and said his prayers like another, and not to have spent his days in
seeking amongst [among NO] the Immortal Powers what he could have found in his own
deeds and days had he willed. Ah, yes, it were better to have *said* . . . NO to 1913.
147 *beads!'* His eyes lit upon *the* . . . NO.

looking at it a thrush, who had alighted among the boughs that
150 were piled against the window, began to sing.

THE CURSE OF THE FIRES AND OF
THE SHADOWS

One summer night, when there was peace, a score of Puritan
troopers, under the pious Sir Frederick Hamilton, broke through
the door of the Abbey of the White Friars at Sligo. As the door fell
with a crash they saw a little knot of friars gathered about the altar,
5   their white habits glimmering in the steady light of the holy candles. All the monks were kneeling except the abbot, who stood
upon the altar steps with a great brass crucifix in his hand. 'Shoot
them!' cried Sir Frederick Hamilton, but nobody stirred, for all
were new converts, and feared the candles and the crucifix. For a
10   little while all were silent, and then five troopers, who were the
bodyguard of Sir Frederick Hamilton, lifted their muskets, and

---

[In NO, the story is signed W. B. Yeats.]
Printings: *The National Observer*, August 5, 1893; 1897; 1908; 1913; 1914; 1925; 1927.
Text from 1932.
Title: . . . SHADOWS. 1913.
1   *One* old-world *summer* . . . NO.
1   *peace* upon earth and in the heavens, *a* . . . NO, 1897.
2   *troopers under* . . . NO to 1914, 1925A.
2   *Hamilton broke* . . . NO.
3   *Friars* which stood by the Shelly River. *As* . . . 1897.
3   *Friars* which stood over the Gara Lough *at* . . . 1908, 1913.
6   *except the* prior *who* . . . NO, 1897.
7   *great* brazen *crucifix* . . . NO to 1913.
7–8   *Shoot* down the enemies of your God,' *cried* . . . NO, 1897.
8   *but* none *stirred* . . . NO to 1913.
9   *were* recent *converts* . . . NO.
9   *feared the* crucifix and the holy candles. The white lights from the altar threw the
shadows of the troopers up on to roof and wall. As the troopers moved about, [~ ∧ NO]
the shadows began a fantastic dance among the corbels and the memorial tablets.
For . . . NO to 1913.
9   *crucifix*. The white lights from the altar threw the shadows of the troopers up on to roof
and wall. As the troopers moved about, the shadows began to dance among the corbels and
the memorial tablets. *For* . . . 1914.
10   *all* was *silent* . . . NO to 1914.
10   *troopers who* . . . NO to 1914.
11   *bodyguard* 1925E, 1927; *body-guard* NO to 1914, 1925A.
11   *Frederick lifted* . . . NO.*
11   *Hamilton lifted* . . . 1897 to 1914.

shot down five of the friars. The noise and the smoke drove away
the mystery of the pale altar lights, and the other troopers took
courage and began to strike. In a moment the friars lay about the
15   altar steps, their white habits stained with blood. 'Set fire to the
house!' cried Sir Frederick Hamilton, and a trooper carried in a
heap of dry straw, and piled it against the western wall, but did not
light it, because he was still afraid of crucifix and of candles. Seeing
this, the five troopers who were Sir Frederick Hamilton's body-
20   guard went up to the altar, and taking each a holy candle set the
straw in a blaze. The red tongues of fire rushed up towards the
roof, and crept along the floor, setting in a blaze the seats and
benches, and making the shadows of the troopers dance among the
corbels and the memorial tablets.
25   For a time the altar stood safe and apart in the midst of its white
light; the eyes of the troopers turned upon it. The abbot whom
they had thought dead had risen to his feet and now stood before it
with the crucifix lifted in both hands high above his head. Suddenly
he cried with a loud voice, 'Woe unto all who have struck down
30   those who have lived in the Light of the Lord, for they shall wander

---

12   *the* monks. *The . . .* NO, 1897.
12–13   *smoke* broke *the mystery . . .* NO.
13–14   *troopers* found again their courage and their new convictions, *and . . .* NO.
14   *the* little knot of *friars . . .* NO.
16   *house* of the enemies of your God,' *cried . . .* NO, 1897.
16–17   *Frederick,* and at his word one went out, and came in again carrying *a heap . . .* NO;
Frederick Hamilton, and at his word one went out, and came in again carrying *a heap . . .* 1897
to 1913.
17–18   *wall,* and, having done this, [∼ ∧ NO] fell back, for the fear of the crucifix and of
the holy candles was still in his heart. *Seeing . . .* NO to 1913.
19   *this the . . .* NO.
19–20   *Sir* Frederick's body-guard darted forward, *and . . .* NO; *Sir Frederick Hamilton's
body-guard* darted forward, *and . . .* 1897 to 1913.
19–20   *body- / guard; body-guard* NO to 1914, 1925A; *bodyguard* 1925E, 1927.
21–22   *up* and flickered from corbel to corbel and from tablet [and tablet NO] to tablet,
and crept . . . NO to 1913.
23–25   *benches.* The dance of the shadows passed away, and the dance of the fires began.
The troopers fell back towards the door in the southern wall, and watched those yellow
dancers springing hither and thither. ¶The altar for a time *stood . . .* NO.
23–25   *benches.* The dance of the shadows passed away, and the dance of the fires began.
The troopers fell back towards the door in the southern wall, and watched those yellow
dancers springing hither and thither. ¶*For . . .* 1897 to 1914.
25   *safe apart . . .* NO.*
26   *light.* Their eyes turned to it instinctively. The prior *whom . . .* NO.
26   *The* prior *whom . . .* 1897.
29–30   *who* smite *those . . .* NO to 1913.
30   *who* dwell within *the Light . . .* NO to 1913.
30   *Lord for . . .* NO.

among shadows, and among fires!' And having so cried he fell on his face dead, and the brass crucifix rolled down the steps of the altar. The smoke had now grown very thick, so that it drove the troopers out into the open air. Before them were burning houses.
35 Behind them shone the Abbey windows filled with saints and martyrs, awakened, as from a sacred trance, into an angry and animated life. The eyes of the troopers were dazzled, and for a while could see nothing but the flaming faces of saints and martyrs. Presently, however, they saw a man covered with dust who came run-
40 ning towards them. 'Two messengers,' he cried, 'have been sent by the defeated Irish to raise against you the whole country about Manor Hamilton, and if you do not stop them you will be overpowered in the woods before you reach home again! They ride north-east between Ben Bulben and Cashel-na-Gael.'
45 Sir Frederick Hamilton called to him the five troopers who had first fired upon the friars and said, 'Mount quickly, and ride through the woods towards the mountain, and get before these men, and kill them.'

In a moment the troopers were gone, and before many moments
50 they had splashed across the river at what is now called Buckley's Ford, and plunged into the woods. They followed a beaten track that wound along the northern bank of the river. The boughs of the birch and mountain ash mingled above, and hid the cloudy moonlight, leaving the pathway in almost complete darkness. They

---

31   *among* the ungovernable shadows, and follow the ungovernable *fires* . . . NO to 1913.
31–32   *fell* upon *his* . . . NO.
32   *the* brazen *crucifix* . . . NO to 1913.
32   *rolled* crashing *down* . . . NO.
33   *thick,* and a sudden puff of *it* . . . NO.
35   *the* painted windows of the Abbey *filled* . . . NO to 1913.
35   *with* flame-illumined *saints* . . . NO.
35–36   *martyrs,* awaked, *as* . . . NO.
36–37   *and* vehement life. For a time the dazzled *eyes* . . . NO.
36–37   *and* vehement *life* . . . 1897.
37–38   *troopers could* . . . NO.*
38–39   *see* naught but these things. *Presently* . . . NO.
44–45   *between* Bulben and Cope's Mountain!' ¶*Sir* . . . NO; *between* the Mountain of Gulben and the Strong Place of the Strangers!' ¶*Sir* . . . 1897.
45–46   *who* did him such good service in the abbey *and said* . . . NO.
46   *the* monks *and said* . . . 1897 to 1914.
46   *said* 'Mount . . . NO.
49   *gone and* . . . NO.
49–50   *many* minutes *they* . . . NO.
53   *and* quicken trees *mingled* . . . NO to 1914.
53   *hid* out *the* . . . NO.

55 rode at a rapid trot, now chatting together, now watching some stray weasel or rabbit scuttling away in the darkness. Gradually, as the gloom and silence of the woods oppressed them, they drew closer together, and began to talk rapidly; they were old comrades and knew each other's lives. One was married, and told how glad
60 his wife would be to see him return safe from this harebrained expedition against the White Friars, and to hear how fortune had made amends for rashness. The oldest of the five, whose wife was dead, spoke of a flagon of wine which awaited him upon an upper shelf; while a third, who was the youngest, had a sweetheart watch-
65 ing for his return, and he rode a little way before the others, not talking at all.

Suddenly the young man stopped, and they saw that his horse was trembling. 'I saw something,' he said, 'and yet it may have been but a shadow. It looked like a great worm with a silver crown upon
70 his head.' One of the five put his hand up to his forehead as if about to cross himself, but remembering that he had changed his religion he put it down, and said, 'I am certain it was but a shadow, for there are a great many about us, and of very strange kinds.' Then they rode on in silence. It had been raining in the earlier part
75 of the day, and the drops fell from the branches, wetting their hair and their shoulders. In a little they began to talk again. They had been in many battles against many a rebel together, and now told

---

59   *knew* the details of *each* . . . NO.
61   *against* Sligo *and* . . . NO.
62   *rashness.* Another, *the* oldest . . . NO.
62-63 *five* was a widower, but talked *of a* . . . NO.
64   *third,* the youngest, who *had* . . . NO.
64   *third who* . . . 1897.
65   *return rode* . . . NO.*
65   *little before* . . . NO.*
65   *others not* . . . NO.
66-67 *all. Suddenly* this *young* . . . NO.
66-67 *all. Suddenly* . . . 1897 to 1914.
68   *trembling 'I* . . . 1927.
68-69 *said,* 'but I do not know but that it may be one of the shadows. *It* . . . NO.
68-69 *yet* I do not know but it may have been one of the shadows. *It* . . . 1897 to 1914.
71-72 *remembering* his changed religion *put* . . . NO.
72-73 *said:* 'Undoubtedly it must have been one of the shadows of [shadows, of 1897] which *there* . . . NO, 1897.
72   *said: 'I* . . . 1908 to 1927.
73   *many* all *about* . . . NO, 1897.
73   *us and* . . . NO.
73   *of* many *strange* . . . NO, 1897.
73-74 *kinds.' They* . . . NO.*

each other over again the story of their wounds, and half forgot the terrible solitude of the woods.

80   Suddenly the first two horses neighed, and then stood still, and would go no further. Before them was a glint of water, and they knew by the rushing sound that it was a river. They dismounted, and after much tugging and coaxing brought the horses to the river-side. In the midst of the water stood a tall old woman with

85   grey hair flowing over a grey dress. She stood up to her knees in the water, and stooped from time to time as though washing. Presently they could see that she was washing something that half floated. The moon cast a flickering light upon it, and they saw that it was the dead body of a man, and, while they were looking at it,

90   the eddy of the river turned the face towards them, and each of the five troopers recognised at the same moment his own face. While they stood dumb and motionless with horror, the woman began to speak, saying slowly and loudly, 'Did you see my son? He has upon his head a crown of silver.' Then the oldest of the troopers, he who

95   had been most often wounded, drew his sword and said, 'I have fought for the truth of my God, and need not fear the shadows of Satan,' and with that rushed into the water. In a moment he returned. The woman had vanished, and though he had thrust his sword into air and water he had found nothing.

100   The five troopers remounted, and set their horses at the ford,

---

78   *other* anew *the story* . . . NO.
78   *and* by thus awakening in their hearts that strongest of all fellowships, the fellowship of the sword, they *half* . . . NO; *and* so awakened in their hearts the strongest of all fellowships, the fellowship of the sword, and *half* . . . 1897 to 1914.
80   *the* two first *horses* . . . NO, 1897.
84   *river- / side*. They soon discovered the cause of the fright of the horses, for *in the midst* . . . NO.
84   *tall* elderly *woman* . . . NO.
88   *it and* . . . NO.
89–90   *at it*, an *eddy* . . . NO to 1914.
90   *face, towards* . . . NO.
91   *recognized* . . . 1897, 1908.
93   *loudly: 'Did* . . . NO to 1927.
93–94   *has* a crown of silver on his head, and there are rubies in the crown.' *Then* . . . NO to 1913.
95   *and* cried: *'I* . . . NO to 1913.
95   *said: 'I* . . . 1914 to 1927.
96   *God and* . . . NO.
98   *vanished* utterly at his approach, *and* . . . NO.
99   *water* alike *he* . . . NO.
100   *remounted and* . . . 1925A.
100   *and* endeavoured to make their horses cross through *the* . . . NO.

but all to no purpose. They tried again and again, and went plunging hither and thither, the horses foaming and rearing. 'Let us,' said the old trooper, 'ride back a little into the wood, and strike the river higher up.' They rode in under the boughs, the ground-ivy
105 crackling under the hoofs, and the branches striking against their steel caps. After about twenty minutes' riding they came out again upon the river, and after another ten minutes found a place where it was possible to cross without sinking above the stirrups. The wood upon the other side was very thin, and broke the moonlight
110 into long streams. The wind had arisen, and had begun to drive the clouds rapidly across the face of the moon, so that thin streams of light were dancing among scattered bushes and small fir-trees. The tops of the trees began also to moan, and the sound of it was like the voice of the dead in the wind; and the troopers remem-
115 bered that the dead in Purgatory are said to be spitted upon the points of the trees and upon the points of the rocks. They turned a little to the south, in the hope that they might strike the beaten path again, but they could find no trace of it.

Meanwhile, the moaning grew louder and louder, and the danc-
120 ing of the moonlight seemed more and more rapid. Gradually they began to be aware of a sound of distant music. It was the sound of a bagpipe, and they rode towards it with great joy. It came from the bottom of a deep, cuplike hollow. In the midst of the hollow was an old man with a red cap and withered face. He sat beside a fire of

---

102   *thither,* their *horses* . . . NO.
103   *a* piece *into* . . . NO.
106   *minutes they* . . . NO.*
107   *minutes'* riding *found* . . . NO.
108   *sinking* below *the* . . . NO to 1914, 1925A.
110   *and begun* . . . NO.*
112   *light* seemed to be dancing a grotesque dance among the *scattered* . . . NO to 1913.
112   *fir-trees* 1908 to 1927; *fir trees* NO; *fir- / trees* 1897.
113–14   *was* as the *voice* . . . NO.
114   *dead* coming down the *wind* . . . NO.
114–15   *remembered* fearfully the legend that tells how *the dead* . . . NO; *remembered* the legend that tells how *the dead* . . . 1897; *remembered* the belief that tells how *the dead* . . . 1908, 1913.
115   *purgatory* . . . NO to 1927.
115   *are spitted* . . . NO to 1913.*
117   *south in* . . . NO.
119–20   *and louder, and the* dance *of* . . . NO to 1913.
120   *the* white moon-fires *more and* . . . NO to 1913.
122   *rode* toward *it* . . . NO.
123   *cuplike* 1925, 1927; *cup-like* NO to 1913; *cup- / like* 1914.
123–24   *the hollow* they found an elderly *man* . . . NO.

125   sticks, and had a burning torch thrust into the earth at his feet, and played an old bagpipe furiously. His red hair dripped over his face like the iron rust upon a rock. 'Did you see my wife?' he said, looking up a moment; 'she was washing! she was washing!' 'I am afraid of him,' said the young trooper; 'I fear he is not a right man.'

130   'No,' said the old trooper, 'he is a man like ourselves, for I can see the sun-freckles upon his face. We will compel him to be our guide'; and at that he drew his sword, and the others did the same. They stood in a ring round the piper, and pointed their swords at him, and the old trooper then told him that they must kill two

135   rebels, who had taken the road between Ben Bulben and the great mountain spur that is called Cashel-na-Gael, and that he must get up on the horse before one of them and be their guide, for they had lost their way. The piper pointed to a neighbouring tree, and they saw an old white horse ready bitted, bridled, and saddled. He slung

140   the pipe across his back, and, taking the torch in his hand, got upon the horse, and started off before them, as hard as he could go.

    The wood grew thinner now, and the ground began to slope up toward the mountain. The moon had already set, but the stars shone brightly between the clouds. The ground sloped more and

145   more until at last they rode far above the woods upon the wide top of the mountain. The woods lay spread out mile after mile below, and away to the south shot up the red glare of the burning town. The guide drew rein suddenly, and pointing upwards with the hand

---

125   *torch* jammed down *into* . . . NO.
127-28   *he* cried, *looking* . . . NO to 1913.
129   *him!' said* . . . NO, 1897.
129   *trooper, 'I* . . . 1897 to 1927.
129-30   *is* one of the Sidhe [shee NO; Shee 1897].' *'No* . . . NO to 1913.
130   *man, for* . . . NO to 1913.*
132   *guide;' and at* . . . NO, 1897.
134   *him.* The *old* . . . NO.
135-36   *between* Bulben and Cope Mountain, *and that* . . . NO; *between* the Mountain of Gulben and the mountain that is called the Strong Place of the Strangers, *and that* . . . 1897.
136-37   *must* up *before* . . . NO; *must get up before* . . . 1897 to 1913.*
137   *be guide* . . . NO.*
138   *piper* turned, and *pointed* . . . NO to 1913.
139   *He* then *slung* . . . NO.
140   *pipe* on to *his back* . . . NO.
141   *them,* running *as hard* . . . NO.
142   *thinner* and thinner, *and* . . . NO to 1913.
142-43   *up* towards *the mountain* . . . NO.
143-44   *set,* and the little white flames of the stars had come out everywhere. *The* . . . NO to 1913.
146   *of* Cope's *Mountain* . . . NO.
147-48   *town.* But before and above them were the little white flames. *The* . . . NO to 1913.

150 that did not hold the torch, shrieked out, 'Look; look at the holy candles!' and then plunged forward at a gallop, waving the torch hither and thither. 'Do you hear the hoofs of the messengers?' cried the guide. 'Quick, quick! or they will be gone out of your hands!' and he laughed as with delight of the chase. The troopers thought they could hear far off, and as if below them, rattle of

155 hoofs; but now the ground began to slope more and more, and the speed grew more headlong moment by moment. They tried to pull up, but they could not, for the horses seemed to have gone mad. The guide had thrown the reins on to the neck of the old white horse, and was waving his arms and singing in Gaelic.

160 Suddenly they saw the thin gleam of a river, at an immense distance below, and knew that they were upon the brink of the abyss that is now called Lugnagall, or in English the Stranger's Leap. The six horses sprang forward, and five screams went up into the air, and a moment later five men and horses fell with a dull crash upon the

165 green slopes at the foot of the rocks.

---

149   *Look! look* ... NO.
150   *gallop. waving* ... 1913.
151   *thither.* The other horses galloped after. *'Do* ... NO.
152-53   *will* escape you!' *and* ... NO.
154   *them, the rattle* ... NO, 1897.
155   *hoofs, but* they soon had no time to listen, for *the* ... NO.
155-56   *slope* down *and the* ... NO.
157   *but* in vain, *for* ... NO to 1913.
159   *arms* about *and* ... NO.
159-60   *singing* a wild Gaelic song. *Suddenly* ... NO to 1913.
160   *saw* a gleam of water *at* ... NO.
161-62   *they* rushed towards the terrible brink of Lugnagall. Their *six* ... NO.
162   *called* the Steep Place of the Strangers. *The* ... 1897.
162   *called* Lug-na-Gael, *or* ... 1908 to 1927.
163-64   *sprang* into the abyss. *A moment* ... NO.
163   *air,* [~; 1897] *a* ... 1897 to 1914.*
164-65   *later* the lake sent up five columns of spray, and after a second's uproar smoothed itself out and began again to fondle and murmur over the countless little white flames of the stars. NO.
[In NO, the story is signed W. B. Yeats.]

WHERE THERE IS NOTHING, THERE IS GOD

The little wicker houses at Tullagh, where the Brothers were accustomed to pray, or bend over many handicrafts, when twilight had driven them from the fields, were empty, for the hardness of the winter had brought the brotherhood together in the little
5   wooden house under the shadow of the wooden chapel; and Abbot Malathgeneus, Brother Dove, Brother Bald Fox, Brother Peter, Brother Patrick, Brother Bittern, Brother Fair-Brows, and many too young to have won names in the great battle, sat about the fire with ruddy faces, one mending lines to lay in the river for eels, one
10   fashioning a snare for birds, one mending the broken handle of a spade, one writing in a large book, and one shaping a jewelled box to hold the book; and among the rushes at their feet lay the scholars, who would one day be Brothers, and whose school-house it was, and for the succour of whose tender years the great fire was
15   supposed to leap and flicker. One of these, a child of eight or nine years, called Olioll, lay upon his back looking up through the hole

---

Printings: *The Sketch*, October 21, 1896; 1897; 1908; 1913; 1914.
Text from 1932. [In 1914, Yeats made a very extensive revision of this story; apparently, however, he was still dissatisfied with it, for it did not appear in the 1925 or 1927 volumes. When he was preparing the text of *Mythologies* he decided to include it once again. In selecting the version of the story to use as the basis for his reprint, he either forgot the 1914 story or chose to ignore it, returning to the 1908/1913 form of the story. There are only three places in which the 1913 revision brought the text to final form, all of them extremely insignificant (see lines 7, 62, 156-57); the fact that these variants from the 1908 text are so few and so minor means that that text is almost as likely as the 1913 text to have been the version Yeats worked on in making his final revisions.]
Change of name: Olioll 1897 to 1932 [except line 131]; Aodh S.
Title: ... GOD. S, 1908, 1913.
[Lines 1-4 and part of line 5 are absent from 1914, which begins 'Abbot Malathgeneus. ...']
1   *houses*, where the Brothers of Tallagh *were* ... S; *houses,* where the Brothers of the Grave of the People of Partholan *were* ... 1897.
2   *pray or* ... S.
2   *handicrafts when* ... S.
3   *for the* severity *of* ... S.
4-5 *in the* square *wooden house* ... S.
5-7 *and* Coarb Malathgeneus, Brother Moal Columb, Brother Moal Melruan, Brother Peter, Brother Patrick, Brother Fintain, *and* ... S.
5-6 *and* Coarb *Malathgeneus* ... 1897.
7   *brows* ... 1897, 1908.
7-8 *Fair- / Brows sat* ... 1914.*
8-9 *fire, one mending* ... 1914.*
11-12 *and one* hammering at the corner of a gold box that was *to* ... 1914.
13   *scholars,* brothers to be, *whose* ... S.
13-15 *Brothers. One* ... 1914.*
16   *back* gazing *up* ... S.

48

in the roof, through which the smoke went, and watching the stars
appearing and disappearing in the smoke with mild eyes, like the
eyes of a beast of the field. He turned presently to the Brother who
20 wrote in the big book, and whose duty was to teach the children,
and said, 'Brother Dove, to what are the stars fastened?' The
Brother, rejoicing to see so much curiosity in the stupidest of his
scholars, laid down the pen and said, 'There are nine crystalline
spheres, and on the first the Moon is fastened, on the second the
25 planet Mercury, on the third the planet Venus, on the fourth the
Sun, on the fifth the planet Mars, on the sixth the planet Jupiter,
on the seventh the planet Saturn; these are the wandering stars;
and on the eighth are fastened the fixed stars; but the ninth sphere
is a sphere of the substance on which the breath of God moved in
30 the beginning.'

'What is beyond that?' said the child.

'There is nothing beyond that; there is God.'

And then the child's eyes strayed to the jewelled box, where one
great ruby was gleaming in the light of the fire, and he said, 'Why
35 has Brother Peter put a great ruby on the side of the box?'

'The ruby is a symbol of the love of God.'

'Why is the ruby a symbol of the love of God?'

'Because it is red, like fire, and fire burns up everything, and
where there is nothing, there is God.'

40 The child sank into silence, but presently sat up and said, 'There
is somebody outside.'

'No,' replied the Brother. 'It is only the wolves; I have heard
them moving about in the snow for some time. They are growing
very wild, now that the winter drives them from the mountains.
45 They broke into a fold last night and carried off many sheep, and if
we are not careful they will devour everything.'

'No, it is the footstep of a man, for it is heavy; but I can hear the
footsteps of the wolves also.'

---

17   *smoke* poured, *watching* . . . S.
18–19   *smoke. He* . . . 1914.*
21   *Brother* Moal Columb, *to* . . . S.
22   *Brother*, pleased to find *so* . . . 1914.
23   *the* style *and* . . . S.
24   *moon* . . . S.
26   *sun* . . . S.
27   *Saturn (these* . . . S.
27–28   *stars), and* . . . S.
29–31   *sphere* made out of the First Substance.' ¶ '*What* . . . 1914.
31   *that* sphere?' *said* . . . S.
33–34   *to the* gold box, *and* . . . 1914.
35   *of* his *box* . . . 1914.

He had no sooner done speaking than somebody rapped three
50   times, but with no great loudness.

'I will go and open, for he must be very cold.'

'Do not open, for it may be a man-wolf, and he may devour us all.'

But the boy had already drawn back the heavy wooden bolt, and
55   all the faces, most of them a little pale, turned towards the slowly=
opening door.

'He has beads and a cross, he cannot be a man-wolf,' said the
child, as a man with the snow heavy on his long, ragged beard, and
on the matted hair that fell over his shoulders and nearly to his
60   waist, and dropping from the tattered cloak that but half-covered
his withered brown body, came in and looked from face to face
with mild, ecstatic eyes. Standing some way from the fire, and with
eyes that had rested at last upon the Abbot Malathgeneus, he cried
out, 'O blessed abbot, let me come to the fire and warm myself and
65   dry the snow from my beard and my hair and my cloak; that I may
not die of the cold of the mountains and anger the Lord with a
wilful martyrdom.'

'Come to the fire,' said the abbot, 'and warm yourself, and eat the
food the boy Olioll will bring you. It is sad indeed that any for
70   whom Christ has died should be as poor as you.'

The man sat over the fire, and Olioll took away his now dripping
cloak and laid meat and bread and wine before him; but he would
eat only of the bread, and he put away the wine, asking for water.

50–51   *times. ¶I* . . . 1914.*
52   *and* might *devour* . . . S.
54   *already* shot *back* . . . S.
54   *drawn* the *bolt* . . . 1914.
55   *all* faces, the most *a* . . . S.
55–56   *slowly-opening* 1897, 1914; *slowly opening* S; *slowly- / opening* 1908, 1913.
57   *cross,* and *cannot* . . . S.
58   *man, with* . . . S.
59   *on* his *matted* . . . 1914.
59   *hair, that* . . . S to 1914.
60   *and* upon *the* . . . 1914.
61   *looked* slowly *from* . . . 1914.
61–62   *to face. Standing* . . . 1914.*
62   *eyes.' Standing* . . . 1908.
63   *the* Coarb *Malathgeneus* . . . S, 1897.
63–64   *he* said, 'O . . . 1914.
64   *blessed* Coarb, *let* . . . S, 1897.
64–65   *myself; that* . . . 1914.*
66   *cold and* . . . 1914.*
68   *said the* Coarb, *'and warm* . . . S, 1897.
68–69   *abbot.* 'It is a pitiful thing surely *that* . . . 1914.
72–73   *would* only eat *of* . . . S.
73–74   *water* in its stead. *When* . . . S.

When his beard and hair had begun to dry a little and his limbs had
75 ceased to shiver with the cold, he spoke again.

'O blessed abbot, have pity on the poor, have pity on a beggar
who has trodden the bare world this many a year, and give me
some labour to do, the hardest there is, for I am the poorest of
God's poor.'

80 Then the Brothers discussed together what work they could put
him to, and at first to little purpose, for there was no labour that
had not found its labourer in that busy community; but at last one
remembered that Brother Bald Fox, whose business it was to turn
the great quern in the quern-house, for he was too stupid for
85 anything else, was getting old for so heavy a labour; and so the
beggar was put to the quern from the morrow.

The cold passed away, and the spring grew to summer, and the
quern was never idle, nor was it turned with grudging labour, for
when any passed the beggar was heard singing as he drove the
90 handle round. The last gloom, too, had passed from that happy
community, for Olioll, who had always been stupid and unteacha-
ble, grew clever, and this was the more miraculous because it had
come of a sudden. One day he had been even duller than usual,
and was beaten and told to know his lesson better on the morrow or
95 be sent into a lower class among little boys who would make a joke
of him. He had gone out in tears, and when he came the next day,
although his stupidity, born of a mind that would listen to every
wandering sound and brood upon every wandering light, had so
long been the byword of the school, he knew his lesson so well that

---

74 *dry and* . . . 1914.*
75 *shiver, he* . . . 1914.*
75–78 *again.* ¶'Set me to some labour, *the hardest* . . . 1914.
76 *blessed* Coarb, *have pity on the* . . . S, 1897.
80 *the* brethren *discussed* . . . S.
82 *labourer; but* . . . 1914.*
83 *Brother* Melruan, *whose* . . . S.
84 *quern-house—for he* . . . S.
84–85 *for* aught *else—was* . . . S.
84–85 *for* aught *else* . . . 1897.
85–87 *old;* and so he could go to the quern-house in the morning. ¶*The* . . . 1914.
86 *was* bid labour at *the quern* . . . S, 1897.
90–91 *last* reason for gloom passed from the brotherhood, *for* . . . 1914.
92 *clever* and alert, *and* . . . S, 1897.
94 *beaten and* bid *know* . . . S, 1897.
94 *lesson* the *better* . . . S.
94 *better* in future *or* . . . 1914.
95–96 *make a* jeer *of* . . . S, 1897.
97–98 *stupidity had* . . . 1914.*
99 *knew* it with such perfection *that* . . . S.

The Secret Rose

100 he passed to the head of the class, and from that day was the best of
scholars. At first Brother Dove thought this was an answer to his
own prayers to the Virgin, and took it for a great proof of the love
she bore him; but when many far more fervid prayers had failed to
add a single wheat-sheaf to the harvest, he began to think that the
105 child was trafficking with bards, or druids, or witches, and resolved
to follow and watch. He had told his thought to the abbot, who bid
him come to him the moment he hit the truth; and the next day,
which was a Sunday, he stood in the path when the abbot and the
Brothers were coming from vespers, with their white habits upon
110 them, and took the abbot by the habit and said, 'The beggar is of
the greatest of saints and of the workers of miracle. I followed
Olioll but now, and by his slow steps and his bent head I saw that
the weariness of his stupidity was over him, and when he came to
the little wood by the quern-house I knew by the path broken in the
115 underwood and by the footmarks in the muddy places that he had
gone that way many times. I hid behind a bush where the path
doubled upon itself at a sloping place, and understood by the tears
in his eyes that his stupidity was too old and his wisdom too new to
save him from terror of the rod. When he was in the quern-house I
120 went to the window and looked in, and the birds came down and
perched upon my head and my shoulders, for they are not timid in
that holy place; and a wolf passed by, his right side shaking my
habit, his left the leaves of a bush. Olioll opened his book and
turned to the page I had told him to learn, and began to cry, and
125 the beggar sat beside him and comforted him until he fell asleep.
When his sleep was of the deepest the beggar knelt down and
prayed aloud, and said, "O Thou Who dwellest beyond the stars,

---

101   *Brother* Moal Columb thought the change *an* . . . S.
102-3 *prayers* and grew proud; *but* . . . 1914.
103-4 *prayers* for more important things had failed, he convinced himself *that* . . . 1914.
104   *wheat- / sheaf; wheat-sheaf* S, 1897; *wheatsheaf* 1908, 1913.
106   *the* Coarb, *who* . . . S, 1897.
106-7 *who* told him to *come* . . . 1914.
108   *when the* Coarb *and* . . . S, 1897.
108-9 *and the* brethren *were* . . . S.
109-10 *vespers, and took* . . . 1914.*
110   *the* Coarb *by* . . . S, 1897.
110   *by the* sleeve *and* . . . 1914.
112-113 *now, and when* . . . 1914.*
113   *when* we *came* . . . S.
115   *underwood* S, 1897; *under- / wood* 1908; *under-wood* 1913, 1914.
115   *footmarks; foot-marks* S to 1908, 1914; *foot- / marks* 1913.
118-19 *to* bring him peace unshaken by *terror* . . . S, 1897.
124   *had* bid him *learn* . . . S, 1897.

52

show forth Thy power as at the beginning, and let knowledge sent
from Thee awaken in his mind, wherein is nothing from the world,
130 that the nine orders of angels may glorify Thy name"; and then a
light broke out of the air and wrapped Olioll, and I smelt the
breath of roses. I stirred a little in my wonder, and the beggar
turned and saw me, and, bending low, said, "O Brother Dove, if I
have done wrong, forgive me, and I will do penance. It was my pity
135 moved me"; but I was afraid and I ran away, and did not stop
running until I came here.'
    Then all the Brothers began talking together, one saying it was
such and such a saint, and one that it was not he but another; and
one that it was none of these, for they were still in their brother-
140 hoods, but that it was such and such a one; and the talk was as near
to quarrelling as might be in that gentle community, for each would
claim so great a saint for his native province. At last the abbot said,
'He is none that you have named, for at Easter I had greeting from
all, and each was in his brotherhood; but he is Aengus the Lover of
145 God, and the first of those who have gone to live in the wild places
and among the wild beasts. Ten years ago he felt the burden of
many labours in a brotherhood under the Hill of Patrick and went
into the forest that he might labour only with song to the Lord; but
the fame of his holiness brought many thousands to his cell, so that
150 a little pride clung to a soul from which all else had been driven.
Nine years ago he dressed himself in rags, and from that day none
has seen him, unless, indeed, it be true that he has been seen living
among the wolves on the mountains and eating the grass of the

---

129   *in* this *mind* . . . S.
129-30 *world"; and* . . . 1914.*
130   *name;" and* . . . 1897.
131   *air and I* . . . 1914.*
131   *wrapped* Aodh, *and* . . . S to 1913.
132   *little, and* . . . 1914.*
133   *Brother* Moal Columb, *if* . . . S.
135   *me;" but* . . . 1897.
135   *but* terror had taken hold of me, and I fled, *and did* . . . S, 1897.
136-37 *came* hither.' ¶*Then* . . . S, 1897.
137   *brothers* . . . S.
138   *he, but* . . . S, 1897.
140-41 *talk was* near to quarrelling, *for* . . . 1914.
141-42 *each* had begun to *claim* . . . 1914.
142   *the* Coarb *said* . . . S, 1897.
144   *Angus* . . . S, 1897.
144-46 *the* Walker to Nowhere. *Ten* . . . 1914.
146-47 *he went* . . . 1914.*
147   *under* Croagh *Patrick* . . . S.
151-52 *day* nobody *has seen* . . . 1914.

fields. Let us go to him and bow down before him; for at last, after
155 long seeking, he has found the nothing that is God; and bid him
lead us in the pathway he has trodden.'

They passed in their white habits along the beaten path in the
wood, the acolytes swinging their censers before them, and the
abbot, with his crozier studded with precious stones, in the midst of
160 the incense; and came before the quern-house and knelt down and
began to pray, awaiting the moment when the child would wake,
and the Saint cease from his watch and come to look at the sun
going down into the unknown darkness, as his way was.

THE OLD MEN OF THE TWILIGHT

At the place, close to the Dead Man's Point, at the Rosses, where
the disused pilot-house looks out to sea through two round windows like eyes, a mud cottage stood in the last century. It also was a
watchhouse, for a certain old Michael Bruen, who had been a smug-
5 gler, and was still the father and grandfather of smugglers, lived
there, and when, after nightfall, a tall French schooner crept over
the bay from Roughley, it was his business to hang a horn lantern in
the southern window, that the news might travel to Dorren's Island, and thence, by another horn lantern, to the village of the

---

155 *God.'* 1914 [1914 version ends here].
156-57 *trodden.'* [~. ∧ 1908] *They* ... S to 1908.
158-59 *and the* Coarb, *with his* ... S, 1897.
162 *come* forth *and look* ... S, 1897.

Printings: *The Weekly Sun Literary Supplement,* December 1, 1895; *The Chap Book* (Chicago),
June 1, 1896; 1897; 1908; 1913; 1914; 1925; 1927.
Text from 1932.
Title: ST. PATRICK AND THE PEDANTS. WS;
S. ... PEDANTS CB; ... TWILIGHT. 1913.
1 *Point, at* Rosses, *where* ... WS, CB; *Point, at the* Three Headlands, *where* ... 1897.
4 *watchhouse* 1897 to 1927; *watch- / house* WS; *watch-house* CB.
4 *watch-house; for* ... CB.
4 *Bruin* ... WS, CB.
4-5 *smuggler* n [*sic*] his day, *and was* ... WS; *smuggler* in his day, *and was* ... CB to 1913.
6 *there; and* ... CB.
6 *when,* under the shadow of night, *a* ... WS to 1897.
6 *tall schooner* ... WS to 1913.*
7 *bay, from* ... 1897.
7 *from Rougley* O'Byrne *it* ... WS; *from Roughley* O'Byrne, *it* ... CB; *from Roughley* of the
Children of Byrne, *it* ... 1897.
7 *lanthorn* ... WS to 1927.
9 *and* from *thence* ... WS to 1914, 1925A.
9 *lanthorn* ... WS to 1927.
9-10 *of Rosses. But for* ... WS; *of Rosses;* and *but for* ... CB; *of the* Headlands. *But
for* ... 1897.

10 Rosses. But for this glimmering of messages, he had little business with mankind, for he was very old, and had no thought for anything but for the making of his soul, bent double over his Spanish beads. One night he had watched hour after hour, because a gentle and favourable wind was blowing, and *La Mère de Miséricorde* was
15 much overdue. At last he was about to lie down upon his heap of straw, for he knew that she would not dare to round Roughley and come to an anchor after daybreak, when he saw a long line of herons flying slowly from Dorren's Island and towards the pools which lie, half choked with reeds, behind what is called the Second
20 Rosses. He had never before seen herons flying over the sea, for they are shore-keeping birds, and partly because this had startled him out of his drowsiness, and more because the long delay of the schooner had emptied his cupboard, he took down his rusty shot=gun, of which the barrel was tied on with a piece of string, and set
25 out for the pools.

In a little he came upon the herons, of which there were a great

---

10-11 *little* communion *with* . . . WS to 1913.
11-12 *anything, but* . . . 1897.
12 *but the* . . . WS, CB.*
12-13 *soul,* [~ ∧ CB] at the foot of the Spanish crucifix of carved oak that hung by his chimney, or bent double over the rosary of stone beads brought to him in a cargo of silks and laces out of France. *One* . . . WS to 1913.
14 *blowing, and* 'La Mére [*sic*] de Miséricorde' *was* . . . WS, CB.
15 *overdue;* and *he was* [and *was* WS, CB] . . . WS to 1914.
16 *straw,* seeing that the dawn was whitening the east [East WS], and that the schooner *would* . . . WS to 1913; *straw,* because the dawn was whitening the east, and *he knew that she would* . . . 1914.
16-17 *round Roughley* O'Byrne and swing at *anchor* . . . WS; *round Roughly* O'Byrne and lie at *anchor* . . . CB; *round Roughley* of the Children of Byrne and swing at *anchor* . . . 1897.
17 *anchor* by the second Rosses, except [second Headland, except 1897] under the shadow of night; [~, CB] *when* . . . WS to 1897.
17 *daybreak; when* . . . 1908 to 1927.
19 *which* are *half-choked* . . . CB.
19 *half choked* WS, 1897 to 1927; *half-choked* CB.
19-20 *reeds,* [~ ∧ CB] in the midst of *Rosses. He* . . . WS, CB; *reeds,* behind the Headlands. *He* . . . 1897.
23 *schooner* kept his cupboard empty, *he* . . . WS to 1913.
23-24 *shot-gun* WS, 1897 to 1913, 1925, 1927; *shotgun* CB; *shot- / gun* 1914.
24-26 *and* followed them towards the pools. ¶When he came close enough to hear the sighing of the rushes in the outermost pool, the morning was grey over the world, so that the tall rushes, the still waters, the vague clouds, the thin mist [mists 1913] lying among the sand-heaps [sand heaps WS, CB], seemed carved out of an enormous pearl. *In* . . . WS to 1913.
24-25 *and* followed the herons towards *the* . . . 1914.
26 *of* whom *there* . . . WS to 1914, 1925A.

number, standing with lifted legs in the shallow water; and crouching down behind a bank of rushes, looked to the priming of his
gun, and bent for a moment over his rosary to murmur, 'Holy S.
30   Patrick, I have a great desire for heron-pie; and if you keep me from
missing I will say a rosary to you every night until the pie is eaten.'
Then he lay down, and, resting his gun upon a large stone, turned
towards a heron which stood upon a bank of smooth grass over a
little stream that flowed into the pool; for he feared to take the
35   rheumatism by wading, as he would have to do if he shot one of
those which stood in the water. But when he looked along the
barrel the heron was gone, and, to his wonder and terror, a man
that seemed of an infinitely great age stood in its place. He lowered
the gun, and once more the heron stood there with bent head and
40   motionless feathers. He raised the gun, and no sooner did he look
along the barrel than the old man was again before him, only to
vanish when he lowered the gun for the second time. He laid the
gun down, and crossed himself three times, and said a *Paternoster*
and an *Ave Maria,* and muttered half aloud, 'Some enemy of God is
45   fishing in the blessed water,' and thereupon he aimed very carefully and slowly. He fired, and when the smoke had gone saw an
old man, huddled upon the grass, and a long line of herons flying

---

27-28   *water, and, crouching* . . . CB.
29   *gun; and* . . . WS.
29-30   *murmur:* 'Patron Patrick, [~ ʌ WS] let me shoot a heron; made into a pie it will
support me for nearly four days, for I no longer eat as in my youth. *If you* . . . WS to 1914.
29   *murmur:* 'Holy . . . 1925, 1927.
29   *St.* . . . 1925, 1927.
33   *heron* who *stood* . . . WS, CB.
34   *pool, for* . . . CB.
34-35   *take rheumatism* . . . WS, CB.*
36   *those* who *stood* . . . WS, CB.
37-38   *man* of *infinitely* . . . WS to 1914.
38   *age* and infirmity *stood* . . . WS to 1914.
39   *and the* . . . WS to 1914.*
40   *feathers,* as though it had slept from the beginning of the world. *He* . . . WS to 1914.
41   *along the* iron than that enemy of all enchantment brought the old man *again* . . . WS
to 1913.
41   *along the* iron *than* . . . 1914.
43-44   *a* 'Paternoster' *and an* . . . WS.
44   *an* 'Ave Maria,' *and* . . . WS.
44   *Maria and* . . . 1897 ['*Maria*' italic in 1897].
44   *aloud:* 'Some . . . CB to 1927.
44-45   *God* and of my patron is standing upon the smooth place and *fishing* . . . WS to
1914.
45   *and then aimed* . . . WS to 1914.
46   *slowly* and with an exultant heart. *He* . . . WS to 1897.
47   *man huddled* . . . CB.
47   *grass and* . . . WS, 1897 to 1913.
47-48   *flying* with clamour [clamor CB] *towards* . . . WS to 1913.

towards the sea. He went round a bend of the pool, and coming to the little stream looked down on a figure wrapped in faded clothes
50 of an ancient pattern and spotted with blood. He shook his head at the sight of so great a wickedness. Suddenly the clothes moved and an arm was stretched upwards towards the rosary which hung about his neck, and long wasted fingers almost touched the cross. He started back, crying: 'Wizard, I will let no wicked thing touch my
55 blessed beads.'

'If you listen to me,' replied a voice so faint that it was like a sigh, 'you will know that I am not a wizard, and you will let me kiss the cross before I die.'

'I will listen to you,' he answered, 'but I will not let you touch my
60 blessed beads,' and sitting on the grass a little way from the dying man, he reloaded his gun and laid it across his knees and composed himself to listen.

'I do not know how many generations ago we, who are now herons, were men of learning; we neither hunted, nor went to
65 battle, nor said prayers, nor sang songs, nor made love. The Druids told us, many a time, of a new Druid Patrick; and most among them were angry with him, while a few thought his doctrine merely their own doctrine set out in new images, and were for giving him wel-

---

48 *and, coming* . . . CB.
49 *stream, looked* . . . CB.
49 *down* at *a* . . . WS, CB.
50 *of* black and green of *an* . . . WS to 1913.
50 *pattern, and* . . . CB.
51 *moved, and* . . . WS, CB.
52 *stretched* upward *towards* . . . WS, CB.
53 *long, wasted* . . . CB.
54 *crying 'Wizard* . . . WS.
55–56 *beads';* [~!' CB; ~;' 1897] and the sense of a great danger just evaded made [just escaped made 1908 to 1914] him tremble. ¶*'If* . . . WS to 1914.
60 *beads;' and* . . . CB.
60 *and, sitting* . . . CB.
63 *I* know not *how* . . . WS to 1913.
64 *were* Ollamhs of King Leaghaire; *we* . . . WS, CB; *were* the men of learning of the King [of King 1914] Leaghaire; *we* . . . 1897 to 1914.
65–66 *battle, nor* listened to the Druids preaching by their grey stones, [~ ∧ WS] and even love, if it came to us at all, was but a transitory fire. The Druids and the poets *told* . . . WS to 1897; *battle, nor* listened to the Druids preaching, and even love, if it came to us at all, was but a passing fire. The [but a brief trivial thing. The 1914] Druids and the poets *told* . . . 1908 to 1914.
65 *druids* . . . 1925, 1927.
66 *us,* [~ ∧ CB] *many* and many *a time* . . . WS to 1913.
66 *time of* . . . CB.
66 *druid* . . . 1925, 1927.
66 *Patrick, and* . . . CB.
67 *were* fierce against *him* . . . WS to 1913.
67 *few* held *his* . . . WS to 1897.
67–68 *merely* the doctrine of the gods set out in new symbols, *and* . . . WS to 1914.

70 come; but we yawned when they spoke of him. At last they came crying that he was coming to the king's house, and fell to their dispute, but we would listen to neither party, for we disputed concerning prosody and the relative importance of rhyme and assonance, syllable and accent; nor were we disturbed when they passed our door with sticks of enchantment under their arms, travelling

75 towards the forest, nor when they returned after nightfall with pale faces and despairing cries; for the click of our knives writing our thoughts in Ogham delighted us. The next day crowds passed going to the king's house, and one of us, who had laid down his knife to yawn and stretch himself, heard a voice speaking far off;

80 but our hearts were deaf, and we carved and disputed and read, and laughed together. In a little we heard many feet coming towards the house, and presently two tall figures stood in the door, the one in white, the other in a crimson coat; and we knew the Druid Patrick and our king. We laid down the slender knives and

85 bowed before the king, but it was not the loud rough voice of our king that spoke to us, but a voice of rapture: "I preached the

---

69 *yawned* in the midst of their tale. *At* . . . WS to 1913.
70 *the* foss of [*the* liss of 1897] the king *and* . . . WS to 1897.
71-73 *for we* were busy with a dispute about the merits of the Great and of the Little Metre [great and little metres WS, CB]; *nor* . . . WS to 1914.
74 *with* staves *of* . . . WS to 1897.
74 *traveling* . . . CB.
75 *forest* to contend against his coming, *nor* . . . WS to 1913; *forest* to drive him away, *nor* . . . 1914.
75-76 *with* torn robes *and* [torn coats *and* 1914] . . . WS to 1914.
76 *cries, for* . . . CB.
76 *click,* click [~! 1897] *of* . . . WS to 1897.
76-78 *knives* filled [*knives writing our thoughts in Ogham* filled 1908 to 1914] us with peace and our dispute filled us with joy; nor even when in the morning crowds passed us to hear the strange Druid preaching the commandments of his God [god 1908, 1913]. The crowds [hear the preaching of the new Druid. The crowds 1914] passed, and one, [~ ∧ CB] *who* . . . WS to 1914.
77 *ogham* . . . 1925, 1927.
79 *himself heard* . . . CB.
79-80 *off,* and knew that the Druid Patrick was preaching within the foss of [the liss of 1897] the king; [~, CB] *but* . . . WS to 1897; *off,* and knew that the Druid Patrick was preaching within the king's house; *but* . . . 1908, 1913; *off* in the king's house; *but* . . . 1914.
81 *laughed* a thin laughter *together* . . . WS to 1913.
83 *crimson* robe; [~, CB] like a great lily and a heavy poppy; *and* . . . WS to 1913.
84 *druid* . . . 1925, 1927.
84 *our King* Leaghaire. *We* . . . WS to 1914.
85 *but* when the black and green robes had ceased to rustle, [~ ∧ CB] *it* . . . WS to 1913.
85 *loud, rough* . . . WS, CB.
85-86 *of* King Leaghaire *that* . . . WS to 1914.
86-87 *a* strange voice in which there was a rapture as of one speaking from behind a battlement of Druid flame: "I preached the commandments of the Maker of the world," *it* . . . WS to 1913.
86 *voice* in which there seemed to be a strange *rapture* . . . 1914.

commandments of God," it said; "within the king's house, and from the centre of the earth to the windows of Heaven there was a great silence, so that the eagle floated with unmoving wings, and the fish
90 with unmoving fins, while the linnets and the wrens and the sparrows stilled their ever-trembling tongues, and the clouds were like white marble, and the shrimps in the far-off sea-pools became still, enduring eternity in patience, although it was hard. But your slender knives kept up their clicking, and, all else being silent, the
95 sound is not to be endured. Because you have lived where the feet of the angels cannot touch your heads, nor the hair of the demons sweep your feet-soles, I shall make you an example for ever and ever; you shall become grey herons and stand pondering in grey pools and flit over the world in that hour when it is most full of
100 sighs; and your deaths shall come by chance and unforeseen, for you shall not be certain about anything for ever and ever."'

---

87 said: "within . . . 1897.
87 the foss of [the liss of 1897] the king and . . . WS to 1897.
87 house and . . . 1908 to 1914, 1925E, 1927.
89 wings in the white air, and . . . WS to 1913.
90 fins in the dim water, while . . . WS to 1913.
91 stilled there ever-trembling . . . 1913.
91 tongues in the heavy boughs, and . . . WS to 1913.
92 marble, and the rivers became their motionless mirrors, and . . . WS to 1913.
92 sea-pools 1908 to 1927; sea pools WS to 1897.
92-93 sea pools [sea-pools 1908, 1913] were still [~, 1897, 1908] enduring . . . WS to 1913.
93 hard." And as he named these things, [~ ʌ CB] it was like a king numbering his people. "But . . . WS to 1914.
94 knives went click, click! [~ ʌ WS, CB] upon the oaken staves, and . . . WS to 1913.
95-97 sound shook the angels with anger. O [Oh CB], little roots, nipped by the winter, who do not wake although [not awake although 1908, 1913] the summer pass above you with innumerable feet. O [Oh CB], men who have no part in love, who have no part in song, who have no part in wisdom, but dwell with the shadows of memory where the feet of angels cannot touch you as they pass over your heads, where the hair of demons cannot sweep about you as they pass under your feet, I lay [feet, lay WS, CB] upon you a curse, and change you to an . . . WS to 1913.
96-97 of angels cannot touch your heads, where the hair of demons cannot sweep about you as they pass under your feet, I . . . 1914.
99 world, in . . . WS.
100 sighs, having forgotten the flame of the stars and not yet perceived the [yet found the 1908, 1913] flame of the sun; [~, CB] and you shall preach to the other herons until they also are like you, and are an example for ever and ever; [~, CB] and your . . . WS to 1913; sighs; and you shall preach to the other herons until they also are like you, and are an example for ever; and your . . . 1914.
100 your death shall . . . 1925A.
100 come to you by . . . WS to 1914.
100-2 unforeseen [~, 1908, 1913] that no fire of certainty may visit your hearts."' ¶The . . . WS to 1913.
101-2 and ever.' [The additional quotation mark to indicate closing of the internal quotation is missing.] ¶The . . . 1925A.

The Secret Rose

The voice became still, but the voteen bent over his gun with his eyes upon the ground, too stupid to understand what he had heard; and he had remained so, it may be for a long time, had not a
105 tug at his rosary aroused him. The old man of learning had crawled along the grass, and was now trying to draw the cross down low enough for his lips to reach it.

'You must not touch my blessed beads,' cried the voteen, and struck the long withered fingers with the barrel of his gun. He need
110 not have struck him, for the old man fell back upon the grass with a sigh and was quiet. He bent down and began to consider the discoloured clothes, for his fear had grown less when he understood that he had something the man of learning wanted, and now that the blessed beads were safe, his fear had nearly all gone; and surely,
115 he thought, if that cloak be warm and without holes, S. Patrick would take the enchantment out of it and leave it fit for use. But the old discoloured cloth fell away wherever his fingers touched it,

---

102   *voice* of the old Ollamh *became* . . . WS, CB; *voice* of the old man of learning *became* . . . 1897 to 1913.
103-4   *ground,* trying in vain to understand something of this tale; *and* . . . WS to 1913.
104   *and he had* so bent for no little while [~, 1897] *had* . . . WS to 1897.
104   *and he had* so bent, *it* . . . 1908, 1913.
105   *rosary* made him start out of his dream [his puzzled dream 1914]. *The* . . . WS to 1914.
105   *old* Ollamh *had* . . . WS, CB.
108   *beads,' [~!' CB] he cried, and* . . . WS, CB.
109   *long, withered* . . . CB.
110   *have* trembled, *for* . . . WS to 1927.
111   *sigh and* [sigh, and CB] *was* still for ever. *He* . . . WS, CB; *sigh and was* still. *He* . . . 1897 to 1913.
111-12   *the* black and green *clothes* . . . WS to 1913.
112   *fear had* begun to pass *when* . . . WS, 1897; *fear* began to pass *when* . . . CB; *fear had* begun to pass away *when* . . . 1908, 1913; *fear* grew less *when* . . . 1914.
112   *he* came to understand *that* . . . WS to 1913.
112   *understood* clearly *that* . . . 1914.
113   *the* Ollamh *wanted* . . . WS, CB.
113   *wanted* and pleaded for, *and* . . . WS to 1913.
114   *safe,* it was *nearly* . . . WS to 1897.
115   *that* ample cloak, and that little tight-fitting cloak under it, were *warm* . . . WS to 1897; *that* big cloak, and that little tight-fitting cloak under [tight-fitting shirt under 1914] it, were *warm* . . . 1908 to 1914.
115   *warm and* goodly, St. *Patrick* . . . WS to 1897.
115   *St.* . . . WS to 1897; *Saint* . . . 1908 to 1927.
116   *of* them and leave them fit for human *use* [for use 1914] . . . WS to 1914.
116-17   *use.* Unhappily the [use. But the 1908, 1913] black and green clothes *fell* . . . WS to 1913.
117   *discoloured* clothes *fell* . . . 1914.
117-18   *touched* them, and while this was a new wonder, *a* . . . WS to 1913.
117-18   *touched* them, *and presently* . . . 1914.

60

and presently a slight wind blew over the pool and crumbled the
old man of learning and all his ancient gear into a little heap of
120 dust, and then made the little heap less and less until there was
nothing but the smooth green grass.

PROUD COSTELLO, MACDERMOT'S DAUGHTER, AND THE BITTER TONGUE

Costello had come up from the fields and lay upon the ground
before the door of his square tower, resting his head upon his
hands and looking at the sunset, and considering the chances of the
weather. Though the customs of Elizabeth and James, now going
5   out of fashion in England, had begun to prevail among the gentry,
he still wore the great cloak of the native Irish; and the untroubled
confidence of his face and his big body had the pride and strength
of a simpler age. His eyes wandered from the sunset to where the
long white road lost itself over the south-western horizon and to a

119   old Ollamh and ... WS, CB.
[In WS and CB, the story is signed W. B. Yeats.]

Printings: *The Pageant,* 1896; 1897; 1908; 1913; 1914; 1925; 1927.
Text from 1932.
Spellings and changes of name: Daly 1897 to 1932; O'Daly ['O'Dalys' at line 75] P. Loch
Gara 1908 to 1932; Lough Garra 1914 to 1932; MacDermott P;
Dermott 1897 to 1913 [but 'Dermot' at lines 222–23 in 1897]. MacNamara 1914 to 1932;
Macnamara P; Namara 1897 to 1913. Una 1914 to 1932; Oona P to 1913. [In 1908 and
1913 Yeats changed the name to 'Winny' as recorded below, but a number of occurrences
of 'Oona' (including that in the title) were apparently overlooked.] whisky 1925, 1927,
1932; whiskey P to 1914. [The varying uses of 'daughter of,' 'of the Sheep,' 'of the Lake,'
etc., and the expansions of proper names in 1897 are recorded individually below.]
Title: COSTELLO THE PROUD, OONA MACDERMOTT, AND THE BITTER
TONGUE P; OF COSTELLO THE PROUD, OF OONA THE DAUGHTER OF
DERMOTT [~, 1913] AND OF THE BITTER TONGUE [TONGUE. 1908, 1913] 1897
to 1913; ... DAUGHTER AND ... 1914 to 1927.
1   *fields, and* ... P.
2   *tower,* supporting *his head* ... P.
3   *hands, looking* ... P.*
6   *native* Irishry; *and* ... P.
6–8   *and the* sensitive outlines of his face and the greatness of his indolent body had a
[body showed a P] commingling of pride and strength which belonged to a ... P to 1913.
6–7   *and the* sensitive outlines of ... 1914.
8   *eyes* strayed in a little *from* ... P.
9   *horizon, and* then falling, lit upon a ... P.
9   *horizon, and* ... 1897.

10   horseman who toiled slowly up the hill. A few more minutes and the horseman was near enough for his little shapeless body, his long Irish cloak, and the dilapidated bagpipes hanging from his shoulders, and the rough-haired garron under him, to be seen distinctly in the grey dusk. So soon as he had come within earshot,

15   he began crying, 'Is it sleeping you are, Tumaus Costello, when better men break their hearts on the great white roads? Get up out of that, proud Tumaus, for I have news! Get up out of that, you great omadhaun! Shake yourself out of the earth, you great weed of a man!'

20   Costello had risen to his feet, and as the piper came up to him seized him by the neck of his jacket, lifted him out of his saddle and shook him.

'Let me alone, let me alone,' said the other, but Costello still shook him.

25   'I have news from MacDermot's daughter Una.' The great fingers were loosened, and the piper fell gasping.

'Why did you not tell me,' said Costello, 'that you came from her? You might have railed your fill.'

'I have come from her, but I will not speak until I am paid for the

30   shaking.'

Costello fumbled at the bag in which he carried his money, and it

---

11   *little* and *shapeless* . . . P to 1914.
12   *cloak and* . . . P.
13-14   *to* stand out distinctly in the gathering greyness. *So* . . . P.
14-15   *earshot he* . . . P.
15   *crying* in Gaelic, ¶'*Is* . . . P; *crying:* ¶'*Is* . . . 1897; *crying: 'Is* . . . 1908 to 1927.
15-16   *Costello,* while better folk [folks 1897] *break* . . . P, 1897.
16-31   *roads?* Listen to me, Tumaus Costello the Proud, for I come out of Coolavin, and bring a message from Oona MacDermott, and it is the good pay I must have, for the saddle was bitter under me.' ¶He was close to the door by now, and began slowly dismounting, cursing the while by God, and Bridget and the devil; for riding in all weathers from wake to wedding and wedding to wake had made him rheumatic. Costello had risen to his feet, and was fumbling at the mouth of the leather *bag, in* . . . P; *roads?* Listen to me, Tumaus Costello the Proud, for I come out of the Corner of the Children of Finn and bring a message from Oona the daughter of Dermott, and I must have good pay, for the saddle was bitter under me.' ¶He was close to the door by now, and began slowly to dismount, cursing the while by God, and Bridget, and the devil, for riding in all weathers from wake to wedding and wedding to wake had made him rheumatic. Costello had risen to his feet and was fumbling at the mouth of the leather *bag in* . . . 1897.
21   *jacket,* and lifting *him* . . . 1908 to 1914.
21-23   *saddle* threw him on to the ground. ¶'*Let* . . . 1908 to 1914.
25   *daughter,* Winny. [~, 1913]' *The* . . . 1908, 1913; *daughter, Una.' The* . . . 1914, 1925A.
26   *piper* rose *gasping* . . . 1908 to 1914.
29   *speak* unless *I* . . . 1908, 1913.
29-30   *for* my *shaking* . . . 1908, 1913.
31   *money,* but *it* . . . P, 1897.

was some time before it would open, for his hand trembled. 'Here
is all the money in my bag,' he said, dropping some French and
Spanish money into the hand of the piper, who bit the coins before
35 he would answer.

'That is right, that is a fair price, but I will not speak till I have
good protection, for if the MacDermots lay their hands upon me in
any boreen after sundown, or in Cool-a-vin by day, I will be left to
rot among the nettles of a ditch, or hung where they hung the
40 horse-thieves last Beltaine four years.' And while he spoke he tied
the reins of his garron to a bar of rusty iron that was mortared into
the wall.

'I will make you my piper and my body-servant,' said Costello,
'and no man dare lay hands upon a man or upon a dog if he belong
45 to Tumaus Costello.'

'And I will only tell my message,' said the other, flinging the
saddle on the ground, 'with a noggin of whisky in my hand, for

---

32 *for* the hand that had thrown so many in wrestling shook with excitement.
¶'*Here* . . . P; *for* the hand that had thrown so many in wrestling shook with fear and with
hope. ¶'*Here* . . . 1897; *for* the hand that had overcome many men shook with fear and
hope. '*Here* . . . 1908, 1913; *for his hand* shook. '*Here* . . . 1914.
33-34 *said,* [~ ∧ 1897] at last [~, 1897] dropping a stream of French and Spanish silver
into . . . P, 1897.
33 *dropping* a stream of French . . . 1908, 1913.
34-37 *piper.* 'I got it for a heifer down at Ballysumaghan last week!' The other bit a
shilling between his teeth, and went on, ¶'And it is the good protection I must have,
for . . . P; *piper.* 'I got it for a heifer down at the Fall of the Oak Trees last week!' The other
bit a shilling between his teeth and then went on: ¶'And I must *have good protection,*
for . . . 1897.
38 *sundown or* . . . 1897.
38 *in* the Corner of the Children of Finn *by* . . . 1897.
38 *Cool-a-vin* 1908 to 1927; *Coolavin* P.
38 *by* broad *day* . . . P, 1897.
38-39 *be* flung *among* . . . P, 1897.
39 *nettles* in *a* . . . P, 1897.
39 *or* hanged upon the sycamore, [~ ∧ 1897] where they hanged *the* . . . P, 1897.
39 *hung* on the great sycamore, *where* . . . 1908, 1913.
40 *horse- / thieves; horse thieves* P, 1897; *horse-thieves* 1908 to 1927.
40 *thieves* out by Leitram [out of Leitram 1897] last Great *Beltan* [*Beltane* 1897] . . . P,
1897.
40 *years!' And* . . . P, 1897.
43 *body-servant; body servant* P; *body- / servant* 1897 to 1927.
44 *upon* the *man* . . . P, 1897 to 1913.
44-46 *man, or* the goat, or the horse, or the dog that is Tumaus Costello's.' ¶'*And* . . . 1897
to 1913.
44 *man, or* . . . 1914, 1925A.
44-45 *or* the goat, or the horse or the dog protected by *Tumaus* . . . P.
46 *other flinging* . . . P.
47 *ground,* 'in the corner of the chimney with a noggin of Spanish ale in my hand, and a
jug of Spanish ale beside me, *for* . . . P; *ground,* 'in the corner of the chimney with a noggin

though I am ragged and empty, my old fathers were well clothed
and full, until their house was burnt down and their cattle driven
50 away seven centuries ago by the Dillons, whom I shall yet see on the
hob of Hell, and they screeching.'

Costello led him up a narrow winding stone stair into a rush=
strewn chamber, where were none of the comforts which had
begun to grow common among the gentry, and pointed to a seat in
55 the great chimney; and when the piper had sat down, filled up a
horn noggin and set it on the floor beside him, and a jug beside
that, and then turned towards him and said, 'Will MacDermot's
daughter come to me, Duallach, son of Daly?'

'MacDermot's daughter will not come to you, for her father has
60 set women to watch her, but I am to tell you that this day week will

---

in my hand, and a jug of the Brew of the Little Pot beside me, *for* . . . 1897 to 1913; *ground,*
'with a noggin in my hand, and a jug of the Poteen beside me, *for* . . . 1914.
48   *empty my* . . . P.
48   *my* forbears [forebears 1908] *were* . . . P to 1913.
49   *full until* . . . P to 1914.
49-50 *burnt,* [~ ∧ 1897] and their cattle harried in the time of Cathal of the Red Hand
by . . . P, 1897.
49-50 *burnt* and their cattle harried *seven* . . . 1908, 1913.
49   *burnt and* . . . 1914.*
51   *hell* . . . P to 1927.
51   *hell and* . . . 1897.
51-53   'screeching,' and while he spoke the little eyes gleamed and the thin hands clenched.
¶Costello brought him into the great rush-strewn hall *where* . . . P; *screaching;'* and while he
spoke the little eyes gleamed and the thin hands clenched. ¶Costello led him into the great
rush- / strewn hall, *where* . . . 1897; *screeching';* and while he spoke the little eyes gleamed
and the thin hands clenched. ¶Costello led him into the great rush-strewn hall,
where . . . 1908, 1913.
52-53   *him* into the rush-strewn hall, *where* . . . 1914.
54-57   *gentry,* but a feudal gauntness and bareness, and pointed to [and led him to P] the
bench in the great chimney; and when he had sat down, filled up a horn noggin [~, P] and
set it on the bench beside him, and set a great black jack [black-jack P] of leather beside the
noggin, and lit a torch that slanted out from a ring in the wall, his hands trembling the
while; *and then* . . . P to 1913; *gentry,* but a mediæval gauntness and bareness, and pointed
to the bench in the great chimney; and when the piper had sat down, filled up a horn
noggin and set it on the bench beside him, and jug beside that, and lit a torch that slanted
out from a ring in the wall; *and then* . . . 1914.
57-58   *said,* ¶'*Will* Oona MacDermott *come* . . . P; *said:* ¶'*Will* Oona the daughter of
Dermott *come* . . . 1897; *said:* 'Will Dermott's *daughter come* . . . 1908, 1913; *said:* 'Will
MacDermot's *daughter come* . . . 1914 to 1927.
58-59   *me, Dualloch* O'Daly of the Pipes?' ¶'Oona MacDermott *will* . . . P; *me, Duallach* the
son of Daly?' ¶'Oona the daughter of Dermott *will* . . . 1897.
59   *father,* Teig MacDermott of the Sheep, *has* . . . P; *father* Dermott, the son of Dermott,
has . . . 1897.
60   *but* she bid me *tell* . . . P to 1913.
60   *day* sennight *will* . . . P to 1913.

be the Eve of S. John and the night of her betrothal to MacNamara of the Lake, and she wants you to be there that, when they tell her to drink to him she loves best, she may drink to you, Tumaus Costello, and let all know where her heart is; and I myself advise
65   you to go with good men about you, for I have seen the horse= thieves with my own eyes.' And then he held the now empty noggin towards Costello, and cried: 'Fill my noggin again, for I wish the day had come when all the water in the world is to shrink into a periwinkle-shell, that I might drink nothing but whisky.'
70   Finding that Costello made no reply, but sat in a dream, he burst out: 'Fill my noggin, I tell you, for no Costello is so great in the world that he should not wait upon a Daly, even though the Daly travel the road with his pipes and the Costello have a bare hill, an empty house, a horse, and a handful of cows.'
75   'Praise the Dalys if you will,' said Costello as he filled the noggin, 'for you have brought me a kind word from my love.'
      For the next few days Duallach went here and there trying to raise a bodyguard, and every man he met had some story of Costello: one told how he killed the wrestler when but a boy by so

---

61   *eve* . . . P to 1927.
61   *St.* . . . P to 1927.
62   *she* would have you *there* . . . P to 1913.
62   *there, that* . . . P.
62-63   *they* bid her *drink to him* . . . P to 1913.
63   *best,* as the way is, *she* . . . P to 1913.
63   *you,* oh *Tumaus* . . . P.
64-65   *is,* [~ ∧ P] *and* how little of gladness is in her marriage; and [her marrying: and P] I myself bid you *go* . . . P to 1913.
65-66   *I* saw the horse thieves [horse-thieves 1908, 1913] with my own eyes, and they dancing the blue pigeon in [the "Blue Pigeon" in 1908, 1913] the air.' *And* . . . P to 1913.
65-66   *horse-thieves* 1908 to 1927; *horse thieves* P, 1897.
67   *Costello,* his hand closing round it like the claw of a bird, *and cried:* [~, ¶ P; ~: ¶ 1897] *'Fill* . . . P to 1913.
67   *I* would *the* . . . P to 1913.
69   *periwinkle-shell* 1897, 1913 to 1927; *periwinkle shell* P; *periwinkle- / shell* 1908.
69-70   *but* the poteen.' *Finding* . . . P; *but* the Brew of the Little Pot.' ¶*Finding* . . . 1897; *but* Poteen.' ¶*Finding* . . . 1908 to 1914.
71   *out,* [~: 1897] ¶*'Fill* . . . P, 1897.
72   *upon* an O'Daly, *even* . . . P.
74   *horse,* a herd of goats, [~ ∧ P] *and* . . . P to 1913.
77   *went* hither and thither [~, P] *trying* . . . P to 1913.
78   *bodyguard* 1908 to 1927; *body guard* P; *body- / guard* 1897.
78   *body guard; and* . . . P.
78-79   *Costello, how* . . . P to 1914.*
79   *wrestler, when* . . . P.
79   *boy, by* . . . P.

80 straining at the belt that went about them both that he broke the big
wrestler's back; another how he dragged fierce horses through a
ford for a wager; another how when grown to be a man he broke
the steel horseshoe in Mayo; but none who would trust himself with
a man so passionate and poor in a quarrel with careful and wealthy
85 persons like MacDermot of the Sheep and MacNamara of the Lake.
Then Costello went out himself, and brought in a big half-witted
fellow, a farm-labourer who worshipped him for his strength, a fat
farmer whose forefathers had served his family, and a couple of
lads who looked after his goats and cows; and marshalled them
90 before the fire. They had brought with them their heavy sticks, and
Costello gave them an old pistol apiece, and kept them all night
drinking and shooting at a white turnip which he pinned against
the wall with a skewer. Duallach sat on the bench in the chimney
playing 'The Green Bunch of Rushes', 'The Unchion Stream', and
95 'The Princes of Breffny' on his old pipes, and abusing now the

---

80 *belt, that went* . . . P.
80 *both, that* . . . P.
80–81 *the* back of his opponent; how, [~ ∧ 1897] when somewhat older, [~ ∧ 1897]
he . . . P, 1897.
81 *back;* how when somewhat older *he* . . . 1908 to 1914.
81 *dragged* the fierce horses of the Dunns of Shancough *through* [of the Dunns of the
Tower *through* 1897] . . . P, 1897.
82 *ford* in the Unchion *for* . . . P to 1913.
82 *wager;* how [~, P] when he came to manhood *he* [to maturity, *he* P] . . . P to 1914.
83 *horseshoe* 1908 to 1927; *horse shoe* P; *horse- / shoe* 1897.
83–84 *Mayo;* how he drove many men before him through Rushy Meadow at
Drum-an-air because [through Drumlease and Cloonbougher and Druma- / hair,
because P; through the Rushy Meadow and the Ridge of the Two Demons of the Air
because 1897] of a malevolent song they had about his poverty; and of many another deed
of his strength and pride; but he could find none who would trust themselves with any
so . . . P to 1913; *Mayo;* and of many another deed of his strength and pride; but he could
find none who would trust themselves with any *so* . . . 1914.
85 *persons, like* . . . P.
85 *Sheep, and* . . . P.
86 *and* [~, P] after listening to many excuses and in many places, *brought* . . . P to 1914.
87 *fellow,* [~ ∧ P] who followed him like a dog, *a farm-labourer* [*farm labourer* P] . . . P to
1913.
87 *farm-labourer* 1897 to 1914, 1927; *farm labourer* P; *farm- / labourer* 1925.
89 *cows, and* . . . P.
90 *fire* in the empty hall. *They* . . . P to 1913.
90 *their* stout alpeens, *and* . . . P; *their* stout cudgels, *and* . . . 1897 to 1913.
91 *apiece* 1908 to 1927; *a-piece* P, 1897.
92 *drinking* Spanish ale [~, P] *and* . . . P to 1913.
93 *skewer.* O'Daly *sat* . . . P; *skewer. Duallach* of the Pipes [pipes 1913] *sat* . . . 1897 to 1913.
94 *Rushes,' 'The* . . . P to 1914, 1925A, 1927.
94 *Stream,' and* . . . P to 1914, 1925A, 1927.
95 *Beffeny* . . . P; *Breffeny* . . . 1897 to 1927.
95 *and* railing now at *the* . . . P to 1913.

appearance of the shooters, now their clumsy shooting, and now Costello because he had no better servants. The labourer, the half-witted fellow, the farmer and the lads were well accustomed to Duallach's abusiveness, but they wondered at the forbearance of
100 Costello, who seldom came either to wake or wedding, and if he had would not have been patient with a scolding piper.

On the next evening they set out for Cool-a-vin, Costello riding a tolerable horse and carrying a sword, the others upon rough= haired ponies, and with their cudgels under their arms. As they
105 rode over the bogs and in the boreens among the hills they could see fire answering fire from hill to hill, from horizon to horizon, and everywhere groups who danced in the red light of the turf. When they came to MacDermot's house they saw before the door an unusually large group of the very poor, dancing about a fire, in
110 the midst of which was a blazing cart-wheel, and from the door and through the loopholes on either side came the light of candles and the sound of many feet dancing a dance of Elizabeth and James.

They tied their horses to bushes, for the number so tied already

---

96   *now* at *their* ... P to 1913.
96–97   *now* at *Costello* ... P to 1913.
98   *were* all *well* ... P to 1913.
98–99   *to Duallach's* railing [O'Daly's unquenchable railing P; Duallach's unquenchable railing 1897], for it was as inseparable from wake or wedding as the squealing of his pipes, *but* ... P to 1913.
99   *abusiveness,* for it was as inseparable from wake or wedding as the squealing of his pipes, *but* ... 1914.
100–1   *and, if he had, would* ... P.
101   *would* scarce *have* ... P to 1913.
102   *for* the Corner of the Children of Finn, *Costello* ... 1897.
102   *Cool-a-vin* 1914, 1927; *Coolavin* P; *Cool-a- / vin* 1908, 1913; *Cool- / a-vin* 1925.
103–4   *rough-haired* 1908 to 1914, 1927; *rough haired* P; *rough- / haired* 1897, 1925.
103–4   *rough-haired* [*rough haired* P; *rough- / haired* 1897] garrons, *and* ... P to 1913.
104   *their* stout alpeens *under* ... P; *their* stout *cudgels under* ... 1897 to 1913.
105   *bogs, and* ... P.
105   *hills, they* ... P.
107   *the* ruddy *light* ... P.
107   *light* on *the* ... 1897 to 1913.
107–8   *turf,* celebrating the bridal of life and fire. *When* ... P to 1913.
110   *cart-wheel* 1927; *cartwheel* P to 1914; *cart- / wheel* 1925.
110   *cartwheel,* that circular dance which is so ancient that the gods, long dwindled to be but fairies, dance no other in their secret places. *From* [other. *From* 1914] *the* ... P to 1914.
110   *door, and* ... P.
111   *the* long *loop-holes* ... P to 1913.
111   *loopholes* 1925E, 1927; *loop-holes* P, 1908 to 1914, 1925A; *loop- / holes* 1897.
111   *side, came* ... P.
111   *came the* pale *light* ... P to 1913.
111   *candles, and* ... P.

showed that the stables were full, and shoved their way through a
115 crowd of peasants who stood about the door, and went into the big
hall where the dance was. The labourer, the half-witted fellow, the
farmer and the two lads mixed with a group of servants who were
looking on from an alcove, and Duallach sat with the pipers on
their bench, but Costello made his way through the dancers to
120 where MacDermot stood pouring out whisky, MacNamara at his
side.

'Tumaus Costello,' said the old man, 'you have done a good deed
to forget what has been, and come to the betrothal of my daughter.'

'I come,' answered Costello, 'because when in the time of Costello
125 De Angalo my ancestors overcame your ancestors and afterwards
made peace, a compact was made that a Costello might go with his
body-servants and his piper to every feast given by a MacDermot
for ever, and a MacDermot with his body-servants and his piper to
every feast given by a Costello for ever.'

130 'If you come with evil thoughts and armed men,' said MacDermot, flushing, 'no matter how good you are with your weapons, it
shall go badly with you, for some of my wife's clan have come out of
Mayo, and my three brothers and their servants have come down
from the Ox Mountains'; and while he spoke he kept his hand
135 inside his coat as though upon the handle of a weapon.

115-16 *into the* great *hall* . . . P to 1913.
117 *farmer, and* . . . P.
117 *servants, who* . . . P.
119 *bench; but* . . . P.
120-22 *where* Dermott [MacDermott P] of the Sheep stood with Namara [Macnamara P]
of the Lake [~, P] pouring Poteen [poteen P; pouring the Brew of the Little Pot 1897]
out of a porcelain jug into horn noggins with silver rims. ¶ *Tumaus* . . . P to 1913; *where*
MacDermot stood with MacNamara pouring Poteen out of a porcelain jug into horn noggins.
¶ *Tumaus* . . . 1914.
123 *been,* and to fling away enmity *and* . . . P to 1913.
123-24 *daughter* to Namara [Macnamara P; MacNamara 1914] of the Lake.' ¶ *'I* . . . P to
1914.
124 *because, when* . . . P.
124-25 *of* Eoha of the Heavy Sighs *my* . . . P.
125 *my* forbears [forebears 1908] overcame your forbears [~, P; forebears 1908]
and . . . P to 1913.
127 *body-servants* 1897 to 1927; *body servants* P.
128 *body-servants* 1897 to 1927; *body servants* P.
130-31 *said MacDermott flushing* . . . P; *said the son of Dermott flushing* . . . 1897 to 1913;
said MacDermot flushing . . . 1914 to 1927.
131 *how* strong your hands to wrestle and to swing the sword, *it* . . . P to 1913.
134 *the* Mountains of the Ox,' [~;' 1897] *and* . . . P, 1897.
134 *Mountains;' and* . . . 1925A.

Proud Costello, MacDermot's Daughter, and the Bitter Tongue

'No,' answered Costello, 'I but come to dance a farewell dance with your daughter.'

MacDermot drew his hand out of his coat and went over to a pale girl who was now standing but a little way off with her mild eyes
140 fixed upon the ground.

'Costello has come to dance a farewell dance, for he knows that you will never see one another again.'

As Costello led her among the dancers her gentle and humble eyes were fixed in love upon his pride and violence. They took
145 their place in the Pavane, that stately dance which, with the Saraband, the Gallead, and the Morris dances, had driven out, among all but the most Irish of the gentry, the quicker rhythms of the verse-interwoven, pantomimic dances of earlier days; and while they danced there came over them the weariness with the world,
150 the melancholy, the pity one for the other, which is the exultation of love. And when a dance ended and the pipers laid down the pipes and lifted the noggins, they stood a little from the others waiting pensively and silently for the dance to begin again and the fire in their hearts to leap up and to wrap them anew; and so they
155 danced Pavane and Saraband and Gallead and Morris the night long, and many stood still to watch them, and the peasants came about the door and peered in, as though they understood that they

---

136   *Costello, 'but I come* . . . 1925A.
138   *a tall pale* . . . P to 1913.
139   *who* had been standing a little way off for the last few moments, *with* . . . P.
142-43   *again.' ¶The girl lifted her eyes and gazed at Costello, and in her gaze was that trust of the humble in the proud, the gentle in the violent, which has been the tragedy of woman from the beginning. Costello* . . . P to 1914.
143-45   *dancers,* and they were soon drawn into the [soon absorbed in the P] rhythm of *the Pavane* . . . P to 1914.
145   *in Pavane* . . . 1925, 1927.*
146   *Morrice* . . . P to 1914.
149   *danced came* . . . P.*
149-50   *them the* unutterable melancholy, the weariness with the world, the poignant and bitter pity for one another, the vague [pity, the vague P] anger against common hopes and fears, *which* . . . P to 1913.
150   *other,* the vague anger against common hopes and fears, *which* . . . 1914.
151-52   *down* their *pipes* . . . P to 1913.
152   *lifted* their horn *noggins* . . . P to 1913.
152-53   *others, waiting* . . . P.
155   *danced* and danced through *Pavane* . . . P; *danced* and danced *Pavane* . . . 1897 to 1913.
155-56   *Gallead* the night through, *and many* . . . P; *Gallead and Morrice* through [*Morrice* and through 1897] *the night long, and many* . . . 1897 to 1913.
155   *Morrice* . . . 1897 to 1914.

69

would gather their children's children about them long hence, and
tell how they had seen Costello dance with MacDermot's daughter
160 Una; and through all the dancing and piping MacNamara went
hither and thither talking loudly and making foolish jokes that all
might seem well, and old MacDermot grew redder and redder,
waiting for the dawn.

At last he saw that the moment to end had come, and, in a pause
165 after a dance, cried out that his daughter would now drink the cup
of betrothal; then Una came over to where he was, and the guests
stood round in a half-circle, Costello close to the wall, and the
piper, the labourer, the farmer, the half-witted man and the two
farm lads close behind him. The old man took out of a niche in the
170 wall the silver cup from which her mother and her mother's
mother had drunk the toasts of their betrothals, filled it with
Spanish wine and handed the cup to his daughter with the custom-
ary words, 'Drink to him whom you love the best.'

She held the cup to her lips for a moment, and then said in a
175 clear soft voice, 'I drink to my true love, Tumaus Costello.'

And then the cup rolled over and over on the ground, ringing
like a bell, for the old man had struck her in the face and the cup
had fallen, and there was a deep silence.

There were many of MacNamara's people among the servants

159-60 *with* Dermott's daughter Oona, and [with Oona MacDermott, and P; with Oona
the daughter of Dermott, and 1897; with MacDermot's daughter Una, and 1914] become
[~, P] by the telling [~, P] themselves a portion of ancient romance; but *through* ... P to
1914.
160 *piping* Namara [Macnamara P] of the Lake *went* ... P to 1913.
161 *jokes, that* ... P.
162 *well* with him, and old Dermott [MacDermott P] of the Sheep *grew* ... P to 1913.
162-63 *redder and redder,* and looked oftener and oftener at the doorway to see [doorway
to to see P] if the candles there grew yellow in *the* ... P to 1914.
165 *out* from where the horn noggins stood, [~ ∧ 1908, 1913] *that* ... P to 1913.
167 *half-circle* 1897 to 1927; *half circle* P.
167-68 *wall* to the right, and the *labourer* ... P.
167 *wall* to the right, *and* ... 1897 to 1914.
168 *man, and* ... P.
169 *behind. The* ... P.*
170 *cup, from* ... P, 1897.
171-72 *betrothals,* and poured into it a little of the poteen out of a porcelain jug,
and ... P; *betrothals,* and poured some of the Brew of the Little Pot out of a porcelain jug
and ... 1897; *betrothals,* and poured Poteen out of a porcelain jug *and* ... 1908 to
1914.
172 *handed* it *to* ... P.
175 *clear, soft* ... P.
175 *voice, ¶'I* ... P; *voice:* [~: ¶ 1897] *'I* ... 1897 to 1927.
177-78 *face,* and it had fallen in her confusion; *and there* ... P.
178-79 *silence. There* ... P.
179-80 *servants, now* ... P.

180   now come out of the alcove, and one of them, a story-teller and
poet, who had a plate and chair in MacNamara's kitchen, drew a
French knife out of his girdle, but in a moment Costello had struck
him to the ground. The click of steel had followed quickly, had not
there come a muttering and shouting from the peasants about the
185   door and from those crowding up behind them; for all knew that
these were no children of Queen's Irish, but of the wild Irish about
Lough Gara and Lough Cara, Kellys, Dockerys, Drurys, O'Regans,
Mahons, and Lavins, who had left the right arms of their children
unchristened that they might give the better blows, and were even
190   said to have named the wolves godfathers to their children.

Costello's knuckles had grown white upon the handle of his
sword, but now he drew his hand away, and, followed by those who
were with him, went towards the door, the dancers giving way
before him, the most angrily and slowly, and with glances at the
195   muttering and shouting peasants, but some gladly and quickly,
because the glory of his fame was over him. He passed through the
fierce and friendly peasant faces, and came where his horse and the

---

180   *story-teller* 1897 to 1927; *story teller* P.
181   *poet*, a last remnant of the bardic order, who had a chair and a platter *in* . . . P to
1913.
182–83   *girdle* [~, P] and made as though he would strike at Costello, but in a moment a
blow had hurled him to the [him on the P] ground, his shoulder sending the cup rolling
and ringing again. *The* . . . P to 1913; *girdle* and seemed as though he would strike at
Costello, but in a moment had been hurled to the ground, his shoulder sending the cup
rolling and ringing again. *The* . . . 1914.
183   *quickly had* . . . P.
185   *door, and* . . . P.
185   *them;* and *all* . . . P to 1913.
186–88   *Queen's Irish* or friendly Macnamaras [Namaras 1897] and MacDermotts
[Dermotts 1897], but wild Lavells and Quinns and Dunns from about Lough Garra, who
[from the Lough of the Little Wood, who 1897] rowed their skin coracles, and had masses
of hair over their eyes, and *left* . . . P, 1897.
186   *Queen's Irish* or friendly Namaras and Dermotts, *but* . . . 1908, 1913.
187–88   *Cara*, who rowed their skin coracles, and had masses of hair over their eyes, and
left . . . 1908, 1913.
189   *unchristened, that* . . . P.
189–91   *the* stouter blows, and swore only by St. Atty and sun and moon, and worshipped
beauty and strength more than St. Atty or sun and moon. ¶*Costello's* . . . P to 1913.
191–92   *Costello's* hand had rested [hand rested 1914] upon the handle of his sword
[~, P, 1914] and his knuckles had grown white, but now he drew it *away* [*drew his hand
away* 1914] . . . P to 1914.
193   *him*, strode *towards* . . . P to 1913.
193–94   *giving before* . . . P.*
194   *slowly and* . . . P.
195–96   *quickly because* . . . P.
196   *him;* [~, 1897] and *passed* . . . P, 1897.
197–98   *his* good horse and the rough-haired garrons *were* . . . P to 1913.

ponies were tied to bushes; and mounted and made his bodyguard mount also and ride into the narrow boreen. When they had gone a
200 little way, Duallach, who rode last, turned towards the house where a little group of MacDermots and MacNamaras stood next to a bigger group of countrymen, and cried, 'MacDermot, you deserve to be as you are this hour, for your hand was always niggardly to piper and fiddler and to poor travelling people.' He had not done
205 before the three old MacDermots from the Ox Mountains had run towards their horses, and old MacDermot himself had caught the bridle of a pony belonging to the MacNamaras and was calling to the others to follow him; and many blows and many deaths had been had not the countrymen caught up still blazing sticks from the
210 ashes of the fires and thrown them among the horses so that they broke away from those who held them and scattered through the fields, and before they could be gathered again Costello was far off.

For the next few weeks Costello had no lack of news of Una, for now a woman selling eggs, and now a man or a woman going to the

---

198   *mounted and* bade his ungainly *body-guard* [*bodyguard* 1908, 1913] ... P to 1913.
198   *bodyguard* 1908 to 1927; *body-guard* P, 1897.
199   *also, and* rode *into* ... P.
199   *borreen* ... P.
200   *way* the *Duallach* ... 1897.
201-2   *to a* far more [*a* more 1897] numerous group of peasants, *and* ... P, 1897.
201-2   *to a* more numerous *group* ... 1908, 1913.
202-3   *cried,* [~: 1897] ¶'Well do you deserve, Teig MacDermott [deserve, Dermott, the son of Dermott 1897], *to be* ... P, 1897.
202   *cried:* 'Dermott, *you* ... 1908, 1913; *cried:* 'MacDermot, *you* ... 1914 to 1927.
203   *hour,* a lantern without a candle, a purse without a penny, a sheep without wool, *for* ... P to 1913.
203   *was* ever *niggardly* ... P to 1913.
203-4   *niggardly to a piper* ... 1925A.
204   *fiddler* and story-teller [story teller P] *and* ... P to 1913.
204   *travelling* folk.' *He* ... P, 1897.
205   *Three Old* ... 1925A.
205   *from the* Mountains of the Ox *had* ... P, 1897.
207   *a* garron of the Namaras [Macnamaras, P] *and* ... P to 1913.
207-8   *calling to others* ... P.*
209   *been, had* ... P, 1897.
209   *the* Lavells and Dunns and Quinns *caught* ... P, 1897.
209   *still* glowing brands *from* ... P, 1897; *still* glowing *sticks from* ... 1908, 1913.
210   *the* fire, *and* ... P.
210   *and* hurled *them* ... P to 1913.
210-13   *horses* with loud cries, making all plunge and rear, and some break from those who held them, the [from their owners with the P] whites of their eyes gleaming in the dawn. ¶*For* ... P to 1914.
214   *eggs* or fowls, *and* ... P to 1913.
214   *or woman* ... 1925A.*
214-15   *woman* on pilgrimage to the Well of the Rocks, *would* [the holy well of Tubbernalty, *would* P] ... P to 1913.

215 Holy Well, would tell him how his love had fallen ill the day after
S. John's Eve, and how she was a little better or a little worse.

---

216   *St.* . . . P to 1927.
216–17   *worse*, as it might be; and though he looked to his horses and his cows and goats as
usual, the common and uncomely, the [uncomely things, the P] dust upon the roads, the
songs of men returning from fairs and wakes, men playing cards in the corners of fields on
Sundays and Saints' Days, the rumours of battles and changes in the great world, the
deliberate purposes of those about him, troubled him with an inexplicable trouble; and the
country people still [trouble; but the peasants still P; trouble; and the peasants still 1897]
remember how when night had fallen he would bid Duallach of the Pipes tell, to [Duallach
O'Daly recite, to P] the chirping of the crickets, 'The Son of Apple,' 'The Beauty of the
World,' 'The Feast of Bricriu [Briarind 1897],' or [World,' 'The King of Ireland's Son,'
or 1908, 1913] some other of those traditional tales [~, P] which were as much a piper's
business as 'The Green Bunch of Rushes,' 'The Unchion Stream,' or 'The Chiefs of
Breffany [Breffeny 1908, 1913]'; and [~, P] while the boundless and phantasmal world of
the legends was a-building, would abandon himself to the dreams of his sorrow. ¶Duallach
would often pause to tell how the Lavells or Dunns or Quinns or O'Dalys [Dalys 1897], or
other tribe near [other clan near 1897] his heart, had come from some Lu, god of the
leaping lightning, or incomparable [how some clan of the wild Irish had descended from
an incomparable 1908, 1913] King of the Blue Belt, [~ ∧ P] or Warrior of the Ozier
Wattle, or to tell with many railings how [many curses how 1908, 1913] all the strangers
and most of the Queen's Irish were the seed of the misshapen [of some misshapen P] and
horned Fomoroh or servile [horned People from under the Sea or of the servile 1897;
horned People from Under the Sea or of the servile 1908, 1913] and creeping Ferbolg;
but [creeping Firbolg; but P; creeping Men of the Bog; but 1897] Costello cared only for
the love sorrows, and no matter whither the stories wandered, whether to the Isle of the
Red Lough, [Loch ∧ P; Loch, 1897] where the blessed are, or to the malign country of the
Hag of the East, Oona alone endured their shadowy hardships; for it was she [~, P] and
no king's [King's P] daughter of old [~, P] who was hidden in the steel tower under the
water with the folds of the Worm of Nine Eyes round and about her prison; and it was she
who won [~, P] by seven years of service [~, P] the right to deliver from hell all she could
carry, and carried away multitudes clinging with worn fingers to the hem of her dress; and
it was she who endured dumbness for a year because of the little thorn of enchantment the
fairies had thrust into her tongue; and it was a lock of her hair, coiled in a little carved box,
which gave so great a light that men threshed by it from sundown to sunrise, and awoke so
great a wonder that kings spent years in wandering [~, P] or fell before unknown armies
in seeking [~, P] to discover her hiding-place [hiding place P]; for there was no beauty in
the world but hers, no tragedy in the world but hers: and when at last the voice of the
piper, grown gentle with the wisdom of old [wisdom or old P] romance, was silent, and his
rheumatic steps had toiled upstairs [up-stairs 1897] and to bed, and Costello had dipped
his fingers into the little delf font of holy water [~, P] and begun to pray to Maurya
[Mary 1908, 1913] of the Seven Sorrows, the blue eyes and star-covered dress of the
painting in the chapel faded from his imagination, and the brown eyes and homespun
dress of Dermott's daughter Winny came [of Oona MacDermott came P; of Oona the
daughter of Dermott came 1897] in their stead; for there was no tenderness in the world
but hers. He was of those ascetics of passion who keep their hearts pure for love or for
hatred [~, P] as other men for God, for Mary and for the saints [Saints 1908, 1913], and
who, when the hour of their visitation arrives, come to the Divine Essence by the bitter
tumult, the Garden of Gethsemane, and the desolate Rood ordained [rood, ordained P]
for immortal passions in mortal hearts. ¶One day *a serving-man [serving man P] rode* . . . P
to 1913.
216–17   *worse;* and the country people still remember how when night had fallen he
would bid Duallach of the Pipes tell out, 'The Son of Apple,' 'The Beauty of the World,'

73

At last a serving-man rode up to Costello, who was helping his two lads to reap a meadow, and gave him a letter, and rode away; and the letter contained these words in English: 'Tumaus Costello,
220 my daughter is very ill. She will die unless you come to her. I therefore command you come to her whose peace you stole by treachery.'

Costello threw down his scythe, and sent one of the lads for Duallach, and himself saddled his horse and Duallach's pony.
225 When they came to MacDermot's house it was late afternoon, and Lough Gara lay down below them, blue and deserted; and though they had seen, when at a distance, dark figures moving about the door, the house appeared not less deserted than the

---

'The King of Ireland's Son,' or some like tale; and while the world of the legends was a-building, would abandon himself to the dreams of his sorrow. ¶Costello cared only for the love sorrows, and no matter where the stories wandered, Una alone endured their shadowy hardships; for it was she and no king's daughter who was hidden in the steel tower under the water with the folds of the Worm of Nine Eyes round and about her prison; and it was she who won by seven years of service the right to deliver from hell all she could carry, and carried away multitudes clinging with worn fingers to the hem of her dress; and it was she who endured dumbness for a year because of the little thorn of enchantment the fairies had thrust into her tongue; and it was a lock of her hair, coiled in a little carved box, which gave so great a light that men threshed by it from sundown to sunrise, and awoke so great a wonder that kings spent years in wandering or fell before unknown armies in seeking to discover her hiding-place. There was no beauty in the world but hers, no tragedy in the world but hers; for he was of those ascetics of passion who keep their hearts pure for love or for hatred as other men for God, for Mary and for the Saints. ¶One day *a* ... 1914.

217   *serving-man* 1897 to 1927; *serving man* P.
218   *meadow, gave* ... P.*
218   *letter and* ... P.
218-19   *away* without a word; *and* ... P to 1913.
220   *ill.* The wise woman from Knock-na-Sidhe has [from Knock-na-shee has P; from the Mountain of the Shee has 1897] seen her, and says *she will* ... P to 1913.
221   *therefore* bid you *to* ... P; *therefore* bid *you come to* ... 1897 to 1913.
221   *you to come* ... 1925A.
221   *her, whose* ... P to 1908.
222-23   *treachery*—Teig MacDermott.' ¶*Costello* ... P; *treachery.*—Dermott [Dermot 1897], the son of Dermott.' ¶*Costello* ... 1897 to 1913.
223   *scythe, sent* ... P.*
224   *Duallach,* who had become associated in his mind with Oona, *and himself* ... P; *Duallach,* who had become woven into his mind with Oona [Una 1914], *and himself* ... 1897 to 1914.
224   *his* great *horse* ... P to 1913.
224-25   *Duallach's* garron. ¶*When* ... P to 1913.
225   *to* the son of Dermott's *house* ... 1897.
226   *Lough* of the Little Wood *lay* ... 1897.
226   *blue,* mirror-like [mirrorlike P], *and deserted* ... P to 1913.
226   *blue, and deserted* ... 1914 to 1927.
228-29   *than the* lake. *The* ... P.

Lough. The door stood half open, and Costello knocked upon it
230 again and again, but there was no answer.

'There is no one here,' said Duallach, 'for MacDermot is too
proud to welcome Proud Costello,' and he threw the door open,
and they saw a ragged, dirty, very old woman, who sat upon the
floor leaning against the wall. Costello knew that it was Bridget
235 Delaney, a deaf and dumb beggar; and she, when she saw him,
stood up and made a sign to him to follow, and led him and his
companion up a stair and down a long corridor to a closed door.
She pushed the door open and went a little way off and sat down as
before; Duallach sat upon the ground also, but close to the door,
240 and Costello went and gazed upon Una sleeping upon a bed. He sat
upon a chair beside her and waited, and a long time passed and still
she slept, and then Duallach motioned to him through the door to
wake her, but he hushed his very breath, that she might sleep on.
Presently he turned to Duallach and said, 'It is not right that I stay
245 here where there are none of her kindred, for the common people
are always ready to blame the beautiful.' And then they went down
and stood at the door of the house and waited, but the evening
wore on and no one came.

229 *half open* 1897 to 1927; *half-open* P.
229 *Costello* rapped *upon* . . . P.
230 *and again,* so that a number of lake gulls flew up [again and again, making a number
of lake gulls fly up P] out of the grass and circled [grass, and circle P] screaming over his
head, *but* . . . P to 1913.
231 *for* Dermott [MacDermott P] of the Sheep *is* . . . P to 1913.
232 *welcome* Costello the Proud;' *and* . . . P to 1913.
232 *and,* flinging *the* . . . P.
232-33 *open,* showed *a* . . . P.
233 *dirty,* and very ancient *woman* . . . P, 1897.
233 *woman who* . . . 1897.
234 *Costello* recognised *Bridget* . . . P.
236 *up, made* . . . P.*
238 *open, and went* . . . P.
239 *before. Duallach* . . . P.
240 *upon Oona* MacDermott asleep *upon* . . . P; *upon Oona* the daughter of Dermott asleep
upon . . . 1897.
240 *upon* Winny *sleeping* . . . 1908, 1913.
241 *passed, and* . . . P.
242 *slept* on, *and* . . . P to 1913.
242 *motioned him* . . . 1925A.*
243 *breath that* . . . P, 1925A.
243-44 *on,* for his heart was full of that ungovernable pity which makes the fading heart
of the lover a shadow of the divine heart. *Presently* . . . P to 1913.
244 *he* returned *to* . . . P.
244 *said,* ¶'*It* . . . P; *said:* [~: ¶ 1897] '*It* . . . 1897 to 1927.
246 *are* ever *ready* . . . P.

'It was a foolish man that called you Proud Costello,' Duallach
250 said at last; 'had he seen you waiting and waiting where they left
none but a beggar to welcome you, it is Humble Costello he would
have called you.'

Then Costello mounted and Duallach mounted, but when they
had ridden a little way Costello tightened the reins and made his
255 horse stand still. Many minutes passed, and then Duallach cried, 'It
is no wonder that you fear to offend MacDermot, for he has many
brothers and friends, and though he is old, he is a strong and
stirring man, and he is of the Queen's Irish, and the enemies of the
Gael are upon his side.'

260 And Costello answered flushing and looking towards the house,
'I swear by the Mother of God that I will never return there again if
they do not send after me before I pass the ford in the Brown
River,' and he rode on, but so very slowly that the sun went down
and the bats began to fly over the bogs. When he came to the river
265 he lingered awhile upon the edge, but presently rode out into the
middle and stopped his horse in a shallow. Duallach, however,
crossed over and waited on a further bank above a deeper place.
After a good while Duallach cried out again, and this time very
bitterly, 'It was a fool who begot you and a fool who bore you, and
270 they are fools who say you come of an old and noble stock, for you

---

249   *you* Costello the Proud,' *Duallach* . . . P, 1897.
249-50   *Duallach cried at* . . . P to 1913.
251   *is* Costello the Humble *he* . . . P, 1897.
254   *way, Costello* . . . P.
255   *passed and* . . . 1897.
255   *cried,* ¶'*It* . . . P; *cried:* [~: ¶ 1897] '*It* . . . 1897 to 1927.
256   *offend* Dermott [offend Teig MacDermott P; offend MacDermot 1914] of the Sheep, *for* . . . P to 1914.
257   *old he* . . . P.
257-60   *strong* man, and ready with his hands.' ¶*And* . . . P.
257-58   *strong* man and ready with his hands, *and he* . . . 1897 to 1913.
260   *answered, flushing* . . . P.
260-61   *house:* ¶'*I swear* . . . P, 1897; *house: 'I swear* . . . 1908 to 1927.
261   *by* Maurya of the Seven Sorrows *that* . . . P, 1897.
262-63   *in the* Donogue,' *and* . . . P.
263   *slowly, that* . . . P.
265   *awhile* 1897 to 1927; *a while* P.
265   *upon the* bank among the flowers of the flag, *but* [the purple flag-flowers, *but* P] . . . P to 1913.
266   *middle, and* . . . P.
266   *a* foaming *shallow* . . . P to 1913.
267   *on* the *further* . . . P, 1897.
268   *while, Duallach* . . . P.
269   *bitterly:* [~: ¶ P, 1897] '*It* . . . P to 1927.
270   *fools* of all fools *who* . . . P to 1913.
270   *and a noble* . . . 1897.

76

come of whey-faced beggars who travelled from door to door, bowing to serving-men.'

With bent head, Costello rode through the river and stood beside
him, and would have spoken had not hoofs clattered on the further
275 bank and a horseman splashed towards them. It was a serving-man
of MacDermot's, and he said, speaking breathlessly like one who
had ridden hard, 'Tumaus Costello, I come to bring you again to
MacDermot's house. When you had gone, his daughter Una awoke
and called your name, for you had been in her dreams. Bridget
280 Delaney the Dummy saw her lips move, and came where we were
hiding in the wood above the house and took MacDermot by the
coat and brought him to his daughter. He saw the trouble upon
her, and bid me ride his own horse to bring you the quicker.'

Then Costello turned towards the piper Duallach Daly, and tak-
285 ing him about the waist lifted him out of the saddle and threw him
against a big stone that was in the river, so that he fell lifeless into a
deep place. Then plunging his spurs into the horse, he rode away
furiously towards the north-west, along the edge of the river, and
did not pause until he came to another and smoother ford, and saw
290 the rising moon mirrored in the water. He paused for a moment

---

271 *beggars, who* . . . P.
271-72 *bowing* to gentles and *to* . . . P to 1913.
272 *serving-men* 1897 to 1927; *serving men* P.
272-73 *serving-men.* ¶*With* . . . 1913.
273 *head Costello* . . . P, 1925A.
275 *serving-man* 1897 to 1925; *serving man* P; *serving- | man* 1927.
276 *of* Teig MacDermott's, *and* . . . P; *of* the son of Dermott's, *and* . . . 1897.
277 *hard:* [~, P] ¶*Tumaus* . . . P, 1897.
277 *to* bid *you* . . . P to 1913.
277-78 *again to* Teig MacDermott's. *When* . . . P; *again to* Dermott the son of Dermott's.
When . . . 1897.
278 *gone,* Oona MacDermott *awoke* . . . P; *gone,* Oona the daughter of Dermott
awoke . . . 1897.
278 *daughter* Winny *awoke* . . . 1908, 1913.
280 *Delaney, the dummy, saw* . . . P.
280 *move* and the trouble upon her, *and* . . . P to 1913.
281 *house, and* . . . P.
281 *took* Teig MacDermott *by* . . . P; *took* Dermott of the Sheep *by* . . . 1897 to 1913.
284 *Duallach* O'Daly *and* . . . P.
284-85 *and, taking* . . . P.
285 *waist, lifted* . . . P.
285 *saddle, and* . . . P.
285-86 *and* hurled him against a grey rock that rose up out of *the* . . . P to 1913.
286-87 *into* the *deep* . . . P to 1913.
287 *place,* and the waters swept over the tongue which God had made [tongue which had
been made 1914] bitter, [~ ∧ P] that [bitter, it may be, that 1914] there might be a story
in men's ears in after time. Then plunging [time; and plunging P] *his* . . . P to 1914.
288 *furiously* toward *the north-west* . . . 1897 to 1914, 1925E, 1927.
289 *ford and* . . . P.

irresolute, and then rode into the ford and on over the Ox Mountains, and down towards the sea; his eyes almost continually resting upon the moon. But now his horse, long dark with sweat and breathing hard, for he kept spurring it, fell heavily, throwing 295 him on the roadside. He tried to make it stand up, and failing in this, went on alone towards the moonlight; and came to the sea and saw a schooner lying there at anchor. Now that he could go no further because of the sea, he found that he was very tired and the night very cold, and went into a shebeen close to the shore and 300 threw himself down upon a bench. The room was full of Spanish and Irish sailors who had just smuggled a cargo of wine, and were waiting a favourable wind to set out again. A Spaniard offered him a drink in bad Gaelic. He drank it and began talking wildly and rapidly.

305   For some three weeks the wind blew inshore or with too great violence, and the sailors stayed drinking and talking and playing cards, and Costello stayed with them, sleeping upon a bench in the shebeen, and drinking and talking and playing more than any. He soon lost what little money he had, and then his long cloak and his 310 spurs and even his boots. At last a gentle wind blew towards Spain, and the crew rowed out to their schooner, and in a little while the sails had dropped under the horizon. Then Costello turned home-

---

291-92   *over the* Mountains of the Ox, *and* ... P, 1897.
292   *sea, his* ... P.
293   *moon* [~, P] which glimmered in the dimness like a great white rose hung on the lattice of some boundless and phantasmal world. *But* ... P to 1913.
293   *long* dank *with* ... P.
294-95   *it* to an extreme speed [to utmost speed P], fell heavily, hurling him into the grass at *the* ... P to 1913.
295   *roadside* 1914 to 1927; *road side* P; *road-side* 1897; *road-* / *side* 1908, 1913.
295-96   *and, failing this* ... P.*
296   *sea, and* ... P.
297-98   *no* farther *because* ... 1925A.
299   *shore, and* ... P.
301   *sailors, who* ... P.
301   *wine* and ale, *and* ... P to 1913.
303   *it* greedily [~, P] *and began* ... P to 1914.
305   *blew* still *inshore* ... P.
305   *inshore* P, 1914 to 1927; *in shore* 1897; *in-* / *shore* 1908, 1913.
306   *stayed, drinking* ... P.
309   *and* then his horse, which some one had brought from the mountain boreen, to a Spaniard, [~ ∧ 1897] who sold it to a farmer from the mountains for a score of silver crowns, and [mountains, and 1908, 1913] *then his long* ... P to 1913.
310   *and* his boots of soft leather. *At* ... P to 1913.
311   *schooner,* [~ ∧ P] singing Gaelic and Spanish songs, and lifted the anchor, *and* ... P to 1913.
311   *little the* ... P.*
311-12   *while the* white *sails* ... P to 1913.

ward, his life gaping before him, and walked all day, coming in the
early evening to the road that went from near Lough Gara to the
315 southern edge of Lough Cay. Here he overtook a crowd of peasants and farmers, who were walking very slowly after two priests
and a group of well-dressed persons, certain of whom were carrying a coffin. He stopped an old man and asked whose burying it
was and whose people they were, and the old man answered, 'It is
320 the burying of Una, MacDermot's daughter, and we are the Mac-
Namaras and the MacDermots and their following, and you are
Tumaus Costello who murdered her.'
     Costello went on towards the head of the procession, passing
men who looked angrily at him, and only vaguely understood what
325 he had heard. Presently he stopped and asked again whose burying
it was, and a man answered, 'We are carrying MacDermot's
daughter Una, whom you murdered, to her burying upon Insula
Trinitatis,' and the man picked up a stone and threw it at Costello,
striking him on the cheek and making the blood flow out over his
330 face. Costello went on, scarcely feeling the blow, and coming to
those about the coffin, shouldered his way into the midst of them,
and laying his hand upon the coffin, asked in a loud voice, 'Who is
in this coffin?'

---

313   *his* empty *life* . . . P, 1897.
314   *near* the Lough of the Little Wood *to* . . . 1897.
315   *a* great *crowd* . . . P to 1913.
316-17   *priests, and* . . . P.
317   *well-dressed* 1908 to 1914, 1925A, 1927; *well dressed* P; *well- / dressed* 1897,
1925E.
317   *persons* who *were* . . . P.
319   answered, ¶'It . . . P; answered: [~: ¶ 1897] 'It . . . 1897 to 1927.
320   *of Oona* MacDermott, *and* . . . P; *of Oona* the daughter of Dermott, *and* . . . 1897.
324   *looked* at him with fierce eyes, [~ ∧ 1913] *and* . . . P to 1913.
324   *vaguely* understanding *what* . . . P to 1913.
325   *heard,* for [~, P] now that he had lost the understanding that belongs to good health
[lost the quick apprehension of perfect health P, 1897], it seemed impossible that a
gentleness and a beauty which had been so long the world's heart [~, 1897] could
[impossible that so much gentleness and beauty could 1914] pass away. *Presently* . . . P to
1914.
326   answered, ¶'We . . . P; answered: [~: ¶ 1897] 'We . . . 1897 to 1927.
326-27   *carrying* Oona MacDermott, *whom* . . . P; *carrying* Oona the daughter of Dermott,
whom . . . 1897; *carrying* Dermott's daughter Winny *whom* . . . 1908, 1913.
327-28   *to* be buried in the island of the Holy Trinity,' *and the* . . . P to 1914.
328   *man* stooped and *picked* . . . P to 1913.
328   *stone and* cast *it* . . . P to 1913.
329   *cheek, and* . . . P.
330   *on* scarcely . . . P to 1927.
330   *and, coming* . . . P.
332   *and, laying* . . . P.
332   voice, ¶'Who . . . P; voice: [~: ¶ 1897] 'Who . . . 1897 to 1927.

The three old MacDermots from the Ox Mountains caught up
335 stones and told those about them to do the same; and he was driven
from the road, covered with wounds.

When the procession had passed on, Costello began to follow
again, and saw from a distance the coffin laid upon a large boat,
and those about it get into other boats, and the boats move slowly
340 over the water to Insula Trinitatis; and after a time he saw the boats
return and their passengers mingle with the crowd upon the bank,
and all scatter by many roads and boreens. It seemed to him that
Una was somewhere on the island smiling gently, and when all had
gone he swam in the way the boats had been rowed and found the
345 new-made grave beside the ruined Abbey, and threw himself upon
it, calling to Una to come to him.

He lay there all that night and through the day after, from time
to time calling her to come to him, but when the third night came
he had forgotten that her body lay in the earth beneath, but only
350 knew she was somewhere near and would not come to him.

Just before dawn, the hour when the peasants hear his ghostly
voice crying out, he called loudly, 'If you do not come to me, Una, I

---

334   *Three* ... 1914, 1925A.
334   *Old* ... 1913, 1914, 1925A.
334   *the* Mountains of the Ox *caught* ... P, 1897.
335   *and* bid those about them *do* ... P to 1913.
336   *road covered* ... P.
336-37 *wounds,* and but for the priests would surely have [would have 1914] been killed.
¶*When* ... P to 1914.
337   *on Costello* ... P.
338-39 *boat and those* ... P.
339   *boats and* ... P.
341-42 *bank and all* ... P.
342   *all* disperse *by* ... P to 1913.
342-43 *that* Winny *was* ... 1908, 1913.
343   *gently* as of old, *and* ... P to 1913.
343   *and, when* ... P.
344   *gone, he* ... P.
345   *Abbey* of the Holy Trinity [the Trinity P], *and* ... P to 1913.
346-47 *him.* Above him the square ivy leaves trembled [the three-cornered leaves of the
ivy trembled P], and all about him white moths moved over white flowers, [~ ʌ P] and
sweet odours drifted through the dim air. ¶*He* ... P to 1913.
349   *forgotten,* worn out with hunger and sorrow, *that* ... P to 1914.
349   *beneath;* and *only* ... P; *beneath;* but *only* ... 1897 to 1914.
352   *out,* his pride awoke and *he* ... P to 1913.
352   *loudly,* ¶'Oona MacDermott, *if* ... P; *loudly:* ¶'Oona the daughter of Dermott,
if ... 1897; *loudly:* 'Winny, daughter of Dermott of the Sheep, *if* ... 1908, 1913; *loudly:*
'*If* ... 1914 to 1927.
352   *me I* ... P to 1913.*

will go and never return,' and before his voice had died away a cold
and whirling wind had swept over the island and he saw women of
355 the Sidhe rushing past; and then Una, but no longer smiling, for
she passed him swiftly and angrily, and as she passed struck him
upon the face, crying, 'Then go and never return.'

Costello got up from the grave, understanding nothing but that
he had made his sweetheart angry and that she wished him to go,
360 and wading out into the lake, began to swim. He swam on, but his
limbs seemed too weary to keep him afloat, and when he had gone
a little way he sank without a struggle.

The next day a fisherman found him among the reeds upon the
lake shore, lying upon the white lake sand, and carried him to his
365 own house. And the peasants lamented over him and sang the
keen, and laid him in the Abbey on Insula Trinitatis with only the
ruined altar between him and MacDermot's daughter, and planted
above them two ash-trees that in after days wove their branches
together and mingled their leaves.

---

353 *return* to the island of the Holy Trinity, [~; P]' *and* [~, P] *before* ... P to 1914.
353 *away, a* ... P.
354 *island, and* ... P.
354-55 *saw* many figures rushing past, women of the Sidhe [Shee P, 1897] with crowns
of silver and dim floating drapery; *and* ... P to 1914.
355 *then Oona* MacDermott, *but* ... P.
355 *smiling* gently, *for* ... P to 1913.
357 *face crying,* ¶*'Then* ... P; *face* [~, 1925E, 1927] *crying:* [~: ¶ 1897] *'Then* ... 1897 to
1927.
357-58 *return.'* ¶He would have followed, [~ ∧ P] and was calling out her name, when
the whole glimmering company rose up [whole company went up 1914] into the air, and,
rushing together in the [together into the P] shape of a great silvery rose, faded into the
ashen dawn. ¶*Costello* ... P to 1914.
359 *his* beloved *angry* [~, P] *and* ... P to 1913.
360 *and, wading* ... P.
360 *swam on* and on, *but* ... P to 1913.
361 *limbs* were *too* ... P to 1913.
361 *him* long *afloat* ... P.
361 *afloat,* and her anger was heavy about him, *and* [~, P] *when* ... P to 1913.
362 *way, he* ... P.
362-63 *struggle,* [~ ∧ P] like a man passing into sleep and dreams. ¶*The* ... P to 1913.
363 *a poor fisherman* ... P to 1913.
364 *sand* with his arms flung out as though he lay upon a rood, *and* ... P to 1913.
365 *the* very poor *lamented* ... P to 1914.
366 *and* [~, P] when the time had come, *laid* ... P to 1914.
367 *and* Oona MacDermott, *and* ... P; *and* Oona the daughter of Dermott, *and* ... 1897.
368 *ash-trees* 1897 to 1927; *ash trees* P.
369 *their* trembling *leaves.* P to 1914.
[In P, the story is signed W. B. Yeats.]

STORIES OF RED HANRAHAN

(1897, REWRITTEN IN 1907 WITH LADY GREGORY'S HELP)

RED HANRAHAN

Hanrahan, the hedge schoolmaster, a tall, strong, red-haired young man, came into the barn where some of the men of the village were sitting on Samhain Eve. It had been a dwelling-house, and when the man that owned it had built a better one, he had put
5   the two rooms together, and kept it for a place to store one thing or another. There was a fire on the old hearth, and there were dip candles stuck in bottles, and there was a black quart bottle upon some boards that had been put across two barrels to make a table. Most of the men were sitting beside the fire, and one
10 of them was singing a long wandering song, about a Munster man

---

Section title. Printings: 1925; 1927.
Text from 1932.
[No variants. In 1927, the section title is followed by the poem 'Sailing to Byzantium,' dedicated to Norah McGuinness, the illustrator of the volume.]
[General note on *Stories of Red Hanrahan:* in the 1905 edition the first words of new paragraphs are not indented, though new paragraphs always begin on a new line. This feature is not recorded in the collations. Ampersands occasionally used for 'and' are not treated as variants.]
Printings: *The Independent Review,* December, 1903; 1905; 1908; 1913; 1914; 1925; 1927.
Text from 1932.
[The story is divided into two sections, the second beginning with line 244. In *The Independent Review,* the sections are numbered I and II. In all other printings the same division is made by extra space between lines 243 and 244.]
Title: ... HANRAHAN. 1913.
1-2 *schoolmaster,* that was tall and strong and red-haired, *came* ... IR.
3 *dwelling-house* IR, 1908 to 1927; *dwelling house* 1905.
5 *kept* them *for* ... IR.
5 *place* where he could *store* ... IR.
10 *song about* ... IR.

and a Connaught man that were quarrelling about their two provinces.

Hanrahan went to the man of the house and said, 'I got your message'; but when he had said that, he stopped, for an old

15 mountainy man that had a shirt and trousers of unbleached flannel, and that was sitting by himself near the door, was looking at him, and moving an old pack of cards about in his hands and muttering. 'Don't mind him,' said the man of the house; 'he is only some stranger came in a while ago, and we bade him welcome, it

20 being Samhain night, but I think he is not in his right wits. Listen to him now and you will hear what he is saying.'

They listened then, and they could hear the old man muttering to himself as he turned the cards, 'Spades and Diamonds, Courage and Power; Clubs and Hearts, Knowledge and Pleasure.'

25 'That is the kind of talk he has been going on with for the last hour,' said the man of the house, and Hanrahan turned his eyes from the old man as if he did not like to be looking at him.

'I got your message,' Hanrahan said then; '"He is in the barn with his three first cousins from Kilchreist," the messenger said,

30 "and there are some of the neighbours with them."'

'It is my cousin over there is wanting to see you,' said the man of the house, and he called over a young frieze-coated man, who was listening to the song, and said, 'This is Red Hanrahan you have the message for.'

---

11   *man* who *were* . . . IR.
11–13 *provinces. Hanrahan* . . . IR.
14   *message;' but* . . . 1905.
14   *that he* . . . IR.
16   *door was* . . . 1905.
17   *hands, and* . . . IR.
18   *muttering.* ¶*'Don't* . . . IR.
18   *mind* that one,' *said* . . . IR.
19   *stranger* come *in* . . . IR.
19   *a while; awhile* IR to 1927.
20   *night; but* . . . IR.
21   *now, and* . . . IR.
23–25 *cards:* 'Diamonds and Hearts, courage and pleasure; Spades and Clubs, knowledge and power.' ¶*That* . . . IR.
26   *house; and* . . . IR.
27   *the* mountainy *man* . . . IR.
27–28 *him. 'I* . . . IR.
28   *message,' he said* . . . IR.
28   *then. 'He* . . . IR; *then;* '"*he* . . . 1905 to 1914, 1925A.
29   *Kilchreist* . . . IR to 1927.
29–30 *the* woman *said:* 'and . . . IR.
33   *said:* 'This . . . IR; *said,* 'this . . . 1905.

35 'It is a kind message, indeed,' said the young man, 'for it comes
from your sweetheart, Mary Lavelle.'
'How would you get a message from her, and what do you know
of her?'
'I don't know her, indeed, but I was in Loughrea yesterday, and a
40 neighbour of hers that had some dealings with me was saying that
she bade him send you word, if he met any one from this side in the
market, that her mother has died from her, and if you have a mind
yet to join with herself, she is willing to keep her word to you.'
'I will go to her indeed,' said Hanrahan.
45 'And she bade you make no delay, for if she has not a man in the
house before the month is out, it is likely the little bit of land will be
given to another.'
When Hanrahan heard that, he rose up from the bench he had
sat down on. 'I will make no delay indeed,' he said; 'there is a full
50 moon, and if I get as far as Kilchreist to-night, I will reach to her
before the setting of the sun to-morrow.'
When the others heard that, they began to laugh at him for being
in such haste to go to his sweetheart, and one asked him if he would
leave his school in the old lime-kiln, where he was giving the chil-
55 dren such good learning. But he said the children would be glad
enough in the morning to find the place empty, and no one to keep
them at their task; and as for his school he could set it up again in
any place, having as he had his little inkpot hanging from his neck
by a chain, and his big Virgil and his primer in the skirt of his coat.

35   *message indeed* . . . 1905.
36   *sweetheart Mary* . . . 1905.
37   *her and* . . . 1905.
39   *her indeed* . . . IR, 1905.
40–41   *me* said *she* . . . IR.
41   *send* word to you, *if* . . . IR.
41   *any one* IR, 1908, 1913, 1925, 1927; *anyone* 1905, 1914.
42   *and* that *if* . . . IR.
44   *her, indeed* . . . IR.
45   *delay; for* . . . IR.
48   *he* stood *up* . . . IR.
49   *delay, indeed* . . . IR.
49   said, 'there . . . 1905 to 1914, 1925A.
50   *Kilchriest* . . . IR to 1908, 1927; *Gilchreist* . . . 1913, 1914, 1925A.
52   *that,* some of them *began* . . . IR.
53   *sweetheart; and* . . . IR.
54   *lime-kiln* IR to 1913; *lime- / kiln* 1914, 1925; *limekiln* 1927.
58   *having, as* . . . IR.
58   *had, his little* . . . IR.
59   *Primer* . . . IR.
59–60   *coat. Some* . . . IR.

60 Some of them asked him to drink a glass before he went, and a young man caught hold of his coat, and said he must not leave them without singing the song he had made in praise of Venus and of Mary Lavelle. He drank a glass of whisky, but he said he would not stop but would set out on his journey.

65 'There's time enough, Red Hanrahan,' said the man of the house. 'It will be time enough for you to give up sport when you are after your marriage, and it might be a long time before we will see you again.'

'I will not stop,' said Hanrahan; 'my mind would be on the roads
70 all the time, bringing me to the woman that sent for me, and she lonesome and watching till I come.'

Some of the others came about him, pressing him that had been such a pleasant comrade, so full of songs and every kind of trick and fun, not to leave them till the night would be over, but he
75 refused them all, and shook them off, and went to the door. But as he put his foot over the threshold, the strange old man stood up and put his hand that was thin and withered like a bird's claw on Hanrahan's hand, and said, 'It is not Hanrahan, the learned man and the great songmaker, that should go out from a gathering like
80 this, on a Samhain night. And stop here, now,' he said, 'and play a hand with me; and here is an old pack of cards has done its work many a night before this, and old as it is, there has been much of the riches of the world lost and won over it.'

One of the young men said, 'It isn't much of the riches of the
85 world has stopped with yourself, old man,' and he looked at the old man's bare feet, and they all laughed. But Hanrahan did not laugh, but he sat down very quietly, without a word. Then one of them

---

60   *went; and* ... IR.
61   *coat and* ... IR.
63   *whiskey* ... 1905 to 1914.
64   *stop, but* ... IR.
70   *time bringing* ... IR.
73–74   *kind of* tricks *and* ... IR.
74   *over; but* ... IR.
75   *But, as* ... IR.
77   *hand, that* ... IR.
77   *claw, on* ... IR, 1905.
78   *and* he *said* ... IR.
78   *said: 'It* ... IR to 1927.
80   *here now* ... IR, 1905.
82   *and, old* ... IR.
83–84   *it.' One* ... IR.
84   *said: 'It* ... IR.
85   *man'; and* ... IR.

said, 'So you will stop with us after all, Hanrahan'; and the old man said, 'He will stop indeed, did you not hear me asking him?'

90 They all looked at the old man then as if wondering where he came from. 'It is far I am come,' he said; 'through France I have come, and through Spain, and by Lough Greine of the hidden mouth, and none has refused me anything.' And then he was silent and nobody liked to question him, and they began to play. There

95 were six men at the boards playing, and the others were looking on behind. They played two or three games for nothing, and then the old man took a fourpenny bit, worn very thin and smooth, out from his pocket, and he called to the rest to put something on the game. Then they all put down something on the boards, and little

100 as it was it looked much, from the way it was shoved from one to another, first one man winning it and then his neighbour. And sometimes the luck would go against a man and he would have nothing left, and then one or another would lend him something, and he would pay it again out of his winnings, for neither good nor

105 bad luck stopped long with any one.

And once Hanrahan said as a man would say in a dream, 'It is time for me to be going the road'; but just then a good card came to him, and he played it out, and all the money began to come to him. And once he thought of Mary Lavelle, and he sighed; and that time

110 his luck went from him, and he forgot her again.

88 said: 'So . . . IR.
88 Hanrahan?'; and . . . IR; Hanrahan;' and . . . 1905.
89 said: 'He . . . IR to 1927.
89 indeed; did . . . IR.
90 then, as . . . IR.
91 said, 'through . . . IR to 1927.
91-92 have gone, and through . . . IR.
92 Spain, and to Loch . . . IR.
93 none have refused . . . IR.
93-94 silent, and nobody . . . IR.
94 him; and . . . IR.
99 and, little . . . IR.
100 was, it looked . . . IR.
100 much from the . . . IR.
102 man, and . . . IR.
104 it back again . . . IR.
105 any one IR, 1925, 1927; anyone 1905 to 1914.
105-6 one. And . . . IR.
106 said, like a man . . . IR.
106 dream: 'It . . . IR.
107 road;' but . . . 1905.
109 sighed, and . . . IR.
110-11 again. But . . . IR.

But at last the luck went to the old man and it stayed with him, and all they had flowed into him, and he began to laugh little laughs to himself, and to sing over and over to himself, 'Spades and Diamonds, Courage and Power,' and so on, as if it was a verse of a
115 song.

And after a while any one looking at the men, and seeing the way their bodies were rocking to and fro, and the way they kept their eyes on the old man's hands, would think they had drink taken, or that the whole store they had in the world was put on the cards; but
120 that was not so, for the quart bottle had not been disturbed since the game began, and was nearly full yet, and all that was on the game was a few sixpenny bits and shillings, and maybe a handful of coppers.

'You are good men to win and good men to lose,' said the old
125 man; 'you have play in your hearts.' He began then to shuffle the cards and to mix them, very quick and fast, till at last they could not see them to be cards at all, but you would think him to be making rings of fire in the air, as little lads would make them with whirling a lighted stick; and after that it seemed to them that all the room
130 was dark, and they could see nothing but his hands and the cards.

And all in a minute a hare made a leap out from between his hands, and whether it was one of the cards that took that shape, or whether it was made out of nothing in the palms of his hands, nobody knew, but there it was running on the floor of the barn, as
135 quick as any hare that ever lived.

Some looked at the hare, but more kept their eyes on the old man, and while they were looking at him a hound made a leap out between his hands, the same way as the hare did, and after that

---

113-14 *himself:* 'Diamonds and Hearts, courage and pleasure,' *and so* . . . IR.
114 *and* Pleasure,' *and so* . . . 1905, 1908.
115-16 *song. And* . . . IR.
116 *any one* IR, 1925, 1927; *anyone* 1905 to 1914.
120 *been* stirred *since* . . . IR, 1905.
122 *sixpenny bits* 1908 to 1914; 1927; *sixpenny-bits* IR; *six- / penny bits* 1905, 1925.
125 *man, 'you* . . . IR to 1927.
125 *hearts,* you have play in your hearts.' *He* . . . IR, 1905.
129 *and then it* . . . IR.
130-31 *cards. And* . . . IR.
131 *And, all* . . . IR.
131 *minute, a hare* . . . IR.
134 *knew; but* . . . IR.
135-36 *lived. Some* . . . IR.
137 *man; and* . . . IR.
137 *and, while* . . . IR.
137 *him, a hound* . . . IR.

another hound and another, till there was a whole pack of them
140 following the hare round and round the barn.

The players were all standing up now, with their backs to the
boards, shrinking from the hounds, and nearly deafened with the
noise of their yelping, but as quick as the hounds were they could not
overtake the hare, but it went round, till at the last it seemed as if a
145 blast of wind burst open the barn door, and the hare doubled and
made a leap over the boards where the men had been playing, and
went out of the door and away through the night, and the hounds
over the boards and through the door after it.

Then the old man called out, 'Follow the hounds, follow the
150 hounds, and it is a great hunt you will see to-night,' and he went out
after them. But used as the men were to go hunting after hares,
and ready as they were for any sport, they were in dread to go out
into the night, and it was only Hanrahan that rose up and that said,
'I will follow, I will follow on.'

155 'You had best stop here, Hanrahan,' the young man that was
nearest him said, 'for you might be going into some great danger.'
But Hanrahan said, 'I will see fair play, I will see fair play,' and he
went stumbling out of the door like a man in a dream, and the door
shut after him as he went.

160 He thought he saw the old man in front of him, but it was only
his own shadow that the full moon cast on the road before him, but
he could hear the hounds crying after the hare over the wide green

---

139   *was whole* . . . 1925A.*
140-41   *barn. The* . . . IR.
142   *shrinking* back *from* . . . IR.
142-43   *with the* great *noise* . . . IR.
143   *yelping; but* . . . IR.
143   *but, as quick* . . . IR.
143   *were, they* . . . IR.
144   *round* and round, till at *last* . . . IR.
147   *out* at *the door* . . . IR.
148   *the* board *and* . . . IR.
148-49   *it. Then* . . . IR.
149   *out: 'Follow* . . . IR.
150   *to-night'; and* . . . IR.
151   *But, used* . . . IR.
153-54   *said: 'I will follow, I* . . . IR.
154-55   *on.' 'You* . . . IR [Because "on.'" comes at the end of the line of type in 1905, it is
not possible to tell whether or not a paragraph break was intended in that version.].
157   *said: 'I will see fair play, I* . . . IR.
157   *fair play'; and* . . . IR.
158   *out* at *the door like* . . . IR.
159-60   *went* out. ¶*He* . . . IR.
160   *him,* though *it* . . . IR.
161   *him; but* . . . IR.

fields of Granagh, and he followed them very fast, for there was
nothing to stop him; and after a while he came to smaller fields that
165 had little walls of loose stones around them, and he threw the
stones down as he crossed them, and did not wait to put them up
again; and he passed by the place where the river goes underground at Ballylee, and he could hear the hounds going before him
up towards the head of the river. Soon he found it harder to run,
170 for it was uphill he was going, and clouds came over the moon, and
it was hard for him to see his way, and once he left the path to take
a short cut, but his foot slipped into a bog-hole and he had to come
back to it. And how long he was going he did not know, or what way
he went, but at last he was up on the bare mountain, with nothing
175 but the rough heather about him, and he could neither hear the
hounds nor any other thing. But their cry began to come to him
again, at first far off and then very near, and when it came quite
close to him, it went up all of a sudden into the air, and there was
the sound of hunting over his head; then it went away northward
180 till he could hear nothing at all. 'That's not fair,' he said, 'that's not
fair.' And he could walk no longer, but sat down on the heather
where he was, in the heart of Slieve Echtge, for all the strength had
gone from him, with the dint of the long journey he had made.

And after a while he took notice that there was a door close to
185 him, and a light coming from it, and he wondered that being so

---

163   *fast for* ... 1905 to 1927.
164   *him. And* ... IR.
167   *again, and* ... IR.
167–68   *river* rises *at* ... IR.
167–68   *underground* 1925E, 1927; *under ground* 1905 to 1914, 1925A.
171   *was* not easy *for* ... IR.
171   *way; and* ... IR.
171–72   *path to* make *a short* ... IR.
172   *into bog-hole* ... 1925A.*
172   *bog-hole* 1925, 1927; *boghole* IR to 1913; *bog- / hole* 1914.
175   *him; and* ... IR.
177   *near; and* ... IR.
178   *him it* ... IR.
179   *head,* and *then* ... IR.
180   *nothing* more *at* ... IR to 1914.
181   *fair.'* ¶*And* ... IR.
181   *longer; but* ... IR.
181–82   *heather, where* ... IR.
182   *was in* ... IR.
182   *Echtge. For* ... IR.
183   *him with* ... IR.
185   *him and a* ... IR.
185   *it; and* ... IR.
185–86   *that,* so close as it was, *he had* ... IR.

close to him he had not seen it before. And he rose up, and tired as he was he went in at the door, and although it was night time outside, it was daylight he found within. And presently he met with an old man that had been gathering summer thyme and yellow flag-flowers, and it seemed as if all the sweet smells of the summer were with them. And the old man said: 'It is a long time you have been coming to us, Hanrahan the learned man and the great songmaker.'

And with that he brought him into a very big shining house, and every grand thing Hanrahan had ever heard of, and every colour he had ever seen, was in it. There was a high place at the end of the house, and on it there was sitting in a high chair a woman, the most beautiful the world ever saw, having a long pale face and flowers about it, but she had the tired look of one that had been long waiting. And there were sitting on the step below her chair four grey old women, and the one of them was holding a great cauldron in her lap; and another a great stone on her knees, and heavy as it was it seemed light to her; and another of them had a very long spear that was made of pointed wood; and the last of them had a sword that was without a scabbard.

Hanrahan stood looking at them for a long time, but none of them spoke any word to him or looked at him at all. And he had it in his mind to ask who that woman in the chair was, that was like a

---

186 *up, and, tired* ... IR.
187 *was, he* ... IR.
187 *door. And* ... IR.
188 *within, and* ... IR.
191 *them, and* he *said* ... IR.
192 *Hanrahan, the learned* ... IR.
193-94 *songmaker.' And* ... IR.
194 *house; and* ... IR.
196 *seen,* were *in* ... IR to 1927.
197 *woman the* ... IR.
199 *it; but* ... IR.
199-200 *been* a long time *waiting* ... IR.
200 *there* was *sitting* ... 1908 to 1914, 1925A.
200 *sitting, on* ... IR.
200 *chair, four* ... IR.
201 *women; and* ... IR.
202 *lap, and another* ... IR.
202 *knees, and, heavy* ... IR.
203 *was, it* ... IR.
203 *her, and* ... IR.
204 *wood, and* ... IR.
205-6 *scabbard.* And *Hanrahan* ... IR.
206 *them* all *for* ... IR.

queen, and what she was waiting for; but ready as he was with his
210 tongue and afraid of no person, he was in dread now to speak to so
beautiful a woman, and in so grand a place. And then he thought to
ask what were the four things the four grey old women were holding like great treasures, but he could not think of the right words to
bring out.
215 Then the first of the old women rose up, holding the cauldron
between her two hands, and she said, 'Pleasure,' and Hanrahan said
no word. Then the second old woman rose up with the stone in her
hands, and she said 'Power'; and the third old woman rose up with
a spear in her hand, and she said 'Courage'; and the last of the old
220 women rose up having the sword in her hands, and she said
'Knowledge.' And every one, after she had spoken, waited as if for
Hanrahan to question her, but he said nothing at all. And then the
four old women went out of the door, bringing their four treasures
with them, and as they went out one of them said, 'He has no wish
225 for us'; and another said, 'He is weak, he is weak'; and another said,
'He is afraid'; and the last said, 'His wits are gone from him.' And
then they all said, 'Echtge, daughter of the Silver Hand, must stay
in her sleep. It is a pity, it is a great pity.'

---

209   *what* it was *she* . . . IR.
209   *but, ready* . . . IR.
211   *woman and* . . . IR.
213   *treasures; but* . . . IR.
214-15   *out.* And *then* . . . IR.
216   *said* [~: IR] *'Pleasure* . . . IR, 1908 to 1927.
216   *Pleasure'; and* . . . IR.
217   *word.* And *then* . . . IR.
218   *said: 'Power'; and* . . . IR; *said 'Power;' and* . . . 1905.
218-19   *with* the *spear* . . . IR to 1914, 1925A.
219   *said: 'Courage'; and* . . . IR; *said 'Courage;' and* . . . 1905.
220   *up, having* . . . IR.
220-21   *said: 'Knowledge* . . . IR.
221   *every one* 1925, 1927; *everyone* IR to 1914.
222   *her; but* . . . IR.
223   *door, taking their* . . . IR.
224   *them; and* . . . IR.
224   *and, as* . . . IR.
224   *out, one* . . . IR.
224   *said: 'He* . . . IR; *said 'he* . . . 1905.
225   *us;' and* . . . 1905.
225   *said: 'He is weak, he* . . . IR; *said 'he is weak, he* . . . 1905.
225-26   *weak;' and another said 'he* . . . 1905.
225-26   *said: 'He* . . . IR.
226   *afraid;' and* . . . 1905.
226   *said: 'His* . . . IR; *said 'his* . . . 1905.
227   *said* [~: IR] *'Echtge* . . . IR to 1913.
228-29   *great pity.' And* . . . IR.

And then the woman that was like a queen gave a very sad sigh,
230 and it seemed to Hanrahan as if the sigh had the sound in it of
hidden streams; and if the place he was in had been ten times
grander and more shining than it was, he could not have hindered
sleep from coming on him; and he staggered like a drunken man
and lay down there and then.
235 When Hanrahan awoke, the sun was shining on his face, but
there was white frost on the grass around him, and there was ice on
the edge of the stream he was lying by, and that goes running on
through Daire-caol and Druim-da-rod. He knew by the shape of
the hills and by the shining of Lough Greine in the distance that he
240 was upon one of the hills of Slieve Echtge, but he was not sure how
he came there; for all that had happened in the barn had gone
from him, and all of his journey but the soreness of his feet and the
stiffness in his bones.

It was a year after that, there were men of the village of Cap-
245 paghtagle sitting by the fire in a house on the roadside, and Red
Hanrahan that was now very thin and worn and his hair very long
and wild, came to the half-door and asked leave to come in and rest
himself; and they bid him welcome because it was Samhain night.
He sat down with them, and they gave him a glass of whisky out of a
250 quart bottle; and they saw the little inkpot hanging about his neck,
and knew he was a scholar, and asked for stories about the Greeks.
He took the Virgil out of the big pocket of his coat, but the cover

---

233 *him, and* . . . IR.
233–34 *man, and lay* . . . IR.
236 *the* ground *around* . . . IR.
237–38 *that* was the same that runs *through* . . . IR.
238 *knew, by* . . . IR.
239 *hills, and* . . . IR.
239 *Loch* . . . IR.
239 *distance, that* . . . IR.
240 *Echtge; but* . . . IR.
241 *there, for* . . . IR.
243–44 *bones./II/It* . . . IR [see head-note].
245 *house* by *the* . . . IR.
246 *Hanrahan, that* . . . IR, 1905.
246 *worn, and* . . . IR.
247 *half-door* IR, 1908 to 1927; *half door* 1905.
247 *half-door, and asked* . . . IR.
249 *whiskey* . . . 1905 to 1914.
250 *bottle, and* . . . IR.
251–52 *Greeks. He* . . . IR.

was very black and swollen with the wet, and the page when he opened it was very yellow, but that was no great matter, for he
255 looked at it like a man that had never learned to read. Some young man that was there began to laugh at him then, and to ask why did he carry so heavy a book with him when he was not able to read it.

It vexed Hanrahan to hear that, and he put the Virgil back in his pocket and asked if they had a pack of cards among them, for cards
260 were better than books. When they brought out the cards he took them and began to shuffle them, and while he was shuffling them something seemed to come into his mind, and he put his hand to his face like one that is trying to remember, and he said, 'Was I ever here before, or where was I on a night like this?' and then of a
265 sudden he stood up and let the cards fall to the floor, and he said, 'Who was it brought me a message from Mary Lavelle?'

'We never saw you before now, and we never heard of Mary Lavelle,' said the man of the house. 'And who is she,' he said, 'and what is it you are talking about?'
270 'It was this night a year ago, I was in a barn, and there were men playing cards, and there was money on the table, they were pushing it from one to another here and there—and I got a message, and I was going out of the door to look for my sweetheart that wanted me, Mary Lavelle.' And then Hanrahan called out very loud,
275 'Where have I been since then? Where was I for the whole year?'

'It is hard to say where you might have been in that time,' said the oldest of the men, 'or what part of the world you may have travelled; and it is like enough you have the dust of many roads on your

---

254   *yellow. But* . . . IR.
257-58   *it. It* . . . IR.
259   *pocket, and* . . . IR.
260   *cards, he* . . . IR.
261   *shuffle them; and, while* . . . IR.
261-62   *was* doing that, *something* . . . IR.
261-62   *shuffling them, something* . . . 1905.
262   *hand* over *his* . . . IR.
263   *said: 'Was* . . . IR to 1927.
264   *this?' And* . . . IR.
265   *up, and let* . . . IR.
265-66   *said: 'Who* . . . IR.
266-67   *Lavelle?' 'We* . . . IR.
268   *she?' he* . . . IR.
272   *there* . . . *and I got* [The suspension points are in Yeats's text.] . . . IR.
273   *out the door* . . . IR.*
274   *Lavelle* . . .' *And* [The suspension points are in Yeats's text.] . . . IR.
274-75   *loud: 'Where have* . . . IR to 1927.

feet; for there are many go wandering and forgetting like that,' he
280 said, 'when once they have been given the touch.'

'That is true,' said another of the men. 'I knew a woman went
wandering like that through the length of seven years; she came
back after, and she told her friends she had often been glad
enough to eat the food that was put in the pig's trough. And it is
285 best for you to go to the priest now,' he said, 'and let him take off
you whatever may have been put upon you.'

'It is to my sweetheart I will go, to Mary Lavelle,' said Hanrahan;
'it is too long I have delayed, how do I know what might have
happened her in the length of a year?'

290 He was going out of the door then, but they all told him it was
best for him to stop the night, and to get strength for the journey;
and indeed he wanted that, for he was very weak, and when they
gave him food he ate it like a man that had never seen food before,
and one of them said, 'He is eating as if he had trodden on the
295 hungry grass.' It was in the white light of the morning he set out,
and the time seemed long to him till he could get to Mary Lavelle's
house. But when he came to it, he found the door broken, and the
thatch dropping from the roof, and no living person to be seen.
And when he asked the neighbours what had happened her, all
300 they could say was that she had been put out of the house, and had
married some labouring man, and they had gone looking for work
to London or Liverpool or some big place. And whether she found
a worse place or a better he never knew, but anyway he never met
with her or with news of her again.

---

279 *feet. For* ... IR.
282 *years. She came* ... IR.
286 *whatever* IR to 1914, 1925E, 1927; *what ever* 1925A.
287–88 Hanrahan, *'it* ... 1905.
288 *delayed; how* ... IR.
289–90 year.' ¶*He* ... 1905.
292 *weak; and* ... IR.
293 *food, he* ... IR.
293 *he eat it* ... IR to 1914.
294 *said: 'He* ... IR.
294 *had been treading on* ... IR.
295 *hungry grass* 1905 to 1927; *hungry-grass* IR.
295 *hungry-grass.' ¶It* ... IR.
297 *when he got to* ... IR.
297 *it he* ... IR.
299 *And, when* ... IR.
301 *gone away looking* ... IR.
302 *London, or Liverpool, or* ... IR.
[In IR the story is signed W. B. Yeats.]

THE TWISTING OF THE ROPE

Hanrahan was walking the roads one time near Kinvara at the fall of day, and he heard the sound of a fiddle from a house a little way off the roadside. He turned up the path to it, for he never had the habit of passing by any place where there was music or dancing

5 or good company, without going in. The man of the house was standing at the door, and when Hanrahan came near he knew him and he said, 'A welcome before you, Hanrahan, you have been lost to us this long time.' But the woman of the house came to the door and she said to her husband, 'I would be as well pleased for Hanra-

10 han not to come in to-night, for he has no good name now among the priests, or with women that mind themselves, and I wouldn't wonder from his walk if he has a drop of drink taken.' But the man said, 'I will never turn away Hanrahan of the poets from my door,' and with that he bade him enter.

15 There were a good many neighbours gathered in the house, and some of them remembered Hanrahan; but some of the little lads that were in the corners had only heard of him, and they stood up to have a view of him, and one of them said, 'Is not that Hanrahan that had the school, and that was brought away by Them?' But his

20 mother put her hand over his mouth and bade him be quiet, and not be saying things like that. 'For Hanrahan is apt to grow wicked,' she said, 'if he hears talk of that story, or if any one goes questioning him.' One or another called out then, asking him for a song, but the man of the house said it was no time to ask him for a song,

25 before he had rested himself; and he gave him whisky in a glass, and Hanrahan thanked him and wished him good health and drank it off.

The fiddler was tuning his fiddle for another dance, and the man of the house said to the young men, they would all know what

30 dancing was like when they saw Hanrahan dance, for the like of it

Printings: 1905; 1908; 1913; 1914; 1925; 1927.
Text from 1932.
Title: ... ROPE. 1913.
7   said: [~:— 1905] 'A ... 1905 to 1927.
9   husband: 'I ... 1905 to 1927.
13 said: 'I ... 1905.
18 said: 'Is ... 1905 to 1927.
20 quiet and ... 1905.
22 any one 1925, 1927; any- / one 1905; anyone 1908 to 1914.
25 whiskey ... 1905 to 1914.
30 was when ... 1905.*

had never been seen since he was there before. Hanrahan said he
would not dance, he had better use for his feet now, travelling as he
was through the four provinces of Ireland. Just as he said that,
there came in at the half-door Oona, the daughter of the house,
35 having a few bits of bog deal from Connemara in her arms for the
fire. She threw them on the hearth and the flame rose up, and
showed her to be very comely and smiling, and two or three of the
young men rose up and asked for a dance. But Hanrahan crossed
the floor and brushed the others away, and said it was with him she
40 must dance, after the long road he had travelled before he came to
her. And it is likely he said some soft word in her ear, for she said
nothing against it, and stood out with him, and there were little
blushes in her cheeks. Then other couples stood up, but when the
dance was going to begin, Hanrahan chanced to look down, and he
45 took notice of his boots that were worn and broken, and the ragged
grey socks showing through them; and he said angrily it was a bad
floor, and the music no great things, and he sat down in the dark
place beside the hearth. But if he did, the girl sat down there with
him.
50 The dancing went on, and when that dance was over another was
called for, and no one took much notice of Oona and Red Hanrahan for a while, in the corner where they were. But the mother
grew to be uneasy, and she called to Oona to come and help her to
set the table in the inner room. But Oona that had never refused
55 her before, said she would come soon, but not yet, for she was
listening to whatever he was saying in her ear. The mother grew yet
more uneasy then, and she would come nearer them, and let on to
be stirring the fire or sweeping the hearth, and she would listen for
a minute to hear what the poet was saying to her child. And one
60 time she heard him telling about white-handed Deirdre, and how
she brought the sons of Usna to their death; and how the blush in
her cheeks was not so red as the blood of kings' sons that was shed
for her, and her sorrows had never gone out of mind; and he said it
was maybe the memory of her that made the cry of the plover on
65 the bog as sorrowful in the ear of the poets as the keening of young
men for a comrade. And there would never have been that memory of her, he said, if it was not for the poets that had put her
beauty in their songs. And the next time she did not well understand what he was saying, but as far as she could hear, it had the

33 *the* five *provinces . . .* 1905 to 1914.
34 *half-door* 1908 to 1927; *half door* 1905.
61 *Usnach . . .* 1905 to 1927.

70   sound of poetry though it was not rhymed, and this is what she heard him say: 'The sun and the moon are the man and the girl, they are my life and your life, they are travelling and ever travelling through the skies as if under the one hood. It was God made them for one another. He made your life and my life before the begin-
75   ning of the world, He made them that they might go through the world, up and down, like the two best dancers that go on with the dance up and down the long floor of the barn, fresh and laughing, when all the rest are tired out and leaning against the wall.'

    The old woman went then to where her husband was playing
80   cards, but he would take no notice of her, and then she went to a woman of the neighbours and said, 'Is there no way we can get them from one another?' and without waiting for an answer she said to some young men that were talking together, 'What good are you when you cannot make the best girl in the house come out and
85   dance with you? And go now the whole of you,' she said, 'and see can you bring her away from the poet's talk.' But Oona would not listen to any of them, but only moved her hand as if to send them away. Then they called to Hanrahan and said he had best dance with the girl himself, or let her dance with one of them. When
90   Hanrahan heard what they were saying he said, 'That is so, I will dance with her; there is no man in the house must dance with her but myself.'

    He stood up with her then, and led her out by the hand, and some of the young men were vexed, and some began mocking at
95   his ragged coat and his broken boots. But he took no notice, and Oona took no notice, but they looked at one another as if all the world belonged to themselves alone. But another couple that had been sitting together like lovers stood out on the floor at the same time, holding one another's hands and moving their feet to keep
100   time with the music. But Hanrahan turned his back on them as if angry, and in place of dancing he began to sing, and as he sang he held her hand, and his voice grew louder, and the mocking of the young men stopped, and the fiddle stopped, and there was nothing heard but his voice that had in it the sound of the wind. And what
105   he sang was a song he had heard or had made one time in his

---

75 *he* . . . 1905 to 1927.
81 *said: 'Is* . . . 1905 to 1927.
83 *together: 'What* . . . 1905 to 1927.
83 *What* a *good* . . . 1914.
90 *said: 'That* . . . 1905 to 1927.
91 *her, there* . . . 1905.

wanderings on Slieve Echtge, and the words of it as they can be put into English were like this:

> O Death's old bony finger
> Will never find us there
110 > In the high hollow townland
> Where love's to give and to spare;
> Where boughs have fruit and blossom
> At all times of the year;
> Where rivers are running over
115 > With red beer and brown beer.
> An old man plays the bagpipes
> In a golden and silver wood;
> Queens, their eyes blue like the ice,
> Are dancing in a crowd.

120 And while he was singing it Oona moved nearer to him, and the colour had gone from her cheek, and her eyes were not blue now, but grey with the tears that were in them, and any one that saw her would have thought she was ready to follow him there and then from the west to the east of the world.

125 But one of the young men called out, 'Where is that country he is singing about? Mind yourself, Oona, it is a long way off, you might be a long time on the road before you would reach to it.' And another said, 'It is not to the Country of the Young you will be going if you go with him, but to Mayo of the bogs.' Oona looked at 130 him then as if she would question him, but he raised her hand in his

---

107-20 *this:* ¶
I heard under a ragged hollow wood,
A queen-woman dressed out in silver, cry
When the sun looked out of his golden hood,
O that none ever loved but you and I!

O hurry to the water amid the trees,
For there the tall deer and his leman cry
When they have but looked upon their images,
O that none ever loved but you and I!

O hurry to the ragged wood for there
I will drive out the deer and moon and cry—
O my share of the world, O yellow hair,
No one has ever loved but you and I!

¶*And* ... 1905.
117 *a* gold *and* ... 1908 to 1914.
122 *any one* 1925, 1927; *anyone* 1905 to 1914.
125 *out:* '*Where* ... 1905 to 1927.
128 *said:* '*It* ... 1905 to 1927.

hand, and called out between singing and shouting, 'It is very near us that country is, it is on every side; it may be on the bare hill behind it is, or it may be in the heart of the wood.' And he said out very loud and clear, 'In the heart of the wood; O, death will never
135 find us in the heart of the wood. And will you come with me there, Oona?' he said.

But while he was saying this the two old women had gone outside the door, and Oona's mother was crying, and she said, 'He has put an enchantment on Oona. Can we not get the men to put him out
140 of the house?'

'That is a thing you cannot do,' said the other woman, 'for he is a poet of the Gael, and you know well if you would put a poet of the Gael out of the house, he would put a curse on you that would wither the corn in the fields and dry up the milk of the cows, if it
145 had to hang in the air seven years.'

'God help us,' said the mother, 'and why did I ever let him into the house at all, and the wild name he has!'

'It would have been no harm at all to have kept him outside, but there would great harm come upon you if you put him out by
150 force. But listen to the plan I have to get him out of the house by his own doing, without any one putting him from it at all.'

It was not long after that the two women came in again, each of them having a bundle of hay in her apron. Hanrahan was not singing now, but he was talking to Oona very fast and soft, and he
155 was saying, 'The house is narrow but the world is wide, and there is no true lover that need be afraid of night or morning or sun or stars or shadows of evening, or any earthly thing.' 'Hanrahan,' said the mother then, striking him on the shoulder, 'will you give me a hand here for a minute?' 'Do that, Hanrahan,' said the woman of
160 the neighbours, 'and help us to make this hay into a rope, for you are ready with your hands, and a blast of wind has loosened the thatch on the haystack.'

'I will do that for you,' said he, and he took the little stick in his hands, and the mother began giving out the hay, and he twisting it,

131   shouting: 'It . . . 1905 to 1927.
134   clear: 'In . . . 1905 to 1927.
134   wood; oh, death . . . 1905 to 1927.
138   said: 'He . . . 1905 to 1927.
147-48   has! ¶'It . . . 1925A.
151   any one 1925, 1927; anyone 1905 to 1914.
155   saying: 'The . . . 1905 to 1927.
159   minute.' 'Do . . . 1905.
160   neighbours; 'and . . . 1905.

165 but he was hurrying to have done with it, and to be free again. The women went on talking and giving out the hay, and encouraging him, and saying what a good twister of a rope he was, better than their own neighbours or than any one they had ever seen. And Hanrahan saw that Oona was watching him, and he began to twist
170 very quick and with his head high, and to boast of the readiness of his hands, and the learning he had in his head, and the strength in his arms. And as he was boasting, he went backward, twisting the rope always till he came to the door that was open behind him, and without thinking he passed the threshold and was out on the road.
175 And no sooner was he there than the mother made a sudden rush, and threw out the rope after him, and she shut the door and the half-door and put a bolt upon them.

She was well pleased when she had done that, and laughed out loud, and the neighbours laughed and praised her. But they heard
180 him beating at the door, and saying words of cursing outside it, and the mother had but time to stop Oona that had her hand upon the bolt to open it. She made a sign to the fiddler then, and he began a reel, and one of the young men asked no leave but caught hold of Oona and brought her into the thick of the dance. And when it was
185 over and the fiddle had stopped, there was no sound at all of anything outside, but the road was as quiet as before.

As to Hanrahan, when he knew he was shut out and that there was neither shelter nor drink nor a girl's ear for him that night, the anger and the courage went out of him, and he went on to where
190 the waves were beating on the strand.

He sat down on a big stone, and he began swinging his right arm and singing slowly to himself, the way he did always to hearten himself when every other thing failed him. And whether it was that time or another time he made the song that is called to this day
195 'The Twisting of the Rope,' and that begins, 'What was the dead cat that put me in this place,' is not known.

But after he had been singing a while, mist and shadows seemed to gather about him, sometimes coming out of the sea, and sometimes moving upon it. It seemed to him that one of the shadows was
200 the queen-woman he had seen in her sleep at Slieve Echtge; not in

---

168   *any one* 1914 to 1927; *any-* / *one* 1905; *anyone* 1908, 1913.
177   *half-door* 1908 to 1927; *half door* 1905.
182–83   *began to reel* . . . 1925A.
195   *Rope', and* . . . 1925.
196   *place', is* . . . 1925.
197   *a while* 1905, 1925, 1927; *awhile* 1908 to 1914.

her sleep now, but mocking, and calling out to them that were behind her, 'He was weak, he was weak, he had no courage.' And he felt the strands of the rope in his hand yet, and went on twisting it, but it seemed to him as he twisted that it had all the sorrows of
205 the world in it. And then it seemed to him as if the rope had changed in his dream into a great water-worm that came out of the sea, and that twisted itself about him, and held him closer and closer. And then he got free of it, and went on, shaking and un-steady, along the edge of the strand, and the grey shapes were
210 flying here and there around him. And this is what they were say-ing: 'It is a pity for him that refuses the call of the daughters of the Sidhe, for he will find no comfort in the love of the women of the earth to the end of life and time, and the cold of the grave is in his heart for ever. It is death he has chosen; let him die, let him die, let
215 him die.'

HANRAHAN AND CATHLEEN, THE DAUGHTER
OF HOULIHAN

It was travelling northward Hanrahan was one time, giving a hand to a farmer now and again in the hurried time of the year, and telling his stories and making his share of songs at wakes and at weddings.
5   He chanced one day to overtake on the road to Coloony one Margaret Rooney, a woman he used to know in Munster when he was a young man. She had no good name at that time, and it was the priest routed her out of the place at last. He knew her by her walk and by the colour of her eyes, and by a way she had of putting

---

202   *her: 'He* ... 1905 to 1927.
202   *courage'. And* ... 1925.
204   *twisted, that* ... 1905 to 1914.
208   *closer,* and grew from big to bigger till the whole of the earth and skies were wound up in it, and the stars themselves were but the shining of the ridges of its skin. *And* ... 1905 to 1914.
210-11   *saying, 'It* ... 1908 to 1927.

Printings: 1905; 1908; 1913; 1914; 1925; 1927.
Text from 1932.
Spellings: bocachs 1925 to 1932; bacachs 1905 to 1914. Houlihan 1932; Hoolihan 1905 to 1927.
Title: ... CATHLEEN THE DAUGHTER ... 1905 to 1927; ... HOOLIHAN. 1913.
5   *Coloony* ... 1905; *Collooney* ... 1908 to 1927.

10   back the hair off her face with her left hand. She had been wandering about, she said, selling herrings and the like, and now she was
going back to Sligo, to the place in the Burrough where she was
living with another woman, Mary Gillis, who had much the same
story as herself. She would be well pleased, she said, if he would
15   come and stop in the house with them, and be singing his songs to
the bocachs and blind men and fiddlers of the Burrough. She
remembered him well, she said, and had a wish for him; and as to
Mary Gillis, she had some of his songs off by heart, so he need not
be afraid of not getting good treatment, and all the bocachs and
20   poor men that heard him would give him a share of their own
earnings for his stories and his songs while he was with them, and
would carry his name into all the parishes of Ireland.

He was glad enough to go with her, and to find a woman to be
listening to the story of his troubles and to be comforting him. It
25   was at the moment of the fall of day when every man may pass as
handsome and every woman as comely. She put her arm about
him when he told her of the misfortune of the Twisting of the
Rope, and in the half-light she looked as well as another.

They kept in talk all the way to the Burrough, and as for Mary
30   Gillis, when she saw him and heard who he was, she went near
crying to think of having a man with so great a name in the house.

Hanrahan was well pleased to settle down with them for a while,
for he was tired with wandering; and since the day he found the
little cabin fallen in, and Mary Lavelle gone from it, and the thatch
35   scattered, he had never asked to have any place of his own; and he
had never stopped long enough in any place to see the green leaves
come where he had seen the old leaves wither, or to see the wheat
harvested where he had seen it sown. It was a good change to him
to have shelter from the wet, and a fire in the evening time, and his
40   share of food put on the table without the asking.

He made a good many of his songs while he was living there, so
well cared for and so quiet. The most of them were love songs, but
some were songs of repentance, and some were songs about Ireland and her griefs, under one name or another.

45   Every evening the bocachs and beggars and blind men and
fiddlers would gather into the house and listen to his songs and his
poems, and his stories about the old time of the Fianna, and they
kept them in their memories that were never spoiled with books;

---

28 *half-light; half light* 1905 to 1927.
42 *quiet, The* . . . 1913.

and so they brought his name to every wake and wedding and
50   pattern in the whole of Connaught. He was never so well off or
made so much of as he was at that time.

One evening of December he was singing a little song that he said
he had heard from the green plover of the mountain, about the
fair-haired boys that had left Limerick, and that were wandering
55   and going astray in all parts of the world. There were a good many
people in the room that night, and two or three little lads that had
crept in, and sat on the floor near the fire, and were too busy with
the roasting of a potato in the ashes or some such thing to take
much notice of him; but they remembered long afterwards when
60   his name had gone up, the sound of his voice, and what way he had
moved his hand, and the look of him as he sat on the edge of the
bed, with his shadow falling on the white-washed wall behind him,
and as he moved going up as high as the thatch.

Of a sudden his singing stopped, and his eyes grew misty as if he
65   was looking at some far thing.

Mary Gillis was pouring whisky into a mug that stood on a table
beside him, and she left off pouring and said, 'Is it of leaving us you
are thinking?'

Margaret Rooney heard what she said, and did not know why she
70   said it, and she took the words too much in earnest and came over
to him, and there was dread in her heart that she was going to lose
so good a comrade, and a man that was thought so much of, and
that brought so many to her house.

'You would not go away from us, my heart?' she said, catching
75   him by the hand.

'It is not of that I am thinking,' he said, 'but of Ireland and the
weight of grief that is on her.' And he leaned his head against his
hand, and began to sing these words, and the sound of his voice was
like the wind in a lonely place.

80   The old brown thorn-trees break in two high over Cummen Strand
       Under a bitter black wind that blows from the left hand;
       Our courage breaks like an old tree in a black wind and dies,
       But we have hidden in our hearts the flame out of the eyes
       Of Cathleen, the daughter of Houlihan.

---

62   *white-washed* 1927; *whitewashed* 1905 to 1914; *white- / washed* 1925.
63-64   *thatch.* And they knew then that they had looked upon a king of the poets of the
Gael, and a maker of the dreams of men. ¶*Of . . .* 1905 to 1914.
66   *whiskey . . .* 1905 to 1914.
71-72   *lose* so wonderful a poet and *so good . . .* 1905 to 1914.
80   *thorn-trees; thorn trees* 1905 to 1927.
84   *Cathleen the . . .* 1905 to 1927.

85   The wind has bundled up the clouds high over Knocknarea
And thrown the thunder on the stones for all that Maeve can say.
Angers that are like noisy clouds have set our hearts abeat;
But we have all bent low and low and kissed the quiet feet
Of Cathleen, the daughter of Houlihan.

90   The yellow pool has overflowed high up on Clooth-na-Bare,
For the wet winds are blowing out of the clinging air;
Like heavy flooded waters our bodies and our blood;
But purer than a tall candle before the Holy Rood
Is Cathleen, the daughter of Houlihan.

95   While he was singing, his voice began to break, and tears came
rolling down his cheeks, and Margaret Rooney put down her face
into her hands and began to cry along with him. Then a blind
beggar by the fire shook his rags with a sob, and after that there was
no one of them all but cried tears down.

RED HANRAHAN'S CURSE

One fine May morning a long time after Hanrahan had left
Margaret Rooney's house, he was walking the road near Coloony,
and the sound of the birds singing in the bushes that were white
with blossom set him singing as he went. It was to his own little
5   place he was going, that was no more than a cabin, but that pleased
him well. For he was tired of so many years of wandering from
shelter to shelter at all times of the year, and although he was

---

85   *The* winds was *bundled* ... 1913, 1914; *The* winds have *bundled* ... 1925, 1927.
86–87   *say; / Angers* ... 1905 to 1927.
87–88   *abeat, / But* ... 1905 to 1927.
89   *Cathleen the* ... 1905 to 1927.
90   *up on* 1905, 1914 to 1927; *upon* 1908, 1913.
90   *Clooth-na-Bare* 1925; *Clooth- / na-Bare* [broken at end of the line of type, but not at the end of the verse line] 1905 to 1913; *Cloothna-Bare* 1914; *Clooth-na- / Bare* 1927 [broken at end of the line of type].
92–93   *blood, / But* ... 1905 to 1927.
94   *Cathleen the* ... 1905 to 1927.

Printings: 1905; 1908; 1913; 1914; 1925; 1927.
Text from 1932.
Title: ... CURSE. 1913.
2   *Collooney* ... 1905 to 1927.

seldom refused a welcome and a share of what was in the house, it
seemed to him sometimes that his mind was getting stiff like his
10   joints, and it was not so easy to him as it used to be to make fun and
sport through the night, and to set all the boys laughing with his
pleasant talk, and to coax the women with his songs. And a while
ago, he had turned into a cabin that some poor man had left to go
harvesting and had never come to again. And when he had
15   mended the thatch and made a bed in the corner with a few sacks
and rushes, and had swept out the floor, he was well content to
have a little place for himself, where he could go in and out as he
liked, and put his head in his hands through the length of an
evening if the fret was on him, and loneliness after the old times.
20   One by one the neighbours began to send their children in to get
some learning from him, and with what they brought, a few eggs,
or an oaten cake or a couple of sods of turf, he made out a way of
living. And if he went for a wild day and night now and again to the
Burrough, no one would say a word, knowing him to be a poet,
25   with wandering in his heart.

It was from the Burrough he was coming that May morning,
light-hearted enough, and singing some new song that had come to
him. But it was not long till a hare ran across his path, and made
away into the fields, through the loose stones of the wall. And he
30   knew it was no good sign a hare to have crossed his path, and he
remembered the hare that had led him away to Slieve Echtge the
time Mary Lavelle was waiting for him, and how he had never
known content for any length of time since then. 'And it is likely
enough they are putting some bad thing before me now,' he said.

35   And after he said that he heard the sound of crying in the field
beside him, and he looked over the wall. And there he saw a young
girl sitting under a bush of white hawthorn, and crying as if her
heart would break. Her face was hidden in her hands, but her soft
hair and her white neck and the young look of her put him in mind
40   of Bridget Purcell and Margaret Gillane and Maeve Connelan and
Oona Curry and Celia Driscoll, and the rest of the girls he had

---

16   *and* bushes, *and* . . . 1905 to 1914.
21-22   *eggs or an* . . . 1905 to 1913.
33   *since* them. *'And* . . . 1925E.
34   *now' he* . . . 1905.
35   *that, he* . . . 1905, 1908.
37   *hawthorne* . . . 1925A.
39   *and white* . . . 1925A.*
39   *of her, put* . . . 1905 to 1927.

made songs for and had coaxed the heart from with his flattering tongue.

45 She looked up, and he saw her to be a girl of the neighbours, a farmer's daughter. 'What is on you, Nora?' he said. 'Nothing you could take from me, Red Hanrahan.' 'If there is any sorrow on you it is I myself should be well able to serve you,' he said then, 'for it is I know the history of the Greeks, and I know well what sorrow is and parting, and the hardship of the world. And if I am not able to
50 save you from trouble,' he said, 'there is many a one I have saved from it with the power that is in my songs, as it was in the songs of the poets that were before me from the beginning of the world. And it is with the rest of the poets I myself will be sitting and talking in some far place beyond the world, to the end of life and time,' he
55 said. The girl stopped her crying, and she said, 'Owen Hanrahan, I often heard you have had sorrow and persecution, and that you know all the troubles of the world since the time you refused your love to the queen-woman in Slieve Echtge; and that she never left you in quiet since. But when it is people of this earth that have
60 harmed you, it is yourself knows well the way to put harm on them again. And will you do now what I ask you, Owen Hanrahan?' she said. 'I will do that indeed,' said he.

'It is my father and my mother and my brothers,' she said, 'that are marrying me to old Paddy Doe, because he has a farm of a
65 hundred acres under the mountain. And it is what you can do, Hanrahan,' she said, 'put him into a rhyme the same way you put old Peter Kilmartin in one the time you were young, that sorrow may be over him rising up and lying down, that will put him thinking of Coloony churchyard and not of marriage. And let you make
70 no delay about it, for it is for to-morrow they have the marriage settled, and I would sooner see the sun rise on the day of my death than on that day.'

'I will put him into a song that will bring shame and sorrow over him; but tell me how many years has he, for I would put them in
75 the song?'

'O, he has years upon years. He is as old as you yourself, Red Hanrahan.' 'As old as myself,' said Hanrahan, and his voice was as if broken; 'as old as myself; there are twenty years and more be-

---

55 *she said: 'Owen* . . . 1905.
69 *Colloony* . . . 1905; *Collooney* . . . 1908 to 1927.
75-76 *song?' ¶'Oh, he* . . . 1905.
77 *myself,' san [sic] Hanrahan* . . . 1908.

tween us! It is a bad day indeed for Owen Hanrahan when a young
80 girl with the blossom of May in her cheeks thinks him to be an old
man. And my grief!' he said, 'you have put a thorn in my heart.'
  He turned from her then and went down the road till he came to
a stone, and he sat down on it, for it seemed as if all the weight of
the years had come on him in the minute. And he remembered it
85 was not many days ago that a woman in some house had said: 'It is
not Red Hanrahan you are now but Yellow Hanrahan, for your
hair is turned to the colour of a wisp of tow.' And another woman
he had asked for a drink had not given him new milk but sour; and
sometimes the girls would be whispering and laughing with young
90 ignorant men while he himself was in the middle of giving out his
poems or his talk. And he thought of the stiffness of his joints when
he first rose of a morning, and the pain of his knees after making a
journey, and it seemed to him as if he was come to be a very old
man, with cold in the shoulders and speckled shins and his wind
95 breaking and he himself withering away. And with those thoughts
there came on him a great anger against old age and all it brought
with it. And just then he looked up and saw a great spotted eagle
sailing slowly towards Ballygawley, and he cried out, 'You, too,
eagle of Ballygawley, are old, and your wings are full of gaps, and I
100 will put you and your ancient comrades, the Pike of Dargan Lake
and the Yew of the Steep Place of the Strangers into my rhyme,
that there may be a curse on you for ever.'
  There was a bush beside him to the left, flowering like the rest,
and a little gust of wind blew the white blossoms over his coat. 'May
105 blossoms,' he said, gathering them up in the hollow of his hand,
'you never know age because you die away in your beauty, and I
will put you into my rhyme and give you my blessing.'
  He rose up then and plucked a little branch from the bush, and
carried it in his hand. But it is old and broken he looked going
110 home that day with the stoop in his shoulders and the darkness in
his face.
  When he got to his cabin there was no one there, and he went
and lay down on the bed for a while as he was used to do when he
wanted to make a poem or a praise or a curse. And it was not long
115 he was in making it this time, for the power of the curse-making
bards was upon him. And when he had made it he searched his
mind how he could send it out over the whole countryside.

---

86 *yellow* ... 1905 to 1927.
98 *out:* 'You ... 1905 to 1927.
100 *pike* ... 1905.

Some of the scholars began coming in then, to see if there would be any school that day, and Hanrahan rose up and sat on the bench
120 by the hearth, and they all stood around him.

They thought he would bring out the Virgil or the Mass book or the primer, but instead of that he held up the little branch of hawthorn he had in his hand yet. 'Children,' he said, 'this is a new lesson I have for you to-day.
125 'You yourselves and the beautiful people of the world are like this blossom, and old age is the wind that comes and blows the blossom away. And I have made a curse upon old age and upon the old men, and listen now while I give it out to you.' And this is what he said,—

130 The poet, Owen Hanrahan, under a bush of may
Calls down a curse on his own head because it withers grey;
Then on the speckled eagle cock of Ballygawley Hill
Because it is the oldest thing that knows of cark and ill;
And on the yew that has been green from the times out of mind
135 By the Steep Place of the Strangers and the Gap of the Wind;
And on the great grey pike that broods in Castle Dargan Lake
Having in his long body a many a hook and ache;
Then curses he old Paddy Bruen of the Well of Bride
Because no hair is on his head and drowsiness inside.
140 Then Paddy's neighbour, Peter Hart, and Michael Gill, his friend,
Because their wandering histories are never at an end.
And then old Shemus Cullinan, shepherd of the Green Lands
Because he holds two crutches between his crooked hands;
Then calls a curse from the dark North upon old Paddy Doe,
145 Who plans to lay his withering head upon a breast of snow,
Who plans to wreck a singing voice and break a merry heart;
He bids a curse hang over him till breath and body part,
But he calls down a blessing on the blossom of the may
Because it comes in beauty, and in beauty blows away.

150 He said it over to the children verse by verse till all of them could

---

129-30 said—¶The ... 1905 to 1913.
130 May ... 1905.
132-33 Hill, / Because ... 1905 to 1927.
137-38 ache. / Then ... 1927.
139-40 inside; / Then ... 1927.
141-42 end, / And ... 1927.
142-43 Lands, / Because ... 1927.
146-47 heart, / He ... 1905 to 1914.
147-48 part; / But ... 1905 to 1914, 1927.
148-49 May, / Because ... 1905; may, / Because ... 1908 to 1927.

say a part of it, and some that were the quickest could say the whole
of it.

'That will do for to-day,' he said then. 'And what you have to do
now is to go out and sing that song for a while, to the tune of The
155 Green Bunch of Rushes, to every one you meet, and to the old men
themselves.'

'I will do that,' said one of the little lads; 'I know old Paddy Doe
well. Last S. John's Eve we dropped a mouse down his chimney,
but this is better than a mouse.'

160 'I will go into the town of Sligo and sing it in the street,' said
another of the boys. 'Do that,' said Hanrahan, 'and go into the
Burrough and tell it to Margaret Rooney and Mary Gillis, and bid
them sing it, and to make the beggars and the bocachs sing it
wherever they go.' The children ran out then, full of pride and of
165 mischief, calling out the song as they ran, and Hanrahan knew
there was no danger it would not be heard.

He was sitting outside the door the next morning, looking at his
scholars as they came by in twos and threes. They were nearly all
come, and he was considering the place of the sun in the heavens to
170 know whether it was time to begin, when he heard a sound that was
like the buzzing of a swarm of bees in the air, or the rushing of a
hidden river in time of flood. Then he saw a crowd coming up to
the cabin from the road, and he took notice that all the crowd was
made up of old men, and that the leaders of it were Paddy Bruen,
175 Michael Gill and Paddy Doe, and there was not one in the crowd
but had in his hand an ash stick or a blackthorn. As soon as they
caught sight of him, the sticks began to wave hither and thither like
branches in a storm, and the old feet to run.

He waited no longer, but made off up the hill behind the cabin
180 till he was out of their sight.

After a while he came back round the hill, where he was hidden
by the furze growing along a ditch. And when he came in sight of
his cabin he saw that all the old men had gathered around it, and
one of them was just at that time thrusting a rake with a wisp of
185 lighted straw on it into the thatch.

'My grief!' he said, 'I have set Old Age and Time and Weariness
and Sickness against me, and I must go wandering again. And, O

154-55   *of the Green* . . . 1905 to 1927.
155   *every one* 1925, 1927; *everyone* 1905 to 1914.
158   *Saint* . . . 1905 to 1927.
163   *them* to *sing it, and to* . . . 1905; *them sing* to *it, and to* . . . 1908, 1913.
163   *bacachs* . . . 1905 to 1914, 1925A.
186   *grief,' he* . . . 1905 to 1927.

Blessed Queen of Heaven,' he said, 'protect me from the Eagle of
Ballygawley, the Yew Tree of the Steep Place of the Strangers, the
190 Pike of Castle Dargan Lake, and from the lighted wisps of their
kindred, the Old Men!'

HANRAHAN'S VISION

It was in the month of June Hanrahan was on the road near
Sligo, but he did not go into the town, but turned towards Ben
Bulben; for there were thoughts of the old times coming upon him,
and he had no mind to meet with common men. And as he walked
5 he was singing to himself a song that had come to him one time in
his dreams:

       O Death's old bony finger
       Will never find us there
       In the high hollow townland
10   Where love's to give and to spare;
       Where boughs have fruit and blossom
       At all times of the year;
       Where rivers are running over

Printings: *McClure's Magazine*, March, 1905; 1905; 1908; 1913; 1914; 1925; 1927.
Text from 1932.
Title: RED HANRAHAN'S VISION MM; ... VISION. 1913.
2 *Beinn* ... MM to 1913.
4-5 *walked, he* ... MM.
6-51 *dreams:* ¶ [~:—¶ MM]
    I went out to the hazel wood, [~ ∧ 1905]
    Because a fire was in my head,
    And cut and peeled a hazel rod, [~ ∧ 1905]
    And put a berry on a thread;
    And when white moths were on the wing, [~ ∧ 1905]
    And stars like moths were shining out,
    I dropped the berry in a stream
    And hooked a little silver trout.

    When I had laid it on a stool
    I stooped to blow the fire aflame,
    But something rustled on the floor, [~ ∧ 1905]
    And some one [someone 1905] *called me by my name.*
    It had become a laughing girl,
    With apple blossoms in her hair,
    That called me by my name and ran
    And faded through the brightening air.
    ¶*Hanrahan* ... MM, 1905 [The poem is printed in italic in MM, in roman in 1905.].

The Secret Rose

15 With red beer and brown beer.
An old man plays the bagpipes
In a golden and silver wood;
Queens, their eyes blue like the ice,
Are dancing in a crowd.

20 The little fox he murmured,
'O what of the world's bane?'
The sun was laughing sweetly,
The moon plucked at my rein;
But the little red fox murmured,
'O do not pluck at his rein,
25 He is riding to the townland
That is the world's bane.'

When their hearts are so high
That they would come to blows,
They unhook their heavy swords
30 From golden and silver boughs;
But all that are killed in battle
Awaken to life again.
It is lucky that their story
Is not known among men,
35 For O, the strong farmers
That would let the spade lie,
Their hearts would be like a cup
That somebody had drunk dry.

Michael will unhook his trumpet
40 From a bough overhead,
And blow a little noise
When the supper has been spread.
Gabriel will come from the water
With a fish tail, and talk
45 Of wonders that have happened
On wet roads where men walk,
And lift up an old horn
Of hammered silver, and drink
Till he has fallen asleep
50 Upon the starry brink.

---

16   *a* gold *and* . . . 1908 to 1914.
30-31   *boughs: | But* . . . 1908 to 1914.
32-33   *again: | It* . . . 1908 to 1914.
34-35   *men. | For* . . . 1908 to 1914.
42-43   *spread, | Gabriel* . . . 1925, 1927.

Hanrahan had begun to climb the mountain then, and he gave over singing, for it was a long climb for him, and every now and again he had to sit down and to rest for a while. And one time he was resting he took notice of a wild briar bush, with blossoms on it,
55 that was growing beside a rath, and it brought to mind the wild roses he used to bring to Mary Lavelle, and to no woman after her. And he tore off a little branch of the bush, that had buds on it and open blossoms, and he went on with his song:

> The little fox he murmured,
60 'O what of the world's bane?'
> The sun was laughing sweetly,
> The moon plucked at my rein;
> But the little red fox murmured,
> 'O do not pluck at his rein,
65 He is riding to the townland
> That is the world's bane.'

And he went on climbing the hill, and left the rath, and there came to his mind some of the old poems that told of lovers, good and bad, and of some that were awakened from the sleep of the
70 grave itself by the strength of one another's love, and brought away to a life in some shadowy place, where they are waiting for the Judgment and banished from the face of God.

And at last, at the fall of day, he came to the Steep Place of the Strangers, and there he laid himself down along a ridge of rocks

---

54   bush with ... MM.
54   with roses on ... MM.
55   rath,* and ... MM [The footnote indicated by the asterisk reads: 'Rath—The ruined fortress-dwelling of one of the ancient Irish chiefs.'].
56   Maire ... MM.
58–67   song: ¶ [~:—¶ MM]
     Though I am old with wandering
     Through hilly lands and hollow lands,
     I will find out where she is gone
     And kiss her lips and take her hands;
     And walk and walk through summer grass,
     And pluck till time and times are done
     The silver apples of the moon,
     The golden apples of the sun.
     ¶And ... MM, 1905 [The poem is printed in italic in MM, in roman in 1905.].
67   And then he ... MM.
71   place where ... MM.
72   judgment ... MM to 1927.
73   Steep Gap of ... MM to 1913.
74   he lay himself ... 1905.
74–75   of rock, and ... MM to 1914.

The Secret Rose

75 and looked into the valley, that was full of grey mist spreading from mountain to mountain.

And it seemed to him as he looked that the mist changed to shapes of shadowy men and women, and his heart began to beat with the fear and the joy of the sight. And his hands, that were 80 always restless, began to pluck off the leaves of the roses on the little branch, and he watched them as they went floating down into the valley in a little fluttering troop.

Suddenly he heard a faint music, a music that had more laughter in it and more crying than all the music of this world. And his heart 85 rose when he heard that, and he began to laugh out loud, for he knew that music was made by some who had a beauty and a greatness beyond the people of this world. And it seemed to him that the little soft rose-leaves as they went fluttering down into the valley began to change their shape till they looked like a troop of men and 90 women far off in the mist, with the colour of the roses on them. And then that colour changed to many colours, and what he saw was a long line of tall beautiful young men, and of queen-women, that were not going from him but coming towards him and past him, and their faces were full of tenderness for all their proud 95 looks, and were very pale and worn, as if they were seeking and ever seeking for high sorrowful things. And shadowy arms were stretched out of the mist as if to take hold of them, but could not touch them, for the quiet that was about them could not be broken. And before them and beyond them, but at a distance as if in rev- 100 erence, there were other shapes, sinking and rising and coming and going, and Hanrahan knew them by their whirling flight to be the Sidhe, the ancient defeated gods; and the shadowy arms did

---

75 *looked* down *into* ... MM.
75 *gray* ... MM.
75 *mist, spreading* ... MM.
77 *looked, that* ... 1905.
85 *loud; for* ... MM.
86 *some* that *had* ... MM.
88 *rose-leaves* MM; *rose leaves* 1905 to 1927.
90 *the* mists, *with* ... MM.
90 *color* ... MM.
91 *color* ... MM.
91 *colors* ... MM.
92 *tall, beautiful* ... MM.
95 *and very* ... MM.*
96 *ever seeking* 1905 to 1927; *ever-seeking* MM.
97 *stretched* up *out* ... MM.
102 *gods, and* ... MM.

114

not rise to take hold of the Sidhe, who are of those that can neither
sin nor obey. And they all lessened then in the distance, and they
105 seemed to be going towards the white door that is in the side of the
mountain.

The mist spread out before him now like a deserted sea washing
the mountains with long grey waves, but while he was looking at it,
it began to fill again with a flowing broken witless life that was a
110 part of itself, and arms and pale heads covered with tossing hair
appeared in the greyness. It rose higher and higher till it was level
with the edge of the steep rock, and then the shapes seemed all but
solid, and that new procession half lost in mist passed very slowly
with uneven steps, and in the midst of each shadow there was
115 something shining in the starlight. They came nearer and nearer,
and Hanrahan saw that they also were lovers, and that they had
heart-shaped mirrors instead of hearts, and they were looking and
ever looking on their own faces in one another's mirrors. They
passed on, sinking downward as they passed, and other shapes rose
120 in their place, and these did not keep side by side, but followed
after one another, holding out wild beckoning arms, and he saw
that those who were followed were women, and as to their heads
they were beyond all beauty, but as to their bodies they were but
shadows without life, and their long hair was moving and trembling
125 about them, as if it lived with some terrible life of its own. And then
the mist rose of a sudden and hid them, and then a light gust of
wind blew them away towards the north-east, and covered Hanrahan at the same time with a white wing of cloud.

He stood up trembling and was going to turn away from the
130 valley, when he saw two dark and half-hidden forms standing as if
in the air just beyond the rock, and one of them that had the

---

103 *of* them, for they were *of* . . . MM to 1914.
103 *Sidhe who* . . . 1925, 1927.
105 *white* square *door* . . . MM.
108 *gray* . . . MM.
108 *waves; but* . . . MM.
109 *flowing, broken, witless* . . . MM.
111 *grayness* . . . MM.
112–13 *shapes* grew to be *solid* . . . MM to 1914.
113 *and a new* . . . MM to 1914.
118 *ever looking* 1905 to 1927; *ever-looking* MM.
118 *ever-looking* in one another's mirrors on their own faces. *They* . . . MM.
121 *wild, beckoning* . . . MM.
121 *arms; and* . . . MM.
125 *them as* . . . MM.
127 *the* northwest, *and* . . . MM.
130 *half-hidden* MM, 1908 to 1927; *half hidden* 1905.

sorrowful eyes of a beggar said to him in a woman's voice, 'Speak to me, for no one in this world or any other world has spoken to me for seven hundred years.'

135   'Tell me who are those that have passed by,' said Hanrahan.

'Those that passed first,' the woman said, 'are the lovers that had the greatest name in the old times, Blanid and Deirdre and Grania and their dear comrades, and a great many that are not so well known but are as well loved. And because it was not only the blos-
140 som of youth they were looking for in one another, but the beauty that is as lasting as the night and the stars, the night and the stars hold them for ever from the warring and the perishing, in spite of the death and bitterness their love brought into the world. And those that came next,' she said, 'and that still breathe the sweet air
145 and have the mirrors in their hearts, are not put in songs by the poets, because they sought only to triumph one over the other, and so to prove their strength and beauty, and out of this they made a kind of love. And as to the women with shadow-bodies, they de-sired neither to triumph nor to love but only to be loved, and there
150 is no blood in their hearts or in their bodies until it flows through them from a kiss, and their life is but for a moment. All these are unhappy, but I am the unhappiest of all, for I am Dervagilla, and this is Dermot, and it was our sin brought the Norman into Ireland. And the curses of all the generations are upon us, and none are
155 punished as we are punished. It was but the blossom of the man and of the woman we loved in one another, and so when we died there was no lasting unbreakable quiet about us, and the bitterness of the battles we brought into Ireland turned to our own punish-ment. We go wandering together for ever, but Dermot that was my

---

132 *voice: 'Speak* ... MM, 1905.
136 *passed* the *first* ... MM.
137 *Blanad* ... MM to 1927.
137-38 *and* Grania and Deirdre *and their* ... MM.
139 *known, but* ... MM.
143 *the* wars and the *bitterness* ... MM to 1914.
145 *hearts are* ... MM.
148 *shadow-bodies* 1905 to 1927; *shadow bodies* MM.
149 *love, but* ... MM.
152 *Dervadilla* ... MM to 1914.
153-54 *Ireland, and the curses* ... MM.
156 *another,* the dying beauty of the dust and not the everlasting beauty. *When we* ... MM to 1914.
159 *for ever* 1905 to 1927; *forever* MM.

160 lover sees me always as a body that has been a long time in the
ground, and I know that is the way he sees me. Ask me more, ask
me more, for all the years have left their wisdom in my heart, and
no one has listened to me for seven hundred years.'

A great terror had fallen upon Hanrahan, and lifting his arms
165 above his head he screamed out loud three times, and the cattle in
the valley lifted their heads and lowed, and the birds in the wood at
the edge of the mountain awaked out of their sleep and fluttered
through the trembling leaves. But a little below the edge of the
rock, the troop of rose-leaves still fluttered in the air, for the gate-
170 way of Eternity had opened and shut again in one beat of the heart.

THE DEATH OF HANRAHAN

Hanrahan, that was never long in one place, was back again
among the villages that are at the foot of Slieve Echtge, Illeton and
Scalp and Ballylee, stopping sometimes in one house and sometimes in another, and finding a welcome in every place for the sake
5 of the old times and of his poetry and his learning. There was some
silver and some copper money in the little leather bag under his
coat, but it was seldom he needed to take anything from it, for it
was little he used, and there was not one of the people that would
have taken payment from him. His hand had grown heavy on the
10 blackthorn he leaned on, and his cheeks were hollow and worn, but
so far as food went, potatoes and milk and a bit of oaten cake, he
had what he wanted of it; and it is not on the edge of so wild and
boggy a place as Echtge a mug of spirits would be wanting, with the
taste of the turf smoke on it. He would wander about the big wood
15 at Kinadife, or he would sit through many hours of the day among
the rushes about Lake Belshragh, listening to the streams from the
hills, or watching the shadows in the brown bog pools; sitting so
quiet as not to startle the deer that came down from the heather to
the grass and the tilled fields at the fall of night. As the days went

---

160   *that* had *been* ... MM.
169   *rose-leaves* MM; *rose leaves* 1905 to 1927.

Printings: 1905; 1908; 1913; 1914; 1925; 1927.
Text from 1932.
Title: ... HANRAHAN. 1913.

20   by it seemed as if he was beginning to belong to some world out of
      sight and misty, that has for its mearing the colours that are beyond
      all other colours and the silences that are beyond all silences of this
      world. And sometimes he would hear coming and going in the
      wood music that when it stopped went from his memory like a
25   dream; and once in the stillness of midday he heard a sound like
      the clashing of many swords, that went on for a long time without
      any break. And at the fall of night and at moonrise the lake would
      grow to be like a gateway of silver and shining stones, and there
      would come from its silence the faint sound of keening and of
30   frightened laughter broken by the wind, and many pale beckoning
      hands.
          He was sitting looking into the water one evening in harvest time,
      thinking of all the secrets that were shut into the lakes and the
      mountains, when he heard a cry coming from the south, very faint
35   at first, but getting louder and clearer as the shadow of the rushes
      grew longer, till he could hear the words, 'I am beautiful, I am
      beautiful. The birds in the air, the moths under the leaves, the flies
      over the water look at me, for they never saw any one so beautiful
      as myself. I am young; I am young: look upon me, mountains; look
40   upon me, perishing woods, for my body will shine like the white
      waters when you have been hurried away. You and the whole race
      of men, and the race of the beasts, and the race of the fish, and
      the winged race, are dropping like a candle that is nearly burned
      out, but I laugh aloud because I am in my youth.' The voice would
45   break off from time to time, as if tired, and then it would begin
      again, calling out always the same words, 'I am beautiful, I am
      beautiful.' Presently the bushes at the edge of the little lake trembled
      for a moment, and a very old woman forced her way among them,
      and passed by Hanrahan, walking with very slow steps. Her face
50   was of the colour of earth, and more wrinkled than the face of any
      old hag that was ever seen, and her grey hair was hanging in wisps,
      and the rags she was wearing did not hide her dark skin that was

---

36   words: 'I am beautiful . . . 1905.
37   beautiful; the birds . . . 1905 to 1914.
38   any one 1908 to 1927; anyone 1905.
39   young, I . . . 1905.
42   beasts and the . . . 1905 to 1914.
42   fish and . . . 1905 to 1914.
43   race are . . . 1905 to 1914.
44   laugh out because . . . 1905 to 1914.
46   words: 'I am beautiful . . . 1905.
48-49 them and . . . 1925A.

roughened by all weathers. She passed by him with her eyes wide
open, and her head high, and her arms hanging straight beside her,
and she went into the shadow of the hills towards the west.

A sort of dread came over Hanrahan when he saw her, for he
knew her to be one Winny Byrne of the Cross Roads, that went
begging from place to place crying always the same cry, and he had
often heard that she had once such wisdom that all the women of
the neighbours used to go looking for advice from her, and that she
had a voice so beautiful that men and women would come from
every part to hear her sing at a wake or a wedding; and that the
Others, the great Sidhe, had stolen her wits one Samhain night
many years ago, when she had fallen asleep on the edge of a rath,
and had seen in her dreams the servants of Echtge of the hills.

And as she vanished away up the hillside, it seemed as if her cry,
'I am beautiful, I am beautiful,' was coming from among the stars
in the heavens.

There was a cold wind creeping among the rushes, and Hanrahan began to shiver, and he rose up to go to some house where
there would be a fire on the hearth. But instead of turning down
the hill as he was used, he went on up the hill, along the little track
that was maybe a road and maybe the dry bed of a stream. It was
the same way Winny had gone, and it led to the little cabin where
she stopped when she stopped in any place at all. He walked very
slowly up the hill as if he had a great load on his back, and at last he
saw a light a little to the left, and he thought it likely it was from
Winny's house it was shining, and he turned from the path to go to
it. But clouds had come over the sky, and he could not well see his
way, and after he had gone a few steps his foot slipped and he fell
into a bog drain, and though he dragged himself out of it, holding
on to the roots of the heather, the fall had given him a great shake,
and he felt better fit to lie down than to go travelling. But he had
always great courage, and he made his way on, step by step, till at
last he came to Winny's cabin, that had no window, but the light was
shining from the door. He thought to go into it and to rest for a
while, but when he came to the door he did not see Winny inside it,
but what he saw was four old grey-haired women playing cards, but
Winny herself was not among them. Hanrahan sat down on a heap

---

57   *Byrne, that* ... 1905 to 1914.*
73   *maybe* 1908 to 1927; *may be* 1905.
73   *maybe* 1908 to 1914, 1925E, 1927; *may be* 1905; *may- / be* 1925A.
76   *hill, as* ... 1905.

119

90   of turf beside the door, for he was tired out and out, and had no
     wish for talking or for card-playing, and his bones and his joints
     aching the way they were. He could hear the four women talking as
     they played, and calling out their hands. And it seemed to him that
     they were saying, like the strange man in the barn long ago, 'Spades
95   and Diamonds, Courage and Power. Clubs and Hearts, Knowledge
     and Pleasure.' And he went on saying those words over and over to
     himself; and whether or not he was in his dreams, the pain that was
     in his shoulder never left him. And after a while the four women in
     the cabin began to quarrel, and each one to say the other had not
100 played fair, and their voices grew from loud to louder, and their
     screams and their curses, till at last the whole air was filled with the
     noise of them around and above the house, and Hanrahan, hearing
     it between sleep and waking, said, 'That is the sound of the fighting
     between the friends and the ill-wishers of a man that is near his death.
105 And I wonder,' he said, 'who is the man in this lonely place that is
     near his death.'
         It seemed as if he had been asleep a long time, and he opened his
     eyes, and the face he saw over him was the old wrinkled face of
     Winny of the Cross Roads. She was looking hard at him, as if to
110 make sure he was not dead, and she wiped away the blood that had
     grown dry on his face with a wet cloth, and after a while she partly
     helped him and partly lifted him into the cabin, and laid him down
     on what served her for a bed. She gave him a couple of potatoes
     from a pot on the fire, and, what served him better, a mug of
115 spring water. He slept a little now and again, and sometimes he
     heard her singing to herself as she moved about the house, and so
     the night wore away. When the sky began to brighten with the
     dawn he felt for the bag where his little store of money was, and
     held it out to her, and she took out a bit of copper and a bit of silver
120 money, but she let it drop again as if it was nothing to her, maybe
     because it was not money she was used to beg for, but food and
     rags; or maybe because the rising of the dawn was filling her with
     pride and a new belief in her own great beauty. She went out and
     cut a few armfuls of heather, and brought it in and heaped it over
125 Hanrahan, saying something about the cold of the morning, and
     while she did that he took notice of the wrinkles in her face, and the

---

94   *ago: 'Spades* . . . 1905 to 1927.
103 *said: 'That* . . . 1905 to 1927.
104 *ill-wishers* 1908 to 1914, 1925E, 1927; *illwishers* 1905; *ill- / wishers* 1925A.
109 *Cross* Road. *She* . . . 1913, 1914.
114 *and what* . . . 1905.

120

greyness of her hair, and the broken teeth that were black and full
of gaps. And when he was well covered with the heather she went
out of the door and away down the side of the mountain, and he
130 could hear the cry, 'I am beautiful, I am beautiful,' getting less and
less as she went, till at last it died away altogether.

Hanrahan lay there through the length of the day, in his pains
and his weakness, and when the shadows of the evening were falling he heard her voice again coming up the hillside, and she came
135 in and boiled the potatoes and shared them with him the same way
as before. And one day after another passed like that, and the
weight of his flesh was heavy about him. But little by little as he
grew weaker he knew there were some greater than himself in the
room with him, and that the house began to be filled with them;
140 and it seemed to him they had all power in their hands, and that
they might with one touch of the hand break down the wall the
hardness of pain had built about him, and take him into their own
world. And sometimes he could hear voices, very faint and joyful,
crying from the rafters or out of the flame on the hearth, and other
145 times the whole house was filled with music that went through it
like a wind. And after a while his weakness left no place for pain,
and there grew up about him a great silence like the silence in the
heart of a lake, and there came through it, like the flame of a
rushlight, the faint joyful voices ever and always.

150 One morning he heard music somewhere outside the door, and
as the day passed it grew louder and louder until it drowned the
faint joyful voices, and even Winny's cry upon the hillside at the fall
of evening. About midnight and in a moment, the walls seemed to
melt away and to leave his bed floating on a pale misty light that
155 shone on every side as far as the eye could see; and after the first
blinding of his eyes he saw that it was full of great shadowy figures
rushing here and there.

At the same time the music came very clearly to him, and he
knew that it was but the continual clashing of swords.

160 'I am after my death,' he said, 'and in the very heart of the music
of Heaven. O Cherubim and Seraphim, receive my soul!'

At his cry the light where it was nearest to him filled with sparks
of yet brighter light, and he saw that these were the points of

---

130   *hear* her *cry* . . . 1905 to 1914.
144   *hearth,* aud [*sic*] *other* . . . 1905.
148   *it like* . . . 1905 to 1914.
149   *rushlight the* . . . 1908 to 1914.
149   *voices, ever* . . . 1905.

swords turned towards his heart; and then a sudden flame, bright
165 and burning like God's love or God's hate, swept over the light and
went out and he was in darkness. At first he could see nothing, for
all was as dark as if there was black bog earth about him, but all of a
sudden the fire blazed up as if a wisp of straw had been thrown
upon it. And as he looked at it, the light was shining on the big pot
170 that was hanging from a hook, and on the flat stone where Winny
used to bake a cake now and again, and on the long rusty knife she
used to be cutting the roots of the heather with, and on the long
blackthorn stick he had brought into the house himself. And when
he saw those four things, some memory came into Hanrahan's mind,
175 and strength came back to him, and he rose sitting up in the bed,
and he said very loud and clear, 'The Cauldron, the Stone, the
Sword, the Spear. What are they? Who do they belong to? And I
have asked the question this time.'

And then he fell back again, weak, and the breath going from
180 him.

Winny Byrne, that had been tending the fire, came over then,
having her eyes fixed on the bed; and the faint laughing voices
began crying out again, and a pale light, grey like a wave, came
creeping over the room, and he did not know from what secret
185 world it came. He saw Winny's withered face and her withered
arms that were grey like crumbled earth, and weak as he was he
shrank back farther towards the wall. And then there came out of
the mud-stiffened rags arms as white and as shadowy as the foam on
a river, and they were put about his body, and a voice that he could
190 hear well but that seemed to come from a long way off said to him
in a whisper, 'You will go looking for me no more upon the breasts
of women.'

'Who are you?' he said then.

'I am one of the lasting people, of the lasting unwearied Voices,
195 that make my dwelling in the broken and the dying, and those that
have lost their wits; and I came looking for you, and you are mine
until the whole world is burned out like a candle that is spent. And
look up now,' she said, 'for the wisps that are for our wedding are
lighted.'

200 He saw then that the house was crowded with pale shadowy

---

176 *clear: 'The* ... 1905 to 1927.
178-79 *time,' he said. ¶And* ... 1905 to 1914.
191 *whisper: 'You* ... 1905 to 1927.
195 *dying and* ... 1905.

hands, and that every hand was holding what was sometimes like a wisp lighted for a marriage, and sometimes like a tall white candle for the dead.

When the sun rose on the morning of the morrow Winny of the Cross Roads rose up from where she was sitting beside the body, and began her begging from townland to townland, singing the same song as she walked, 'I am beautiful, I am beautiful. The birds in the air, the moths under the leaves, the flies over the water look at me. I am young: look upon me, mountains; look upon me, perishing woods, for my body will be shining like the white waters when you have been hurried away. You and the whole race of men, and the race of the beasts, and the race of the fish, and the winged race, are dropping like a candle that is nearly burned out. But I laugh aloud, because I am in my youth.'

She did not come back that night or any night to the cabin, and it was not till the end of two days that the turf-cutters going to the bog found the body of Red Owen Hanrahan, and gathered men to wake him and women to keen him, and gave him a burying worthy of so great a poet.

208–10 *water look at me.* Look at me, *perishing* . . . 1905 to 1914.
210–11 *the* lake water after *you* . . . 1905 to 1914.
211 *the* old *race* . . . 1908 to 1914.
213 *are* wearing away like a candle that has been *burned* . . . 1905 to 1914.
214 *laugh* out loud, *because* . . . 1905 to 1914.
216 *turf-cutters; turf cutters* 1905 to 1927.

ROSA ALCHEMICA

THE TABLES OF THE LAW

AND

THE ADORATION OF THE MAGI

(1897)

'O blessed and happy he who, knowing the mysteries of the gods, sanctifies his life, and purifies his soul, celebrating orgies in the mountains with holy purifications.'—EURIPIDES

TO

A. E.

Section Title. Printings: 1925.
Text from 1932.
[Date lacking: 1925]
Epigraph. Printings: 1897; 1908; 1913; 1914; 1925. [Note: 'The Tables of the Law' and 'The Adoration of the Magi' are not in 1897 and 1914.]
Text from 1932.
[In 1908 to 1914, the quotation is in roman, the source in italics; the quotation is not set off by quotation marks in 1897 to 1914; a period follows the source in 1897 to 1925.]
1   *he, who knowing* . . . 1897 to 1914.
3   *purifications.* Euripides. 1897; *purifications.'* Euripides. 1925.
Dedication. Printings: 1925.
Text from 1932.
[No variants; but see 'Dedications and Notes not in *Mythologies*,' p. 233.]

The Secret Rose

ROSA ALCHEMICA

I

It is now more than ten years since I met, for the last time, Michael Robartes, and for the first time and the last time his friends and fellow-students; and witnessed his and their tragic end, and passed through strange experiences, which have changed me so that my writings have grown less popular and less intelligible, and may compel me to take refuge in the habit of S. Dominic. I had just published *Rosa Alchemica*, a little work on the Alchemists, somewhat in the manner of Sir Thomas Browne, and had received many letters from believers in the arcane sciences, upbraiding what they called my timidity, for they could not believe so evident sympathy but the sympathy of the artist, which is half pity, for everything which has moved men's hearts in any age. I had discovered, early in my researches, that their doctrine was no merely chemical phantasy, but a philosophy they applied to the world, to the elements and to man himself; and that they sought to fashion gold out of common metals merely as part of an universal transmutation of all things into some divine and imperishable substance; and this enabled me to make my little book a fanciful reverie over the transmutation of life into art, and a cry of measureless desire for a world made wholly of essences.

Printings: *The Savoy*, April, 1896; 1897; 1908; 1913; 1914; 1925.
Text from 1932.
Title: [in roman, S to 1925]; ALCHEMICA. 1913.
1–6 A few years ago an extraordinary religious frenzy took hold upon the peasantry of a remote Connemara headland; and a number of eccentric men and women, who had turned an old custom-house into a kind of college, were surprised at prayer, as it was then believed, by a mob of fishermen, stone masons, and small farmers, and beaten to death with stones, which were heaped up close at hand to be ready for the next breach in the wave-battered pier. Vague rumours of pagan ceremonies and mysterious idolatries had for some time drifted among the cabins; and the indignation of the ignorant had been further inflamed by a priest, unfrocked for drunkenness, who had preached at the road-side of the secret coming of the Antichrist. I first heard of these unfortunates, on whom the passion for universal ideas, which distinguishes the Celtic and Latin races, was to bring so dreadful a martyrdom, but a few weeks before the end; and the change in my opinions which has made my writings so much less popular and intelligible, and driven me to the verge of taking the habit of St. Dominic, was brought about by the strange experiences I endured in their presence.¶*I* . . . S.
3 *fellow-students; fellow students* 1897 to 1925.
3–4 *end, and* endured those *strange* . . . 1897 to 1914.
5–6 *intelligible, and* driven me almost to the verge of taking *the* . . . 1897 to 1914.
6 *St.* . . . 1897 to 1925.
7 *published* 'Rosa Alchemica,' *a* . . . S.
7 *alchemists* . . . S.
13–14 *phantasy but* . . . S.
14–15 *elements, and to man* . . . S.

I was sitting dreaming of what I had written, in my house in one
of the old parts of Dublin; a house my ancestors had made almost
famous through their part in the politics of the city and their
friendships with the famous men of their generations; and was
25 feeling an unwonted happiness at having at last accomplished a
long-cherished design, and changed my rooms into an expression
of this favourite doctrine. The portraits, of more historical than
artistic interest, had gone; and tapestry, full of the blue and bronze
of peacocks, fell over the doors, and shut out all history and activity
30 untouched with beauty and peace; and now when I looked at my
Crevelli and pondered on the rose in the hand of the Virgin,
wherein the form was so delicate and precise that it seemed more
like a thought than a flower, or my Francesca, so full of ghostly
astonishment, I knew a Christian's ecstasy without his slavery to
35 rule and custom. When I pondered over the antique bronze gods
and goddesses, which I had mortgaged my house to buy, I had all a
pagan's delight in various beauty and without his terror at sleepless
destiny and his labour with many sacrifices; and I had but to go to
my bookshelf, where every book was bound in leather, stamped
40 with intricate ornament, and of a carefully chosen colour: Shakespeare in the orange of the glory of the world, Dante in the dull red
of his anger, Milton in the blue-grey of his formal calm; to know
what I would of human passions without their bitterness and without satiety. I had gathered about me all gods because I believed in
45 none, and experienced every pleasure because I gave myself to
none, but held myself apart, individual, indissoluble, a mirror of

---

21   *sitting, dreaming* . . . S.
22   *Dublin, a* . . . S.
23   *city, and* . . . S.
26   *long-cherished* 1913 to 1925; *long cherished* S; *long- / cherished* 1897, 1908.
26   *and* made my rooms *an* . . . S to 1914.
28   *and old Flemish tapestry* . . . S.
29–30 *all* common history and all unbeautiful activity; and now, I repeated to myself, *when* . . . S.
31   *Crevelli, and* . . . S.
33–34 *flower,* [~; 1897] *or* at the grey [gray S] dawn and rapturous faces of my Francesca, I knew all *a* . . . S to 1914.
35   *custom; when I* . . . S to 1914.
37   *beauty, and* . . . S.
38   *destiny, and his* . . . S.
38   *sacrifices: and* . . . S.
38   *had* only *to go* . . . S to 1914.
39   *bookshelf* 1908 to 1914; *book-shelf* S, 1897; *book- / shelf* 1925.
40–41 *colour; Shakespeare* . . . S, 1897.
42   *blue-grey; blue-gray* S; *blue grey* 1897 to 1925.
42   *blue-gray* . . . S.
42–43 *calm;* and I could experience *what* . . . S to 1914.

polished steel. I looked in the triumph of this imagination at the
birds of Hera, glittering in the light of the fire as though of Byzantine mosaic; and to my mind, for which symbolism was a necessity,
50 they seemed the doorkeepers of my world, shutting out all that was
not of as affluent a beauty as their own; and for a moment I
thought as I had thought in so many other moments, that it was
possible to rob life of every bitterness except the bitterness of
death; and then a thought which had followed this thought, time
55 after time, filled me with a passionate sorrow. All those forms: that
Madonna with her brooding purity, those delighted ghostly faces
under the morning light, those bronze divinities with their passion-
less dignity, those wild shapes rushing from despair to despair,
belonged to a divine world wherein I had no part; and every ex-
60 perience, however profound, every perception, however exquisite,
would bring me the bitter dream of a limitless energy I could never
know, and even in my most perfect moment I would be two selves,
the one watching with heavy eyes the other's moment of content. I
had heaped about me the gold born in the crucibles of others; but
65 the supreme dream of the alchemist, the transmutation of the
weary heart into a weariless spirit, was as far from me as, I doubted
not, it had been from him also. I turned to my last purchase, a set of
alchemical apparatus which, the dealer in the Rue Le Peletier had
assured me, once belonged to Raymond Lully, and as I joined the
70 *alembic* to the *athanor* and laid the *lavacrum maris* at their side, I
understood the alchemical doctrine, that all beings, divided from
the great deep where spirits wander, one and yet a multitude, are

---

47   *steel: I* . . . 1897 to 1914.
48-49   *Hera,* glowing in the firelight as though they were wrought of jewels; *and* . . . S to
1914.
48-49   *Bizantine* . . . 1925.
49   *mozaic* . . . 1925A.
50   *doorkeepers* 1908 to 1925; *door-keepers* S, 1897.
55   *forms;* [~, 1897] *that* . . . S, 1897.
56-57   *those* rapturous faces singing in *the* . . . S to 1914.
58-59   *to despair; belonged* . . . S.
62   *know; and* . . . S.
64   *born* on *the* . . . S.
64   *others, but* . . . S.
65   *the* alchemists, *the transmutation* . . . S.
67   *from* them *also* . . . S.
68   *apparatus, which* . . . S.
68   *le* . . . S to 1925.
69   *and, as* . . . S.
70   *athanor, and* . . . S ['*athanor*' italic in S].
70   *mare* . . . S ['*mare*' italic in S].
72   *deep, where* the spirits wander *one* . . . S.

weary; and sympathised, in the pride of my connoisseurship, with
the consuming thirst for destruction which made the alchemist veil
75 under his symbols of lions and dragons, of eagles and ravens, of
dew and of nitre, a search for an essence which would dissolve all
mortal things. I repeated to myself the ninth key of Basilius Valen-
tinus, in which he compares the fire of the last day to the fire of the
alchemist, and the world to the alchemist's furnace, and would have
80 us know that all must be dissolved before the divine substance,
material gold or immaterial ecstasy, awake. I had dissolved indeed
the mortal world and lived amid immortal essences, but had ob-
tained no miraculous ecstasy. As I thought of these things, I drew
aside the curtains and looked out into the darkness, and it seemed
85 to my troubled fancy that all those little points of light filling the sky
were the furnaces of innumerable divine alchemists, who labour
continually, turning lead into gold, weariness into ecstasy, bodies
into souls, the darkness into God; and at their perfect labour my
mortality grew heavy, and I cried out, as so many dreamers and
90 men of letters in our age have cried, for the birth of that elaborate
spiritual beauty which could alone uplift souls weighted with so
many dreams.

II

My reverie was broken by a loud knocking at the door, and I
wondered the more at this because I had no visitors, and had bid
95 my servants do all things silently, lest they broke the dream of an all
but secret life. Feeling a little curious, I resolved to go to the door
myself, and, taking one of the silver candlesticks from the mantelpiece, began to descend the stairs. The servants appeared to be out,
for though the sound poured through every corner and crevice of
100 the house there was no stir in the lower rooms. I remembered that
because my needs were so few, my part in life so little, they had

---

73   *sympathized* . . . S to 1914.
74   *the* alchemists *veil* . . . S.
78–79   *to the fire of* an *alchemist* . . . S.
79   *to* an *alchemist's* . . . S.
82   *world, and* . . . S.
88   *labour, my* . . . S, 1897.
95   *servants* to *do* . . . S.
95–96   *of* my inner *life* . . . S to 1914.
97–98   *mantlepiece* . . . 1897 to 1914.
100   *house, there* . . . S.
100–101   *that my needs* . . . S.*
101   *little,* that *they* . . . S.

begun to come and go as they would, often leaving me alone for
hours. The emptiness and silence of a world from which I had
driven everything but dreams suddenly overwhelmed me, and I
105 shuddered as I drew the bolt. I found before me Michael Robartes,
whom I had not seen for years, and whose wild red hair, fierce
eyes, sensitive, tremulous lips and rough clothes, made him look
now, just as they used to do fifteen years before, something between a debauchee, a saint, and a peasant. He had recently come to
110 Ireland, he said, and wished to see me on a matter of importance:
indeed, the only matter of importance for him and for me. His
voice brought up before me our student years in Paris, and remembering the magnetic power he had once possessed over me, a
little fear mingled with much annoyance at this irrelevant intru-
115 sion, as I led the way up the wide staircase, where Swift had passed
joking and railing, and Curran telling stories and quoting Greek, in
simpler days, before men's minds, subtilised and complicated by
the romantic movement in art and literature, began to tremble on
the verge of some unimagined revelation. I felt that my hand
120 shook, and saw that the light of the candle wavered more than it
need have upon the gods and nymphs set upon the wall by some
Italian plasterer of the eighteenth century, making them look like
the first beings slowly shaping in the formless and void darkness.
When the door had closed, and the peacock curtain fell between us
125 and the world, I felt, in a way I could not understand, that some
singular and unexpected thing was about to happen. I went over to
the mantelpiece, and finding that a little chainless bronze censer,

103   world, from . . . S.
104   dreams, suddenly . . . S, 1897.
104   me and . . . S.
107   clothes made . . . 1897, 1908.
108   now just . . . S.
110-11   importance, indeed, the . . . S; importance; indeed [~, 1908] the . . . 1897, 1908.
111   and me . . . S.*
112   brought visibly before . . . S.
112-13   remembering a mesmeric power . . . S.
116   Greek in . . . S.
117   subtilized . . . S to 1914.
120   shook and . . . S.
120   wavered and quivered more . . . S to 1914.
121   have, upon . . . S, 1897.
121-22   upon the Mænads [meanids S] on the old French panels, making . . . S to 1914.
124   curtain, glimmering like many-coloured flame, fell . . . S to 1914.
125   felt in . . . S.
127   mantlepiece . . . 1897 to 1914.
127   mantelpiece and set the candlestick upon it, and . . . S.
127-28   little painted bowl from the workshop of Orazio . . . S.

set, upon the outside, with pieces of painted china by Orazio Fon-
tana, which I had filled with antique amulets, had fallen upon its
130 side and poured out its contents, I began to gather the amulets into
the bowl, partly to collect my thoughts and partly with that habitual
reverence which seemed to me the due of things so long connected
with secret hopes and fears. 'I see,' said Michael Robartes, 'that you
are still fond of incense, and I can show you an incense more
135 precious than any you have ever seen,' and as he spoke he took the
censer out of my hand and put the amulets in a little heap between
the *athanor* and the *alembic*. I sat down, and he sat down at the side
of the fire, and sat there for a while looking into the fire, and
holding the censer in his hand. 'I have come to ask you something,'
140 he said, 'and the incense will fill the room, and our thoughts, with
its sweet odour while we are talking. I got it from an old man in
Syria, who said it was made from flowers, of one kind with the
flowers that laid their heavy purple petals upon the hands and
upon the hair and upon the feet of Christ in the Garden of
145 Gethsemane, and folded Him in their heavy breath, until He cried
against the cross and His destiny.' He shook some dust into the
censer out of a small silk bag, and set the censer upon the floor and
lit the dust, which sent up a blue stream of smoke, that spread out
over the ceiling, and flowed downwards again until it was like Mil-
150 ton's banyan tree. It filled me, as incense often does, with a faint
sleepiness, so that I started when he said, 'I have come to ask you
that question which I asked you in Paris, and which you left Paris
rather than answer.'

---

129 *I* used for holding *antique* . . . S.
129 *fallen* on *its* . . . S.
130 *side, and* . . . S.
130-31 *I* lingered partly to collect my thoughts, and partly to gather the amulets into the
bowl *with* . . . S.
131 *bowl partly to* . . . 1897.
131 *thoughts, and* . . . 1897.
133-51 *and* terrors. When I turned I saw Robartes standing in the middle of the room
and looking straight before him as though he saw some one or something I could not, and
whispering to himself. He heard me move, and coming toward the fire, sat down and
began gazing at the flame. I turned my chair towards him and sat down also and waited for
him to speak. He watched the rising and falling of the flame for a moment and began. ¶'*I*
have . . . S.
138 *a while* 1914, 1925; *awhile* 1897 to 1913.
140 *said, and the incense* . . . 1908.
144 *Christ, in* . . . 1897.
145 *he* . . . 1913, 1914.
146 *his* . . . 1897 to 1914.
148 *dust which* . . . 1897 to 1925.
152 *in* the Café de la Paix, *and* . . . S.

The Secret Rose

He had turned his eyes towards me, and I saw them glitter in the
155 firelight, through the incense cloud, as I replied, 'You mean, will I
become an initiate of your Order of the Alchemical Rose? I would
not consent in Paris, when I was full of unsatisfied desire, and now
that I have at last fashioned my life according to my desire, am I
likely to consent?'
160 'You have changed greatly since then,' he answered. 'I have read
your books, and now I see you among all these images, and I
understand you better than you do yourself, for I have been with
many and many dreamers at the same crossways. You have shut
away the world and gathered the gods about you, and if you do not
165 throw yourself at their feet, you will be always full of lassitude, and
of wavering purpose, for a man must forget he is miserable in the
bustle and noise of the multitude in this world and in time; or seek
a mystical union with the multitude who govern this world and
time.' And then he murmured something I could not hear, and as
170 though to some one I could not see.
For a moment the room appeared to darken, as it used to do
when he was about to perform some singular experiment, and in
the darkness the peacocks upon the doors seemed to glow with a
more intense colour. I cast off the illusion, which was, I believed,
175 merely caused by memory, and by the twilight of incense, for I
would not acknowledge that he could overcome my now mature
intellect; and I said, 'Even if I grant that I need a spiritual belief
and some form of worship, why should I go to Eleusis and not to
Calvary?' He leaned forward and began speaking with a slightly
180 rhythmical intonation, and as he spoke I had to struggle again with
the shadow, as of some older night than the night of the sun, which

---

154   *me and* . . . S.
155   *firelight as* . . . S*; *firelight,* and through the incense, *as* . . . 1897 to 1914.
155   *replied:* ¶*'You* . . . S, 1897; *replied: 'You* . . . 1908 to 1925.
157   *desire and* . . . S.
163   *crossways*   1925A; *cross ways* S; *cross-ways*   1897 to 1914, 1925E.
165   *lassitude and* . . . S.
166   *purpose; for* . . . S.
167   *and time, or* . . . S.*
167-71   *in time.'* ¶*For* . . . S.*
170   *some one*   1897, 1925; *someone*   1908 to 1914.
174-75   *was, I* believe, *merely* . . . 1908 to 1914.
174-75   *believed,* caused merely by memory, *for* . . . S.
177   *intellect,* [~; 1897] *and said:* ¶*'Even* . . . S, 1897.*
177   *said: 'Even* . . . 1908 to 1925.
178   *Eleusis, and* . . . S.
181   *shadow; as* . . . S.
181   *sun; which* . . . S.

began to dim the light of the candles and to blot out the little
gleams upon the corner of picture-frames and on the bronze divinities, and to turn the blue of the incense to a heavy purple; while
185 it left the peacocks to glimmer and glow as though each separate
colour were a living spirit. I had fallen into a profound dream-like
reverie in which I heard him speaking as at a distance. 'And yet
there is no one who communes with only one god,' he was saying,
'and the more a man lives in imagination and in a refined under-
190 standing, the more gods does he meet with and talk with, and the
more does he come under the power of Roland, who sounded in
the Valley of Roncesvalles the last trumpet of the body's will and
pleasure; and of Hamlet, who saw them perishing away, and
sighed; and of Faust, who looked for them up and down the world
195 and could not find them; and under the power of all those countless divinities who have taken upon themselves spiritual bodies in
the minds of the modern poets and romance writers, and under the
power of the old divinities, who since the Renaissance have won
everything of their ancient worship except the sacrifice of birds and
200 fishes, the fragrance of garlands and the smoke of incense. The
many think humanity made these divinities, and that it can unmake
them again; but we who have seen them pass in rattling harness,
and in soft robes, and heard them speak with articulate voices while
we lay in deathlike trance, know that they are always making and
205 unmaking humanity, which is indeed but the trembling of their
lips.'
He had stood up and begun to walk to and fro, and had become
in my waking dream a shuttle weaving an immense purple web
whose folds had begun to fill the room. The room seemed to have
210 become inexplicably silent, as though all but the web and the weav-

182 *candles, and* ... 1925A.
183 *the* corners *of* ... S.
183 *picture- / frames* 1897; *picture frames* S; *picture-frames* 1908 to 1925.
183-84 *divinities, while* ... S.*
186 *dream-like* 1897 to 1914; *dreamlike* S; *dream- / like* 1925.
187 *reverie, in* ... S.
191-96 *of* Lear, and Hamlet, and Lancelot, and Faust, and Beatrice, and Quixote,
divinities who took *upon* ... S.
195 *them; and of* ... 1897.*
196 *who* took *upon* ... 1897.
197 *romance writers* 1897 to 1925; *romance-writers* S.
198 *who, since* ... S.
198 *Renaissance, have* ... S.
199-200 *birds* and beasts *and fishes* ... S.
206-7 *lips.' He* ... S.
208 *immense web* ... S.*

ing were at an end in the world. 'They have come to us; they have come to us,' the voice began again; 'all that have ever been in your reverie, all that you have met with in books. There is Lear, his head still wet with the thunder-storm, and he laughs because you
215 thought yourself an existence who are but a shadow, and him a shadow who is an eternal god; and there is Beatrice, with her lips half parted in a smile, as though all the stars were about to pass away in a sigh of love; and there is the mother of the God of humility, He who has cast so great a spell over men that they have
220 tried to unpeople their hearts that He might reign alone, but she holds in her hand the rose whose every petal is a god; and there, O swiftly she comes! is Aphrodite under a twilight falling from the wings of numberless sparrows, and about her feet are the grey and white doves.' In the midst of my dream I saw him hold out his left
225 arm and pass his right hand over it as though he stroked the wings of doves. I made a violent effort which seemed almost to tear me in two, and said with forced determination, 'You would sweep me away into an indefinite world which fills me with terror; and yet a man is a great man just in so far as he can make his mind reflect
230 everything with indifferent precision like a mirror.' I seemed to be perfectly master of myself, and went on, but more rapidly, 'I command you to leave me at once, for your ideas and phantasies are but the illusions that creep like maggots into civilisations when they

---

211   *us. They have* . . . S.
212   *come us* . . . 1897.*
212   *began, 'all* . . . S.*
213-14   *his* beard *still* . . . S.
214   *thunder- / storm; thunderstorm* S, 1925E; *thunder-storm* 1897 to 1914, 1925A.
217   *half parted* 1897 to 1925; *half-parted* S.
218   *mother of* that *god of* . . . S.
218   *god* . . . 1897.
219   *humility who cast* . . . S to 1913.*
219   *he* . . . 1914.
220   *he* . . . S to 1914.
221-22   *O! swiftly* . . . S.
222   *comes, is* . . . S.
223   *gray* . . . S.
227   *with* a forced determination, 'Your philosophy is charming as a phantasy, but, carried to the point of belief, it is a supreme delusion, and, enforced by mesmeric glamour, a supreme crime. You* . . . S.
227   *determination: 'You* . . . 1897 to 1925.
229   *is great, just* . . . S.*
231   *rapidly: 'I* . . . 1897 to 1925.
232   *and* your *phantasies* . . . S.
233   *that* eat the world like maggots; they creep *into* . . . S.
233   *civilizations* . . . S to 1914.
233-34   *they decline* . . . S.*

begin to decline, and into minds when they begin to decay.' I had
235 grown suddenly angry, and seizing the *alembic* from the table, was
about to rise and strike him with it, when the peacocks on the door
behind him appeared to grow immense; and then the *alembic* fell
from my fingers and I was drowned in a tide of green and blue and
bronze feathers, and as I struggled hopelessly I heard a distant
240 voice saying: 'Our master Avicenna has written that all life pro-
ceeds out of corruption.' The glittering feathers had now covered
me completely, and I knew that I had struggled for hundreds of
years, and was conquered at last. I was sinking into the depth when
the green and blue and bronze that seemed to fill the world became
245 a sea of flame and swept me away, and as I was swirled along I
heard a voice over my head cry, 'The mirror is broken in two
pieces,' and another voice answer, 'The mirror is broken in four
pieces,' and a more distant voice cry with an exultant cry, 'The
mirror is broken into numberless pieces'; and then a multitude of
250 pale hands were reaching towards me, and strange gentle faces
bending above me, and half-wailing and half-caressing voices uttering words that were forgotten the moment they were spoken. I was
being lifted out of the tide of flame, and felt my memories, my
hopes, my thoughts, my will, everything I held to be myself, melt-
255 ing away; then I seemed to rise through numberless companies of
beings who were, I understood, in some way more certain than
thought, each wrapped in his eternal moment, in the perfect lifting
of an arm, in a little circlet of rhythmical words, in dreaming with
dim eyes and half-closed eyelids. And then I passed beyond these

---

234 *they decay* . . . S.*
235 *and, seizing* . . . S.
235 ['alembic' roman in S]
236 *and* fling *it* . . . S.
237 ['alembic' roman in S]
238 *fingers, and I* . . . S.
238–39 *green and bronze* . . . S.*
239 *heard* his *distant* . . . S.
240 *saying, 'Our* . . . S.
240 *master, Avicenna, has* . . . S.
243 *years and* . . . S.
244 *green and bronze* . . . S.*
247 *pieces;' and* . . . S.
249 *pieces;' and* . . . S, 1897.
250 *me and* . . . S.
251 *half-wailing* S; *half wailing* 1897 to 1914, 1925A; *half- / wailing* 1925E.
251 *half-caressing* S, 1925E; *half caressing* 1897 to 1914, 1925A.
257 *thought; each* . . . S.
259 *half- / closed* 1913; *half-closed* S, 1908, 1914, 1925; *half closed* 1897.
259 *eyelids: And* . . . S.

260 forms, which were so beautiful they had almost ceased to be, and,
having endured strange moods, melancholy, as it seemed, with the
weight of many worlds, I passed into that Death which is Beauty
herself, and into that Loneliness which all the multitudes desire
without ceasing. All things that had ever lived seemed to come and
265 dwell in my heart, and I in theirs; and I had never again known
mortality or tears, had I not suddenly fallen from the certainty of
vision into the uncertainty of dream, and become a drop of molten
gold falling with immense rapidity, through a night elaborate with
stars, and all about me a melancholy exultant wailing. I fell and fell
270 and fell, and then the wailing was but the wailing of the wind in the
chimney, and I awoke to find myself leaning upon the table and
supporting my head with my hands. I saw the *alembic* swaying from
side to side in the distant corner it had rolled to, and Michael
Robartes watching me and waiting. 'I will go wherever you will,' I
275 said, 'and do whatever you bid me, for I have been with eternal
things.' 'I knew,' he replied, 'you must needs answer as you have
answered, when I heard the storm begin. You must come to a great
distance, for we were commanded to build our temple between the
pure multitude by the waves and the impure multitude of men.'

III

280   I did not speak as we drove through the deserted streets, for my
mind was curiously empty of familiar thoughts and experiences; it
seemed to have been plucked out of the definite world and cast
naked upon a shoreless sea. There were moments when the vision
appeared on the point of returning, and I would half-remember,
285 with an ecstasy of joy or sorrow, crimes and heroisms, fortunes and
misfortunes; or begin to contemplate, with a sudden leaping of the
heart, hopes and terrors, desires and ambitions, alien to my orderly
and careful life; and then I would awake shuddering at the thought
that some great imponderable being had swept through my mind.

261   *moods melancholy* ... S.
263   *into* this *Loneliness* ... S.
265   *heart and I in* ... S.
272   ['alembic' roman in S]
273-74   *and Robartes* ... S.*
276   *knew* you could not help yourself,' he replied, 'but *must* ... S.
276   *need* ... S to 1925.
279   *multitude* of *the waves* ... S.
281   *experiences: it* ... S.
284-85   *half-remember* [*half-* / *remember* 1897] *with* ... S, 1897.
286   *misfortunes, or* ... S, 1897.
286   *contemplate with* ... S, 1897.

290 It was indeed days before this feeling passed perfectly away, and
even now, when I have sought refuge in the only definite faith, I
feel a great tolerance for those people with incoherent per-
sonalities, who gather in the chapels and meeting-places of certain
obscure sects, because I also have felt fixed habits and principles
295 dissolving before a power, which was *hysterica passio* or sheer madness, if you will, but was so powerful in its melancholy exultation
that I tremble lest it wake again and drive me from my new-found
peace.

When we came in the grey light to the great half-empty terminus,
300 it seemed to me I was so changed that I was no more, as man is, a
moment shuddering at eternity, but eternity weeping and laughing
over a moment; and when we had started and Michael Robartes
had fallen asleep, as he soon did, his sleeping face, in which there
was no sign of all that had so shaken me and that now kept me
305 wakeful, was to my excited mind more like a mask than a face. The
fancy possessed me that the man behind it had dissolved away like
salt in water, and that it laughed and sighed, appealed and denounced at the bidding of beings greater or less than man. 'This is
not Michael Robartes at all: Michael Robartes is dead; dead for ten,
310 for twenty years perhaps,' I kept repeating to myself. I fell at last
into a feverish sleep, waking up from time to time when we rushed
past some little town, its slated roofs shining with wet, or still lake
gleaming in the cold morning light. I had been too preoccupied to
ask where we were going, or to notice what tickets Michael
315 Robartes had taken, but I knew now from the direction of the sun
that we were going westward; and presently I knew also, by the way
in which the trees had grown into the semblance of tattered beggars flying with bent heads towards the east, that we were ap-
proaching the western coast. Then immediately I saw the sea be-
320 tween the low hills upon the left, its dull grey broken into white
patches and lines.

---

290 *was, indeed, days* ... S.
291 *now when* ... S.
295 *passio, or* ... S ['*passio*' italic in S].
299–303 *peace.* ¶We were not long in the train before Michael Robartes was asleep, and,
to my excited mind, his *face* ... S.
305 *was more* ... S.*
307–8 *denounced, at* ... S.
310 *years, perhaps* ... S.
313 *preoccupied* S, 1914, 1925; *pre-occupied* 1897, 1913; *pre-* / *occupied* 1908.
316 *westward* S to 1913, 1925; *west-ward* 1914.
320 *upon the* right, *its* ... S, 1897.
320 *gray* ... S.

The Secret Rose

When we left the train we had still, I found, some way to go, and
set out, buttoning our coats about us, for the wind was bitter and
violent. Michael Robartes was silent, seeming anxious to leave me to
325 my thoughts; and as we walked between the sea and the rocky side
of a great promontory, I realised with a new perfection what a
shock had been given to all my habits of thought and of feeling, if
indeed some mysterious change had not taken place in the substance of my mind, for the grey waves, plumed with scudding
330 foam, had grown part of a teeming, fantastic inner life; and when
Michael Robartes pointed to a square ancient-looking house, with a
much smaller and newer building under its lee, set out on the very
end of a dilapidated and almost deserted pier, and said it was the
Temple of the Alchemical Rose, I was possessed with the phantasy
335 that the sea, which kept covering it with showers of white foam, was
claiming it as part of some indefinite and passionate life, which had
begun to war upon our orderly and careful days, and was about to
plunge the world into a night as obscure as that which followed the
downfall of the classical world. One part of my mind mocked this
340 phantastic terror, but the other, the part that still lay half plunged
in vision, listened to the clash of unknown armies, and shuddered
at unimaginable fanaticisms, that hung in those grey leaping waves.
We had gone but a few paces along the pier when we came upon
an old man, who was evidently a watchman, for he sat in an overset
345 barrel, close to a place where masons had been lately working upon
a break in the pier, and had in front of him a fire such as one sees
slung under tinkers' carts. I saw that he was also a voteen, as the

323 *out buttoning* . . . S, 1897.
324 *violent. Robartes* . . . S.*
326 *realized* . . . S to 1914.
327 *and of* feelings, *if* . . . 1897 to 1925.
329 *gray* . . . S.
330 *life, and* . . . S.
330-31 *when Robartes* . . . S.*
331-32 *with a smaller* . . . S.*
332 *lea* . . . S.
334 *temple* . . . S.
334 *alchemical rose* . . . S.
340 *other; the* . . . S.
340 *half plunged* 1897 to 1925; *half-plunged* S.
341 *vision; listened* . . . S.
342 *gray, leaping* . . . S.
342-359 *waves.* ¶Some half a mile to sea, and plunging its bowsprit under at every moment, and lifting it again dripping with foam, was a brown-sailed fishing yawl. ¶'*A* . . . S.
347 *carts; and I* . . . 1897.

138

peasants say, for there was a rosary hanging from a nail on the rim
of the barrel, and as I saw I shuddered, and I did not know why I
350 shuddered. We had passed him a few yards when I heard him cry
in Gaelic, 'Idolaters, idolaters, go down to Hell with your witches
and your devils; go down to Hell that the herrings may come again
into the bay'; and for some moments I could hear him half screaming and half muttering behind us. 'Are you not afraid,' I said, 'that
355 these wild fishing people may do some desperate thing against
you?'
'I and mine,' he answered, 'are long past human hurt or help,
being incorporate with immortal spirits, and when we die it shall be
the consummation of the supreme work. A time will come for these
360 people also, and they will sacrifice a mullet to Artemis, or some
other fish to some new divinity, unless indeed their own divinities
set up once more their temples of grey stone. Their reign has never
ceased, but only waned in power a little, for the Sidhe still pass in
every wind, and dance and play at hurley, but they cannot build
365 their temples again till there have been martyrdoms and victories,
and perhaps even that long-foretold battle in the Valley of the
Black Pig.'
Keeping close to the wall that went about the pier on the seaward
side, to escape the driving foam and the wind, which threatened
370 every moment to lift us off our feet, we made our way in silence to
the door of the square building. Michael Robartes opened it with a
key, on which I saw the rust of many salt winds, and led me along a
bare passage and up an uncarpeted stair to a little room surrounded
with bookshelves. A meal would be brought, but only of fruit, for I

351-52 *your* she dhowls; *go* . . . 1897.
353 *bay;' and* . . . 1897.
360 *also,'* said Robartes, pointing towards the yawl, '*and* . . . S.
361 *divinity; unless, indeed, their* . . . S.
361-62 *divinities,* the Dagda [~, 1897] with his overflowing cauldron, Lu [~, 1897]
with his spear dipped in poppy juice [poppy-juice 1897], lest it rush forth hot for battle,
Angus [~, 1897] with the three birds on his shoulder, Bove Derg and [Bove and 1897] his
red swine-herd, and all the heroic children of Dana [~, 1897] *set* . . . S, 1897; *divinities,* the
Dagda, with his overflowing cauldron, Lug, with his spear dipped in poppy-juice lest it
rush forth hot for battle, Aengus, with the three birds on his shoulder, Bodb and his red
swineherd, and all the heroic children of Dana, *set* . . . 1908, 1913.
362 *gray* . . . S.
363 *shee* . . . S ['*shee*' italic in S]; *Shee* . . . 1897.
364 *hurley,* and fight their sudden battles in every hollow and on every hill; *but* . . . S to
1913.
369 *side to* . . . S.
371 *building. Robartes* . . . S.*
374 *bookshelves* S, 1908 to 1925; *book-shelves* 1897.

375 must submit to a tempered fast before the ceremony, he explained, and with it a book on the doctrine and method of the Order, over which I was to spend what remained of the winter daylight. He then left me, promising to return an hour before the ceremony. I began searching among the bookshelves, and found one of the

380 most exhaustive alchemical libraries I have ever seen. There were the works of Morienus, who hid his immortal body under a shirt of hair-cloth; of Avicenna, who was a drunkard and yet controlled numberless legions of spirits; of Alfarabi, who put so many spirits into his lute that he could make men laugh, or weep, or fall in

385 deadly trance as he would; of Lully, who transformed himself into the likeness of a red cock; of Flamel, who with his wife Parnella achieved the elixir many hundreds of years ago, and is fabled to live still in Arabia among the Dervishes; and of many of less fame. There were very few mystics but alchemical mystics, and because, I

390 had little doubt, of the devotion to one god of the greater number and of the limited sense of beauty, which Robartes would hold an inevitable consequence; but I did notice a complete set of fac-similes of the prophetical writings of William Blake, and probably because of the multitudes that thronged his illumination and were

395 'like the gay fishes on the wave when the moon sucks up the dew'. I noted also many poets and prose writers of every age, but only those who were a little weary of life, as indeed the greatest have been everywhere, and who cast their imagination to us, as a some-thing they needed no longer now that they were going up in their

400 fiery chariots.

Presently I heard a tap at the door, and a woman came in and laid a little fruit upon the table. I judged that she had once been

---

379 *bookshelves* S, 1913 to 1925; *book-shelves* 1897; *book- / shelves* 1908.
382 *drunkard, and* . . . S.
384–85 *in* deathly *trance, as* . . . S.
386 *Flamell* . . . S.
388 *dervishes* . . . S, 1897.
388 *many of* a *less* . . . S.
389 *were* few mediæval or modern mystics other than the alchemical; *and* . . . S.
390–91 *number, and* . . . S.
391–92 *hold* its *inevitable* . . . S.
394 *the* multitude *that* . . . S.
394 *illumination, and* . . . S.
394–95 *were,* as he delights to describe them, '*like* . . . S.
395 *on the* waves *when* . . . S.
395 *dew.' I* . . . S to 1914, 1925A.
396 , *prose writers* 1897 to 1925; *prose-writers* S.
398 *who* have *cast* . . . S.

handsome, but her cheeks were hollowed by what I would have held, had I seen her anywhere else, an excitement of the flesh and a
405 thirst for pleasure, instead of which it doubtless was an excitement of the imagination and a thirst for beauty. I asked her some question concerning the ceremony, but getting no answer except a shake of the head, saw that I must await initiation in silence. When I had eaten, she came again, and having laid a curiously wrought
410 bronze box on the table, lighted the candles, and took away the plates and the remnants. So soon as I was alone, I turned to the box, and found that the peacocks of Hera spread out their tails over the sides and lid, against a background on which were wrought great stars, as though to affirm that the heavens were a
415 part of their glory. In the box was a book bound in vellum, and having upon the vellum and in very delicate colours, and in gold, the Alchemical Rose with many spears thrusting against it, but in vain, as was shown by the shattered points of those nearest to the petals. The book was written upon vellum, and in beautiful clear
420 letters, interspersed with symbolical pictures and illuminations, after the manner of the *Splendor Solis*.

The first chapter described how six students, of Celtic descent, gave themselves separately to the study of alchemy, and solved, one the mystery of the Pelican, another the mystery of the Green Dra-
425 gon, another the mystery of the Eagle, another that of Salt and Mercury. What seemed a succession of accidents, but was, the book declared, the contrivance of preternatural powers, brought them

---

405   *pleasure,* but that [but was 1897], I doubted not, *an* . . . S, 1897.
407   *but, getting* . . . S.
409   *eaten she* . . . S.
409   *a* curious *wrought* . . . S.
413   *lid,* and *against* . . . S.
413   *background, on* . . . S to 1914, 1925E.
414   *stars as* . . . S.
416   *vellum, and in very* . . . S.
416   *colours and* . . . S.
417   *alchemical rose* . . . S to 1925.
417   *rose, with* . . . S.
418   *shattered* golden *points* . . . S.
418-19   *nearest. The* . . . S, 1897.*
420   *letters interspersed* . . . S.
421-22   *Solis. The* . . . S ['*Solis*' italic in S].
422-23   *of* whom all but one, who was of Cornish descent, were Western Irish, Western Scottish, or French, *gave* . . . S.
423   *alchemy and* . . . 1925A.
424   *green* . . . S to 1914.
426   *a* procession *of* . . . S.
427   *declared,* a *contrivance* . . . S.

together in the garden of an inn in the South of France, and while
they talked together the thought came to them that alchemy was
430 the gradual distillation of the contents of the soul, until they were
ready to put off the mortal and put on the immortal. An owl
passed, rustling among the vine-leaves overhead, and then an old
woman came, leaning upon a stick, and, sitting close to them, took
up the thought where they had dropped it. Having expounded the
435 whole principle of spiritual alchemy, and bid them found the
Order of the Alchemical Rose, she passed from among them, and
when they would have followed was nowhere to be seen. They
formed themselves into an Order, holding their goods and making
their researches in common, and, as they became perfect in the
440 alchemical doctrine, apparitions came and went among them, and
taught them more and more marvellous mysteries. The book then
went on to expound so much of these as the neophyte was permitted to know, dealing at the outset and at considerable length with
the independent reality of our thoughts, which was, it declared, the
445 doctrine from which all true doctrines rose. If you imagine, it said,
the semblance of a living being, it is at once possessed by a wandering soul, and goes hither and thither working good or evil, until the
moment of its death has come; and gave many examples, received,
it said, from many gods. Eros had taught them how to fashion
450 forms in which a divine soul could dwell and whisper what it would
into sleeping minds; and Ate, forms from which demonic beings
could pour madness, or unquiet dreams, into sleeping blood; and
Hermes, that if you powerfully imagined a hound at your bedside it
would keep watch there until you woke, and drive away all but the
455 mightiest demons, but that if your imagination was weakly, the
hound would be weakly also, and the demons prevail, and the

---

428   *south* . . . S.
429   *them, that* . . . S.
430   *soul until* . . . S.
432   *passed rustling* . . . S.
433   *and sitting* . . . S.
433   *them took* . . . S.
437   *followed, was* . . . S.
438   *order* . . . S.
445   *doctrines* sprang. *If* . . . S, 1897.
447   *hither and* hither *working* . . . 1897, 1908.
448   *examples received* . . . S.
449   *gods: Eros* . . . S, 1897.
450   *dwell, and* . . . S to 1914.
450   *what* they *would* . . . S to 1914.
451   *sleeping* ears; *and* . . . S.
453   *bedside, it* . . . S.

hound soon die; and Aphrodite, that if you made, by a strong
imagining, a dove crowned with silver and bade it flutter over your
head, its soft cooing would make sweet dreams of immortal love
460 gather and brood over mortal sleep; and all divinities alike had
revealed with many warnings and lamentations that all minds are
continually giving birth to such beings, and sending them forth to
work health or disease, joy or madness. If you would give forms to
the evil powers, it went on, you were to make them ugly, thrusting
465 out a lip with the thirsts of life, or breaking the proportions of a
body with the burdens of life; but the divine powers would only
appear in beautiful shapes, which are but, as it were, shapes trembling out of existence, folding up into a timeless ecstasy, drifting
with half-shut eyes into a sleepy stillness. The bodiless souls who de-
470 scended into these forms were what men called the moods; and
worked all great changes in the world; for just as the magician or
the artist could call them when he would, so they could call out of
the mind of the magician or the artist, or if they were demons, out
of the mind of the mad or the ignoble, what shape they would, and
475 through its voice and its gestures pour themselves out upon the
world. In this way all great events were accomplished; a mood, a
divinity, or a demon, first descending like a faint sigh into men's
minds and then changing their thoughts and their actions until hair
that was yellow had grown black, or hair that was black had grown
480 yellow, and empires moved their border, as though they were but
drifts of leaves. The rest of the book contained symbols of form,

457-58   *you* imagined *a* . . . S.
458   *silver, and* . . . S.
458   *and* bad *it* . . . 1897 to 1913.
458-59   *your* bed, *its* . . . S.
460   *over* your *mortal* . . . S.
460   *sleep. And* . . . S.
465   *lip, with* . . . S to 1914.
465   *Life* . . . S.
466   *Life* . . . S.
468-69   *drifting, with* . . . S, 1925A.
469   *eyes, into* . . . S to 1925.
470   *forms, were* . . . 1897.
470   *men* call *the* . . . S to 1908.
470   *moods, and* . . . S.
475   *and its* gesture *pour* . . . S.
477   *divinity or* . . . S, 1897.
478   *minds, and then* . . . S.
480   *yellow*, or cities crumbled away and new cities arisen in their places, *and* . . . S.
480   *border as* . . . S.
481   *leaves*. I remembered, as I read, that mood which Edgar Poe found in a wine-cup,
and how it passed into France and took possession of Baudelaire, and from Baudelaire

and sound, and colour, and their attribution to divinities and demons, so that the initiate might fashion a shape for any divinity or
any demon, and be as powerful as Avicenna among those who live
485 under the roots of tears and of laughter.

IV

A couple of hours after sunset Michael Robartes returned and
told me that I would have to learn the steps of an exceedingly
antique dance, because before my initiation could be perfected I
had to join three times in a magical dance, for rhythm was the
490 wheel of Eternity, on which alone the transient and accidental
could be broken, and the spirit set free. I found that the steps,
which were simple enough, resembled certain antique Greek
dances, and having been a good dancer in my youth and the master
of many curious Gaelic steps, I soon had them in my memory. He
495 then robed me and himself in a costume which suggested by its
shape both Greece and Egypt, but by its crimson colour a more
passionate life than theirs; and having put into my hands a little
chainless censer of bronze, wrought into the likeness of a rose, by
some modern craftsman, he told me to open a small door opposite
500 to the door by which I had entered. I put my hand to the handle,
but the moment I did so the fumes of the incense, helped perhaps
by his mysterious glamour, made me fall again into a dream, in
which I seemed to be a mask, lying on the counter of a little Eastern
shop. Many persons, with eyes so bright and still that I knew them
505 for more than human, came in and tried me on their faces, but at
last flung me into a corner laughing; but all this passed in a moment, for when I awoke my hand was still upon the handle. I

---

passed to England and the Pre-Raphaelites, and then again returned to France, and still
wanders the world, enlarging its power as it goes, awaiting the time when it shall be,
perhaps, alone, or, with other moods, master over a great new religion, and an awakener of
the fanatical wars that hovered in the gray surges, and forget the wine-cup where it was
born. *The* . . . S.
484-85   *live* among *the* . . . S.
485   *and laughter* . . . S.*
486   *sunset Robartes* . . . S.*
488   *antique* pantomimic *dance* . . . S.
489-90   *dance;* rhythm being the circle *of* . . . S.
501   *so, the fumes* . . . 1897.
504   *still, that* . . . 1897.
506   *corner* with a little laughter; *but* . . . S to 1914.
507   *awoke, my* . . . 1897.

opened the door, and found myself in a marvellous passage, along
whose sides were many divinities wrought in a mosaic, not less
510 beautiful than the mosaic in the Baptistery at Ravenna, but of a less
severe beauty; the predominant colour of each divinity, which was
surely a symbolic colour, being repeated in the lamps that hung
from the ceiling, a curiously scented lamp before every divinity. I
passed on, marvelling exceedingly how these enthusiasts could
515 have created all this beauty in so remote a place, and half persuaded to believe in a material alchemy, by the sight of so much
hidden wealth; the censer filling the air, as I passed, with smoke of
ever-changing colour.

I stopped before a door, on whose bronze panels were wrought
520 great waves in whose shadow were faint suggestions of terrible
faces. Those beyond it seemed to have heard our steps, for a voice
cried, 'Is the work of the Incorruptible Fire at an end?' and immediately Michael Robartes answered, 'The perfect gold has come
from the *athanor*.' The door swung open, and we were in a great
525 circular room, and among men and women who were dancing
slowly in crimson robes. Upon the ceiling was an immense rose
wrought in mosaic; and about the walls, also in mosaic, was a battle
of gods and angels, the gods glimmering like rubies and sapphires,
and the angels of the one greyness, because, as Michael Robartes
530 whispered, they had renounced their divinity, and turned from the
unfolding of their separate hearts, out of love for a God of humility
and sorrow. Pillars supported the roof and made a kind of circular
cloister, each pillar being a column of confused shapes, divinities, it

---

509   *mosaic not* . . . S.
511   *predominate* . . . 1925A.
511   *each, which* . . . S.*
512   *surely* symbolic, *being* . . . S.
513   *curiously scented* 1925; *curiously-scented* S to 1914.
513   *before* each *divinity* . . . S.
517   *hidden* mysterious *wealth, the censer* . . . S.
517   *censer, filling* . . . 1925A.
518–19   *colour. I* . . . S.
519   *door on* . . . S.
522   *cried: 'Is* . . . S to 1925.
522–23   *immediately Robartes* . . . S.*
523   *answered: 'The* . . . S to 1925.
524   *Athanor* . . . S [roman in S].
524   *open and* . . . S.
527   *mosaic, and* . . . S.
527   *mosaic, a* . . . S.*
529   *grayness* . . . S.
529   *as Robartes* . . . S.*

seemed, of the wind, who in a whirling dance of more than human
535   vehemence, rose playing upon pipes and cymbals; and from among
these shapes were thrust out hands, and in these hands were censers. I was bid place my censer also in a hand and take my place and
dance, and as I turned from the pillars towards the dancers, I saw
that the floor was of a green stone, and that a pale Christ on a pale
540   cross was wrought in the midst. I asked Robartes the meaning of
this, and was told that they desired 'to trouble His unity with their
multitudinous feet'. The dance wound in and out, tracing upon the
floor the shapes of petals that copied the petals in the rose overhead, and to the sound of hidden instruments which were perhaps
545   of an antique pattern, for I have never heard the like; and every
moment the dance was more passionate, until all the winds of the
world seemed to have awakened under our feet. After a little I had
grown weary, and stood under a pillar watching the coming and
going of those flame-like figures; until gradually I sank into a
550   half-dream, from which I was awakened by seeing the petals of the
great rose, which had no longer the look of mosaic, falling slowly
through the incense-heavy air, and, as they fell, shaping into the
likeness of living beings of an extraordinary beauty. Still faint and
cloud-like, they began to dance, and as they danced took a more
555   and more definite shape, so that I was able to distinguish beautiful
Grecian faces and august Egyptian faces, and now and again to
name a divinity by the staff in his hand or by a bird fluttering over
his head; and soon every mortal foot danced by the white foot of an
immortal; and in the troubled eyes that looked into untroubled
560   shadowy eyes, I saw the brightness of uttermost desire as though
they had found at length, after unreckonable wandering, the lost
love of their youth. Sometimes, but only for a moment, I saw a faint
solitary figure with a veiled face, and carrying a faint torch, flit
among the dancers, but like a dream within a dream, like a shadow

---

534   *the* winds, *who* ... S.
534   *who* rose as *in* ... S to 1914.
535   *vehemence,* and *playing* ... S to 1914.
541   *To* ... S to 1914.
542   *feet.' The* ... S to 1925.
544   *instruments, which* ... S.
548   *stood* by *a* ... S.
550   *half-dream* 1897 to 1925; *half dream* S.
552   *incense-heavy* 1897, 1908, 1914, 1925; *incense heavy* S; *incense-* / *heavy* 1913.
552   *and as* ... S, 1897.
552   *fell shaping* ... S.
560   *desire, as* ... S.

565 of a shadow, and I knew by an understanding born from a deeper
fountain than thought, that it was Eros himself, and that his face
was veiled because no man or woman from the beginning of the
world has ever known what love is, or looked into his eyes, for Eros
alone of divinities is altogether a spirit, and hides in passions not of
570 his essence if he would commune with a mortal heart. So that if a
man love nobly he knows love through infinite pity, unspeakable
trust, unending sympathy; and if ignobly through vehement
jealousy, sudden hatred, and unappeasable desire; but unveiled
love he never knows. While I thought these things, a voice cried to
575 me from the crimson figures, 'Into the dance! there is none that can
be spared out of the dance; into the dance! into the dance! that the
gods may make them bodies out of the substance of our hearts';
and before I could answer, a mysterious wave of passion, that
seemed like the soul of the dance moving within our souls, took
580 hold of me, and I was swept, neither consenting nor refusing, into
the midst. I was dancing with an immortal august woman, who had
black lilies in her hair, and her dreamy gesture seemed laden with a
wisdom more profound than the darkness that is between star and
star, and with a love like the love that breathed upon the waters;
585 and as we danced on and on, the incense drifted over us and round
us, covering us away as in the heart of the world, and ages seemed
to pass, and tempests to awake and perish in the folds of our robes
and in her heavy hair.

Suddenly I remembered that her eyelids had never quivered,
590 and that her lilies had not dropped a black petal, nor shaken from
their places, and understood with a great horror that I danced with
one who was more or less than human, and who was drinking up

565   knew, by ... S.
568   Love ... S.
568   is or ... S.
568   eyes; for ... S.
569   spirit; and ... S.
570   essence, if he ... S.
571   knows Love through ... S.
572   ignobly, through ... S.
574   Love ... S.
575   figures: 'Into ... 1897 to 1925.
575   dance, there ... S, 1897.
576   dance; into the dance, into the dance, that ... S, 1897.
577–78   hearts;' and ... S, 1897.
580   me and ... S.
586   away, as ... 1897.
589–90   quivered and ... S.
590   petal, or shaken ... S to 1914.

my soul as an ox drinks up a wayside pool; and I fell, and darkness passed over me.

v

595   I awoke suddenly as though something had awakened me, and saw that I was lying on a roughly painted floor, and that on the ceiling, which was at no great distance, was a roughly painted rose, and about me on the walls half-finished paintings. The pillars and the censers had gone; and near me a score of sleepers lay wrapped

600 in disordered robes, their upturned faces looking to my imagination like hollow masks; and a chill dawn was shining down upon them from a long window I had not noticed before; and outside the sea roared. I saw Michael Robartes lying at a little distance and beside him an overset bowl of wrought bronze which looked as

605 though it had once held incense. As I sat thus, I heard a sudden tumult of angry men and women's voices mix with the roaring of the sea; and leaping to my feet, I went quickly to Michael Robartes, and tried to shake him out of his sleep. I then seized him by the shoulder and tried to lift him, but he fell backwards, and sighed

610 faintly; and the voices became louder and angrier; and there was a sound of heavy blows upon the door, which opened on to the pier. Suddenly I heard a sound of rending wood, and I knew it had

---

593   *wayside* S, 1908 to 1925; *way-side* 1897.
593   *pool, and I* . . . S.
594–96   *me.* /V/ ¶When I awoke *I was* . . . S.
596   *and on* . . . S.*
598   *the* wall a half-finished painting. *The* . . . S.
599–600   *and* about me, wrapped in disordered robes, lay a score of sleepers, *their* . . . S.
602   *them, from* . . . S.
603   *roared* angrily. *I* . . . S.
603   *distance, and* . . . S.
604   *wrought bronze* S, 1908 to 1925; *wrought- / bronze* 1897.
605–47   *incense.* ¶I had no thought but to get away, and to forget all. The door of the room opened with a push, and hurrying along the passage, where the bare boards clattered under my feet, I found the front door by the light of a single oil lamp, that hung from the ceiling, mingling its yellow flame with the morning light. I hurried along the pier, between brown nets and old spars, the spray driving in my face; but had not gone far before I met a group of stonemasons going to their morning work. They went a few yards past me and then one of them, an old man with iron-gray hair, turned and cried: 'Idolater, idolater, go back to your she dhoules, go down to hell with your she dhoules!' I scarcely heard them, for other voices were in my ears. Voices uttering reproaches that were forgotten the moment they were spoken, as a dream is forgotten on waking. ¶From that day I have never failed to carry the rosary about my neck, and whenever the indefinite world, which has but half lost its empire over my heart and my intellect, though my conscience and my soul are free, is about to claim a new mastery, I press the cross *to my heart* . . . S.
610   *angrier; and a* . . . 1897.*
611–12   *pier,* began to mingle with the voices. *Suddenly* . . . 1897.

begun to give, and I ran to the door of the room. I pushed it open and came out upon a passage whose bare boards clattered under my
615 feet, and found in the passage another door which led into an empty kitchen; and as I passed through the door I heard two crashes in quick succession, and knew by the sudden noise of feet and the shouts that the door which opened on to the pier had fallen inwards. I ran from the kitchen and out into a small yard, and from
620 this down some steps which descended the seaward and sloping side of the pier, and from the steps clambered along the water's edge, with the angry voices ringing in my ears. This part of the pier had been but lately refaced with blocks of granite, so that it was almost clear of seaweed; but when I came to the old part, I found it
625 so slippery with green weed that I had to climb up on to the roadway. I looked towards the Temple of the Alchemical Rose, where the fishermen and the women were still shouting, but somewhat more faintly, and saw that there was no one about the door or upon the pier; but as I looked, a little crowd hurried out of the door and
630 began gathering large stones from where they were heaped up in readiness for the next time a storm shattered the pier, when they would be laid under blocks of granite. While I stood watching the crowd, an old man, who was, I·think, the voteen, pointed to me, and screamed out something, and the crowd whitened, for all the
635 faces had turned towards me. I ran, and it was well for me that pullers of the oar are poorer men with their feet than with their arms and their bodies; and yet while I ran I scarcely heard the following feet or the angry voices, for many voices of exultation and lamentation, which were forgotten as a dream is forgotten the
640 moment they were heard, seemed to be ringing in the air over my head.

There are moments even now when I seem to hear those voices of exultation and lamentation, and when the indefinite world, which has but half lost its mastery over my heart and my intellect,
645 seems about to claim a perfect mastery; but I carry the rosary about my neck, and when I hear, or seem to hear them, I press it to my heart and say, 'He whose name is Legion is at our doors deceiving our intellects with subtlety and flattering our hearts with beauty,

---

627   *shouting but* ... 1897.
642   *now, when* ... 1897.
647   *say: 'He* ... S to 1925.
647   *legion* ... S.
647   *doors, deceiving* ... S.
648–49 *beauty,* so that *we* ... S.

and we have no trust but in Thee'; and then the war that rages
650 within me at other times is still, and I am at peace.

THE TABLES OF THE LAW

I

'Will you permit me, Aherne,' I said, 'to ask you a question, which
I have wanted to ask you for years, and have not asked because we
have grown nearly strangers? Why did you refuse the biretta, and
almost at the last moment? When you and I lived together, you
5   cared neither for wine, women, nor money, and had thoughts for
nothing but theology and mysticism.' I had watched through
dinner for a moment to put my question, and ventured now, because he had thrown off a little of the reserve and indifference
which, ever since his last return from Italy, had taken the place of
10 our once close friendship. He had just questioned me, too, about
certain private and almost sacred things, and my frankness had
earned, I thought, a like frankness from him.

When I began to speak he was lifting a glass of that wine which
he could choose so well and valued so little; and while I spoke, he
15 set it slowly and meditatively upon the table and held it there, its
deep red light dyeing his long delicate fingers. The impression of

---

649   Thee.' And . . . S; Thee;' and . . . 1897.
649-50   that wages within . . . S.
650   at all other . . . S.
650   still and . . . S.
[In S, the story is signed W. B. Yeats.]

Printings: The Savoy, November, 1896; 1897T; 1904T; 1908; 1914T; 1925.
Text from 1932.
Title: The Tables of the Law 1904T.
1   [The ornate initial letter in S necessitated omission of the opening quotation mark.]
2   years; and . . . S.
3   strangers. Why . . . S.
3   the cassock and the berretta, and . . . S, 1897T.
3   berretta . . . 1904T to 1925.
4   moment? I never expected you, of all men, to become 'a spoilt priest.' When . . . S.
5-6   and were absorbed in theological and mystical studies.' I . . . S.
5-6   and were absorbed in theology . . . 1897T.
8-9   indifference, which . . . S to 1904T, 1925.
10   me too . . . S, 1897T.
13   lifting to his lips a . . . S to 1914T.
13   that old wine . . . S to 1914T.

his face and form, as they were then, is still vivid with me, and is
inseparable from another and fanciful impression: the impression
of a man holding a flame in his naked hand. He was to me, at that
20 moment, the supreme type of our race, which, when it has risen
above, or is sunken below, the formalisms of half-education and the
rationalisms of conventional affirmation and denial, turns away,
unless my hopes for the world and for the Church have made me
blind, from practicable desires and intuitions towards desires so
25 unbounded that no human vessel can contain them, intuitions so
immaterial that their sudden and far-off fire leaves heavy darkness
about hand and foot. He had the nature, which is half monk, half
soldier of fortune, and must needs turn action into dreaming, and
dreaming into action; and for such there is no order, no finality, no
30 contentment in this world. When he and I had been students in
Paris, we had belonged to a little group which devoted itself to
speculations about alchemy and mysticism. More orthodox in most
of his beliefs than Michael Robartes, he had surpassed him in a
fanciful hatred of all life, and this hatred had found expression in
35 the curious paradox—half borrowed from some fanatical monk,
half invented by himself—that the beautiful arts were sent into the
world to overthrow nations, and finally life herself, by sowing
everywhere unlimited desires, like torches thrown into a burning
city. This idea was not at the time, I believe, more than a paradox, a
40 plume of the pride of youth; and it was only after his return to
Ireland that he endured the fermentation of belief which is coming
upon our people with the reawakening of their imaginative life.
    Presently he stood up, saying, 'Come, and I will show you why,
you at any rate will understand,' and taking candles from the table,
45 he lit the way into the long paved passage that led to his private
chapel. We passed between the portraits of the Jesuits and

---

20 *which when* ... 1897T.
22–24 *away from* ... S.*
23 *church* ... 1897T, 1904T.
24 *intuitions, towards* ... S.
27 *half* alchemist, *half* ... S.
30–32 *world.* At the Jesuit school in Paris he had made one of the little group, which used
to gather in corners of the playing field, or in remote class rooms, to hear the speculative
essays which we wrote and read in secret. *More* ... S.
35 *paradox, half* ... S, 1897T.
36 *himself; that* ... S; *himself, that* ... 1897T.
40–41 *his* leaving school *that* ... S.
43 *saying:* ¶*'Come* ... S to 1904T, 1925; *saying: 'Come* ... 1908, 1914T.
43–44 *show you, for you* ... S to 1914T.

priests—some of no little fame—his family had given to the
Church; and engravings and photographs of pictures that had
especially moved him; and the few paintings his small fortune,
50 eked out by an almost penurious abstinence from the things most
men desire, had enabled him to buy in his travels. The photographs and engravings were from the masterpieces of many
schools; but in all the beauty, whether it was a beauty of religion, of
love, or of some fantastical vision of mountain and wood, was the
55 beauty achieved by temperaments which seek always an absolute
emotion, and which have their most continual, though not most
perfect expression in the legends and vigils and music of the Celtic
peoples. The certitude of a fierce or gracious fervour in the enrap-
tured faces of the angels of Francesca, and in the august faces of
60 the sibyls of Michael Angelo; and the incertitude, as of souls

---

47 *priests, some* ... S, 1897T.
47 *fame, whom his* ... S, 1897T.
48 *Church; and* framed photographs of the pictures which *had* ... S, 1897T.
51–64 *The* pictures that I knew best, for they had hung there longest, whether
reproductions or originals, were of the Sienese School, which he had studied for a long
time, claiming that it alone of the schools of the world pictured not the world but what is
revealed to saints in their dreams and visions. The Sienese alone among Italians, he would
say, could not or would not represent the pride of life, the pleasure in swift movement or
sustaining strength, or voluptuous flesh. They were so little interested in these things that
there often seemed to be no human body at all under the robe of the saint, but they could
represent by a bowed head, or uplifted face, man's reverence before Eternity as no others
could, and they were at their happiest when mankind had dwindled to a little group
silhouetted upon a golden abyss, as if they saw the world habitually from far off. When I
had praised some school that had dipped deeper into life, he would profess to discover a
more intense emotion than life knew in those dark outlines. 'Put, [~∧ 1914T] even
Francesca, who felt the supernatural as deeply,' he would say, 'beside the work of Siena,
and one finds a faint impurity in his awe, a touch of ghostly terror, where love and
humbleness had best been all.' He had often told me of his hope that by filling his mind
with those holy pictures he would help himself to attain at last to vision and ecstasy, and of
his disappointment at never getting more than dreams of a curious and broken beauty. But
of late he had added pictures of a different kind, French symbolistic pictures which he had
bought for a few pounds from little-known painters, English and French pictures of the
School of the English Pre-Raphaelites; and now he stood for a moment and said, 'I have
changed my taste. I am fascinated a little against my will by these faces, where I find the
pallor of souls trembling between the excitement of the flesh and the excitement of the
spirit, and by landscapes that are created by heightening the obscurity and disorder of
nature. These landscapes do not stir the imagination to the energies of sanctity but as to
orgaic dancing and prophetic frenzy.' I saw with some resentment new images where the
old ones *had* ... 1908, 1914T.
51–52 *photographs* of pictures *were* ... S, 1897T.
53 *all, the* ... S.
55–56 *absolute* of emotion, and *have* ... S.
56 *and* who have ... 1897T, 1904T.
57 *expression, in* ... S.
57 *and* music and vigils *of* ... S, 1897T.
59 *of* Francesca's and Crivelli's Madonnas, *and* ... S; *of the* Madonnas of Francesca,
and ... 1897T.

trembling between the excitement of the spirit and the excitement
of the flesh, in wavering faces from frescoes in the churches of
Siena, and in the faces like thin flames, imagined by the modern
symbolists and Pre-Raphaelites, had often made that long, grey,
65 dim, empty, echoing passage become to my eyes a vestibule of
eternity.

Almost every detail of the chapel, which we entered by a narrow
Gothic door, whose threshold had been worn smooth by the secret
worshippers of the penal times, was vivid in my memory; for it was
70 in this chapel that I had first, and when but a boy, been moved by
the mediaevalism which is now, I think, the governing influence in
my life. The only thing that seemed new was a square bronze box
which stood upon the altar before the six unlighted candles and the
ebony crucifix, and was like those made in ancient times of more
75 precious substances to hold the sacred books. Aherne made me sit
down on an oak bench, and having bowed very low before the
crucifix, took the bronze box from the altar, and sat down beside
me with the box upon his knees.

'You will perhaps have forgotten,' he said, 'most of what you
80 have read about Joachim of Flora, for he is little more than a name
to even the well-read. He was an abbot in Cortale in the twelfth
century, and is best known for his prophecy, in a book called *Ex-
positio in Apocalypsin,* that the Kingdom of the Father was passed,
the Kingdom of the Son passing, the Kingdom of the Spirit yet to
85 come. The Kingdom of the Spirit was to be a complete triumph of
the Spirit, the *spiritualis intelligentia* he called it, over the dead letter.
He had many followers among the more extreme Franciscans, and
these were accused of possessing a secret book of his called the
Liber inducens in Evangelium aeternum. Again and again groups of

---

62   *in* the wavering faces Sodoma made for *the* ... S.
64   *pre-Raphaelites* ... S to 1904T, 1925.
64   *long gray* ... 1908, 1914T.
64-65   *gray, dim,* echoing passage seem to me like *a* ... S.
65   *empty echoing* ... 1897T.
66   *Eternity* ... 1908, 1914T.
71   *mediævalism* ... S to 1925.
71-72   *influence* on *my* ... S.
72-75   *box;* like those made in ancient times of more precious substances to hold the
sacred books; which stood before the six unlighted candles and the ebony crucifix upon the
altar. *Aherne* ... S.
76   *on* a long oaken *bench* ... S.
81   *the* best *read* ... S.
81   *well-read* 1925; *well read* 1897T to 1914T.
81   *abbot in* Corace *in* ... S.
89   *Inducens* ... S to 1914T.
89   *Æternum* ... S to 1914T.

90 visionaries were accused of possessing this terrible book, in which
the freedom of the Renaissance lay hidden, until at last Pope Alexander IV. had it found and cast into the flames. I have here the
greatest treasure the world contains. I have a copy of that book; and
see what great artists have made the robes in which it is wrapped.
95 This bronze box was made by Benvenuto Cellini, who covered it
with gods and demons, whose eyes are closed to signify an absorption in the inner light.' He lifted the lid and took out a book bound
in leather, covered with filigree work of tarnished silver. 'And this
cover was bound by one of the binders that bound for Canevari;
100 while Giulio Clovio, an artist of the later Renaissance, whose work is
soft and gentle, took out the beginning page of every chapter of the
old copy, and set in its place a page surmounted by an elaborate
letter and a miniature of some one of the great whose example was
cited in the chapter; and wherever the writing left a little space
105 elsewhere, he put some delicate emblem or intricate pattern.'
I took the book in my hands and began turning over the gilded,
many-coloured pages, holding it close to the candle to discover
the texture of the paper.
'Where did you get this amazing book?' I said. 'If genuine, and I
110 cannot judge by this light, you have discovered one of the most
precious things in the world.'
'It is certainly genuine,' he replied. 'When the original was de-
stroyed, one copy alone remained, and was in the hands of a lute=

---

93   *book, and* ... S.
94-106   *wrapped.* The greater portion of the book itself is illuminated in the Byzantine
style, which so few care for to-day, but which moves me because these tall, emaciated angels
and saints seem to have less relation to the world about us than to an abstract pattern of
flowing lines, [~ ∧ 1914T] that suggest an imagination absorbed in the contemplation of
Eternity. Even if you do not care for so formal an art, you cannot help seeing that work
where there is so much gold, and of that purple colour which has gold dissolved in it, was
valued at a great price in its day. But it was only at the Renaissance the labour was spent
upon it which has made it the priceless thing it is. The wooden boards of the cover show by
the astrological allegories painted upon them, as by the style of painting itself, some
craftsman of the school of Francesco Cossi of Ferrara, but the gold clasps and hinges are
known to be the work of Benvenuto Cellini, who made likewise the bronze box and covered
it with gods and demons, whose eyes are closed, to signify an absorption in the inner light.'
¶*I* ... 1908, 1914T.
98   *in* old *leather* ... S.
99   *cover bound for* ... S.*
100-101   *Clovio,* the one artist of the later Renaissance who could give to his work the
beauty of a hidden hope, tore *out* [hope, *took out* 1897T] ... S, 1897T.
102   *copy and* ... S, 1897T.
102   *page, surmounted* ... S, 1897T.
103   *letter, and* ... S, 1897T.
106-7   *over the* jewel-like *pages* ... S.
113-14   *lute-player* 1897T, 1914, 1925; *lute player* S; *lute- / player* 1904T, 1908.

player of Florence, and from him it passed to his son, and so from
115   generation to generation until it came to the lute-player who was
father to Benvenuto Cellini, and from him it passed to Giulio
Clovio, and from Giulio Clovio to a Roman engraver; and then
from generation to generation, the story of its wandering passing
on with it, until it came into the possession of the family of Aretino,
120   and so Giulio Aretino, an artist and worker in metals, and student
of the kabalistic reveries of Pico della Mirandola. He spent many
nights with me at Rome, discussing philosophy; and at last I won
his confidence so perfectly that he showed me this, his greatest
treasure; and, finding how much I valued it, and feeling that he
125   himself was growing old and beyond the help of its teaching, he
sold it to me for no great sum, considering its great preciousness.'
   'What is the doctrine?' I said. 'Some mediaeval straw-splitting
about the nature of the Trinity, which is only useful to-day to show
how many things are unimportant to us, which once shook the
130   world?'
   'I could never make you understand,' he said with a sigh, 'that
nothing is unimportant in belief, but even you will admit that this
book goes to the heart. Do you see the tables on which the commandments were written in Latin?' I looked to the end of the room,
135   opposite to the altar, and saw that the two marble tablets were gone,
and that two large empty tablets of ivory, like large copies of the
little tablets we set over our desks, had taken their place. 'It has
swept the commandments of the Father away,' he went on, 'and
displaced the commandments of the Son by the commandments of
140   the Holy Spirit. The first book is called *Fractura Tabularum*. In the
first chapter it mentions the names of the great artists who made
them graven things and the likeness of many things, and adored

115   *to generation, until* . . . S, 1897T.
115   *lute-player* 1897T to 1908, 1925; *lute player* S; lute- / player 1914T.
115   *lute player* [*lute-player* 1897T], *who* . . . S, 1897T.
116–18   *from* Benvenuto Cellini to that Cardinal of Ferrara who released him from
prison, and from him to a natural son, so *from* . . . 1908, 1914T.
120   *and so to Giulio* . . . S, 1897T; *and to Giulio* . . . 1908, 1914T.
121   *kabalistic* heresies *of* . . . S to 1914T.
122   *Rome discussing* . . . S, 1897T.
125   *its* mysterious *teaching* . . . S.
126   *it me* . . . S, 1897T.*
127   *mediæval* . . . S to 1925.
131   *said, with* . . . 1908, 1914T.
131   *a* deep *sigh* . . . S.
134–35   *room opposite* . . . S.
136   *and two* . . . S, 1897T.*

155

them and served them; and the second the names of the great wits
who took the name of the Lord their God in vain; and that long
145 third chapter, set with the emblems of sanctified faces, and having
wings upon its borders, is the praise of breakers of the seventh day
and wasters of the six days, who yet lived comely and pleasant days.
Those two chapters tell of men and women who railed upon their
parents, remembering that their god was older than the god of
150 their parents; and that which has the sword of Michael for an
emblem commends the kings that wrought secret murder and so
won for their people a peace that was *amore somnoque gravata et
vestibus versicoloribus,* "heavy with love and sleep and many-coloured
raiment"; and that with the pale star at the closing has the lives of
155 the noble youths who loved the wives of others and were transformed into memories, which have transformed many poorer
hearts into sweet flames; and that with the winged head is the
history of the robbers who lived upon the sea or in the desert, lives
which it compares to the twittering of the string of a bow, *nervi
160 stridentis instar;* and those two last, that are fire and gold, and devoted to the satirists who bore false witness against their neighbours
and yet illustrated eternal wrath, and to those that have coveted
more than other men wealth and woman, and have thereby and
therefore mastered and magnified great empires.

165   'The second book, which is called *Straminis Deflagratio,* recounts
the conversations Joachim of Flora held in his monastery at Cortale, and afterwards in his monastery in the mountains of La Sila,
with travellers and pilgrims, upon the laws of many countries; how
chastity was a virtue and robbery a little thing in such a land, and
170 robbery a crime and unchastity a little thing in such a land; and of

---

143   *served them; and* in *the second* . . . S.
147-48   *six days. Those* . . . S.*
150   *that, which* . . . S, 1897T.
151   *emblem, commends* . . . S, 1897T.
152   *for* the *people* S.
153   *versicoloribus, heavy* . . . 1908, 1914T ['*versicoloribus*' italic in 1908, 1914T].
154   *raiment;*" [~; ∧ 1908, 1914T] *and* . . . S to 1914T.
158   *robbers, who* . . . S, 1897T, 1925A.
158   *lived, upon* . . . S, 1897T.
160-61   *gold,* are *devoted* . . . S to 1925.
162   *wrath; and* . . . S.
163-65   *men* the house of God, and all things that are His [his S, 1897T], which no man
has seen and handled, except in madness and in dreams. ¶'*The* [in dreaming. ¶'*The* S] . . . S
to 1914T.
165-73   *book* is called *Lex* . . . 1908, 1914T ['*Lex*' italic in 1908, 1914T].
166-67   *at* Corace, *and* . . . S.
167-68   *of* Sylae, *with* . . . S.

the persons who had flung themselves upon these laws and become *decussa veste Dei sidera,* stars shaken out of the raiment of God.

'The third book, which is the close, is called *Lex Secreta,* and describes the true inspiration of action, the only Eternal Evangel;

175 and ends with a vision, which he saw among the mountains of La Sila, of his disciples sitting throned in the blue deep of the air, and laughing aloud, with a laughter that was like the rustling of the wings of Time: *Coelis in coeruleis ridentes sedebant discipuli mei super thronos: talis erat risus, qualis temporis pennati susurrus.'*

180 'I know little of Joachim of Flora,' I said, 'except that Dante set him in Paradise among the great doctors. If he held a heresy so singular, I cannot understand how no rumours of it came to the ears of Dante; and Dante made no peace with the enemies of the Church.'

185 'Joachim of Flora acknowledged openly the authority of the Church, and even asked that all his published writings, and those to be published by his desire after his death, should be submitted to the censorship of the Pope. He considered that those whose work was to live and not to reveal were children and that the Pope was

190 their father; but he taught in secret that certain others, and in always increasing numbers, were elected, not to live, but to reveal that hidden substance of God which is colour and music and softness and a sweet odour; and that these have no father but the Holy Spirit. Just as poets and painters and musicians labour at their

195 works, building them with lawless and lawful things alike, so long as they embody the beauty that is beyond the grave, these children of the Holy Spirit labour at their moments with eyes upon the shining substance on which Time has heaped the refuse of creation; for the

---

172   *veste dei sidera,* "stars . . . S ['*veste dei sidera*' italic in S].
172-73   God." 'The third . . . S.
173   *which is the* finish, *is* . . . S.
175-76   *of* Sylae, *of his* . . . S.
176   air *and* . . . S.
177   *laughter* which it compares to *the rustling* . . . S.
178-80   Time.' ¶'*I know* . . . S.*
178   *Cœlis* . . . 1897T to 1914T.
178   *cœruleis* . . . 1908, 1914T.
179   *qualis emporis pennati* . . . 1925A.
188   *those, whose* . . . S to 1904T, 1925.
189   *reveal, were* . . . S to 1904T, 1925.
190   *Father* . . . 1908, 1914T.
191   *not* for life's sake, *but* . . . S.
195   *alike so* . . . S, 1897T.
196   *grave; these* . . . S, 1897T.

world only exists to be a tale in the ears of coming generations; and
200 terror and content, birth and death, love and hatred, and the fruit
of the Tree, are but instruments for that supreme art which is to
win us from life and gather us into eternity like doves into their
dove-cots.

'I shall go away in a little while and travel into many lands, that I
205 may know all accidents and destinies, and when I return, will write
my secret law upon those ivory tablets, just as poets and romance
writers have written the principles of their art in prefaces; and will
gather pupils about me that they may discover their law in the
study of my law, and the Kingdom of the Holy Spirit be more
210 widely and firmly established.'

He was pacing up and down, and I listened to the fervour of his
words and watched the excitement of his gestures with not a little
concern. I had been accustomed to welcome the most singular
speculations, and had always found them as harmless as the Persian
215 cat, who half closes her meditative eyes and stretches out her long
claws, before my fire. But now I would battle in the interests of
orthodoxy, even of the commonplace: and yet could find nothing
better to say than:

'It is not necessary to judge every one by the law, for we have also
220 Christ's commandment of love.'

He turned and said, looking at me with shining eyes:

'Jonathan Swift made a soul for the gentlemen of this city by
hating his neighbour as himself.'

'At any rate, you cannot deny that to teach so dangerous a doc-
225 trine is to accept a terrible responsibility.'

---

199 generations and . . . 1925A.
200 hatred and . . . S, 1897T.
201 Tree are . . . S, 1897T.
205 return will . . . 1914T.
207–11 and when I know what principle of life, discoverable at first by imagination and
instinct, I am to express, I will gather my pupils that they may discover their law in the
study of my law, as poets and painters discover their own art of expression by the study of
some Master. I know nothing certain as yet but this—I am to become completely alive, that
is, completely passionate, for beauty is only another name for perfect passion. I shall create
a world where the whole lives of men shall be articulated and simplified as if seventy years
were but one moment, or as they were the leaping of a fish or the opening of a flower.'
¶He . . . 1908, 1914T.
215 cat who . . . 1908, 1914T.
216 claws before . . . 1908, 1914T.
216 I longed to battle . . . S.
218–19 than, ¶'It . . . 1897T, 1904T; than: 'It . . . 1908, 1914T.
219 every one 1897T, 1904T, 1925; everyone S, 1908, 1914T.
221–22 eyes, ¶'Jonathan . . . 1897T, 1904T; eyes: 'Jonathan . . . 1908, 1914T.

'Leonardo da Vinci,' he replied, 'has this noble sentence: "The hope and desire of returning home to one's former state is like the moth's desire for the light; and the man who with constant longing awaits each new month and new year, deeming that the things he
230 longs for are ever too late in coming, does not perceive that he is longing for his own destruction." How then can the pathway which will lead us into the heart of God be other than dangerous? why should you, who are no materialist, cherish the continuity and order of the world as those do who have only the world? You do
235 not value the writers who will express nothing unless their reason understands how it will make what is called the right more easy; why then will you deny a like freedom to the supreme art, the art which is the foundation of all arts? Yes, I shall send out of this chapel saints, lovers, rebels, and prophets: souls that will surround
240 themselves with peace, as with a nest made with grass; and others over whom I shall weep. The dust shall fall for many years over this little box; and then I shall open it; and the tumults, which are, perhaps, the flames of the last day, shall come from under the lid.'

I did not reason with him that night, because his excitement was
245 great and I feared to make him angry; and when I called at his house a few days later, he was gone and his house was locked up and empty. I have deeply regretted my failure both to combat his heresy and to test the genuineness of his strange book. Since my conversion I have indeed done penance for an error which I was
250 only able to measure after some years.

II

I was walking along one of the Dublin quays, on the side nearest the river, about ten years after our conversation, stopping from time to time to turn over the works upon an old book-stall, and

226 sentence, "The . . . S, 1897T.
227 state, is . . . S to 1904T, 1925.
228 man, who . . . S to 1904T, 1925.
229 year—deeming . . . S.
230 coming—does . . . S.
231 How, then, can . . . 1908, 1914T.
237 why, then, will . . . 1908, 1914T.
239 rebels and . . . 1908, 1914T.
239 souls which will . . . S to 1904T; souls who will . . . 1908, 1914T.
240 made of grass . . . S, 1897T.
240 and perhaps others . . . S.
251–52 quays, about . . . S.*
253 the books upon . . . S, 1908, 1914T.
253 book-stall 1925; bookstall S, 1897T, 1908, 1914T; book- / stall 1904T.

255 thinking, curiously enough, of the terrible destiny of Michael Robartes, and his brotherhood; when I saw a tall and bent man walking slowly along the other side of the quay. I recognised, with a start, in a lifeless mask with dim eyes, the once resolute and delicate face of Owen Aherne. I crossed the quay quickly, but had not gone many yards before he turned away, as though he had seen

260 me, and hurried down a side street; I followed, but only to lose him among the intricate streets on the north side of the river. During the next few weeks I inquired of everybody who had once known him, but he had made himself known to nobody; and I knocked, without result, at the door of his old house; and had nearly per-

265 suaded myself that I was mistaken, when I saw him again in a narrow street behind the Four Courts, and followed him to the door of his house.

I laid my hand on his arm; he turned quite without surprise; and indeed it is possible that to him, whose inner life had soaked up the

270 outer life, a parting of years was a parting from forenoon to afternoon. He stood holding the door half open, as though he would keep me from entering; and would perhaps have parted from me without further words had I not said:

'Owen Aherne, you trusted me once, will you not trust me again,

275 and tell me what has come of the ideas we discussed in this house

---

254-61   *the* destinies of the little group of fellow-students who had shared so many speculations at the school in Paris, and particularly of the terrible destiny of Michael Robartes and his disciples, when I saw a tall, bent man walking slowly in front of me. He stopped presently at a little shop, in the window of which were blue and white statues of the Virgin, and gilded statues of St. Patrick and his crozier. His face was now half turned towards me, and I recognized in the lifeless mask with dim eyes what had been the resolute, delicate face of Owen Aherne. I walked towards him, but had not gone many yards before he turned away, as though he had seen me, and went hastily down a side street. ¶*During* . . . S.
256   *recognized* . . . 1897T to 1914T.
262   *of* all *who* . . . S.
263-64   *to* no one, and knocked without result *at* . . . S.
264   *house.* I *had* . . . S.
265-66   *again,* and this time in a back *street* . . . S.
266   *him* until he stopped at *the* . . . S.
268   *hand* upon *his* . . . S.
268   *turned* round, and *quite* . . . S.
268-69   *and, indeed, it* . . . S.
270   *of* many *years* . . . S.
272   *entering, and* . . . S.
272   *would, perhaps, have* . . . S.
272-73   *from me* with no *further* . . . S.
273-74   *said:* ¶*'Aherne* . . . S.*
273-74   *said:* 'Owen . . . 1908, 1914T.
275-76   *discussed ten* . . . S.*

ten years ago? —but perhaps you have already forgotten them.'
'You have a right to hear,' he said, 'for since I have told you the
ideas, I should tell you the extreme danger they contain, or rather
the boundless wickedness they contain; but when you have heard
280 this we must part, and part for ever, because I am lost, and must be
hidden!'

I followed him through the paved passage, and saw that its corners were choked with dust and cobwebs; and that the pictures
were grey with dust and shrouded with cobwebs; and that the dust
285 and cobwebs which covered the ruby and sapphire of the saints on
the window had made it very dim. He pointed to where the ivory
tablets glimmered faintly in the dimness, and I saw that they were
covered with small writing, and went up to them and began to read
the writing. It was in Latin, and was an elaborate casuistry, illus-
290 trated with many examples, but whether from his own life or from
the lives of others I do not know. I had read but a few sentences

---

276   *ago? but* . . . S.
276   *have* long *forgotten* . . . S.
277–82   *he* answered; 'for having told you the ideas, it is necessary that I tell you the
terrible danger they contain; but when you have heard, we part for good and all: I must be
hidden away, for I am lost.' ¶*I* . . . S.
278   *ideas I* . . . 1897T.
283–84   *choked,* and the pictures gray, with dust and cobwebs; *and that* . . . 1908, 1914T.
284   *were* shrouded with cobwebs and gray with dust; and, when he opened the door of
the chapel, I saw *that* . . . S.
285–86   *saints* in *the window* . . . S.
286   *window, had* . . . 1897T.
286   *He* sat down wearily, not seeming to notice whether I was standing or sitting, and
pointed . . . S.
287   *the* deep gloom. *I* . . . S.
288   *with* very *small* . . . S.
288–89   *read* them. The writing was *an* . . . S.
289–90   *illustrated* apparently *with* . . . S.
290   *life, or* . . . S.
291   *the* life *of* . . . S.
291   *others, I do* . . . S.
291–376   *know.* Before I had done more than read a sentence here and there, I turned
from them, for Aherne had begun to speak in a low monotonous voice. ¶'I am outside the
salvation of Him who died for sinners, because I have lost the power of committing a sin. I
found the secret law of my life, and, finding it, no longer desired to transgress, because it
was my own law. Whatever my intellect and my soul commanded, I did, and sin passed
from me, and I ceased to be among those for whom Christ died.' And at the name of Christ
he crossed himself with that involuntary gesture which marks those who have crossed
themselves from childhood. 'At first I tried to sin by breaking my law, although without
desire; but the sin without desire is shadowy, like the sins of some phantom one has not
visited even in dreams. You who are not lost, who may still speak to men and women, tell
them that it is necessary to make an arbitrary law that one may be among those for whom
Christ has died.' ¶I went over and stood beside him, and said: ¶'Prayer and penance will

when I imagined that a faint perfume had begun to fill the room, and turning round asked Owen Aherne if he were lighting the incense.

295 'No,' he replied, and pointed where the thurible lay rusty and empty on one of the benches; as he spoke the faint perfume seemed to vanish, and I was persuaded I had imagined it.

'Has the philosophy of the *Liber inducens in Evangelium aeternum* made you very unhappy?' I said.

300 'At first I was full of happiness,' he replied, 'for I felt a divine ecstasy, an immortal fire in every passion, in every hope, in every desire, in every dream; and I saw, in the shadows under leaves, in the hollow waters, in the eyes of men and women, its image, as in a mirror; and it was as though I was about to touch the Heart of God.

305 Then all changed and I was full of misery; and in my misery it was revealed to me that man can only come to that Heart through the sense of separation from it which we call sin, and I understood that I could not sin, because I had discovered the law of my being, and could only express or fail to express my being, and I understood

310 that God has made a simple and an arbitrary law that we may sin and repent!'

He had sat down on one of the wooden benches and now became silent, his bowed head and hanging arms and listless body having more of dejection than any image I have met with in life or in any

315 art. I went and stood leaning against the altar, and watched him, not knowing what I should say; and I noticed his black closely=buttoned coat, his short hair, and shaven head, which preserved a memory of his priestly ambition, and understood how Catholicism had seized him in the midst of the vertigo he called philosophy; and

---

make you like other men.' ¶'Not,' he replied, 'unless they can take from me my knowledge of the secret law.' ¶I used some argument, which has passed out of my memory, but his strong intellect, which seemed all the stronger and more active from contrast with the weary monotony of his voice, tore my argument in pieces. I had gone on to heap argument on argument, had he not risen and led me from the chapel, repeating, 'We part for good and all; for I must be hidden away.' ¶I followed, intending to come to him again the next day; but as I stood in the door of the house a sudden hope came into my mind, and I said: ¶'Will you lend me the *Liber Inducens in Evangelium Æternum* for a few days, that I may have it examined by an expert?' ¶'I have burned the book and flung the box into the sea.' ¶When I came the next day with a Jesuit Father from the College of St. Francis Xavier, the house was locked up and apparently empty once more. S [S ends here].
298 *Inducens* . . . 1897T to 1914T.
298 *Æternum* . . . 1897T to 1914T.
305 *misery*, and I said to myself that I was caught in the glittering folds of an enormous serpent, and was falling with him through a fathomless abyss, and that henceforth the glittering folds were my world; *and in* . . . 1897T to 1914T.
318 *catholicism* . . . 1897T, 1904T, 1925.

320 I noticed his lightless eyes and his earth-coloured complexion, and understood how she had failed to do more than hold him on the margin: and I was full of an anguish of pity.

'It may be,' he went on, 'that the angels who have hearts of the Divine Ecstasy, and bodies of the Divine Intellect, need nothing but
325 a thirst for the immortal element, in hope, in desire, in dreams; but we whose hearts perish every moment, and whose bodies melt away like a sigh, must bow and obey!'

I went nearer to him and said, 'Prayer and repentance will make you like other men.'

330 'No, no,' he said, 'I am not among those for whom Christ died, and this is why I must be hidden. I have a leprosy that even eternity cannot cure. I have seen the whole, and how can I come again to believe that a part is the whole? I have lost my soul because I have looked out of the eyes of the angels.'

335 Suddenly I saw, or imagined that I saw, the room darken, and faint figures robed in purple, and lifting faint torches with arms that gleamed like silver, bending above Owen Aherne; and I saw, or imagined that I saw, drops, as of burning gum, fall from the torches, and a heavy purple smoke, as of incense, come pouring
340 from the flames and sweeping about us. Owen Aherne, more happy than I who have been half initiated into the Order of the Alchemical Rose, or protected perhaps by his great piety, had sunk again into dejection and listlessness, and saw none of these things; but my knees shook under me, for the purple-robed figures were
345 less faint every moment, and now I could hear the hissing of the gum in the torches. They did not appear to see me, for their eyes were upon Owen Aherne; now and again I could hear them sigh as though with sorrow for his sorrow, and presently I heard words which I could not understand except that they were words of sor-
350 row, and sweet as though immortal was talking to immortal. Then one of them waved her torch, and all the torches waved, and for a moment it was as though some great bird made of flames had fluttered its plumage, and a voice cried as from far up in the air,

---

323-25 *angels* whose hearts are shadows of the Divine Heart, and whose bodies are made of the Divine Intellect, may come to where their longing is always by a thirst for the divine ecstasy, the immortal fire, that is in passion, *in hope* ... 1897T to 1914T.
328 *said: 'Prayer* ... 1897T to 1925.
337 *bending, above* ... 1897T to 1925.
341 *order* ... 1904T.
342 *Rose,* and *protected* ... 1897T to 1914T.
347 *Aherne;* and *now* ... 1897T, 1914T.
353-54 *air: 'He* ... 1897T to 1925.

'He has charged even his angels with folly, and they also bow and
355 obey; but let your heart mingle with our hearts, which are wrought
of divine ecstasy, and your body with our bodies, which are
wrought of divine intellect.' And at that cry I understood that the
Order of the Alchemical Rose was not of this earth, and that it was
still seeking over this earth for whatever souls it could gather within
360 its glittering net; and when all the faces turned towards me, and I
saw the mild eyes and the unshaken eyelids, I was full of terror, and
thought they were about to fling their torches upon me, so that all I
held dear, all that bound me to spiritual and social order, would be
burnt up, and my soul left naked and shivering among the winds
365 that blow from beyond this world and from beyond the stars; and
then a voice cried, 'Why do you fly from our torches that were
made out of the trees under which Christ wept in the Garden of
Gethsemane? Why do you fly from our torches that were made out
of sweet wood, after it had perished from the world?'
370 It was not until the door of the house had closed behind my
flight, and the noise of the street was breaking on my ears, that I
came back to myself and to a little of my courage; and I have never
dared to pass the house of Owen Aherne from that day, even
though I believe him to have been driven into some distant country
375 by the spirits whose name is legion, and whose throne is in the
indefinite abyss, and whom he obeys and cannot see.

THE ADORATION OF THE MAGI

I was sitting reading late into the night a little after my last
meeting with Aherne, when I heard a light knocking on my front
door; and found upon the doorstep three very old men with stout

---

356   *bodies which* ... 1897T.
361   *eyelids I* ... 1897T.
363   *order would* ... 1897T.
364   *up and my* ... 1897T.
365-66   *stars; and* a faint *voice* ... 1897T.
366   *a* faint *voice* ... 1904T to 1925.
369-70   *world* and come to us who made it of old times with our breath?' ¶*It* ... 1897T to
1914T.
[In S, the story is signed W. B. Yeats.]

Printings: 1897T; 1904T; 1908; 1914T; 1925.
Text from 1932.
Title: ... MAGI. 1897T; The Adoration of the Magi 1904T.
3   *door. I found* ... 1908, 1914T.

sticks in their hands, who said they had been told I would be up and
5   about, and that they were to tell me important things. I brought
them into my study, and when the peacock curtains had closed
behind us, I set their chairs for them close to the fire, for I saw that
the frost was on their great-coats of frieze and upon the long beards
that flowed almost to their waists. They took off their great-coats,
10   and leaned over the fire warming their hands, and I saw that their
clothes had much of the country of our time, but a little also, as
it seemed to me, of the town life of a more courtly time. When they
had warmed themselves—and they warmed themselves, I thought,
less because of the cold of the night than because of a pleasure in
15   warmth for the sake of warmth—they turned towards me, so that
the light of the lamp fell full upon their weather-beaten faces, and
told the story I am about to tell. Now one talked and now another,
and they often interrupted one another, with a desire, like that of
countrymen, when they tell a story, to leave no detail untold. When
20   they had finished they made me take notes of whatever conversation they had quoted, so that I might have the exact words, and got
up to go, and when I asked them where they were going, and what
they were doing, and by what names I should call them, they would
tell me nothing, except that they had been commanded to travel
25   over Ireland continually, and upon foot and at night, that they
might live close to the stones and the trees and at the hours when
the immortals are awake.

    I have let some years go by before writing out this story, for I am
always in dread of the illusions which come of that inquietude of
30   the veil of the temple, which M. Mallarmé considers a characteristic
of our times; and only write it now because I have grown to believe
that there is no dangerous idea which does not become less
dangerous when written out in sincere and careful English.

    The three old men were three brothers, who had lived in one of
35   the western islands from their early manhood, and had cared all
their lives for nothing except for those classical writers and old

---

4   *I should be* . . . 1897T to 1914T.
6   *and, when* . . . 1897T.
13   *themselves; and* . . . 1897T.
15   *of warmth; they* . . . 1897T.
18   *desire like* . . . 1914T.
18–19   *of* peasants, *when they* . . . 1897T.
22   *go. When* . . . 1908, 1914T.*
22   *going and* . . . 1897T.
23   *doing and* . . . 1897T.
30   *Temple* . . . 1897T to 1925.
32   *idea, which* . . . 1897T.

Gaelic writers who expounded an heroic and simple life. Night
after night in winter, Gaelic story-tellers would chant old poems to
them over the poteen; and night after night in summer, when the
40 Gaelic story-tellers were at work in the fields or away at the fishing,
they would read to one another Virgil and Homer, for they would
not enjoy in solitude, but as the ancients enjoyed. At last a man,
who told them he was Michael Robartes, came to them in a
fishing-boat, like S. Brandan drawn by some vision and called by
45 some voice; and told them of the coming again of the gods and the
ancient things; and their hearts, which had never endured the body
and pressure of our time, but only of distant times, found nothing
unlikely in anything he told them, but accepted all simply and were
happy. Years passed, and one day, when the oldest of the old men,
50 who had travelled in his youth and thought sometimes of other
lands, looked out on the grey waters, on which the people see the
dim outline of the Islands of the Young—the Happy Islands where
the Gaelic heroes live the lives of Homer's Phaeacians—a voice
came out of the air over the waters and told him of the death of
55 Michael Robartes. While they were still mourning, the next oldest
of the old men fell asleep whilst he was reading out the Fifth Ec-
logue of Virgil, and a strange voice spoke through him, and bid
them set out for Paris, where a dying woman would give them
secret names and thereby so transform the world that another Leda

---

37   *life; night* . . . 1897T to 1914T.
42   *solitude but* . . . 1897T.
42-43   *man who* . . . 1897T.
43   *Robartes came* . . . 1897T.
44   *fishing-boat* 1897T to 1908, 1925; *fishing boat* 1914T.
44   *St.* . . . 1897T to 1925.
45   *and* spoke *of the coming* . . . 1908, 1914T.
47   *time but* . . . 1897T.
49   *day; when* . . . 1897T.
50   *who travelled* . . . 1904T to 1914T.
51   *which the* peasants *see* . . . 1897T.
52   *Young, the* . . . 1897T.
53   *live the* life *of* . . . 1897T.
53   *Phæacians; a* . . . 1897T; *Phæacians—a* . . . 1904T to 1925.
55   *Robartes. They* . . . 1908, 1914T.*
55   *mourning when the* . . . 1908, 1914T.
56   *asleep* while *reading* . . . 1908, 1914T.
58-62   *a* woman lay dying, who would reveal to them the secret names of the gods, which
[the immortals, which 1897T] can be perfectly spoken only when the mind is steeped in
certain colours and certain sounds and certain odours; but at whose perfect speaking the
immortals cease to be cries and shadows, and walk and talk with one like men and
women. ¶*They* . . . 1897T to 1914T.

60   would open her knees to the swan, another Achilles beleaguer
Troy.

They left their island, and were at first troubled at all they saw in
the world, and came to Paris, and there the youngest met a person
in a dream, who told him they were to wander about at hazard until

65   those who had been guiding their footsteps had brought them to a
street and a house, whose likeness was shown him in the dream.
They wandered hither and thither for many days, until one morning they came into some narrow and shabby streets, on the south of
the Seine, where women with pale faces and untidy hair looked at

70   them out of the windows; and just as they were about to turn back
because Wisdom could not have alighted in so foolish a neighbourhood, they came to the street and the house of the dream. The
oldest of the old men, who still remembered some of the modern
languages he had known in his youth, went up to the door and

75   knocked, and when he had knocked, the next in age to him said it
was not a good house, and could not be the house they were looking for, and urged him to ask for somebody who could not be there
and go away. The door was opened by an old over-dressed woman,
who said, 'O you are her three kinsmen from Ireland. She has been

80   expecting you all day.' The old men looked at one another and
followed her upstairs, passing doors from which pale and untidy
women thrust out their heads, and into a room where a beautiful
woman lay asleep, another woman sitting by her.

The old woman said: 'Yes, they have come at last; now she will be

85   able to die in peace,' and went out.

'We have been deceived by devils,' said one of the old men,

---

62   *island, at first* much *troubled* ... 1908, 1914T.
64-65   *until* the immortals, who would guide their *footsteps, had* ... 1897T.
66   *house,* which the person showed *him* ... 1897T.
67   *days,* but *one* ... 1908, 1914T.
68   *they* wandered *into* ... 1897T.
75   *knocked,* but *when* ... 1908, 1914T.
75   *next* oldest of the old men *said* ... 1897T.
77   *ask* for some one who they [one that they 1908; one they 1914T] knew was not
there ... 1897T to 1914T.
79   *O, you* ... 1908, 1914T.
79   *three* cousins *from* ... 1897T.
81   *upstairs* 1908, 1914T, 1925E; *up-stairs* 1897T, 1904T, 1925A.
83   *asleep* in a bed, with *another* ... 1897T to 1914T.
84   *Yes they* ... 1914T.
84   *last, now* ... 1897T.
86   *by* Dhouls,' *said* ... 1897T.

'for the Immortals would not speak through a woman like this.'

'Yes,' said another, 'we have been deceived by devils, and we must go away quickly.'

90 'Yes,' said the third, 'we have been deceived by devils, but let us kneel down for a little, for we are by the deathbed of one that has been beautiful.' They knelt down, and the woman sitting by the bed whispered, and as though overcome with fear, and with lowered head, 'At the moment when you knocked she was suddenly con-
95 vulsed and cried out as I have heard a woman in childbirth and fell backward as though in a swoon.' Then they watched for a little the face upon the pillow and wondered at its look, as of unquenchable desire, and at the porcelain-like refinement of the vessel in which so malevolent a flame had burned.

100 Suddenly the second oldest of them crowed like a cock, till the room seemed to shake with the crowing. The woman in the bed still slept on in her death-like sleep, but the woman who sat by her head crossed herself and grew pale, and the youngest of the old men cried out: 'A devil has gone into him, and we must begone or it will
105 go into us also.' Before they could rise from their knees, a resonant chanting voice came from the lips that had crowed and said:

'I am not a devil, but I am Hermes the Shepherd of the Dead, I run upon the errands of the gods, and you have heard my sign. The woman who lies there has given birth, and that which she bore
110 has the likeness of a unicorn and is most unlike man of all living things, being cold, hard and virginal. It seemed to be born dancing; and was gone from the room wellnigh upon the instant, for it is of

---

87   immortals . . . 1897T to 1925.
88   by Dhouls, and . . . 1897T.
90   by Dhouls, but . . . 1897T.
91–92   one who was beautiful . . . 1897T.
92–96   woman [~, 1897T] who sat by the bed, [~ ʌ 1897T] and seemed to be overcome [seemed overcome 1897T] with fear and awe, lowered her head. They watched . . . 1897T to 1914T.
100   of the old men crowed . . . 1897T.
100   cock, and until the . . . 1897T to 1914T.
104   A Dhoul has . . . 1897T.
105   knees a . . . 1914T.
106–7   said: 'I am not . . . 1897T, 1908, 1914T.
107   a Dhoul, but . . . 1897T.
107   Dead, and I . . . 1897T to 1914T.
108–18   sign, that has been my sign from the old days. Bow down before her from whose lips the secret names of the immortals, and of the things near their hearts, are about to come, [~ ʌ 1897T] that the immortals may come again into the world. Bow down, and understand that when they are [when the immortals are 1897T] about to overthrow . . . 1897T to 1914T.

the nature of the unicorn to understand the shortness of life. She
does not know it has gone, for she fell into a stupor while it danced,
115 but bend down your ears that you may learn the names that it must
obey.' Neither of the other two old men spoke, but doubtless
looked at the speaker with perplexity, for the voice began again:
'When the Immortals would overthrow the things that are to-day
and bring the things that were yesterday, they have no one to help
120 them, but one whom the things that are to-day have cast out. Bow
down and very low, for they have chosen this woman in whose
heart all follies have gathered, and in whose body all desires have
awaked; this woman who has been driven out of Time and has lain
upon the bosom of Eternity.'
125 The voice ended with a sigh, and immediately the old man awoke
out of sleep, and said, 'Has a voice spoken through me, as it did
when I fell asleep over my Virgil, or have I only been asleep?'
The oldest of them said, 'A voice has spoken through you. Where
has your soul been while the voice was speaking through you?'
130 'I do not know where my soul has been, but I dreamed I was
under the roof of a manger, and I looked down and I saw an ox
and an ass; and I saw a red cock perching on the hay-rack; and a
woman hugging a child; and three old men in chain armour kneeling with their heads bowed very low in front of the woman and the
135 child. While I was looking the cock crowed and a man with wings
on his heels swept up through the air, and as he passed me, cried
out, "Foolish old men, you had once all the wisdom of the stars." I
do not understand my dream or what it would have us do, but you
who have heard the voice out of the wisdom of my sleep know what
140 we have to do.'
Then the oldest of the old men told him they were to take the
parchments they had brought with them out of their pockets and

114   *gone for* . . . 1925.
117   *perplexity for* . . . 1925A.
121   *chosen* for their priestess [~, 1897T] *this* . . . 1897T to 1914T.
123   *Time, and* . . . 1914T.
124-25   *Eternity.* After you have bowed down the old things shall be again, and
another Argo shall carry heroes over sea, and [over the deep, and 1897T, 1904T] another
Achilles beleaguer another Troy.' ¶*The voice* . . . 1897T to 1914T.
126   *said:* 'Has . . . 1897T to 1925.
127-28   *asleep?'* ¶'A voice has spoken through you,' said the oldest of the old men.
'Where . . . 1897T.
128   *said:* 'A . . . 1904T to 1925.
133-34   *men, in* armour [~, 1914T] studded with rubies, *kneeling* . . . 1897T to 1914T.
137   *out:* "Foolish . . . 1897T to 1925.
142-43   *and to* spread them on the ground. When . . . 1897T.

spread them on the ground. When they had spread them on the
ground, they took out of their pockets their pens, made of three
145 feathers, which had fallen from the wing of the old eagle that is
believed to have talked of wisdom with S. Patrick.

'He meant, I think,' said the youngest, as he put their ink-bottles
by the side of the rolls of parchment, 'that when people are good
the world likes them and takes possession of them, and so eternity
150 comes through people who are not good or who have been forgotten. Perhaps Christianity was good and the world liked it, so now it
is going away and the Immortals are beginning to awake.'

'What you say has no wisdom,' said the oldest, 'because if there
are many Immortals, there cannot be only one Immortal.'

155 'Yet it seems,' said the youngest, 'that the names we are to take

---

144   *ground they* . . . 1897T.
145   *eagle, that* . . . 1897T.
146   *St.* . . . 1897T to 1925.
147   *youngest* of the old men, *as* . . . 1897T.
152   *immortals* . . . 1897T to 1925.
153   *oldest* of the old men, *'because* . . . 1897T.
154   *immortals there* . . . 1897T.
154   *immortals* . . . 1904T to 1925.
154–166   *one immortal.'* ¶Then the woman in the bed sat up and looked about her with
wild eyes; and the oldest of the old men said: 'Lady, we have come to write down the names
of the immortals,' and at his words a look of great joy came into her face. Presently she
began to speak slowly, and yet eagerly, as though she knew she had but a little while to live,
and, in English, with the accent of their own country; and she told them the secret names
of the immortals of many lands, and of the colours, and odours, and weapons, and
instruments of music and instruments of handicraft they held dearest; but most about the
immortals of Ireland and of their love for the cauldron, and the whetstone, and the sword,
and the spear, and the hills of the Shee, and the horns of the moon, and the Grey Wind,
and the Yellow Wind, and the Black Wind, and the Red Wind. Then she tossed feebly a
while and moaned, and when she spoke again it was in so faint a murmur that the woman
who sat by the bed leaned down to listen, and while she was listening the spirit went out of
the body. ¶Then the oldest of the old men said in French to the woman who was still
bending over the bed: *'There* . . . 1897T; *one immortal.'* ¶Then the woman in the bed sat up
and looked about her with wild eyes; and the oldest of the old men said: 'Lady, we have
come to write down the secret names,' and at his words a look of great joy came into her
face. Presently she began to speak slowly, and yet eagerly, as though she knew she had but
a little while to live, and [~, 1904T] in the Gaelic of their own country; and she spoke to
them [she told them 1904T] many secret powerful names, and of the colours, and odours,
and weapons, and instruments of music and instruments of handicraft belonging to the
owners of those names; but most about the Sidhe of Ireland and of their love for the
Cauldron, and the Whetstone, and the Sword, and the Spear. Then she tossed feebly for a
while and moaned, and when she spoke again it was in so faint a murmur that the woman
who sat by the bed leaned down to listen, and while she was listening the spirit went out of
the body. ¶Then the oldest of the old men said in French to the woman who was still
bending over the bed: *'There* . . . 1904T to 1914T.
154   *immortal* . . . 1925.

170

down are the names of one, so it must be that he can take many forms.'

Then the woman on the bed moved as in a dream, and held out her arms as though to clasp the being that had left her, and mur-
160 mured names of endearment, and yet strange names, 'Harsh sweetness', 'Dear bitterness', 'O solitude', 'O terror', and after lay still for awhile. Then her voice changed, and she, no longer afraid and happy but seeming like any dying woman, murmured a name so faintly that the woman who sat by the bed bent down and put her
165 ear close to her mouth.

The oldest of the old men said in French, 'There must have been yet one name which she had not given us, for she murmured a name while the spirit was going out of the body,' and the woman said, 'She was merely murmuring over the name of a symbolist
170 painter she was fond of. He used to go to something he called the Black Mass, and it was he who taught her to see visions and to hear voices.'

This is all the old men told me, and when I think of their speech and of their silence, of their coming and of their going, I am almost
175 persuaded that had I followed them out of the house, I would have found no footsteps on the snow. They may, for all I or any man can say, have been themselves Immortals:immortal demons, come to put an untrue story into my mind for some purpose I do not understand. Whatever they were, I have turned into a pathway
180 which will lead me from them and from the Order of the Alchemi- cal Rose. I no longer live an elaborate and haughty life, but seek to

---

162 awhile 1925; a while 1897T to 1914T.
163 happy, but . . . 1925A.
163 woman, she murmured . . . 1925A.
166 French: 'There . . . 1925.
169 was but murmuring . . . 1908, 1914T.
172-73 voices. She met him for the first time a few months ago,.and we have had no peace from that day because of her talk about visions and about voices. Why! it was only last night that I dreamed I saw a man with a red beard and red hair, [~ ʌ 1897T] and dressed in red, [~ ʌ 1897T] standing by my bedside. He held a rose in one hand, [~ ʌ 1897T] and tore it in pieces with the other hand, and the petals drifted about the room, and became beautiful people who began to dance slowly. When I woke up I was all in a heat with terror.' ¶This . . . 1897T to 1914T.
173 old man told . . . 1897T.
175 had I gone out of the house [~, 1897T] after they had gone out of it, I should have . . . 1897T to 1914T.
177 immortals . . . 1897T to 1925.
179 were I . . . 1914T.
180 them, and . . . 1897T.

lose myself among the prayers and the sorrows of the multitude. I pray best in poor chapels, where frieze coats brush against me as I kneel, and when I pray against the demons I repeat a prayer which
185 was made I know not how many centuries ago to help some poor Gaelic man or woman who had suffered with a suffering like mine.

> *Seacht b-páidreacha fó seacht*
> *Chuir Muire faoi n-a Mac,*
> *Chuir Brighid faoi n-a brat,*
190 *Chuir Dia faoi n-a neart,*
> *Eidir sinn 'san Sluagh Sidhe,*
> *Eidir sinn 'san Sluagh Gaoith.*

> Seven paters seven times,
> Send Mary by her Son,
195 Send Bridget by her mantle,
> Send God by His strength,
> Between us and the faery host,
> Between us and the demons of the air.

NOTES

I have left out a few passages in *The Celtic Twilight*, which was first published in 1893. The *Stories of Red Hanrahan*, page 197 to page 245, were published with the stories now called *The Secret Rose* and

---

183 *chapels where* ... 1897T.
183 *where* the *frieze* ... 1908, 1914T.
183 *brush* by *me* ... 1908, 1914T.
184 *prayer, which* ... 1897T.
189 *Brighid* ... 1914T.
192-93 *Gaoith.* / [*Seven Paters* ... 1897T ['*Gaoith*' italic in 1897T].
192-93 *Gaoith,* / *Seven* ... 1925A ['*Gaoith*' italic in 1925A].
196 *his* ... 1897T.
198 *air.*] 1897T.

Printings: 1925.
Text from 1932.
[The 1925 version of this note begins with a long passage concerning the poems in *Early Poems and Stories;* this was omitted in 1932.]
1 *in* 'The Celtic Twilight', *which* ... 1925E; *in* 'The Celtic Twilight,' *which* ... 1925A.
2 ['*The*' italic in 1925]
2-3 *page* 395 to page 459, *were* ... 1925.

Rosa Alchemica in a book called *The Secret Rose* in 1897, and they owe
5   much of their merit to Lady Gregory. They were, as first published,
written in that artificial, elaborate English so many of us played
with in the 'nineties, and I had come to hate them. When I was
changing the first story in the light of a Sligo tale about 'a wild old
man in flannel' who could change a pack of cards into the likeness
10   of a pack of hounds, I asked Lady Gregory's help. We worked
together, first upon that tale, and after upon all the others, she
now suggesting a new phrase or thought, and now I, till all had been
put into that simple English she had learned from her Galway
country-men, and the thought had come closer to the life of the
15   people. If their style has merit now, that merit is mainly hers. Dr.
Hyde had already founded the first Gaelic play ever performed in
a theatre upon one of the stories, and but the other day Lady
Gregory made a Hanrahan play upon an incident of her own in-
vention. *The Tables of the Law* and *The Adoration of the Magi* were
20   intended to be part of *The Secret Rose,* but the publisher, A. H.
Bullen, took a distaste to them and asked me to leave them out, and
then after the book was published liked them and put them into a
little volume by themselves. In these as in most of the other stories I
have left out or rewritten a passage here and there. (1925).

[A note concerning *The Irish Dramatic Movement* is not reproduced.]

4   *called* 'The Secret Rose' *in* ... 1925.
7   *nineties* ... 1925A.
14   *country-men; countrymen* 1925.
19   *Magi,* page 498 to page 526, *were* ... 1925 ['*Magi*' italic in 1925].
20   *of* 'The Secret Rose', *but* ... 1925.
24   *here and* here.... 1925A.
24   *there. / W. B. Y.* [date lacking] 1925.

Other Texts

The basic text for stories in this section is taken from *The Secret Rose* (1897). No emendations have been made.

THE BINDING OF THE HAIR

The men-at-arms of the young and wise Queen Dectira, and of
the old and foolish King Lua, had lighted a line of fires from the
mountain of Gulben to the sea and set watchmen by every fire; and
built close to the place where the Liss of the Blindman was built in
5 later times, a large house with skin-covered wattles for the assembly, and smaller houses to sleep in, and dug round all a deep ditch:
and now they sat in the large house, waiting the attack of certain
nations of the People of the Bag coming up out of the south, and
listened to the bard Aodh, who spoke to them a story of the wars of
10 Heber and Heremon. The tale was written upon thin slips of wood,
which the bard held before him like a fan, grasping them above the
brazen pivot, and only laid down when he would take up the five=
stringed cruit from the ground and chaunt hastily, and with vehement gesture, one of the many songs woven into the more massive
15 measure of the tale. Though the bard was famous, and claimed to
be descended from the bard for whom the nations of Heber and
Heremon cast lots at the making of the world, the old and foolish
king did not listen, but leaned his head upon the middle pillar and
snored fitfully in a wine-heavy sleep; but the young queen sat
20 among her women, straight and still like a white candle, and listened as though there was no tale in the world but this tale of
Aodh's, for the enchantment of his dream-heavy voice was in her
ears; the enchantment of his dream-distraught history in her mind:
how he would live now in the raths of kings, now alone in the great

Printings: *The Savoy*, January, 1896; 1897.
Text from 1897; all variants from S.
1   *young queen Dectira . . .**
2-3   *from* Bulben *to . . .*
4-7   *built* a long house with skin-covered wattles for the assembly, and smaller houses to
sleep in, and dug round them a deep ditch, close to the place where the Lis of the
Blindman was built in later times; *and . . .*
7   *the* long *house waiting . . .*
7-8   *of* the clans coming down from the plain of Ith, *and . . .*
9   *who* recited a battle-tale *of the . . .*
13   *ground* at his feet *and chaunt . . .*
14   *many* lyrics *woven . . .*
15-17   *famous, the old . . .**
18   *the* central *pillar . . .*
21-22   *this* one, *for . . .*
22   *his* dreamy *voice . . .*
23   *his* changing *history . . .*
23-24   *her* memory: *how . . .*
24   *Raths . . .*

25   forest; how, despite the grey hairs mingling before their time with the dark of his beard, he was blown hither and thither by love and anger; how, according to his mood, he would fly now from one man and with blanched face, and would now show an extreme courage one man against many; and, above all, how he had sat
30   continually by her great chair telling of forays and battles, to hearten her war-weary men-at-arms, or chaunting histories and songs laden with gentler destinies for her ears alone, or, more often still, listening in silence to the rustling of her dress.

    He sang now of anger and not of love, for it was needful to fill
35   the hearts of her men-at-arms with thirst of battle that her days might have peace; yet over all the tale hovered a mournful beauty not of battle, and from time to time he would compare the gleam of a sword to the brightness of her eyes; or the dawn breaking on a morning of victory to the glimmering of her breast. As the tale, and
40   its songs, which were like the foam upon a wave, flowed on, it wrapped the men-at-arms as in a tide of fire, and its vehement passages made them clash their swords upon their shields and shout an always more clamorous approval. At last it died out in a chaunt of triumph over battle-cars full of saffron robes and orna-
45   ments of gold and silver, and over troops of young men and young girls with chains of bronze about their ankles; and the men shouted and clashed their swords upon their shields for a long time. The queen sat motionless for a little, and then leaned back in her chair so that its carved back made one dark tress fall over her cheek.
50   Sighing a long, inexplicable sigh, she bound the tress about her head and fastened it with a golden pin. Aodh gazed at her, the fierce light fading in his eyes, and began to murmur something over to himself, and presently, taking the five-stringed cruit from the ground, half knelt before her, and softly touched the strings.
55   The shouters fell silent, for they saw that he would praise the queen, as his way was when the tales were at an end; and in the silence he struck three notes, as soft and sad as though they were the cooing of doves over the Gates of Death.

---

25 *forest;* how rumour held him of the race of the bard for whom the tribes of Heber and Heremon cast lots at the making of the world; *how, despite* . . .
28-29 *face, and* now prove himself of a preternatural bravery alone *against* . . .
30 *battles to* . . .
31 *her* war-beaten *men-at-arms* . . .
40 *its* lyrics, *which* . . .
43 *an* ever-more *clamorous* . . .
45-46 *over* long lines of youths and maidens with brazen chains *about* . . .
48 *a* while, *and* . . .
53 *presently taking* . . .

Before he could begin his song, the door which led from the long
60 room into the open air burst open and a man rushed in, his face
red with running, and cried out:
'The nations with ignoble bodies and ragged beards have driven
us from the fires and have killed many!'
The words were scarcely from his mouth before another man
65 struck against him, making him reel from the door, and this man
was followed by another and another and another, until all that
remained of the watchmen stood in the middle of the hall, muddy
and breathless, some pouring wine into horns from the great stone
flagon that stood there, and some unhooking their bronze helmets
70 and shields and swords from the wall and from the pillars, and all
cursing the nations of the People of the Bag. The men about the
queen also unhooked their bronze helmets and shields and swords
from the walls and from the pillars: but the queen sat there straight
and still; and Aodh half knelt before her, with bowed head, and
75 slowly touched the five-stringed cruit as though he were half sunk
into a Druid sleep.
At last he rose with a sigh, and was about to pass into the crowd
of the men-at-arms when the queen leaned forward, and, taking
him by the hand, said, in a low voice:
80 'O Aodh, promise me to sing the song out before the morning,
whether we overcome them or they overcome us.'
He turned, with a pale face, and answered:
'There are two little verses in my heart, two little drops in my
flagon, and I swear by the Red Swineherd that I will pour them out
85 before the morning for the Rose of my Desire, the Lily of my Peace,
whether I live or be with Orchil and her faded multitude!'
Then he took down from a pillar his shield of wicker and hide,
and his bronze helmet and sword, and passed among the crowd

---

62   *The* races *with* . . .
62   *beards,* from beyond the Red Cataract, *have* . . .
65-66   *door,* only to be thrust aside *by* . . .
67   *in the* centre *of the* . . .
70-71   *swords* from the pillars. *The* . . .
72-73   *queen* had already taken their helmets and shields and swords from pillars and
walls, and were now armed; *but* . . .
73   *sat* on *straight* . . .
74-75   *head, and touched* . . .*
75-77   *cruit* slowly and dreamily. ¶*At* . . .
77-78   *to* mix among *the men-at- / arms* . . .
80   *song before* . . .*
81-82   *we* be victors or weary fugitives!' ¶*He* . . .
86-87   *I* have living lips or fade among the imponderable multitudes!' ¶*Then* . . .
87-88   *down* his wicker shield covered with hide, and his helmet and sword, from a pillar,
and mixed *among* . . .

that went, shouting, through the wide door; and there was no one
90   left in the room except the queen and her women and the foolish
king, who slept on, with his head against a pillar.

After a little, they heard a far-off ringing of bronze upon bronze,
and the dull thud of bronze upon hide, and the cries of men, and
these continued for a long time, and then sank into the silence.
95   When all was still, the queen took the five-stringed cruit upon her
knees and began touching the strings fitfully and murmuring
vague words out of the love songs of Aodh; and so sat until about
two hours before dawn, when she heard the trampling of the feet
of the men-at-arms. They came in slowly and wearily, and threw
100 themselves down, clotted with blood as they were, some on the
floor, some on the benches.

'We have slain the most, and the rest fled among the mountains,'
said the leader; 'but there is no part of the way where there was not
fighting, and we have left many behind us.'
105 'Where is Aodh?' said one of the women.
'I saw his head taken off with a sword,' said the man.

The queen rose and passed silently out of the room, and, half
crossing the space within the ditch, came where her horses were
tethered, and bade the old man, who had charge of their harness
110 and chariot, tell none, but come with her and seek for a dead man.
They went along the narrow track in the forest that had been trod
by marauders, or by those sent to give them battle, for centuries;
and saw the starlight glimmer upon the helmets and swords of
dead men, troubling a darkness which seemed heavy with a sleep
115 older than the world. At last they came out upon the treeless place
where the nations of the People of the Bag had fought desperately
for the last time before they were scattered. The old man tied the
reins to a tree and lit a torch, and the old man and the queen began
to search among the dead. The crows, which had been tearing the
120 bodies, rushed up into the air before them with a loud cawing, and

---

89   *that* poured, *shouting* . . .
89–90 *the* great door. ¶Nobody remained in the long *room* . . .
96–97 *murmuring* stray lines and phrases *out* . . .
98–99 *when* the tramp of feet told the return *of* . . .
102   *fled* beyond *the* . . .
111   *They* drove *along* . . .
114   *men troubling* . . .
116   *where the* servile tribes *had* . . .
116–17 *fought* their last desperate battle before they broke. *The* . . .
118   *torch, and the* two *began* . . .
120   *with loud* . . .*

here and there the starlight glimmered upon a helmet or a sword, or in pools of blood, or in the eyes of the dead.

Of a sudden, a sweet, tremulous song came from a bush near them. They hurried towards the spot, and saw a head hanging
125 from the bush by its dark hair; and the head was singing, and this was the song it sung;

> Fasten your hair with a golden pin,
> And bind up every wandering tress;
> I bade my heart build these poor rhymes:
130 It worked at them, day out, day in,
> Building a sorrowful loveliness
> Out of the battles of old times.

> You need but lift a pearl-pale hand,
> And bind up your long hair and sigh;
135 And all men's hearts must burn and beat;
> And candle-like foam on the dim sand,
> And stars climbing the dew-dropping sky,
> Live but to light your passing feet.

And then a troop of crows, heavy like fragments of that sleep
140 older than the world, swept out of the darkness, and, as they passed, smote those ecstatic lips with the points of their wings; and the head fell from the bush and rolled over at the feet of the queen.

---

121   *glimmered* on helmet or *sword* . . .
126-27   *sung*—¶*'Fasten* . . .
130   *them day out* . . .
138-39   *feet.'* ¶*And* . . .
141   *wings, and* . . .

The Book of the Great Dhoul
and Hanrahan the Red

AND

The Devil's Book

THE BOOK OF THE GREAT DHOUL
AND HANRAHAN THE RED

Somewhere in the middle of the last century a man, with a frieze coat and a great mass of red hair, strode down a narrow street in the Town of the Grey Lough, and with a slightly unsteady step. The little ink-bottle hanging by a chain from his neck, and his pale vehement face, contradicted his rough weather-beaten hands, and showed him for a hedge school-master before all eyes familiar with the villages.

Presently a puff of wind swept round the corner of a house, and sent a whirl of straws dancing and leaping before his feet, and made him stop and cross himself in momentary fear, for such winds are held to be the passing of a troop of the Shee. At the same moment his eyes fell upon a little shop-window, and in the window were rolls of tobacco, three hats of the old rimless type, the head of a churn cask, a sheaf of tallow candles, certain dusty pieces of soap, a sod of turf with two clay pipes stuck in it crosswise to show there was the Brew of the Little Pot within, and a book whose pages were open and full of singular diagrams. He at once remembered having heard the owner of the shop talking of this book, which had lain in the window a long time in the hope of catching the eyes of some curiosity hunter; and he wondered he had never thought of looking at it, and perhaps of buying it and taking it home. He stooped down, where so many children had stood and nudged each other, and whispered that there was the book of the Great Dhoul which he wrote himself; and looked long and pondered and pondered. Presently he stood up and gave the door of the shop a kick, and called out: 'Come out of that, Little Paddy.'

'Is that you, Hanrahan the Red?' said a big peasant, stooping his head under the lintel. 'I thought you were kept all day at the Fearny Height teaching school, and minding cattle, when school was done, for the Squire the son of Dowda, the red anger of God upon him! and, when the cattle were in the byre, making rhymes about the old giants, and fighting men, and the blessed Maurya, and the four evangelists, and your own light o' loves.'

'My school is gone from me.'

'Did you lose it as you lost the school at the Great Spring because of the women?'

184

THE DEVIL'S BOOK
(*The National Observer,* November 26, 1892)

[This story was so extensively revised for *The Secret Rose* (1897) as to make collation impossible.]

Somewhere about the middle of the last century, a man with a great mass of red hair and a pale, vehement face, stopped in front of a shop window in a back street in Cork. In the window was a roll of tobacco, three hats of the old rimless type, the head of a churn
5   cask, a sheaf of tallow candles, a sod of turf with two clay pipes stuck in it cross-wise to give evidence of unlicensed whiskey within, a coil of rope, a bottle of sweets, and a book for raising the devil. The book had displayed its yellow pages for many a day, in vain hope of catching the eye of some Cork curiosity hunter. The chil-
10   dren had often stood on tip-toe, and looked in and nudged each other, and whispered that there was the devil's book, which 'he wrote himsel' ': but the red-haired-man was the first person old enough to be a buyer who had looked upon the book and pon-dered. This was the third time that day he had come and stared
15   into the window, but now, instead of turning away down the rough-paved street among the children and the ducks and hens, he gave the door of the shop a kick and called out, 'Come out of that, Paudeen; I want to deal with you.' A big peasant came out, stooping his head under the low lintel of the door.
20   'Is that you, O'Sullivan the Red?' he began. 'I thought ye were teachin' school at Shronehill and mindin' cattle for that divil, Squire Thomas, and makin' rhymes over-night about the gi'nts and fightin' men that were.'

'I have no school now.'
25   'Did ye lose it, as ye lost the school at Tailteen and Conroy, and all along o' the women?'

'The truth is on your tongue,' replied Hanrahan, 'for I got into trouble about Maive Lavell, who I made the song to.'

'Owen,' said the other, 'if it is the Brew of the Little Pot you are
40   wanting, you must pay on the nail, for though you are a great poet and know Latin, I will not trust you for another noggin.'

'It is not the Brew of the Little Pot I want, but the book of the Great Dhoul.'

'And how are you going to pay for it?'

45   'I have just come from selling my big brown coat with the cape to Michael the son of Rafferty.'

'You will have to give me two silver shillings; a great price for a book; for it's been long in the family. My poor father, may he rest easy! took it out of a French brigantine. O but my poor father was a
50   fine man: he put a tar-barrel on a rock out by one of the Arran Isles, and he wrecked her for the soap that was aboard.'

The money was paid, and Little Paddy took the book out of the window, and Hanrahan, touching it with the tips of the fingers of one hand, and having made a cross over it with the other hand,
55   thrust it into his breast-pocket.

'And what are you going to do with my book, that has kept the thieves out these four years?'

Hanrahan had not considered this at all, and stood for a moment, shoving his fingers up through his red hair, so that his cap
60   rose a couple of inches; and presently, struck by a sudden idea, poured out a vehement tide of words. 'Be quiet now and I will tell you what I want the Book for, and I will tell you no lies about it, but the truth. Father Gillen says I am a limb of the great Dhoul, but I am going to hold out against him until he has raised the
65   neighbourhood as Father Clancy raised the Great Spring on me. You have heard how the Fianna were sent down into Hell because they were heathens, and worshipped none but Dana and Angus and the Dagda and Lir and Mannanan, and them that were in the sun, and them that were in the moon; but may be you have not
70   heard that God himself, because He admired the great blows they gave, and the songs and the stories they made, put a circle of smooth green grass all round and about the place for them. They rush in their chariots on that green grass for ever and ever, making the sods fly with the hoofs of the horses; and Oscar, the biggest of
75   them, goes before with a flail, and drives the demons from the road. Well, their way is my way, for whatever a man does against me, and wherever I am, I get the best out of things; and now that Father Gillen is turning the neighbours against me, I am going to

186

'The truth is upon your tongue,' replied O'Sullivan; 'for I got into trouble about Molly Casey, her I made the song to.'

'Owen,' said the other, 'if it be poteen ye are after, ye must pay
30 down, for though you are a great poet and know letters, I will not thrust ye for another noggin.'

'It is not the poteen I want, but the Devil's Book.'

'And what do ye want my book for—my book that kept the thieves out these four years? and how are ye goin' to pay for it?'
35 'Whist now, and I'll tell you. Father Gillen says I am a limb o' Satan, but I am goin' to howld out until he has ruz the neighbourhood, as Father Clancey has ruz Conroy on me. Ye heard tell how the Finians were sent down into Hell because they were powerful strong haythens in their day: but may be ye never heard that God
40 himself put a circle of smooth green grass all round and about the place for them, becaze ye see he admired the sperrit that was in them: and on that smooth green grass they rush in their chariots for ever and ever, makin' the scraws fly with the hoofs o' the horses, and Oscar goes before them with a flail and drives the deamons
45 from their road. Well, their way is my way, for whatever men do agin me, and wherever I am, I get the best out of things, whether they be most like Hell or Heaven; and now that Father Gillen is turnin' the neighbours on me, I am goin' to meet them fair and square. They say, ye know, that I got me songs on the Rath of
50 Cruchan. Well, now I am goin' to make them say I get them straight from the Ould Boy himsel', and when they say it I will laugh, and laughter will be like smooth green grass before me and behind.'

'You were ever a wild fellow and a great rhymer, but how are ye goin' to pay for the book?'
55 'The Fairy-Man of Shronehill promised me two shillin' for the book and I'll give you one shillin' when he pays me and sixpence down.'

'Ye must give me the other sixpence too, for the book is long in the family. Me poor ould father took it out of the French brigan-
60 tine, *The Mother o' Misery.*'

'The *Mère de Miséricorde;* I mind the wreck of her.'

'The fine man he was! He hung out a tarbar'l, and he wrecked her on the Arran Islands for the soap that was aboord.'

80 meet him and them and get the best out of things. They say, you
know, that I got my songs from the People of Dana, when I lay
asleep on the Grey Rath; and now I am going to say I got them
from the Great Dhoul himself, and show the Book for a proof, and
when they believe this, I will laugh loudly, and laughter will be
smooth green grass before me and behind.'

85 Having thought of this use for the Book, he was eager to begin,
and with but little of a leave-taking hurried away and walked the
long round to the Fearny Height in a fever of expectancy. He went
first to the village shebeen, and getting into talk with a potato=
digger's wife dropped a hint or two about the Grey Rath, and then

90 about even more dreadful marvels; and last of all he showed the
Book and told sleep-murdering stories of those who had owned it
before him; and then going to his own cabin sat all the evening by a
good turf fire whistling 'The Green Bunch of Rushes,' 'Yellow
Shawn,' 'The Fair White Calf,' and 'Is there Silk in your Wallet?' in

95 a quick succession, and smiling to himself, for he could hear outside a shuffling of feet, and knew that the neighbours were looking
at the Book where it lay, as if by chance, on the ledge of the small
square window.

Several nights passed over, and every night he heard the shuf-
100 fling of always more numerous feet, and his heart rose higher and
higher. As he went along the roads he noticed the people avoided
him; and when at last it was reported that he had been seen drunk
with the Faery man of the Great Spring he saw to his entire happiness that women crossed themselves when he passed. Having at-

105 tained the height of evil repute, he began to weary and hunger to
look at the Book and discover if it was as dreadful as men thought.
He had not touched it since he laid it on the window-ledge, for he
was mortally afraid of it, and now when he took courage he said
three *aves* as a preparation. Holding it close to the fire-light he read

110 the title, 'Grimoire of Pope Honorius,' and then dipping here and
there into the dog-latin read how to destroy your enemies in diverse fashions, and how to make any you would love you. Last of all
his eyes lit on a receipt for making spirits appear, by writing their
names on paper with the blood of a bat and encircling their names

115 with certain squares and triangles and many-pointed stars, drawn
also with the blood, and then burning the paper calling the names
aloud the while. He had often longed to see the Shee, and had really
spent half a night on the Grey Rath in great fear, but quite without
avail, and, now that a sight of them seemed really possible, he

120 began to tremble all over, and in all likelihood his fear had been

A few hours later O'Sullivan was sitting by a good turf fire in his
65   own cabin, whistling 'The Little Green Bench of Rushes,' and smiling softly to himself, for he could hear outside a sound of shuffling
feet, and he knew that the neighbours were looking at the Devil's
Book where it lay, as if by chance, on the ledge of the small square
window. An hour before he had been to the village sheebeen, and
70   getting into chat with a potato-digger's wife had dropped a hint or
two about the Rath of Cruchan, and then about even more dreadful horrors; and last of all he had shown the Book, and told sleep=
murdering stories about the adventures of those who had owned it
before him. Several nights passed over, and every night he sat there
75   whistling now 'Stoca an Varoga,' 'The Fair White Calf,' 'Shawn
Bui,' 'Is There Silk in Your Wallet,' and many another old air, and
listening the while to ever more numerous footsteps without. As he
went along the roads in the day-light he noticed that people
avoided him, and when at last it was reported that he had been seen
80   drunk with the Fairy-Man of Shronehill he saw to his entire happiness that women crossed themselves when he passed. He had now
attained the very height of evil repute, and was beginning to get
weary and to long to look into the Book and see if it were as
dreadful as men thought. He had not touched it since he laid it on
85   the window ledge, for he was afraid of it, and now, when at last he
had taken courage, he said three *Aves* as a preparation. Holding it
close to the fire-light he read the title *Gringoire of Pope Honorius* and
then, dipping here and there into the dog-latin he read how to
destroy your enemies in divers sudden fashions, and how to make
90   any you would love you. Last of all, his eyes lit on a receipt for
making the spirits appear by writing certain words with the blood
of a bat. Now, he had more than once longed to see the spirits, and
had really spent half a night on the Rath of Cruchan, in great fear
and trembling, but quite without avail. And while he was thinking
95   over this receipt, it happened, by I know not what contrivance of

more than his curiosity but for something that redoubled the temptation. A bat fluttered in through the half-closed door, and beat itself against the white-washed canvas under the thatch and the rafters. Moved by a sudden impulse he took the handle of a hoe
125 from a corner and struck at the bat until it fell with a broken wing at his feet. He struck it again, and killed it, and then wrote the first name that came into his head, Cleena of the Wave, the name of the queen of the Southern fairies, on a page torn out of a book, from which he had taught English in his hedge-school, and called 'The
130 Lives of Celebrated Rogues and Rapparees.' Then remembering an old poem, that called Cleena a power of the air, he traced round her name a certain many-angled star, which the Book told him to use when invoking a power of the air, and held the paper in the flame of the turf until it was burnt, calling out 'Cleena! Cleena!
135 Cleena!' The paper had not all fallen into ashes before it seemed to him that the room was sinking away, and an inexplicable silence as of the last sleep creeping over everything. Then suddenly he felt rather than saw, and more as an intellectual presence than as a substantial form, a tall woman, dressed in saffron, like the women
140 of ancient Ireland, who stood a little above the floor, her dark hair falling from under a silver fillet. Then from the shadow of her hair shone eyes of a faint blue, very clear and soft, giving to her whole being a look of unearthly mildness, as though she had never known trouble nor met with any affront. She seemed waiting for Hanra-
145 han to speak, but his fear and his reverence alike kept him silent for very long; at last, feeling that he must ask her some question to justify so daring an invocation, he asked whether Angus the master of love still lived, and whether the three birds he made out of his kisses sang as sweetly as of old? Her lips moved, but he could not
150 hear anything, although he strained to hear, except a faint murmur, for she seemed to be close to him, and yet at a great distance. Finding his question of no avail he sank into a rapturous silence, gazing upon her; and was still gazing when the greyness of the dawn began to gleam through the small window-panes. The
155 woman appeared to see the greyness, and her dæmonic patience, which seemed well nigh as nature's own, gave way, and she faded with the night.

All the next day Owen longed for the night, and when the night came he wrote the word anew and burnt the paper, calling for
160 Cleena of the Wave; and the woman came again, but so much more visibly that he saw the silk stitches in the border of little embroi-

the dim powers, that a bat fluttered in through the half-closed door, and beat itself against the white-washed canvas that hid the thatch and the rafters. He struck it down with the shovel and killed it, and wrote the names on the back of a reading-book used by him 100 in his hedge-school, and called *The Lives of Celebrated Rogues and Rapparees.* Then he cried out that he wished to see Cleona of Ton Cleona, the Queen of the Munster Sheogues, for there was a great fear on him lest, if he did not ask for a particular spirit, the Devil might come himself. He had no sooner called out the name Cleona 105 than the room grew slightly darker, and he felt, rather than saw, a tall woman, dressed in saffron like the women of ancient Ireland, standing in the opposite corner.

From under the shadow of her hair shone eyes burning with a faint blue lustre, very clear and soft, giving to her whole being a 110 look of unearthly mildness, as though she had never known trouble nor met with any obstacle. O'Sullivan asked her if Fintain the Salmon God still lived, and whether, if he did, he had not grown even wiser than he was in the time of Fionr McComhil, for he felt that he must ask something. Her lips moved, but he could not hear any 115 sound, although he strained to hear. She seemed to be quite close to him, and yet at an infinite distance. Finding it useless to try and talk to this beautiful phantom, he sank into a very rapturous silence, gazing upon her. He sat gazing until the first greyness of the dawn began to gleam through the small window-panes. The figure 120 appeared to see the grey, and her demoniac patience, which had seemed well-nigh as Nature's own, gave way, and she faded with the night.

The next day Owen could do nothing but dream of the vision. Perhaps, he thought, if he could only please the Sheogues who 125 obeyed her, she also would be pleased, and would come again when he called her, and perhaps find a way to speak with him. Accordingly, he got another pan and filled it with milk, and put it, with a griddle-cake, under the haunted thorn-tree on the hill above his cabin. All day he longed for night, and when night came he wrote 130 the words anew, and the Lady of the Shee came again, but so much more visibly and clearly that he saw the hem on the saffron robe.

dered roses that went round and about the edge of her robe; and when without waiting for any question her lips began to move he could distinguish a sentence here and there in the midst of the
165 sound as of the rippling of distant waters. She was trying to answer his question, and he could hear many words which seemed to be telling of the high and merry notes and of the low and sobbing notes of the birds of love. The next evening at twilight he wandered along the edge of a coppice with a long cudgel until he had
170 knocked down and killed another bat, and that night Cleena was even more visible and audible, and he listened to many miraculous things concerning the meaning of the notes and how they rose beyond the highest ramparts of heaven, and sank more low than the desolate land where Orchil drives the iron-horned and iron=
175 hoofed deer; and all the while Owen was greatly perturbed at having put so great a lady to so great a trouble, for a thing that mattered to no man.

About a week passed over in this way. At last one day he was so absorbed that the cattle he was minding broke into a barley-field,
180 and when he had gathered them together it was far past his usual hour for breaking off work, and he was very tired; and his nerves, already shaken by his trouble and by his drunkenness, made him start at every sound. When he reached his cabin he threw himself into his chair, and fell into a broken sleep, to be presently awak-
185 ened by hearing some one moving about the room. When the dream had fallen from his eyes he saw a beautiful woman in a pale saffron dress looking at her own foot-mark in the ashes; and at the sight, the memory of all the trouble women had brought upon him passed over his mind, and he cried out, 'Woman, what do you want
190 here?'

She turned toward him a face so full of the tender substance of mortality, and smiled upon him with lips so full of red mortal blood that he did not recognize the immortal of his dreams; and she said to him in a caressing voice: 'You have always loved me better than
195 your own soul, and you have sought for me everywhere and in everything, though without knowing what you sought, and now I have come to you and taken on mortality that I may share your sorrow.' He saw that she was indeed Cleena of the Wave, but so changed that all the trouble he had ever had from women, and all
200 his anger against them were between him and her; and standing up hurriedly he cried: 'Woman, begone out of this. I have had enough of women. I am weary of women. I am weary of life.'

135

140

She moved her lips as if to speak, and without waiting for any question, and now he could hear a faint sound like a distant ripple of water, and even distinguish a word here and there. She was trying to answer his question of the preceding night, and he could hear the name of Fintain the Salmon God more than once. Every evening now he put the milk and the griddle-cake under the thorn, and every night he called Cleona: and every time he called her she grew more visible, and her words were more distinct. He began to hear whole sentences about Fintain, and grew quite ashamed of himself for having given so great a lady so much trouble about a thing that mattered to nobody.

145

150

About a week passed over in this way. At last one day he was so absorbed that the cattle he was minding broke into a barley field, and when he had gathered them together again, it was far past his usual hour for breaking off work, and he was very tired. He put the milk and the griddle-cake under the thorn-tree, and threw himself into his chair, and fell asleep. And presently he was aroused by a touch upon his forehead, and by a soft voice saying: 'Feel, my touch is warm; and look, there is a weight on my feet.' And he opened his eyes, and Cleona was looking at her own foot-marks in the ashes.

155

'Look at me,' she went on; 'I have a mortal body like your own. I saw the sorrowful dhrames o' the world dhriftin' above it, like a say as it slept in the night, and I skimmed the foam o' them with a noggin, and made mesel' a body, and it was love for your love o' me that made me do it, Owen.'

160

He started up and cried out, everything turning round about him, fierce and sudden anger in his breast. 'Had I not sorrow and trouble enough along wid ye?' he said. 'Did I not lose three schools wid ye? I tell you that it was not you, but the Fairy Woman that I loved. She had no sorrows, she had not had to foight wid people, she would not grow ould and git grey hairs like these that are comin' on my head. O, I have lost the Woman o' the Shee!'

165

'Do not drive me away' she said, clinging to his knees and sobbing. 'I have loved ye ever since I saw ye lyin on the Rath of Cruchan and saw ye turnin' from side to side, for the fire in yer heart would not let ye rest. I love ye, for ye are fierce and passionate, now good and now bad, and not free and dim and wave-like as are the Sheogues. I love ye as Eve loved the Serpent.'

170

'I hate ye!' he cried. 'I hate ye—for I hate everybody, and I hate the world, and I want to be out o' it.'

She came over to him, and laying her hand upon his shoulder, said in a half whisper: 'I will surround you with peace, and I will
205 make your days calm, and I will grow old by your side. Do you not see I have always loved you?' and as she spoke her voice was broken with tears. 'I have loved you from the night I saw you lying on the Grey Rath, and saw you turning from side to side, for the fire in your heart would not let you rest. I love you, for you are fierce and
210 passionate, and good and bad, and not dim and wave-like as are the people of the Shee. It was I who put a thought of the Devil's Book into your head, and it was I who drove the bat through the window; and now I will grow old by your side, my beloved.' Her importunity had made him angry, and he flung her from him, crying: 'It was
215 not you I loved, but the woman of the Shee,' and strode towards the door. But now she too was angry, and he heard her voice, musical even in anger, and her words staid long in his ears: 'Owen Hanrahan the Red, you have looked so often upon the dust that when the Rose has blossomed there you think it but a pinch of coloured dust;
220 but now I lay upon you a curse, and you shall see the Rose everywhere, in the noggin, in woman's eye, in drifting phantoms, and seek to come to it in vain; it shall waken a fire in your heart, and in your feet, and in your hands. A sorrow of all sorrows is upon you, Owen Hanrahan the Red.'
225 It was now almost dawn, and a faint green was touching the eastern sky, and as he looked at it he trembled as though it burnt in his own heart.

It was near midnight before he returned: a frightful storm was blowing, and he being very drunk, made way against it with great
230 difficulty, falling many times. He felt about for the door, but it was gone. The door-posts were gone too. The whole cabin was gone, and the fragments lay about the field where it had stood, and a whirlwind was driving bunches of the thatch up into the air; and it seemed to him that faint, shrill voices were talking angrily in the
235 whirlwind, and that if he were sober he would know what they were saying. He looked about him in a dazed way, and saw the Book lying among the fragments of the cabin and close to the still burning embers. He took the Book up and thrust it into his pocket. The next day he sold it to the Faery man of the Great Spring; and by
240 telling him all that had happened through its possession, and by representing the great fame it would bring a Faery man, and how the people whose butter was taken by witches would certainly employ no one but him to charm the butter home again, got a three months' old pig in return. He exchanged the pig for the Brew of

'Do not drive me away, Owen: becaze o' ye I left all my own people weepin' for me. Owen, I have always been good to yer family, and did me best to keep the good luck among ye. And ye
175 were the hard family to help and I done it, Owen O'Sullivan.'

'Begone from me!' he cried, and strode out into the darkness.

It was almost dawn, and a faint citron green was touching the eastern sky when he came again, this time very drunk, to the door of his cabin. He felt about for the door but it was gone. The door=
180 posts were gone too. The whole cabin was gone, and the fragments lay about the field where it had stood, and a whirlwind, such as the peasants ever associated with the Fairies, was driving remnants of the thatch up into the air. Faint but shrill voices were chanting in the whirlwind, and these were the words they chanted: 'Sorrow be
185 upon those who change the sowls that are in them to please another, for they shall lose the heart they would win and shall have little joy of the change that is over them.' O'Sullivan the Red looked about him in a dazed way. The Book was lying among the pieces of his cabin close to a still burning ember of the fire. He took the Book
190 up, and thrust it into his pocket.

The next day he sold the Book to the Fairy-Man of Shronehill: and by telling all that had happened to him through the possession of it, and by representing the fame such a book would bring to a Fairy-Man, and how the people whose butter was taken away by
195 witches would certainly employ no one but the owner of this book to charm it back again, he succeeded in getting a bougeen for it as

245 the Little Pot because a great thirst had come upon him, and drunkenness seemed to promise things he had never dreamed of before. The following Sunday the priest denounced him from the altar, and declared that his house had been thrown down by the wrath of God, and not by the Shee as the foolish supposed. Late at
250 night, a number of men searched for him, and found him lying very drunk beside his roofless hearth; and having beaten him soundly and sprinkled him with holy water, they put him into a cart and dropped him over the border of the next county.

well as the two shillings. He exchanged the bougeen for poteen. The following Sunday the priest denounced him from the altar and declared that his house had been thrown down by the wrath of God
200 and not by the Sheogues, as the foolish supposed. Late at night a number of men who had listened to the sermon searched for him, and found him lying very drunk beside his roofless hearth. And having beaten him soundly and sprinkled him with holy water, they put him into a cart and dropped him over the boundary of the next
205 county.

W.B. Yeats.

Note.—O'Sullivan the Red was really a noted peasant-poet of the last century. His character was much as I have described it. The Gaelic poets were often thought to have a Lianaan Shee or Fairy-mistress. Cleona of Ton Cleona is the Queen of the Munster Fairies.

THE TWISTING OF THE ROPE
AND HANRAHAN THE RED

    Hanrahan having thought over his quarrel with the priest and his angry neighbours, decided that vengeance was not in his power, and resolved to begone westward, for Gaelic Ireland was still alive, and the Gaelic poets were still honoured in the West. He cut a
5   cudgel out of the hedge and journeyed on and on, doing a day's work here and singing a song for his lodging there; and as the English tongue and English manners died behind him, he became a new man: for was he not the last of that mighty line of poets which came down unbroken from Sancan Torpeist (whom the Great Cat
10   well-nigh ate), and mightier Oisin, whose heart knew unappeased three hundred years of dæmonic love? There is a moment at twilight in which all men look handsome, all women beautiful; and day by day as he wandered slowly and aimlessly he passed deeper and deeper into that Celtic twilight, in which heaven and earth so
15   mingle that each seems to have taken upon itself some shadow of the other's beauty. It filled his soul with a desire for he knew not what, it possessed his body with a thirst for unimagined experiences. He bathed at midnight under that round hill where (forgetful of the days when men lifted his eyelids, powerless with age, that
20   his terrible glance might fall upon the Danaan swordsmen and turn them into stone) sleeps Balor of the Evil Eye; and as he swam through the smooth sea he laughed and sang up at the drifting clouds until they seemed but vague passions drifting about his

Printings: *The National Observer*, December 24, 1892; 1897.
Text from 1897; all variants from NO.
Spellings and changes of name: Hanrahan 1897; O'Sullivan NO. Margaret Brien 1897; Margaret O'Brien NO.
Title: THE TWISTING OF THE ROPE
2 *neighbours decided* . . .
3 *to* betake himself into the extreme west, for there *Gaelic* . . .
3-4 *still* upon the earth and the glory of the Gaelic poets was little faded. *He* . . .
4 *cut* him *a* . . .
6-7 *there. And as the* imperfect English of the Munster peasants gave place to the perfect Gaelic of them of Connaught, *he* . . .
11-12 *at* gloaming *in* . . .
14 *that* great *Celtic* . . .
14 *twilight,* that shadowy sunset of the Gaelic world, *in* . . .
15 *each* one *seems* . . .
18-19 *where, forgetful* . . .
21 *stone, sleeps* . . .
22-23 *at the* feather-soft and quietly floating *clouds* . . .
23 *seemed* loves and affections *drifting* . . .

heart; and he longed to feel, as they did, the silvery arrows of the
25 stars shoot through him. He spent a night in the cave where Grania
found a little peace, before the boar slew Dermot, and the fascination of ancient white-haired Finn fell upon him as it had fallen
upon her; and, as he lay there, the immense shadows seemed to be
taking him to themselves, disembodying him away into the dim life
30 of the Powers that have never lived in mortal bodies. All night they
passed through his dreams crowned with rubies, and having roses
in their hands; and in the morning he awoke, a rough-clad peasant,
shivering on the earthen floor.

At last he began to long for the companionship of some human
35 being, and above all for the companionship of some woman. He
knocked one night at the door of a whitewashed farmhouse,
flanked with elder bushes, and asked food and shelter from the big
red-faced woman who opened the door.

'My name is Hanrahan, and men call me "the Red" that I may be
40 known from that ignorant rhymer whom they have named "the
Gaelic," and I have written "Yellow Shawn" and many another
song, known wherever the voice of the Gael finds any to listen; and
I ask you to give me a plate of meat and a bed.'

'Happy are the stones of my house, and happy the yellow thatch
45 upon it, to know that Owen Hanrahan shall sit by the chimney
corner. But why have you come out of your own country to eat
your bread among foreigners?'

'There is a devil in the soles of my feet,' replied the poet as he
bent his head under the lintel. He entered singing in a low voice to
50 himself:

> I never have seen Maid Quiet,
> Nodding her russet hood,

---

24 *heart and . . .*
26–28 *and* upon him there fell the fascination of ancient white-haired Fion; *and . . .*
29 *themselves,* unhumanising *him . . .*
34–35 *last* a longing for human companionship fell upon him, and the longing came to him in the old fatal form he had so often known. *He . . .*
36 *a* long *white-washed . . .*
36 *whitewashed* 1897; *white-washed* NO.
36 *farmhouse* 1897; *farm house* NO.
38–39 *red-faced* farmer's wife who answered his summons. They spoke together in Gaelic. ¶'*My . . .*
39 *me the Red that . . .*
41 *written Shawn Bui and . . .* ['*Shawn Bui*' italic in NO]
42–43 *listen. Give me . . .**
51 *maid . . .*

The Secret Rose

For the winds that awakened the stars
Are blowing through my blood.
I never have seen Maid Quiet,
Nodding alone and apart,
For the words that called up the lightning
Are calling through my heart.

55

He sang his song through, and reached the middle of the room,
60 before he said the usual 'God save all here,' and heard the answering 'God save you kindly,' murmured by many voices. There were
faces all round him, and a fiddler was beginning to play in the
corner. He looked round, and knew by the primroses strewn upon
the threshold that it was May Eve, and that the birth of summer was
65 being awaited with dancing and music. His eyes strayed from the
primroses to a soft dreamy-looking young girl who sat by the fire.
Her great eyes met his, and she blushed. He sat down beside her,
and, before the whisper that he was Hanrahan the Red had gone
the round of the room, he had begun the subtle flattery of his deep
70 musical Gaelic. And before the dancers had tired the fiddler into a
momentary pause and a draught from the earthen jug at his elbow,
he had compared her beauty to the beauty of white Deirdre; and
told her of the dreams that led the feet of Adene into the dim
kingdom of the Shee; and made her feel that she also, because she
75 knew, while he spoke, a joy that was kneaded up with melancholy,
was of the lineage of the king's daughters of old, and the ungainly
dancers about her were shadows haunting the pathway of her
banishment. Before the fiddler had paused again, and again set his
lips to the jug, the big red-faced woman had begun to watch her
80 daughter; and all that evening she watched; and still those two

---

53–54 *awakened the* star, / *Are* ...
55 *maid* ...
61 *kindly' murmured* ...
62 *was* striking up *in* ...
65 *with* dance and string. *His* ...
67–68 *beside her and* ...
69 *room* had began *the* ...
71 *a* deep *draught* ...
73 *of* those *dreams* ...
75–76 *knew* when he spoke of melancholy and of joy in flattering unison, *was* ...
76 *the* rank and *lineage* ...
76 *old and* ...
78 *and set* ...*
79 *red-faced* peasant *had* ...
80 *daughter.* The evening passed; and still *she* ...

200

talked with their heads together, heedless of dance and fiddle; and
still the girl's blushes came and went like a stormy sunset.

Towards midnight a great bush was dragged out into the middle
of the road; and lighted by a flint and steel, for to have carried fire
85   from the hearth would have given the evil spirits power, despite the
strewn primroses, over all under that roof. The bush blazed up,
and the revellers began a slow procession about it, after one who
carried a hoop wreathed with quicken leaves and marsh-marigolds,
and containing two little balls; covered the one with gold and the
90   other with silver paper, to represent the sun and the moon. They
moved with slow steps from left to right, chanting a Gaelic song the
while. Hanrahan and the young girl stood in the door, too wrapped
up in each other to join in the dance. 'The sun and the moon,' he
was saying, 'they are man and woman. They are my soul and yours.
95   They go always through the heavens on and on, wrapped up in
each other. God made them for each other. He made sun and
moon, He made my soul and yours before the beginning of the
world, and He made for them one long sweet dance of love.'

'They say you have been very wicked,' she replied.
100   'But that,' he made answer, 'was because I never met any one
good and pure like you.'

And while this world-old flattery was ringing in her ears, the
dance changed, and casting aside the hoop of marigold and quick-
en, the dancers swept about the fire from right to left with swift
105   serpentine motions, and the song grew louder and wilder.

'Look,' he cried, 'at the serpent dance, the dance made by the wise
Druids. Is it not like the winding and the wandering of passion? Do
you not hear passion cry deep down in your heart: "Away, away,
away, some whither, some whither, some whither?" I hear it always,

---

82   *like* the red rays of *a* . . .
84   *road, and lighted* . . .
84   *steel (for* . . .
86   *roof). The* . . .
88   *marsh-marigolds* 1897; *marsh marigolds* NO.
89   *two* globes—*covered* . . .
90   *paper—to* . . .
92–93   *too* much absorbed *in each* . . .
95   *and on,* absorbed *in* . . .
107–8   *Druids.* Ever wandering serpentine passion! Do ye *not* . . .
108   *hear* it *cry* . . .
108–9   *Away, away—away* . . .
109   *wither, some wither—some* . . .
109–10   *always—always* . . .

The Secret Rose

110   always. We will wander on and on, you and I. Do you not hear the
       song of the great white roads, calling, calling? We will listen to the
       cuckoo, we will see the salmon leap in the rivers, we will sleep under
       the green oak leaves.' And then he sang in a low voice these words
       from a Gaelic love-song:—'Death will never find us in the heart of
115   the wood.' He looked down into her face, and the shadows of the
       dancers now cast it into darkness and now let it brighten with the
       leaping light of the fire. 'And even if death find us, how will it
       matter? Even if the rains beat upon us, how will it matter? Even if
       the winds blow upon us, how will it matter? We shall have found
120   that for which the woods spread their tents of green, and the stars
       light their candles.' He leaned and kissed her forehead, and drew
       her closer to him.
           The farmer's wife had called her croney, Bridget Purcel, aside,
       and the two were in deep talk in the shadow of a haystack, inter-
125   rupting their talk to point to the two figures, when a rare and
       sudden brightening of the fire discovered them. 'Many is the girl's
       heart he has made sore,' she was saying; 'many is the girl's mind he
       has darkened with bitter memories. Ay, many is the girl's life he has
       filled with a light of scornful faces. Many is the girl he has drawn
130   away from her prayers and her sewing and her sweeping, and from
       her place by the chimney corner with that sweet subtle tongue of
       his.'
           'That is true, Margaret Brien,' said the other: 'but if you were to
       drive a poet of the Gael out of your house there would be great
135   talk, and black would be the deed.'
           'O that I had never let him in.'
           'You might indeed have kept him from the house, for one's
       house is one's own; and you may still do this: get him out through
       the door by mother-wit, and shut the door and shoot the bolt. In
140   old days a poet's curse could wither the corn in the earth and make

---

110   and on—you and ...
111   roads—calling, calling ...
114   from the old Gaelic ...
118   matter! Even if the ...
120   their tent of ...
123   Bridget Purcee, aside ...
125   their discourse to point to ...
126   fire revealed them ...
132-33   his.' ¶'Ay, Margaret O'Brien,' said ...
133-36   but great would be the talk, and black would be the deed, if you were to drive a
poet of the Gael out of your house.' ¶'Would that ...
136-37   in!' ¶'Ay, you might ...
138   and this still you may do. Get him ...

202

the milk dry in the udders of the cows; but if you keep to your rights and do no wrong, it may pass you by without hurting. Seven years it must needs hang in the air; but if you be charitable to the poor, and pay the priest his dues, it will pass into the earth and the
145 sea, and melt away, or but fall upon himself when the eighth year comes.'

'Tell me, Bridget, how I will get him from the door; for there is wisdom upon your tongue.'

'Gather up a great bundle of hay, and I will gather up another;
150 and I will tell you how, while the neighbours are getting home to their beds: for they are going now that the dawn is mingling with the glow of the fire.'

In a little while Margaret Brien returned to the house and found it empty except for Hanrahan the Red and the young girl, who sat
155 by the fire talking in whispers. She carried a great bundle of hay under each arm. She laid one down near the door and then spoke: 'Owen Hanrahan, will you help me make these bundles of hay into a rope, for a breath of wind has blown the haystack down, and I would put it to rights before my husband comes home from the
160 fair?'

'Ay, gladly,' said Hanrahan, going over to the bundle by the door and taking out a wisp of hay. When he had twisted it out to about a foot in length, he put one end into the hands of Margaret Brien, and the twisting of the rope began. They kept adding to it from the
165 bundles of hay, and Margaret Brien gradually edged round the while until Hanrahan's back was to the door. The rope grew longer and longer, until at last the poet's feet were upon the threshold; and it grew longer and longer until he was out on the road. Margaret Brien waited until he was standing by the embers of the bush,
170 and then, with a sudden run, shut-to the door and bolted it.

'May the ravens and the crows and the hawks get your body, and the demons get your soul, and may your bed be made for all eter-

---

147-48   *door: for* wisdom is *upon . . .*
150   *how while . . .*
151   *for* see *they . . .*
160-61   *fair* at Boyle.' ¶*'Ay . . .*
162   *wisp.* When . . .*
164   *They* added *to . . .*
164-65   *from* their *bundles . . .*
165-66   *round until . . .**
168   *and* longer and longer still it grew, *until . . .*
168-69   *road.* But *Margaret . . .*
169   *standing* close *by . . .*

nity upon the red hearth-stone of hell!' he cried, and beat upon the door.

175   'It is well for us this night,' said Margaret Brien to her daughter, 'that the primroses are strewn upon the threshold and the quicken bough is woven into the thatch!' Presently the beating ceased, and she heard Hanrahan's feet go rapidly along the road.

He went down towards the sea, and as he went his anger gave
180   way to a profound melancholy. Innumerable thoughts and feelings began to eddy and whirl about in him. He stopped at the sea-shore, and, sitting down on a big stone, began swaying his right arm and singing slowly to himself. He was seeking comfort, where he had so often found it, in verse and in music; for like many of the Gaelic
185   poets, he was scarce better known as a maker of verse than as a maker of music. He was making the verse and the music which are called 'The Twisting of the Rope,' and as he made them his dreams deepened and changed until he was singing about the twisting of the Rope of Human Sorrows. Grey forms, half seen, half felt,
190   seemed to gather about him and to walk upon the sea. And among them Cleena of the Wave passed by, no longer marred by a human body, but laughing and mocking under a crown of rubies. Then it seemed as if the Rope of Human Sorrows changed in his dreams into a great serpent, coiling about him and taking him always more
195   closely in its folds till it filled the whole earth and the heavens, and the stars were the glistening of its scales. He stood up and staggered

---

173   *hell!'* Thus cried O'Sullivan the Red, while he *beat* . . .
174-75   *door.* ¶'Well is it *for* . . .
183   *comfort (where* . . .
184   *it) in* song *and* . . .
184   *music—for, like* . . .
185-86   *as* poet than as composer. *He* . . .
186-87   *making the* song which is called *The Twisting of the Rope, and* . . . ['*The Twisting of the Rope*' italic in NO]
187   *made* it *his* . . .
189   *rope* . . .
189   *human sorrows* . . .
191   *them* passed Cleona of the Wave, *no* . . .
191   *marred by* the soilure of *a* . . .
192   *of* ruby. *Then* . . .
193   *as* though *the* . . .
193   *rope* . . .
193   *human sorrows* . . .
194   *a* vast *serpent coiling* . . .
194   *taking him* ever *more* . . .
195   *folds; till* . . .
196   *stars* became *the* . . .

along the edge of the sea; and now he imagined the grey forms to be flying round and round the coils. And behold! they were sing-ing, 'Sorrow be upon him who rejects the love of the daughters of
200   Dana, for he shall find no comfort in the love of the daughters of Eve. The fire has taken hold upon his heart. Cast him out, cast him out, cast him out.'

KATHLEEN THE DAUGHTER OF HOOLIHAN AND HANRAHAN THE RED

After the twisting of the rope at Margaret Brien's, Owen Hanra-han the Red journeyed northward, doing odd jobs for farmers and telling tales at wakes and weddings, and then south again into Leitrim and so back in the direction of the Town of the Shelly
5   River, through the Ridge of the Two Demons of the Air.

Between the Ridge of the Two Demons of the Air and the Lough of Swords, he overtook, to his surprise, one Margaret Rooney, a vagrant woman he had known in Munster in his youth. She had become notorious over the whole of her native barony, and had at
10   last been hunted out of the place by the priest. He knew her by her walk, by the colour of her eyes, and by a habit she had of brushing her hair back from time to time with her left hand. She had been

---

197   *now the* ...*
197   *forms* seemed *to* ...
199–200   *of the* spirits, *for* ...
200   *shall* seek in vain for *the love* ...
200–201   *of the* children of men. *The* ...
202   *him out.'* That was the song O'Sullivan heard them sing.
[In NO, the story is signed W. B. Yeats.]

Printings: *The National Observer,* August 4, 1894; 1897.
Text from 1897; all variants from NO.
Spellings and changes of name: Hanrahan 1897; O'Sullivan NO.
Title: KATHLEEN-NY-HOOLIHAN
1   *at* Mrs. O'Brien's *Owen* ...
3   *South* ...
4–7   *direction of* Sligo, through Drumahair and Drumease. ¶On the road between Drumease and Sligo and close to Colgagh Lough, *he* ...
9   *barony and* ...
10   *of* sight *by the* ...
10   *Priest* ...
11   *eyes and* ...
12–13   *been* in Drumahair, *she* ...

wandering about, she said, and selling herrings, and was now on
her way home to the corner of the Town of the Shelly River which
15 is called the Burrough, where she lived with her croney, Mary
Gillis, a woman of like character and almost similar history; and
would be right glad, she added, if he would set up house with them
and sing his sweet songs to the bodachs, blind men, beggars and
fiddlers of the Burrough. She had always a kind memory of him,
20 and Mary Gillis had one of his songs by heart, so that he need not
fear any but the best of treatment, and the bodachs, blind men,
beggars and fiddlers would carry his fame into the four corners of
the Province, and not forget to pay him for tales and poems with
tenpenny pieces.
25 He accepted her offer cheerfully enough, for he was tired of
wandering, and desired domestic peace and women to listen to the
tale of his troubles and to comfort him. As they went along together
under the great trees which shaded the footpath at Hazelwood he
told his many sorrows. She heard the story of the Book of the Great
30 Dhoul and of the woman of the Shee with many an awe-struck 'God
bless us!' and more than one pious crossing of herself, and comforted him for the misfortune at the twisting of the rope with a kiss
and an encircling arm.

It was twilight when they reached the Burrough, and Hanrahan
35 noticed that his middle-aged sweetheart looked in the dimness not
at all uncomely.

When Mary Gillis was told the name of her guest, she almost
wept at the thought of entertaining so famous a man.

Hanrahan settled down in his new abode with a great joy. Mar-
40 garet Rooney was almost forty and Mary Gillis little younger, but
they had both some dilapidated remnants of tolerably good looks,

---

13   *said, selling . . .**
13   *herrings and . . .*
14-15   *to the* Burrough of Sligo, *where . . .*
15   *her* crooney, Mary . . .
23   *Province and not . . .*
26   *wandering and desired . . .*
26   *and* a woman or two *to listen . . .*
28   *footpath* 1897; *foot-path* NO.
29-30   *story of the* Devil's book and *the woman . . .*
34   *Burrough and . . .*
37   *guest she . . .*
39-40   *Margaret* Mooney *was . . .*
41   *some* very *dilapidated . . .*
41-42   *looks and had . . .*

Kathleen the Daughter of Hoolihan and Hanrahan the Red

and had outlived jealousy and made good girdle-cakes and knew where the Brew of the Little Pot was to be had for next to nothing, and both were good-tempered in their cups. Helped by the un-
45 wonted peace and order of this kind of life, Hanrahan began making poems rapidly. He sometimes got through several in a day instead of spending a week over a few verses, and the poems, too, were better poems. The most of them were love-songs, but some were songs of penitence, afterwards included in 'Hanrahan's Ros-
50 ary,' a book which is famous among Gaelic scholars. Others again were poems disguising a passionate patriotism under the form of a love-song addressed to the Little Black Rose or Kathleen the Daughter of Hoolihan or some other personification of Ireland.
      Every evening the bodachs, beggars, blind men, and fiddlers
55 would gather together round the fire and listen with admiration to song or vehement recitation. Their tireless memories, unspoiled by print and paper, soon learnt off his songs and tales, and their tireless feet bore his fame to every wake, wedding, and pattern throughout Connaught. Never were his fortunes at so high a pitch.
60   Every one who saw him one November night, sitting on the edge of the great bed, with his shadow flickering behind him on the whitewashed wall and up to the thatched ceiling, singing a love= song to a score and a half of ragged peasants, and watched the ever mobile face and noticed the insistent energy of every gesture, re-
65 membered to his dying day that he had looked upon a king of the poets of the Gael and a ruler of the dreams of men.
      Suddenly he ceased to sing and his eyes became dim, as though he gazed upon distant things.
      Mary Gillis, who was pouring the Brew of the Little Pot into a

---

43   *where* excellent potheen *was* . . .
45   *life* O'Sullivan *began* . . .
46   *poems* at a great rate. *He* . . .
47   *of* lazily *spending* . . .
47-48   *the* quality of the work was higher too. The bulk *of* . . .
49-50   *in* that 'Pious Miscellany' of his which is now so well-known to *Gaelic* . . .
52-53   *to* Rosseen Dubh or Kathleen-Ny-Hoolihan *or* . . .
53   *other* of the personifications *of* . . .
56   *Their* admirable memories, undimmed *by* . . .
57   *tales and* . . .
58   *patern* . . .
59   *throughout* all *Connaught* . . .
61   *bed with* . . .
69   *pouring* some potheen *into* . . .
69-70   *a naggen upon* . . .*

The Secret Rose

70 noggin which stood upon a creepy-stool at his feet, ceased to pour,
and said: 'Are you thinking of leaving us?'
Margaret Rooney heard the words without seeing their cause,
and taking them too seriously, got up from her place by the hearth
and came over to him, her heart full of the fear of renewed pov-
75 erty, of weary tramps with a basket of herrings on her head, and of
the loss of so wonderful a companion and of the importance he
gave her house.
'You would not do that, my honey?' she said, catching him by the
hand.
80 'No,' he said, laying his hand upon her head. 'I am thinking of
Ireland and her sorrows.' Then he began to sing these words to a
wild and fitful air of his own making which rose and fell like the cry
of the wind.

O tufted reeds, bend low and low in pools on the Green Land,
85 Under the bitter Black Winds blowing out of the left hand!
Like tufted reeds our courage droops in a Black Wind and dies:
But we have hidden in our hearts the flame out of the eyes
Of Kathleen the Daughter of Hoolihan.

O tattered clouds of the world, call from the high Cairn of Maive,
90 And shake down thunder on the stones because the Red Winds rave!
Like tattered clouds of the world, passions call and our hearts beat:

---

70 *a* three-legged *stool at* . . .
71 *said, 'Are* . . .
76 *importance* that *he* . . .
82 *wild, fitful* . . .*
82 *own, which* . . .*
83–99 *wind* among the reeds:
Veering, fleeting, fickle, the winds of Knocknarea,
When in ragged vapour they mutter night and day,
Veering, fleeting, fickle, our loves and angers meet:
But we bend together and kiss the quiet feet
Of Kathleen-Ny-Hoolihan.

Weak and worn and weary the waves of Cummen Strand,
When the wind comes blowing across the hilly land;
Weak and worn and weary our courage droops and dies
But our hearts are lighted from the flame in the eyes
Of Kathleen-Ny-Hoolihan.

Dark and dull and earthy the stream of Drumahair
When the rain is pelting out of the wintry air;
Dark and dull and earthy our souls and bodies be:
But pure as a tall candle before the Trinity
Our Kathleen-Ny-Hoolihan.

¶*While* . . .

208

But we have all bent low and low, and kissed the quiet feet
    Of Kathleen the Daughter of Hoolihan.

O heavy swollen waters, brim the Fall of the Oak trees,
95   For the Grey Winds are blowing up, out of the clinging seas!
Like heavy swollen waters are our bodies and our blood:
But purer than a tall candle before the Blessed Rood
    Is Kathleen the Daughter of Hoolihan.

While he sang he became greatly moved, and a tear rolled down
100 his cheek, and Margaret Rooney put her face upon her hands and
wept too. Then a blind beggar by the fire shook his rags with a sob,
and after that every one wept.

THE CURSE OF HANRAHAN
THE RED

One morning in spring, Hanrahan the Red turned into the road
that leads from the Great Field to the mail coach road and so on to
the Townland of the Bridge.

Presently he began to sing, for his heart had been awakened by
5   the soft green grass at the roadside, by the far blue flame of the
Waters of the Speckled Bog, and by the glimmering of the clouds
overhead.

In a little while, however, a magpie flew across his path, and,
darting ahead of him, lit upon the wall of unmortared stone to his
10   left, and at this evil sight he ceased to sing. Again the magpie

---

102 *wept* and tossed about as does Shroon-a-Melea when the tide runs strong and the
wind blows high.
[In NO, the story is signed W. B. Yeats.]

Printings: *The National Observer*, September 29, 1894; 1897.
Text from 1897; all variants from NO.
Spellings and changes of name: Hanrahan 1897; O'Sullivan NO.
Title: THE CURSE OF O'SULLIVAN THE RED UPON OLD AGE
2 *from* Aghamore *to the* . . .
2–4 *on to* Balladrihid. ¶*Presently* . . .
5–6 *of* Lough Naminbrach *and* . . .
6–8 *glimmering* and gleaming of the great burnished *clouds over head.* ¶*In* . . .
7 *overhead* 1897; *over head* NO.
8 *path and* . . .

The Secret Rose

crossed the path and again alighted ahead of him, nor did it turn to its own affairs until it had a third time fluttered before his face, its white feathers shining in the sun.

'Ah,' muttered Hanrahan, 'they are going to work evil upon me
15 again,' and with these words his singing died, and his brows knit angrily for the first time since the beautiful bright weather had begun. By 'they' he meant the faeries, who had stirred up all manner of accidents to beset his path since the day when he refused the love of Cleena of the Wave.
20 There was a time when he would have faced their worst with a light heart, but now age was coming over him and clouding his mind with a love of peaceful indolence and the hope of a placid ending. He had changed greatly of late, and his red hair had faded to yellow and his figure stooped more than when he had made
25 merry with the women and beggars and fiddlers in the Burrough of Sligo. At length he stood still, for a sound of some one sobbing in the field to his right hand caught his quick ear. He had come to where a path led away over the fields to the cabin of a small farmer. He looked over the wall of unmortared stones and saw a young girl
30 with her face down in the long grass of the meadow, sobbing loudly. He could not see her face, for that was resting upon her hands, but her soft wavy hair and her young figure made him remember Bridget Purcell, Margaret Gillen, Maurya Connellan, Oona Curry, Celia Driscoll, and the other beautiful fragile women,
35 whose names he had woven into his verse.

'Colleen,' he said in a voice at once proud and gentle, as though he were a king talking to some good but ill-fated subject. 'Colleen,' he repeated, for the long grass had made her deaf. She looked up,

---

16   *beautiful* warm *weather* . . .
17   *fairies* . . .
19-20 *of Cleena of* TonCleena. ¶*Once he* . . .
20   *worst* endeavours *with* . . .
21   *light* of battle in his eyes, *but* . . .
21-22 *his* heart *with* . . .
23-24 *hair* was more tempered with white *and* . . .
24   *figure* more stooped *than* . . .
24-25 *when* we saw him making *merry* . . .
33   *Purcell,* Pastheen Gillen, Mary *Connellan* . . .
34   *Celea* . . .
34   *Driscoll and* . . .
34   *beautiful, fragile* . . .
35-36 *had* set in his imperishable song. ¶*'Colleen* . . .
38   *for* her sorrow and *the* . . .
38-39 *up and he recognised a* . . .

The Curse of Hanrahan the Red

and he recognized a pretty pink and white face he had passed more
40 than once on his way to and from the Townland of the Bridge.
'Colleen, there is trouble upon you, and ill would it become me to
go by and you weeping. I am Hanrahan the Red, and no mere
common man who cannot help when he pities, for I tend the school
of the Townland of the Bridge and know the Latin tongue, and
45 shall sit, after my death, upon a gold bench with the most mighty of
the singers of Eri listening to the beating of the heart of God. Great
have been my wrongs and my persecutions, but, Colleen, I can send
help after my pity!' The girl had sat up and was now looking
straight at him, her tears rolling down her cheeks the while.
50 'Owen Hanrahan,' she said, 'I know well how great have been
your wrongs and your persecutions, and how many have been the
enemies and evil chances she has wakened against you.' She leant
towards him, resting upon her hand, and her voice became tremulous with eagerness. 'You have had evil done you, and can pity those
55 that have had evil done them; and will you promise me to do what I
ask of you, Owen Hanrahan?'
'I promise,' he answered.
'My father and my mother and my brothers,' she went on, 'are
marrying me to old Paddy Doe because of the hundred acres he
60 rents under the Mountain, and I would have you put him into a
rhyme as you put old Peter Kilmartin in the days when you were
young; that sorrow may be over him, rising up and lying down.'
'I will put him into a little song that shall bring shame and sorrow
over him; but how many years has he, for I would put them into the
65 song?'
'O, he has years upon years—he is as old as you are, Owen Hanrahan.'
'As old as me!' said Hanrahan, in a broken voice. 'There are
twenty years between him and me if there is a day. An evil hour has

---

40–41 *from* Balladrihid. 'Colleen, the trouble is *upon* . . .
41 *you and* . . .
43–44 *the School of* Balladrihid *and know* . . .
44 *tongue and* . . .
55 *have evil* . . .*
55 *me* now that you will do the thing *I* . . .
56 *ask you* . . .*
59 *old* Paudeen Hart *because* . . .
60 *rents* in Bally Sumaghan, *and* . . .
61 *Peter* Bruin *in* . . .
62 *young, that* . . .

70 come for Owen Hanrahan when a colleen with a cheek like the blossom of the May thinks him an old man. Colleen, colleen, an arrow
is in my heart!' He turned away, and went slowly towards the road
with eyes fixed on the ground; and she sat in the meadow grass
looking after him bewildered. But he went towards the Townland
75 of the Bridge with his eyes on the white dust, stooping and seeming
an old man indeed. He went about three-quarters of a mile, and
then, looking up saw a great spotted eagle sailing slowly towards
the Hill of Awley, and standing still, he cried out: 'You, too, eagle
of the Hill of Awley, are old, and your wings are full of gaps. I will
80 put you and your ancient comrades, the pike of Dargan Lake, and
the yew of the Steep Place of the Strangers, into my rhyme that you
may be accursed for ever!'
  To the left of the road was a bush covered with May blossoms,
and a little gust of wind blew the white petals over his coat.
85 'May blossoms!' he said, brushing a number of them into the
hollow of one hand, 'you never know age because you die away in
beauty; and I will put you into my rhyme, and give you a blessing!'
He sat down under the bush, and began making his rhyme, crooning it to himself, the May blossoms falling over him the while. At
90 last he had finished, and this is the rhyme that he made:—

> The poet, Owen Hanrahan, under a bush of May
> Calls down a curse on his own head, because it withers grey;
> Then on the speckled eagle cock that is on Awley's Hill,
> Because it is the oldest thing that knows of cark and ill;
95 > And on the yew that has been green from the times out of mind,
> By the Steep Place of the Strangers, and the Gap of the Wind;
> And on the great grey pike that broods in Castle Dargan Lake,

---

73 *ground. She sat . . .**
74 *him* in a bewildered way. *But . . .*
74-75 *towards* Balladrihid *with . . .*
75 *stooping* greatly *and . . .*
77 *up, saw . . .*
77-78 *towards* Bally Gawley and the surrounding hills, *and . . .*
78 *still,* burst out with, '*You . . .*
78-79 *eagle* of Bally Gawley, *are old . . .*
81 *the* ash-tree of Markree Wood, *into . . .*
87 *and* you will I put *into . . .*
91 *poet,* Red O'Sullivan, *under . . .*
93 *cock* of Bally Gawley *Hill . . .*
94 *of* care *and . . .*
95-97 *on the* leaning, wrinkling ash, that many an age hath stood / Hollow and knarled
and broken to North of Markree Wood; / *And . . .*
97 *that* dwells *in . . .*

The Curse of Hanrahan the Red

Having in his long body a many a pain and ache;
Then curses he old Paddy Bruen of the Well of Bride
100 Because no hair is on his head and drowsiness inside.
Then Paddy's neighbour, Peter Hart, and Michael Gill, his friend,
Because their wandering histories are never at an end.
And then old Shemus Cullinan, shepherd of the Green Lands,
Because he holds two crutches between his crooked hands;
105 Then calls a curse of threefold power upon old Paddy Doe,
Who plans to lay his withering head upon a breast of snow,
Who plans to wreck a singing voice and break a merry heart,
He calls a curse that shall be his until his breath depart;
And he calls down a blessing on the blossom of the May,
110 Because it comes in beauty, and in beauty blows away.

Having made his rhyme, he lighted his small black pipe and sat on under the bush, for the passion of the cursing bards was upon him, and he sought means of sending his curse over the country side. He knew it was fair day in the Town of the Shelly River, and that 115 traffickers must needs pass on their way thither. In a little while a boy came down the road driving a donkey with two creels of turf, and Hanrahan signalled to him to stop.

'Gossoon,' he said, 'I have made a curse upon old age and on the old men, and I would have it sung this day in the Town of the 120 Shelly River.'

'Give it to me, Hanrahan,' said the boy, 'and I will give it to any you will.'

Hanrahan then repeated the rhyme.

'Aye, I know old Michael Gill right well,' said the boy. 'Last St. 125 John's Eve we dropped a mouse down his chimney, but this is better than a mouse!'

99–100   *old* Paudeen Strange, herdsman of Tubber Bride, / *Because* . . .
101   *Then* Paudeen's *neighbour* . . .
101   *Hart and* . . .
102   *their* rambling *histories* . . .
103–4   *Cullinan,* cooper of Scanavin, / *Because* . . .
104–5   *crutches* in his fingers long and thin; / *Then* . . .
105   *of* Druid *power* . . .
105   *old* Paudeen *Doe* . . .
107–8   *heart,* / A threefold curse of Druid power, clinging till *breath* . . .
108–9   *depart;* / But O, *he* . . .
109   *calls a* . . .*
110   *beauty and* . . .
111   *made* the *rhyme* . . .
112–13   *him and* . . .
114   *in* Sligo *and* . . .
119–21   *in* Sligo.' ¶'*Give* . . .

Hanrahan made the boy say the rhyme over and over until he had it perfectly, and then bade him go to the Burrough and tell it to Margaret Rooney and Mary Gillis, and bid them sing it and make
130 the beggars and bodachs sing it, to the tune of 'The Green Bunch of Rushes.'

The boy then hurried upon his way, eager to make the most of his new importance, while Hanrahan knocked the ashes out of his pipe and shook the white petals from his coat and put a spray of the
135 blossom in his button-hole.

When Hanrahan arrived at the dilapidated barn at the Townland of the Bridge, where he taught Latin out of the Mass-book and English out of 'The Lives of Celebrated Rogues and Rapparees,' he had to collect his scholars from the neighbouring hills and valleys.
140 One party was quietly playing 'chanies,' as they called housekeeping with pieces of broken pottery, between two boulders on the sea-shore, and another 'leap-frog' upon the hill-top; and when they were at last together more than half the day had gone. He heard no lessons that day, but, taking the fragment of pink and white blos-
145 som from his button-hole, he laid it upon the desk in front of him.

'Children, you and the beautiful of this world, are like the May, and the wind comes, and you are blown away with it. Children, I have made a curse upon old age and upon the old men, and listen while I sing it to you.' He then sang it, and afterwards made them
150 write it out upon their slates, and sing it to him, and he let them go free for the day.

He slept well that night, and the next morning was at school betimes, and sat in the door smoking and watching his pupils arrive in little groups. They were all in but two or three, and he was
155 considering the place of the sun in the heavens to know whether it was time to begin, when he caught sight of a crowd coming up the boreen from the main road. Presently he noticed that it was a crowd of old men, and that the three who were in front were

---

129   *Margaret* Mooney *and Mary* . . .
129   *Gillis and bid* . . .
130-31   *Green* Floor *of* . . .
136-37   *barn at* Balladrihid, *where* . . .
138-39   *of The Lives of Celebrated Rogues and Rapparees,* he found *he had* . . . ['*The Lives of Celebrated Rogues and Rapparees*' italic in NO]
140   *party* were *quietly* . . .
142   *sea-shore* 1897; *seashore* NO.
142   *leap-frog* 1897; *leap frog* NO.
142   *hill-top* 1897; *hill top* NO.
150   *him, and let* . . .*
158   *the* four *who* . . .

indeed Paddy Bruen, Michael Gill, and Paddy Doe, and that all
160 carried short and heavy cudgels. At the same instant they caught
sight of him, and the cudgels began to wave hither and thither, and
the old feet to run.

He waited for no more, but made off up the hill behind the barn,
and by a great round home again. He paused at a point, where the
165 road turned a corner bringing his cabin in sight; and saw that
another party had surrounded his cabin, and were busy thrusting a
rake, with a wisp of burning straw upon it, into the thatch.

'Ah!' he cried, 'I have set Old Age and Time and Weariness and
Sickness against me, and must to my wandering again! O, Blessed
170 Queen of Heaven! protect me from the Eagle of the Hill of Awley,
the Yew Tree of the Steep Place of the Strangers, the Pike of Castle
Dargan Lake, and from their kindred in Eri!'

THE VISION OF HANRAHAN
THE RED

Hanrahan, after wandering from place to place, sleeping, now in
a barn, now under a hayrick, set out to cross the mountains between
the Strong Place of the Strangers and the Steep Place of the Strangers
with the thought of pushing on into North Leitrim, where, perhaps,
5 his love songs might be known and his satires unknown, and the
little square harp that hung from his shoulders a new delight. Dis-
covering, however, the deserted cabin of a shepherd, well sheltered
by a great rock, and by that yew-tree which men believed to have

---

159   *indeed* Paudeen Strange, Peter Hart, *Michael* ...
159   *and* Paudeen *Doe* ...
160   *short* heavy sticks, 'alpeens' as they are called. *At* ...
161   *the* alpeens *began* ...
164   *great* detour *home* ...
164   *point where* ...
165   *corner, bringing* ...
165–66   *and* it was well for him that he did, for *another* ...
170–71   *Eagle of* Bally Gawley Hill, the Ash Tree of Markree Wood, *the Pike* ...
[In NO, the story is signed W. B. Yeats.]

Printings: *The New Review*, April, 1896; 1897.
Text from 1897; all variants from NR.
Spellings and changes of name: Hanrahan 1897; O'Sullivan NR.
Title: THE VISION OF O'SULLIVAN THE RED
2–4   *cross* Copes Mountain, *with* ...
8–11   *rock, he* ...*

been planted there by a hermit, who was thrice the age of common
10 men, and which was not to die until it was thrice the age of the hermit,
he changed his purpose and set to work plaiting rushes into the
broken thatch and filling the lower half of the window, from which
the glass had been broken, with sods of grass. He had changed it the
more readily because Maive Lavell, a love of his youth and the dearest,
15 perhaps, of any, and who had come out of the South to seek him now
many years ago, lay buried in a little grass-grown cemetery at the
mountain foot; and his heart was heavy at the thought of putting
the whole bulk of the Steep Place of the Strangers and of the
Mountain of Gulben between him and her. He had stopped a while
20 at her grave before beginning to climb, but when twilight was falling, and his work for the day at an end, he took the narrow,
precipitous boreen trodden into brown mud by the donkeys of
generations of turf-cutters, and was soon sitting under the wild=
rose tree that was the only monument of so great passion and
25 beauty. He sat there full of thoughts and memories, amid the
dropping dew, and watched the stars coming out one by one, between the branches of the wild-rose tree, until gradually the old
passion, softened with a new pity and remorse born from the fading of his powers and from the loosening of his hold upon life,
30 began to fill his eyes with tears. His fingers began to play with the
wires of the little square harp and his lips to murmur as the mood
shaped itself into a song; and presently he sang to the now forgotten tune so full of fathomless regret, despite its uncouth name,
'The Herdsmen of the Children of Byrne':—

35   O Colleens, kneeling by your altar rails long hence,

---

11   *purpose, and* . . .
14   *Maiv* . . .
15   *any, who* . . .*
18–19   *bulk of* Bulben and Copes Mountain *between* . . .
20–21   *falling and* . . .
22   *borreen* . . .
22   *the* asses *of* . . .
23   *turf- / cutters* 1897; *turf cutters* NR.
29–30   *life,* had filled *his* . . .
31   *murmur, as* . . .
33   *tune, so* . . .
33   *regret despite* . . .
33–35   *name,* The Herdsmen of Roughley O'Byrne:— ¶*O* . . . ['*The Herdsmen of Roughley O'Byrne*' and '*O*' italic in *NR*]
35–42   [In NR, this poem is printed entirely in italics.]

When song I wove for my beloved hides the prayer,
And smoke from this dead heart drifts through the violet air
And covers away the smoke of myrrh and frankincense;
Bend down and pray for the great sin I wove in song,
40 Till Maurya of the wounded heart cry a sweet cry,
And call to my beloved and me: 'No longer fly
Amid the hovering, piteous, penitential throng.'

When the song was ended, he sat motionless awhile, and then put
up his hand and pulled a frail blossom that hung between three
45 white stars, and having kissed it tenderly wound its stalk among
the wires of his harp. He began to climb the hill again, but found
the journey so long and tiresome that he often sat down upon the
green ditch at the side of the boreen. In one of these rests he found
himself at the edge of a rath, or royalty as he called it, and went
50 over in his mind certain ancient poems that told of sinful lovers,
who were awakened by one another's love from the sleep of the
grave and to a shadowy life in faeryland, where they await the
Judgment banished from the face of God. He wondered if he and
his Maive would so wander and what their punishment might be,
55 and whether the demons would persecute them or wait until they
were judged. He went on with a deep sigh, and when he stopped
again it was to gather rushes for his bed, and with restless hands
that he might not think.
He spread the rushes in a corner of the cabin, and, because it was
60 still early, went on to the Steep Place of the Strangers, and going
down to the edge of the precipice, gazed into the valley and
touched the wires of his harp with aimless fingers. The valley was
full of a grey mist, spreading from mountain to mountain, that
seemed to his awed imagination like a crowd of huddled phantoms,
65 and the fancy made his heart beat with terror and delight. Presently, and only half understanding what he was doing, he began
picking the petals from the rose that still clung to the wires of his

---

42-43 *throng!'* *¶When* . . . ['*throng*' italic in NR]
45 *and, having* . . .
45 *tenderly, wound* . . .
48 *borreen* . . .
53 *Judgment, banished* . . .
54 *Maiv* . . .
54 *wander, and* . . .
55 *and if the* . . .
60 *to* Lug-na-Gall, *and* . . .
63 *mist* spread *from* . . .

harp, and watching them float into the abyss in a little fluttering troop.

70   Suddenly he heard a faint music, a music that had a greater compass of emotion, for it was now of an intolerable merriment, now of an intolerable sadness, than any made by human fingers, and his terror became delight, because he knew that the faeries were somewhere in the abyss. His eyes rested upon the little flutter-

75 ing troop of petals, and while he gazed they changed and began to look like a troop of men and women walking through the darkness and far off, who were yet half rose-petals, and then the twy-nature faded and they were indeed a long line of stately couples walking upon the vapour. Instead of going away from him they were com-

80 ing towards him, they were going past him, and their faces were full of a proud tenderness, and pale as with a quenchless desire of august and mournful things. Shadowy arms were stretched up out of the vapour as if to seize them, but in vain, for they passed in some inviolate peace. Before them and beyond them, but at a dis-

85 tance as though in reverence, were other forms, sinking and rising and plunging and flying, and by their disordered flight Hanrahan knew the once Divine Shee, and to them rose no shadowy arms, for they were of those who can neither sin nor obey. They all grew small in the distance, pacing and flying towards the white square door

90 which is in the side of the Mountain of Gulben. The vapour spread now before him like a deserted sea washing the mountains with fantastic waves, but, while he gazed upon it, it began to fill with a flowing, broken, imperfect life that was a part of itself, and arms and pale heads covered with tossing hair appeared in the greyness.

95 It rose higher and higher until it was level with the edge of the cliff,

---

71   *emotion— for . . .*
72   *sadness— than . . .*
75   *gazed, they . . .*
75   *changed, and . . .*
76   *women, walking . . .*
77   *rose- / petals; and . . .*
78   *faded, and . . .*
79   *him, they . . .*
81   *tenderness and . . .*
86   *flying; and . . .*
87   *devine . . .*
87   *Shee; and . . .*
90   *side* of **Bulben.** *The . . .*
91   *him, like . . .*
94   *grayness . . .*
95   *and higher, until . . .*

and then the shapes became more solid, and a new procession half lost in vapour, passed with uneven steps but very slowly, and in the midst of each shadow was a something glittering in the starlight. They came nearer and nearer, and Hanrahan saw that they also
100 were lovers, and that they had heart-shaped mirrors instead of hearts, and looked in each other's mirrors incessantly pondering upon their own faces. They passed, sinking downward as they passed, and other forms rose in their place, and these did not flit side by side, but followed one another with wild gestures.
105 Those that flew were women, with beautiful heads full of an exquisite life upon shadowy and bloodless bodies, and about them their long hair wavered and trembled as though it lived with some deadly life. A sudden upswelling of the vapour hid them, and then a light momentary wind, come from the mountain, blew them away
110 towards the north-west, and, as it did so, covered Hanrahan with a white wing of vapour.

He stood up trembling, and was about to turn from the abyss, when he saw two dark and half hidden forms standing in the air just beyond the verge, and one of them was looking out of dim,
115 appealing eyes. 'Speak to me,' it said at last in a woman's voice; 'it is five hundred years since any one, among men or among demons, has spoken to me.'

He shook with terror and was silent, and the voice began again: 'I will not harm you. Speak to me and bid me speak. No one has
120 listened to me for five hundred years.'

'Who are those who have passed by?' he said.

'Those that passed the first,' it answered, 'are the famous lovers of old time, Blanid and Deirdre, and Grania, and their dear friends, and a multitude less known, but not less beloved; and because they
125 sought in one another no blossom of mere youth, but a beauty coeval with the night and with the stars, the night and the stars hold them for ever from the unpeaceful and the perishing, despite the

---

96   *solid and . . .*
96   *procession, half . . .*
101   *incessantly, pondering . . .*
102   *faces. ¶They . . .*
104–5   *gestures. Those . . .*
105   *that* fled *were . . .*
105   *women with . . .*
105   *heads, full . . .*
106   *life, upon . . .*
114–15   *looking* from strangely *appealing . . .*
119   *me, and . . .*

battle and the bitterness their love wrought in the world. Those who came next, O man, who still breathe the sweet air, and have the mirrors in their hearts, are sung by no bards, because they sought only to triumph one over the other, and so to prove their strength and beauty, and fashioned out of this a kind of love. The women with shadowy bodies desired neither to triumph nor to love, but only to be loved, and there is no blood in their hearts or in their bodies until it flow through them from a kiss, and their life is but for a moment. All these are unhappy, but I am the unhappiest of all, for I am Dervadilla, and this is Dermond, and our sin brought the Norman into Ireland, and now none are punished as we are punished. We loved only the blossom of manhood and of womanhood in one another, the deciduous blossom of the dust and not the eternal beauty. When we died there was no inviolate world about us, the demons of the battles and bitterness we wrought pronounced our doom. We wander inseparable, but he who was my lover beholds me always as a dead body dropping in decay, and I know that I am so beheld. Ask more, ask more, for the years have poured their wisdom into my heart, and no one has listened to me for five hundred years.'

A great terror had fallen upon Hanrahan, and, lifting his arms above his head, he shrieked three times and the figure faded, and the cattle in the valley heard him and lifted their heads and lowed, and the birds in the woods on the edge of the Mountain of Gulben awoke out of their sleep and flew through the trembling leaves. But a little below the edge of the cliff the troop of petals still fluttered in the air, for the gateway of Eternity had opened and closed in a pulsation of the heart.

---

135 *kiss and* . . .
141 *died, there* . . .
142 *us: the demons* . . .
144 *me* ever *as* . . .
149 *times; and the* . . .
149 *faded* when he shrieked; *and* . . .
150 *him, and lifted* . . .
150-51 *lowed; and* . . .
151-52 *of* Bulben *awoke* . . .
152 *sleep, and* . . .
152-53 *But, a* . . .
153 *cliff, the* . . .
[In NR, the story is signed W. B. Yeats.]

THE DEATH OF HANRAHAN
THE RED

It came about gradually that Hanrahan ceased to stray from the
neighbourhood of the Steep Place of the Strangers, making even his
necessary journeys to the town for food seldomer and seldomer.
The little leather bag in which there was still some silver and copper
5   money, hung by the hearth-side undisturbed; nor did he seem to
endure the pangs of half-starvation, although his hand had grown
heavy on the staff and his cheeks hollow. His favourite business was
to sit looking into the long narrow lake which cherishes the gaunt
image of the Rock of the Bogs, and to wander in a little wood of
10   larch and hazel and ash upon its border; and as the days passed it
was as though he became incorporate with some more poignant and
fragile world whose marchlands are the intense colours and si-
lences of this world. Sometimes he would hear in the little wood a
fitful music which was forgotten like a dream the moment it had
15   ceased, and once in the deep silence of noon he heard there a
sound like the continuous clashing of many swords; while at sundown and at moon-rise the lake grew like a gateway of ivory and
silver, and from its silence arose faint lamentations, a vague shivering laughter, and many pale and beckoning hands.
20   He was sitting looking into the water one autumn evening close
to the place where the sacrilegious men-at-arms had fallen heaped
together, while the piper of the Shee who had lured them over the
edge of the Steep Place of the Strangers, rode through the upper
air whirling his torch; when a cry began towards the east, at first

Printings: *The New Review*, December, 1896; 1897.
Text from 1897; all variants from NR.
Spellings and changes of name: Hanrahan 1897; O'Sullivan NR. Whinny Byrne 1897;
Whinny O'Byrne NR.
Title: THE DEATH OF O'SULLIVAN THE RED
2   *of* Cope's Mountain and Lug-na-gall, *making* . . .
4   *bag, in* . . .
8   *narrow* lough *which* . . .
9   *image of* Crug-na-Moonagh, *and* . . .
9   *in* the *little* . . .
18–19 *vague, shivering* . . .
20–21 *evening* where the lough comes nearest the green slope whereon *the sacrilegious* . . .
22   Shee, *who* . . . ['*Shee*' italic in NR]
23   *edge of* Lug-na-gall, *rode* . . .
24   *torch, when* . . .
24   *the* west, *at* . . .

The Secret Rose

25   distant and indistinct, but getting nearer and louder as the shadows
gathered. 'I am beautiful; I am beautiful,' were the words; 'the
birds in the air, the moths under the leaves, the flies over the water
look at me; for they never saw any one as beautiful as I am. I am
young; I am young; look at me, mountains; look at me, perishing
30   woods; for my body will gleam like the white waters when you have
been hurried away. You and the races of men, and the races of
beasts, and the races of the fish and the winged races are dropping
like a guttering candle; but I laugh aloud remembering my youth!'
The cry would cease from time to time as though in exhaustion and
35   then begin once more, 'I am beautiful, I am beautiful,' and repeat
the same words and in the same monotonous chant. Presently the
hazel-branches at the edge of the little wood trembled for a moment, and an old woman forced her way from among them and
passed Hanrahan with slow deliberate steps. Her face was the col-
40   our of earth and incredibly wrinkled, and her white hair hung
about it in tangled and discoloured locks, and through her tattered
clothes showed here and there her dark, weather-roughened skin.
She passed with wide open eyes and lifted head and arms hanging
straight down; and was lost in the shadow of the mountains towards
45   the west. Hanrahan looked after her with a shudder; for he recognized crazy Whinny Byrne, who went from barony to barony
begging her bread and crying always the same cry; and remembered
that she was once so wise that the women of her village sought her

---

26   *beautiful, I* . . .
26   *words, 'the* . . .
29   *young, I* . . .
29   *am young! Look at me, mountains* . . .
29   *mountains! look* . . .
30   *woods! for* . . .
31–32 *You and the races of men, and the races of* the animals, *and the races of* . . .
32   *fish, and* . . .
32   *races, are* . . .
33   *aloud, remembering* . . .
34   *exhaustion, and* . . .
35   *more: 'I am beautiful, I* . . .
37   *hazel-branches* 1897; *hazel branches* NR.
37–38   *moment and an* . . .
40   *earth, and incredibly* . . .
42   *dark weather-roughened* . . .
43   *wide open* 1897; *wide-open* NR.
43   *head, and* . . .
44   *down, and* . . .
44–45   *towards the* north. O'Sullivan *looked* . . .
45–46   *recognised* . . .
47   *cry, and* . . .

counsel in all things; and had so beautiful a voice that men and
50   women came from a distance of many miles to hear her sing at
wake or wedding; but the people of the Shee stole her wits a summer night fifty years before, while she sat crooning to herself on
the edge of the sea, and dreaming of Cleena, who rushes with
unwrinkled feet among the foam.

55   The cry died away up the hillside, the last faint murmurs coming,
as it seemed, out of the purple deep where the first stars were
glimmering like little fluttering white moths.

A cold wind was creeping among the reeds, and Hanrahan began
to shiver and to sigh, and to think of the hearth where his fire of
60   turf would be still making a little warm and kind, if dwindling,
world under the broken thatch. He toiled slowly up the hill bowed
as by an immense burden that grew the greater as he passed, where
he had seen the unhappy lovers, that are in fairy-land, walking on
the dark air with august feet, because the thought of them made his
65   exile from beauty and from youth so bitterly poignant. The old yew
above his cabin looked the more malignant from dwelling at so
great a height an outcast from among its kind, and seemed to uplift
its dark branches like withered hands threatening the stars, and the
blue deep they swim in, with the coming of decay and shadowy old
70   age.

He mounted upon the rock, whose partial shelter had doubtless
enabled the yew to root itself firmly, before its branches received
the burden of all the winds; and looked towards the south, for
there he had been last loved and made his last verses. A little black
75   spot was moving from the hills and woods, between the Hill of
Awley and the lake of Castle Dargan, and, while he watched, it
grew larger and larger, until he knew it for a wide-winged bird, and
then for a spotted eagle with something glittering in its claws. It
came swiftly towards him, flying straight onward as if upon a long

56   *deep, where* . . .
61   *hill, bowed* . . .
63   *fairy-land* 1897; *fairyland* NR.
67   *height, an* . . .
68   *hands, threatening* . . .
68   *stars and* . . .
68–69 *and the* purple *deep* . . .
69   *they* fluttered *in with* . . .
70–71 *age. He* . . .
71   *rock—whose* . . .
72   *enabled* it to be rooted *firmly* . . .
73   *winds—and* . . .
75–76 *between the* mountain of Balligawley *and the* . . .

80 journey or pondering some hidden purpose; and when it was
    nearly overhead he saw that the glittering thing was a large fish
    which still writhed from side to side. Suddenly the fish made a last
    struggle and leaped out of its claws, and fell with gasping mouth
    into the branches of the yew-tree. Hanrahan had not eaten since
85 the previous morning, and then but little, and, though he had been
    scarcely aware of his hunger hitherto, his hunger came upon him
    now, and so fiercely that he had gladly buried his teeth into the
    living fish. He hurled a heavy stone at the eagle, which had begun
    to circle with great clamour about the tree, and having filled his cap
90 with like stones, drove it screaming over the mountain eastward.
    He began then to climb the tree with a passionate haste, and had
    almost come to where the fish hung in the fork between two
    branches, glittering like a star among the green smoke of some
    malevolent fire lighted by the People from under the Sea, when a
95 branch broke under his hand and he fell heavily upon a rock, and
    from this rebounded again, striking first his back and then his
    head, and becoming unconscious at the last blow. The fire had
    already consumed his goods, and now those creatures of earth and
    air and water, that once endured his curse, had taken him in a
100 subtle ambuscade.
        A face was bent over him when he awoke, and, despite his weak-
    ness and bewilderment and suffering, he shuddered when the turf
    fire, now red and leaping, gleamed on the broken and blackened
    teeth and on the mud-stiffened tatters of Whinny Byrne. She
105 watched him intently a little, for her slow senses appeared to need
    time to assure her that he was not dead; and then laid down the wet
    cloth which had bathed the blood from his face; and began stirring
    a pot, from which she drew presently a couple of potatoes and held
    them towards him with an inarticulate murmur. In so much of the
110 night as was not spent in short and feverish sleep, he saw her
    moving hither and thither, or bending over the hearth with her
    wrinkled hands spread out above its flame; and once or twice he
    caught the words of her monotonous chant, subdued into a feeble

---

81–82 *fish, which* ...
83   *fell, with* ...
83–84 *mouth, into* ...
84   *yew-tree* 1897; *yew tree* NR.
87   *now so* ...*
89   *and, having* ...
89–90 *his* caubeen *with* ...
93–94 *some* Fomorian fire, *when* ...
104   *teeth, and* ...
104   *tatters, of* ...

The Death of Hanrahan the Red

murmur. At the dawn he half raised himself with many pains and
115 pointed to the leather bag by the hearth-side. Whinny opened the
bag and took out a little copper and silver money, but let it fall back
again, not seeming to understand its purpose; perhaps because she
was accustomed to beg, not for money, but for potatoes and for
fragments of bread and meat, and perhaps because the persuasion
120 of her own beauty was coming upon her with a double passion in
the exultation of the dawn. She went out and brought an armful of
heather and heaped it over him, saying something about the morning being 'cold, cold, and cold,' and brought a dozen more armfuls
and heaped them by the first until he was well covered; and went
125 away down the mountain-side; her cry of 'I am beautiful, I am
beautiful,' dying slowly in the distance.
　　Hanrahan lay through the day, enduring much pain; and scarce
able even to wonder if Whinny Byrne had left him for good, or but
to come again and divide with him the gains of her begging. A little
130 after sundown he heard her voice on the hillside, and that night she
made up his fire and cooked her potatoes and divided them with
him as before. Some days passed in this way, and the weight of his
flesh was heavy about him, but gradually as he grew weaker it
seemed to him that there were powers close at hand, and growing
135 always more numerous, who might, in the wink o' an eye, break
down the rampart the sensuality of pain had builded about him,
and receive him into their world. Even as it was he had moments
when he heard faint ecstatic reedy voices, crying from the roof-tree
or from the flame of the earth; while at other moments the room
140 was brimmed with a penetrating music. After a little, weakness
brought a vanishing of pain and a slow blossoming of silence in
which, like faint light through a mist, the ecstatic reedy voices came
continually.
　　One morning he heard music, somewhere outside the door, and
145 as the day passed it grew louder and louder until it drowned the
ecstatic reedy voices and even Whinny's voice upon the hillside at
sundown. About midnight, and in a moment, the walls seemed to

---

114　*dawn, he* ...
125　*mountain-side* 1897; *mountain side* NR.
133　*gradually, as* ...
133　*weaker, it* ...
138　*faint, ecstatic, reedy* ...
138　*roof-tree* 1897; *roof tree* NR.
139　*of the* hearth; *while* ...
141　*silence, in* ...
143-44　*continually. One* ...
146　*voices, and* ...

melt away and to leave his bed floating in a misty and pale light,
which glimmered on each side to an incalculable distance; and after
150 the first blinding of his eyes he saw that it was full of faint and great
figures rushing hither and thither. At the same moment the music
became so distinct, that he understood it was but the continuous
clashing of swords. 'I am dead,' he repeated, 'and in the midst of
the music of heaven. O Cherubim and Seraphim, receive my soul!'
155 At his cry the light where it was nearest filled with sparks of more
intense light; and he saw that these were the points of swords
turned towards his heart, and then a sudden flame, dazzling, as it
seemed, like a divine passion, swept over all the light and went out,
and he was in darkness. At first he could see nothing, for it was as
160 dark as though he were enclosed in black marble; but gradually the
firelight began to glimmer upon Whinny Byrne, who was bending
over it, with her eyes fixed upon the bed. She got up and came
towards him, and the ecstatic reedy voices began crying again,
while a faint dove-grey light crept over the room, coming from he
165 knew not what secret world. He saw the withered earthen face and
withered earthen arms, and for all his weakness shrank further
towards the wall; and then faint white arms, wrought as of glistening cloud, came out of the mud-stiffened tatters and were clasped
about his body; and a voice that sounded faint and far, but was of a
170 marvellous distinctness, whispered in his ears: 'You will seek me no
longer upon the breasts of women.'
   'Who are you?' he murmured.
   'I am of those,' was the answer, 'who dwell in the minds of the
crazy and the diseased and the dying, and you are mine until the
175 world is melted like wax. Look, they have lighted our wedding
tapers!' And he saw that the air was crowded with pale hands, and
that each hand held a long taper like a rushlight.
   Whinny Byrne sat by the body until morning, and then began
begging from barony to barony again, her monotonous chant keep-
180 ing time to the beat of her wrinkled heels in the clinging dust: 'I am
beautiful; I am beautiful; the birds in the air, the moths under the

---

155   light, where ...
155   nearest, filled ...
156   light, and ...
160   marble, but ...
161   firelight 1897; fire-light NR.
163-64   crying, while ...*
167   wall, and ...
170   ears:—'You ...
181   beautiful, I ...

leaves, the flies over the waters look at me, for they never saw any one beautiful as I am. I am young; I am young; look at me, mountains; look at me, perishing woods; for my body will gleam
185 like the white waters when you have been hurried away. You and the races of men, and the races of beasts, and the races of the fish and the winged races are dropping like a guttering candle; but I laugh aloud remembering my youth!' She did not return at nightfall or ever again to the shepherd's cabin; and it was only after some
190 days that turf-cutters found the body of Owen Hanrahan the Red, and gathering a concourse of mourners and of keening women gave him a burying worthy of so great a poet.

THE ROSE OF SHADOW

A violent gust of wind made the roof shake and burst the door open, and Peter Herne got up from his place at the table and shut it again, and slipped the heavy wooden bolt; saying, as he did so: 'One would almost think the house was about to fall upon our
5 heads.' His father and mother were at the table, but his sister, Oona, unmindful of her mother's call to supper, was sitting near the door listening to the wind among the fir-trees upon the mountain. Peter Herne, made lonely by a glimpse of the dishev-

---

182   *over the* water *look* . . .
182   *me; for* . . .
183   *one* as *beautiful* . . .
183   *young, I am young! Look at* . . .
184   *mountains! look* . . .
184   *woods! for* . . .
186   *and the races of* the animals, *and the races of the* . . .
186–87   *fish, and* . . .
188   *aloud, remembering* . . .
190   *Owen* Roe O'Sullivan *the* . . .
191   *and, gathering* . . .
191   *women, gave* . . .
[In NR, the story is signed W. B. Yeats.]

Printings: *The Speaker,* July 21, 1894; 1897.
Text from 1897; all variants from S.
Title: THOSE WHO LIVE IN THE STORM.
3–5   *bolt. His* . . .*
7   *fir-trees* 1897; *fir trees* S.
8   *mountain* slope above them. *Peter* . . .

elled night sky through the open door, turned toward her and said:
10 'It is the blackest storm that ever came out of the heavens.'

'Twelve months ago this night,' answered the girl, 'it was as black and as bitter, and the wind blew then, as now, along the Mountain of Gulben and out to sea.'

Peter Herne and Simon Herne started and looked at each other, 15 and the hand of old Margaret Herne began to tremble. A year that night Peter Herne had killed, with a blow from a boat-hook, one Michael Creed, the master of a coasting smack, who had long been the terror of the little western ports because of his violence and brutality, and the hatred of all peaceful households, because of his 20 many conquests among women, whom he subdued through that love of strength which is deep in the heart of even the subtlest among them.

Until this moment Oona had never alluded, even indirectly, to this quarrel and the blow, and they had hoped she had half forgot- 25 ten, or even come to think of that night as a night of deliverance.

'Mother,' she went on, speaking in a low voice, 'when those who have done crimes, when those who have never confessed, are dead, are they put in a place apart, or do they wander near to us?'

'Child,' replied the old woman, 'my mother told me that some are 30 spitted upon the points of the rocks, and some upon the tops of the trees, but that others wander with the season in the storms over the seas and about the strands and headlands of the world. But, daughter, I bid you think of them no more, for when we think of them they draw near.'

35 'Mother,' said the girl, with a rapt light in her eyes, 'last night when you had all gone to bed, I put my cloak over my night-gown and slipped out, and brought in a sod from his grave and set it on the chair beside my bed; and after I had been in bed a while, I heard it whisper and then speak quite loudly. "Come to me, 40 alanna," it said; and I answered, "How can I come?" And it said, "Come with me when the wind blows along the Mountain of Gulben and out to sea." Then I was afraid, and I put it outside on the window-sill.'

The old woman went over to the little china font which hung 45 upon a nail by the window, and dipped her fingers into it and

9-10 *said* in Gaelic, '*It* . . .
12-13 *along* Bulber *and* . . .
30 *rocks and* . . .
35-36 *night, when* . . .
41-42 *along* Bulber and over the *sea* . . .
45 *and* wet her fingers *and* . . .

sprinkled the holy water over the girl, who thanked her in a low voice. For a moment the brooding look went out of her face, and then the eyes clouded with dreams once more.

'Put such things out of your head,' said Simon Herne angrily.

50 'Had not Peter struck a straight blow the devils had been one less, but the disgraced and shamefaced of the earth one more. I bid you know, colleen, that it is not this house but the bare highway that had been your home on the day when your brawler had tired of you!'

55 The girl did not seem to hear; she seemed to be wholly absorbed in listening to the storm in the fir-trees.

'Come to the table,' cried Peter Herne, 'and eat your supper like another.'

The girl made no answer, but gazed upon the smoke-blacked

60 wall as though she could see through it. With an oath the old man began his supper, and Peter Herne busied himself filling his father's noggin and his own from a jug of Spanish wine out of a recently-smuggled cargo. Margaret Herne kept glancing at the girl from time to time. Meanwhile the wind roared louder and louder,

65 and set the hams that hung from the rafters swaying to and fro. Presently the old woman saw by the girl's moving lips that she was speaking, but the wind drowned her words. Slowly, however, the wind became still, as though the beings that controlled it were listening also.

70 The girl was singing a fitful, exultant air in a low voice. The words were inaudible, but the air they knew well.

'Be silent!' cried the old man, going over and striking her on the mouth with his open hand; 'that is an evil air, and no daughter of mine shall ever sing it. Hanrahan the Red sang it after he had

75 listened to the singing of those who are about the faery Cleena of the Wave, and it has lured, and will lure, many a girl from her hearth and from her peace.'

'Good colleen,' said her mother, 'the host of Cleena sang of a love too great for our perishing hearts, and from that night Hanrahan

80 the Red is always seeking with wild tunes and bewildered words to answer their voices, and a madness is upon his days and a darkness before his feet. His songs are no longer dear to any but to the

---

71–72   *air* was marked and familiar. ¶*'Be* . . .
72   *man going* . . .
74   *it.* O'Sullivan *the* . . .
75–76   *about the fairy Cleena of* Tor Cleena, *and it* . . .
79–80   *night* O'Sullivan *the* . . .
80   *is* ever *seeking* . . .

coasting sailors and to the people of the mountain, and to those that are ill-nurtured and foolish. Look, daughter, to the spinning=
85 wheel, and think of our goods that, horn by horn and fleece by fleece, grow greater as the years go by, and be content.'

The girl heard and saw nothing of the things about her, but sang on as if in a trance. And now some wild words of love became audible from time to time, like a torch in a dim forest, or a star
90 among drifting clouds; and the others could not help themselves but listen while she sang, an icy feeling beginning to creep about the room and into their hearts, as though all the warmth of the world was in that low, exultant song.

'It is very cold,' said Peter Herne, shivering; 'I will put more turf
95 upon the fire.' And going over to the stack in the corner he flung an armful upon the flickering hearth, and then stooped down to stir the embers. 'The fire is going out,' he said; 'I cannot keep it alight. My God! the cold has numbed my feet;' and, staggering to his chair, he sat down. 'One would half think, if one did not know
100 all such things to be but woman's nonsense, that the demons, whose coming kills the body of man, were in the storm listening to this evil song.'

'The fire has gone out,' said the old man.

The eyes of the girl brightened, and she half rose from her chair,
105 and sang in a loud and joyous voice:—

> O, what to me the little room,
>   That was brimmed up with prayer and rest?
> He bade me out into the gloom,
>   And my breast lies upon his breast.
>
> 110 O, what to me my mother's care,
>   The home where I was safe and warm?
> The shadowy blossom of my hair

---

84   *are* its *nurtured* . . .
87   *about, but* . . .*
89-90   *star* amid drear *clouds* . . .
93   *low,* exulting *song* . . .
100   *the* seabar, *whose* . . .
101   *man,* was *in* . . .
101   *to* his *evil* . . .
105-8   *voice:—* ¶*'O, what to me the* firelit room, / Where I have laughed and spun and played? / He . . .
109-10   *my* white breast on his he laid. / ¶*'O* . . .
110-12   *care,* / The milking-place, the sheltered farm? / The . . .

230

Will hide us from the bitter storm.

O, hiding hair and dewy eyes,
115   I am no more with life and death!
My heart upon his warm heart lies;
      My breath is mixed into his breath.

While she had been singing, an intense drowsiness had crept into
the room, as though the gates of Death had moved upon their
120 hinges. The old woman had leaned forward upon the table, for she
had suddenly understood that her hour had come. The young man
had fixed his eyes fiercely on the face of the girl, and the light died
out of them. The old man had known nothing, except that he was
very cold and sleepy, until the cold came to his heart. At the end of
125 the song the storm began again with redoubled tumult, and the
roof shook. The lips of the girl were half-parted in expectation,
and out of her eyes looked all the submission which had been in the
heart of woman from the first day.
Suddenly the thatch at one end of the roof rolled up, and the
130 rushing clouds and a single star flickered before her eyes for a
moment, and then seemed to be lost in a formless mass of flame
which roared but gave no heat, and had in the midst of it the shape
of a man crouching on the storm. His heavy and brutal face and his
partly naked limbs were scarred with many wounds, and his eyes
135 were full of white fire under his knitted brows.

113–14   storm. / ¶'O . . .
117–18   his breath.' ¶While . . .
118   singing an . . .
119   the air, as . . .
124   heart and his head fell backwards, convulsed. At . . .
126   shook violently. The . . .
130   star became visible for . . .
131   moment and . . .
131   then were lost . . .
131   a shapeless mass . . .
132–33   and in the midst of the flame was the form of . . .
133–34   his part naked . . .
135   brows. The rest of the roof rolled up and then fell inward with a crash, and the storm
rushed through the house.
                    *   *   *   *   *
The next day the neighbours found the dead in the ruined house, and buried them
in the barony of Amharlish, and set over them a tombstone to say they were killed by
the great storm of October, 1765.
[In S, the story is signed W. B. Yeats.]

Dedications and Notes

1. [Dedication to 1897, 1908, 1913, 1914; in 1914, it is placed at the end of *Stories of Red Hanrahan*]

My Dear [*dear* 1913, 1914] *A.E.—I dedicate this book to you because, whether you think it well or ill written, you will sympathize with the sorrows and the ecstasies of its personages, perhaps even more than I do myself. Although I wrote these stories at different times and in different manners, and without any definite plan, they have but one subject, the war of spiritual with natural order; and how can I dedicate such a book to anyone* [*any one* 1897] *but to you, the one poet of modern Ireland who has moulded a spiritual ecstasy into verse? My friends in Ireland sometimes ask me when I am going to write a really national poem or romance, and by a national poem or romance I understand them to mean a poem or romance founded upon some famous moment of Irish* [*some moment of famous Irish* 1897] *history, and built up out of the thoughts and feelings which move the greater number of patriotic Irishmen. I on the other hand believe that poetry and romance cannot be made by the most conscientious study of famous moments and of the thoughts and feelings of others, but only by looking into that little, infinite, faltering, eternal flame that we call ourselves. If* [*that one calls one's self. If* 1897] *a writer wishes to interest a certain people among whom he has grown up, or fancies he has a duty towards them, he may choose for the symbols of his art their legends, their history, their beliefs, their opinions, because he has a right to choose among things less than himself, but he cannot choose among the substances of art. So far, however, as this book is visionary it is Irish;* [~ ∧ 1913; ~, 1914] *for Ireland,* [~ ∧ 1914] *which is still predominantly Celtic,* [~ ∧ 1914] *has preserved with some less excellent things a gift of vision, which has died out among more hurried and more successful nations: no shining candelabra have prevented us from looking into the darkness, and when one looks into the darkness there is always something there.*

W. B. YEATS.

London, 1896 [lacking 1897 to 1913]

2. [Note, 1897]

The greater number of these stories have appeared in either *The New Review, The Sketch, The National Observer,* or *The Savoy,* and I have to thank their editors for leave to reprint them.

3. [Note, 1897T]

These stories were originally intended to follow 'Rosa Alchemica' in 'The Secret Rose.'

4. [Note, 1904T]

These stories were privately printed some years ago. I do not think I should have reprinted them had I not met a young man in Ireland the other day, who liked them very much and nothing else that I have written.

W. B. Yeats.

5. [Note, 1905]

A friend has helped me to remake these stories nearer to the mind of the country places where Hanrahan and his like wandered and are remembered.

6. [Note, 1913, 1914]

I owe thanks to Lady Gregory, who helped me to rewrite The Stories of Red Hanrahan *in the beautiful country speech of Kiltartan, and nearer to the tradition of the people among whom he, or some likeness of him, drifted and is remembered.*

7. [Dedication, 1925; prefixed to *Early Poems and Stories* as a whole, rather than to the section devoted to the stories]

DEDICATION

MY DEAR ASHE KING,

A couple of days ago, while correcting the proofs of this book, I remembered a lecture you delivered in the year 1894 to the Dublin National Literary Society; a denunciation of rhetoric, and of Irish rhetoric most of all; and that it was a most vigorous and merry lecture and roused the anger of the newspapers. Thereon I decided to offer the book to you—though I had years ago dedicated various sections to friends, some of whom are long dead—for a distaste for rhetoric was a chief characteristic of my generation, and gave the book its defects and qualities. The Irish form of Victorian rhetoric had declined into a patriotic extravagance that offended all educated minds, but Victor Hugo and Swinburne had so delighted our school days that we distrusted our habitual thoughts. I tried after the publication of 'The Wanderings of Oisin' to write of nothing but emotion, and in the simplest language, and now I have had to go through it all, cutting out or altering passages that are sentimental from lack of thought. Are we not always doomed to see our world as the Stoics foretold, consumed alternately by fire and water. Upon the other hand, I cannot have altogether failed in simplicity, for these poems, written before my seven-and-twentieth year, are still the most popular that I have written. A girl made profound by the first pride of beauty, though all but a child still, once said to me, "Innocence is the highest achievement of the human intellect," and as we are encouraged to believe that our intellects grow with our years I may be permitted the conviction that—grown a little nearer innocence—I have found a more appropriate simplicity.

I published the first edition of 'The Celtic Twilight' when we were founding the National Literary Society, and often when it was time for some committee meeting—how modest and practical you were at those meetings—I rose without regret, for it is pleasanter to talk than to write, from some finished or unfinished story of 'The Secret Rose'. I [Rose.' I 1925A] wrote a good portion of that book while I still shared a lodging with old John O'Leary, the Fenian leader, but 'Rosa Alchemica', 'The [Alchemica,' 'The 1925A] Tables of the Law', and [Law,' and 1925A] 'The Adoration of the Magi' when I had left Dublin in despondency.

W. B. YEATS

May 1925. [May, 1925. in American edition]

235

Appendixes

1. Variants from
Mythologies (1959)

The following list of instances in which the text of the 1959 volume *Mythologies* differs from the text of the 1931–32 page proofs in their corrected state includes all variants except those involving words hyphenated at line-end in one text and either joined or hyphenated within the line in the other text.

[Section Title]

(1897) 1932
1897 1959

[Epigraph]

1–2   L'Isle Adam ... 1932
        L'Isle-Adam ... 1959

To the Secret Rose

16   *Gods ... liss* 1932
        gods ... liss, 1959

The Crucifixion of the Outcast

8   *abiding place* ... 1932
        abiding-place ... 1959
19   *Dathi, who* ... 1932
        Dathi who ... 1959
81   *upside down* ... 1932
        upside-down ... 1959
96   *Connaught* ... 1932
        Connacht ... 1959

Appendix 1

Variants from *Mythologies* (1959)

137-38	*wisdom, for law* ... 1932
	wisdom?—for law ... 1959
141	*things? Men* ... 1932
	things. Men ... 1959

The Heart of the Spring

77	*Ancient Gods* ... 1932
	ancient gods ... 1959
87	*Gods* ... 1932
	gods ... 1959
93	*orange trees* ... 1932
	orange-trees ... 1959

The Curse of the Fires and of the Shadows

31	*shadows, and* ... 1932
	shadows and ... 1959
81	*no* further. *Before* ... 1932
	no farther. *Before* ... 1959
162	*English the* Stranger's Leap. *The* ... 1932
	English the Steep Place of the Strangers. *The* ... 1959

Where there is Nothing, there is God

60	*half-covered* ... 1932
	half covered ... 1959
105	*druids* ... 1932
	Druids ... 1959
110	*said, 'The* ... 1932
	said: 'The ... 1959
138	*such and such* ... 1932
	such-and-such ... 1959
140	*such and such* ... 1932
	such-and-such ... 1959
142-43	*said, 'He* ... 1932
	said: 'He ... 1959

The Old Men of the Twilight

29	*S.* ... 1932
	Saint ... 1959
43	*Paternoster* ... 1932 [roman in 1959]
44	*Ave Maria* ... 1932 [roman in 1959]
54	*crying: 'Wizard* ... 1932
	crying, 'Wizard ... 1959

Appendix 1

87   *said; 'within* . . . 1932
               said, 'within . . . 1959
115   *S.* . . . 1932 [emended version]
               Saint . . . 1959

Proud Costello, MacDermot's Daughter, and the Bitter Tongue

47   *whisky* . . . 1932
               whiskey . . . 1959
61   *S.* . . . 1932 [emended version]
               Saint . . . 1959
69   *whisky* . . . 1932
               whiskey . . . 1959
94   *Rushes', 'The* . . . 1932
               Rushes,' 'The . . . 1959
94   *Stream', and* . . . 1932
               Stream,' and . . . 1959
120   *whisky* . . . 1932
               whiskey . . . 1959
187   *Gara* . . . 1932
               Gabhra . . . 1959
216   *S.* . . . 1932 [emended version]
               Saint . . . 1959
226   *Gara* . . . 1932
               Gabhra . . . 1959
260   *answered flushing* . . . 1932
               answered, flushing . . . 1959
267   *a* further *bank* . . . 1932
               a farther *bank* . . . 1959
274–75   *the* further *bank* . . . 1932
               the farther *bank* . . . 1959
297–98   *no* further *because* . . . 1932
               no farther *because* . . . 1959
314   *Gara* . . . 1932
               Gabhra . . . 1959
[THE END   lacking 1932]
THE END   1959

[Section Title]

(1897, REWRITTEN IN 1907 WITH LADY
GREGORY'S HELP) 1932
1897
REWRITTEN IN 1907 WITH LADY GREGORY'S HELP   1959

242

Variants from *Mythologies* (1959)

Red Hanrahan

11	*Connaught* ... 1932
	Connacht ... 1959
28	*then; '"He* ... 1932
	then, '"He ... 1959
29	*Kilchreist* ... 1932
	Kilchriest ... 1959
50	*Kilchreist* ... 1932
	Kilchriest ... 1959
63	*whisky* ... 1932
	whiskey ... 1959
78	*said, 'It* ... 1932
	said: 'It ... 1959
172	*short cut* ... 1932
	short-cut ... 1959
187	*night time* ... 1932
	night-time ... 1959
191	*said: 'It* ... 1932
	said, 'It ... 1959
218	*said 'Power* ... 1932
	said, 'Power ... 1959
219	*said 'Courage* ... 1932
	said, 'Courage ... 1959
220–21	*said 'Knowledge* ... 1932
	said, 'Knowledge ... 1959
238	*Daire-caol* ... 1932
	Doire-Caol ... 1959
238	*Druim-da-rod* ... 1932
	Drim-na-rod ... 1959
246	*worn and* ... 1932
	worn, and ... 1959
249	*whisky* ... 1932
	whiskey ... 1959

The Twisting of the Rope

25	*whisky* ... 1932
	whiskey ... 1959
35	*bog deal* ... 1932
	bog-deal ... 1959
36	*hearth and the* ... 1932
	hearth, and the ... 1959
36	*up, and* ... 1932
	up and ... 1959

Appendix 1

Hanrahan and Cathleen, the Daughter of Houlihan

Red Hanrahan's Curse

130–31	*may / Calls* . . . 1932
	may, / Calls . . . 1959
132	*eagle cock* . . . 1932
	eagle-cock . . . 1959
136–37	*Lake / Having* . . . 1932
	Lake, / Having . . . 1959
142–43	*Lands / Because* . . . 1932
	Lands, / Because . . . 1959
154–55	*of The Green Bunch of Rushes, to every* . . . 1932
	of "The Green Bunch of Rushes," to every . . . 1959
158	*S.* . . . 1932 [emended version]
	Saint . . . 1959
186	*said, 'I* . . . 1932
	said. 'I . . . 1959

Hanrahan's Vision

6	*dreams: ¶* . . . 1932
	dreams:— ¶ . . . 1959
35	*O, the* . . . 1932
	O the . . . 1959
44	*fish tail* . . . 1932
	fish-tail . . . 1959
54	*briar* . . . 1932
	brier . . . 1959
58	*song: ¶* . . . 1932
	song:— ¶ . . . 1959
137	*Blanid* . . . 1932
	Blanaid . . . 1959
141	*stars, the night* . . . 1932
	stars; the night . . . 1959
152	*Dervagilla* . . . 1932
	Dervorgilla . . . 1959
153	*Dermot* . . . 1932
	Diarmuid . . . 1959
159	*Dermot* . . . 1932
	Diarmuid . . . 1959

The Death of Hanrahan

14	*turf smoke* . . . 1932
	turf-smoke . . . 1959
36	*words, 'I am beautiful* . . . 1932
	words: 'I am beautiful . . . 1959
39	*young; I* . . . 1932
	young, I . . . 1959

Appendix 1

40	*will* shine *like* . . . 1932
	will be shining *like* . . . 1959
44	*out, but* . . . 1932
	out. But . . . 1959
57	*Cross Roads* . . . 1932
	Cross-Roads . . . 1959
64-65	*rath, and* . . . 1932
	rath and . . . 1959
109	*Cross Roads* . . . 1932
	Cross-Roads . . . 1959
205	*Cross Roads* . . . 1932
	Cross-Roads . . . 1959
207	*walked, 'I am beautiful, I* . . . 1932
	walked: 'I am beautiful, I . . . 1959
[THE END	lacking 1932]
THE END	1959

[Epigraph]

'*O blessed* . . . 1932 [italics in text]
'*O, blessed* . . . 1959 [italics in text]

Rosa Alchemica

[title]	*ROSA ALCHEMICA* 1932 [roman in 1959]
6	*S.* . . . 1932
	Saint . . . 1959
13-14	*phantasy* . . . 1932
	fantasy . . . 1959
16	*of an universal* . . . 1932
	of a universal . . . 1959
31	*Crevelli* . . . 1932
	Crivelli . . . 1959
52	*thought as* . . . 1932
	thought, as . . . 1959
70	*alembic* . . . 1932 [roman in 1959]
70	*athanor* . . . 1932 [roman in 1959]
74	*consuming* . . . 1932
	consuminy . . . 1959
78	*last day* . . . 1932
	Last Day . . . 1959
112-13	*and remembering* . . . 1932
	and, remembering . . . 1959
137	*athanor* . . . 1932 [roman in 1959]
137	*alembic* . . . 1932 [roman in 1959]

155	*replied, 'You* . . . 1932
	replied: 'You . . . 1959
197	*romance / writers* . . . 1932
	romance- / writers . . . 1959
221–22	*O swiftly* . . . 1932
	O, swiftly . . . 1959
232	*phantasies* . . . 1932
	fantasies . . . 1959
235	*alembic* . . . 1932 [roman in 1959]
237	*alembic* . . . 1932 [roman in 1959]
240	*saying: 'Our* . . . 1932
	saying, 'Our . . . 1959
272	*alembic* . . . 1932 [roman in 1959]
284	*half- / remember* . . . 1932
	half / remember . . . 1959
334	*phantasy* . . . 1932
	fantasy . . . 1959
340	*phantastic* . . . 1932
	fantastic . . . 1959
386	*Parnella* . . . 1932
	Pernella . . . 1959
395	*dew'. I* . . . 1932
	dew.' I . . . 1959
524	*athanor* . . . 1932 [roman in 1959]
534	*who in* . . . 1932
	who, in . . . 1959
542	*feet'. The* . . . 1932
	feet.' The . . . 1959
568	*love* . . . 1932
	Love . . . 1959
571	*knows* love *through* . . . 1932
	knows Love *through* . . . 1959
574	*love* . . . 1932
	Love . . . 1959
606	*angry* men *and* . . . 1932
	angry men's *and* . . . 1959

The Tables of the Law

43–44	*why, you* . . . 1932
	why; you . . . 1959
57	*perfect expression* . . . 1932
	perfect, expression . . . 1959
60	*Michael Angelo* . . . 1932
	Michaelangelo . . . 1959

Appendix 1

83	*passed* . . . 1932
	past . . . 1959
121	*kabalistic* . . . 1932
	cabbalistic . . . 1959
163	*and woman, and have* . . . 1932
	and women, and have . . . 1959
206-7	*romance writers* . . . 1932
	romance-writers . . . 1959
217	*commonplace: and* . . . 1932
	commonplace; and . . . 1959
218-19	*than: ¶'It* . . . 1932
	than: 'It . . . 1959
232	*why* . . . 1932
	Why . . . 1959
237	*why then will* . . . 1932
	why, then, will . . . 1959
242	*tumults, which* . . . 1932
	tumults which . . . 1959
243	*last day, shall* . . . 1932
	Last Day shall . . . 1959
253	*book-stall* . . . 1932
	bookstall . . . 1959
255	*brotherhood; when* . . . 1932
	brotherhood, when . . . 1959
273-74	*said: ¶'Owen* . . . 1932
	said: 'Owen . . . 1959
356	*divine ecstasy* . . . 1932
	Divine Ecstasy . . . 1959
357	*divine intellect* . . . 1932
	Divine Intellect . . . 1959

The Adoration of the Magi

27	*immortals* . . . 1932
	Immortals . . . 1959
30	*temple* . . . 1932
	Temple . . . 1959
44	*S.* . . . 1932
	Saint . . . 1959
44	*Brandan* . . . 1932
	Brendan . . . 1959
79	*O you* . . . 1932
	O, you . . . 1959
84	*said: 'Yes* . . . 1932
	said, 'Yes . . . 1959
91	*deathbed* . . . 1932
	death-bed . . . 1959

248

104	*out:* 'A ... 1932
	out, 'A ... 1959
106-7	*said:* ¶'I am not ... 1932
	said:— ¶'I am not ... 1959
122-23	*desires have* awaked; *this* ... 1932
	desires have awakened; *this* ... 1959
145	*feathers, which* ... 1932
	feathers which ... 1959
146	*S*. ... 1932
	Saint ... 1959
161	*sweetness', 'Dear* ... 1932
	sweetness,' 'Dear ... 1959
161	*bitterness', 'O solitude* ... 1932
	bitterness,' 'O solitude ... 1959
161	*solitude', 'O* ... 1932
	solitude,' 'O ... 1959
161	*terror', and* ... 1932
	terror,' and ... 1959
162	*awhile* ... 1932
	a while ... 1959
186-87	*mine.* ¶*Seacht* ... 1932 ['*Seacht*' italic in text]
	mine:— ¶*Seacht* ... 1959 ['*Seacht*' italic in text]

[THE END lacking 1932]
THE END 1959

Notes

| [title] NOTES 1932 |
| NOTE 1959 |
2-3	*Hanrahan,* page 197 to page 245, *were* ... 1932 ['Hanrahan' italic in text]
	Hanrahan were ... 1959 ['Hanrahan' italic in text]
11	*and after upon* ... 1932
	and, after, upon ... 1959
14	*country-men* ... 1932
	countrymen ... 1959
23	*these as* ... 1932
	these, as ... 1959
23	*stories I* ... 1932
	stories, I ... 1959
24	*there. (1925).* 1932
	there. / W. B. YEATS / *1925* 1959

[A passage concerning *The Irish Dramatic Movement* (intended in 1932 for *Mythologies*) was deleted in 1959.]

2. Line-End Word Division in the Copy Texts

The following list includes those words hyphenated at line-end in the originals of the basic texts that in all earlier versions were hyphenated if they occurred *within* the line. (Words hyphenated at line-end in the originals of the basic texts and appearing in more than one other form within the line in earlier versions are included in the collations; words hyphenated at line-end in the originals of the basic texts but not listed either below or in the collations were joined within the line in earlier versions.)

Texts from *Mythologies*

Out of the Rose

24	wood- / thieves
75	wood- / thieves

The Heart of the Spring

120	glow- / worm

The Curse of the Fires and of the Shadows

84	river- / side
104	ground- / ivy

Where there is Nothing, there is God

7	Fair- / Brows

Appendix 2

Proud Costello, MacDermot's Daughter, and the Bitter Tongue

13   rough- / haired
148   verse- / interwoven
345   new- / made

The Twisting of the Rope

60   white- / handed

Rosa Alchemica

284   half- / remember
297   new- / found
299   half- / empty

The Tables of the Law

127   straw- / splitting
153   many- / coloured

The Adoration of the Magi

16   weather- / beaten

Other Texts

The Binding of the Hair

31   men-at- / arms
53   five- / stringed
78   men- / at-arms (S has 'men-at- / arms')

The Book of the Great Dhoul and Hanrahan the Red

109   fire- / light

Kathleen the Daughter of Hoolihan and Hanrahan the Red

30   awe- / struck
42   girdle- / cakes

The Curse of Hanrahan the Red

| 137 | Mass- / book |
| 145 | button- / hole |

The Death of Hanrahan the Red

| 17 | moon- / rise |
| 168 | mud- / stiffened |

The Rose of Shadow

| 126 | half- / parted |

In several instances, a word hyphenated at line-end in the 1897 basic text was also hyphenated at line-end in the periodical version, or did not appear in the periodical version. In cases where the hyphen may have been intended as part of the spelling, the hyphen is preserved when the word appears within the line in the Variorum Edition. The following words fall into this category: school- / master, 'The Book of the Great Dhoul and Hanrahan the Red,' line 6; hearth- / side, 'The Death of Hanrahan the Red,' line 115; ill- / nurtured, 'The Rose of Shadow,' line 84. (In the original text of 'The Devil's Book,' line 128, 'griddle- / cake' is hyphenated at line-end; the word does not occur in 1897. In the Variorum Edition, it is hyphenated within the line. 'Fairy- / mistress,' in Yeats's note to the story, has been treated in the same way.)

3. Related Documents

This section contains two documents relevant to the evolution of The Secret Rose: a series of holograph memoranda concerning the contents of *The Secret Rose* (1897); and 'A Very Pretty Little Story,' an unpublished version of 'The Binding of the Hair' rewritten in the same manner as the Hanrahan group.

Memoranda from a Notebook of 1893–95

This notebook, now in the collection of Senator Michael B. Yeats, is inscribed on the flyleaf 'W B Yeats / August 29th / 1893.'[1] The latest dated entry in the book is December 1895. Although it may originally have been intended for fair copies of works drafted elsewhere it was not in fact used exclusively for that purpose, and many of the entries are extraordinarily difficult to read. The transcriptions below are thus highly conjectural.

On the page numbered 97, under the heading 'To be written,' three stories are listed:

The Binding of the Hair
The Death of O Sullivan
The Herons

'The Herons' is presumably 'St. Patrick and the Pedants' (later 'The Old Men of the Twilight'). It was first published in December 1895; the other two stories appeared in 1896. This page also contains two lines of verse that may have some connection with 'The Binding of the Hair.'

On page 98, below a passage of verse beginning 'O woman with the braided hair,' is a list headed 'written.' It includes

[1]For a general description of the notebook, see Curtis Bradford, *Yeats at Work* (Carbondale and Edwardsville: Southern Illinois University Press, 1965), pp. 18–42.

Appendix 3

The Crucifixion of the [Jester ?]
Out of the Rose
The Heart of Spring
The Fires & the Shadows
Wisdom
[Tinker ?] Death & the Devil
O Sullivan & the Woman of the Shee
O Sullivan & the Twisting the Rope
O Sullivan & [illegible]
Curse upon Old Age
The Storm
Costello

The majority of these titles are easily recognizable. Of those which are not, 'O Sullivan & the Woman of the Shee' must be 'The Devil's Book' and the third O'Sullivan story listed is probably 'Kathleen-ny-Houlihan.' The most remarkable entry is '[Tinker ?] Death & the Devil,' which seems to be a reference to the story 'Michael Clancy, the Great Dhoul, and Death.' It had appeared in *The Old Country,* December 1893, but was never included in any of the published volumes of the Secret Rose unit. It made extensive use of the sort of peasant dialect which Yeats rewrote 'The Devil's Book' to eliminate; but he was apparently considering including it (perhaps also rewritten) in the volume the plan of which was being sketched out in these memoranda.

'The Curse of O'Sullivan the Red upon Old Age' was published September 29, 1894; 'Wisdom' in September 1895. Although 'Costello the Proud...' did not appear in print until December 1896, it may have been written a good while earlier, for a surviving manuscript of it is dated (not by Yeats) August 1895. All the other stories in the list had been published before 'The Curse of O'Sullivan...'; it is reasonable to assume, therefore, that this entry in the notebook was made sometime in 1895.

The third entry relating to *The Secret Rose* appears much further on, on an unpaginated leaf that would have been page 363:

1   The Heart of the Spring
2   O Sullivan the Red & the Woman of the Shee
3   The Twisting of the Rope
4   Kathleen ni Hoolihan
5   The Curse of O Sullivan upon Old Age
6   The Storm
7   The Crucifixion of the Outcast
8   Out of the Rose

256

9 Wisdom
10 The Fires & the Shadows
11 The [Braiding ?] of the Hair
12 Costello the Proud
13 The Devil & the Pedlar[2]

This list contains all the stories included in that on page 98; and also 'The Braiding [or 'Binding'] of the Hair.' As that story is one of those referred to on page 97 as 'To be written,' this list would appear to be a later, updated one. 'St. Patrick and the Pedants,' also listed on page 97, and not included here, was published on December 1, 1895. The later list must therefore have been drawn up sometime before that date.

The volume conceived in these memoranda was to undergo considerable change before its publication as *The Secret Rose* in 1897. 'Michael Clancy...' was omitted, and three stories not listed in any of the memoranda ('Where there is Nothing, there is God,' 'The Vision of O'Sullivan the Red,' and 'Rosa Alchemica') were added.[3] In addition, the stories appeared in an order different from that in either list.

A Very Pretty Little Story

The Berg Collection of the New York Public Library has a three-page typescript (carbon) titled 'A Very Pretty Little Story,' which was found among Lady Augusta Gregory's papers. This story is a 'folk' version of 'The Binding of the Hair.' It may represent an abortive attempt to apply the sort of collaborative revision that the Hanrahan stories underwent to the rest of *The Secret Rose*, in the 1897 version of which 'The Binding of the Hair' was the first story. The precise extent (if any) of Yeats's involvement in the writing of 'A Very Pretty Little Story' is unknown; the text contains some holograph alterations, but none in his hand. In any case, the experiment must have been considered a failure, as this story was never published and no similar version of any of the other stories not dealing with Hanrahan ever appeared. The resultant division of the original collection into 'folk' and non-'folk' stories persisted throughout its entire subsequent history.

[2]'The Devil & the Pedlar' seems to be yet another title for 'Michael Clancy...' and perhaps indicates some change in Yeats's conception of the story. But in 1898 he allowed Standish O'Grady to reprint the original version and himself supplied a note concerning its composition.
[3]'The Tables of the Law' and 'The Adoration of the Magi' were also intended for *The Secret Rose* but Yeats was forced by the publisher to leave them out; see 'Census of Other Manuscript and Proof Materials,' item G.

A VERY PRETTY LITTLE STORY.

In the time long ago, when herons made their nests in old men's beards and turkeys chewed tobacco, and the little pigs ran about with knives and forks stuck in them crying out 'Who'll eat me! Who'll eat me! Who'll eat me!' there lived a queen in a golden palace, having [?] the roof thatched with birds wings.

She was as young as the first light of the morning, and as beautiful as a may-bush in summer time, and her cheeks were like a rose where the lily and the rose are fighting for mastery. And there was no one ever saw her but had a wish to be taking care of her.

There was hardly a week from years end to years end but some king from the gardens of the east or from the ~~islands~~ plains of the ~~west~~ south would bring his armies, with their swords and their spears, striving to ~~bring~~ take away the queen that was ~~so~~ the blossom and the branch of the whole ~~of the~~ western world.

Her people put a hundred locks on every door, and they had a hundred hiding places for every key; and if so much as a mouse squeaked out of a corner, a big fighting man had his head off with a sword before the squeak was ended.

Every evening when the fighting was at an end, the queen's men used to unlock the doors and to come in and to tell her all they had done, and how many of her enemies they had killed, and the plans they had made for the nighttime. But they would never let her follow them out, for fear she might be scared by the strange red beard of some enemy, or stung by some bee in a honey-blossom, or so much as touched by the down of a dandelion that might be floating in the air.

A young man that was a stranger came in with the fighting men one night, and the queen looked up from the silver thread she was spinning on her wheel and she saw him. ~~'Wher~~ 'Who are you?, young man'? said she. 'I am a poet, queen' said he. 'What is your country?' said she. 'The Rose of the World' said he. 'What path did you come by?' said she. 'By the road of danger', said he. 'What have you come to do for me?' said she. 'To sing a song for you' said he. 'What will the song be about?' said ~~he~~ she. 'About the Beauty of all Beauties' said he.

When the queen heard that she was very glad, and she clapped her hands and he took his little harp and struck the strings, and put it upon his knee. But the old fighting men were jealous, and one of them said 'There is no time for singing, when we have not made the round of the palace yet that we always make at the darkest hour when the enemy may be creeping up by the ditch'. 'O wait a while' said the queen. 'He is going to sing a song about me, and not one among you all has ever sung a song about me before.!' 'Tat is 'That is good thanks you are giving us' said the old man 'for the nights we have watched and the days we have served you, and the blows and the wounds that have stiffened our bodies'. 'Sing on!' said the queen; and she threw her little ball of silver thread at the old man to quiet him. Then the young man played a little tune, and he began to sing, and it is What he sang:

But then another old man said 'It is no time for singing. We have not made our round of the house and our night attack on the enemy; and there is nothing makes a man sleep so well and so quiet as the head of a king or of a king's son under his pillow'.

And another young man said to the poet 'It is no time for singing.

'You that are young should be ashamed to be sitting there with a harp in your hand in place of a sword. And come out now and strike a blow for the queen' he said.

'I will do that' said the young man, and there was a blush in his face as he said it. 'Do not go' said the queen, 'You made a promise you would sing me that song'. 'I will go' said he, 'but dead or living I will sing you that song through before morning'. 'Men are a hard, ugly, stubborn race' said she.

The men went out then, and the queen sat down to her spinning wheel and she began to spin the silver thread, But the wheel had gone cranky or the thread brittle, or the queen's hand uneasy, and she rose up and gave a little kick at the ball, and went to the door. And then, what she had never done before, she went out into the night after the fighting men.

There was a noise of fighting sure enough as she came to the edge of the wood, and she cried out, 'Whose swords and whose shields are those I hear in the darkness?' And the old men cried out 'We are making an end of the queen's enemies'. And then everything was quiet, and a cloud went off from the moon, and she saw the body of a young man lying straight and stiff, and though the head had been struck from it she knew by the strange foreign clothes and the little harp by his side that it was the stranger that had come from [to?] the castle palace and had gone from it again. She saw then by the light of the moon his head that was hanging by the hair to a thornbush, and while she looked at it the lips of it moved. 'Is the dawn come yet' it said. 'Not yet, it is but the light of the moon'. 'My promise will be kept yet' said the head. And with that it began to sing, and it is what it sang:—

4. Census of Other Manuscript and Proof Materials

Few other manuscript and proof materials related to The Secret Rose seem to have survived, and in no case are *all* the materials for a given story or volume extant. Thus the surviving documents are often interesting, but of little textual value. This section identifies and indicates the location of those currently known to exist; two short fragments are given in their entirety, the others briefly described.

A. Manuscript fragment of 'Those Who Live in the Storm' (Collection of Senator Michael B. Yeats)

A holograph fragment of the ending of 'Those Who Live in the Storm':

> ... hidden by a huge mass of white flame that roared but gave no heat and in the midst of the flame was the form of a man crouching on the storm. His heavy and brutal face and his vast naked limbs were scarred with many wounds and his eyes full of white fire were fixed upon the girl under their knitted brows. The rest of the roof rolled up and then fell with a crash and the storm rushed through the house. [Quoted from Bradford, *Yeats at Work,* pp. 317–18]

There are a number of differences between this text and the corresponding passage of the story as published in *The Speaker* on July 21, 1894, so the fragment may not have been part of the last manuscript version.

B. Holograph manuscript of 'Costello the Proud' (Collection of Senator Michael B. Yeats)

A complete holograph manuscript of 'Costello the Proud,' dated (in an unidentified hand) 'Aug. 1895.' Numerous revisions were made in preparation of this text, which in its final form is basically that of the story's first printing, in *The Pageant* (1896).

C. Corrected page proofs of *The Secret Rose*, 1897
(Collection of Senator Michael B. Yeats)

Pages 1–256, date-stamped 2, 4, 6, 8 Nov 96. Holograph corrections by Yeats, but only in five signatures (of sixteen), so that there must have been another, more fully corrected, set.

D. Page proofs of *Stories of Red Hanrahan*, 1904–1905
(Berg Collection, New York Public Library)

Complete early and late page proofs of *Stories of Red Hanrahan,* with holograph corrections by Lady Gregory throughout, notes on production matters by Lolly Yeats, some suggestions about punctuation and syntax by 'Wm. Russell,' and holograph correction by Yeats of 'William Butler' to 'W. B.' on the title page of the early proofs.

E. A printed copy of *The Tables of the Law and The Adoration of the Magi,* 1904, with holograph revisions by Yeats
(Berg Collection, New York Public Library)

The 1904 text of *The Tables of the Law and The Adoration of the Magi,* with holograph revisions made by Yeats in revising the two stories for inclusion in *Early Poems and Stories.* See also Robert O'Driscoll, 'The Tables of the Law: A Critical Text,' *Yeats Studies* 1 (1971), 87–118.

F. A printed copy of the 'Secret Rose' section of *Stories of Red Hanrahan / The Secret Rose / Rosa Alchemica,* 1914
(Berg Collection, New York Public Library)

Pages 79–188 of the 1914 volume, with holograph revisions made by Yeats in revising the stories for inclusion in *Early Poems and Stories.*

G. A manuscript version of 'NOTES,' 1925
(National Library of Ireland)

A fragmentary holograph manuscript of the 'NOTES' section of *Early Poems and Stories:*

'The Tables of the Law' & 'The Adoration of the Magi'
were [intd ?] to [be ?] a part of 'The Secret Rose' but

the publisher A H Bullen disliked them, & made me
leave them out, & then after they were ~~published~~ printed
liked them, & published them separately. ~~In th~~
~~In them, as in most of the stories that preceded~~ th
In ~~them, as in all the stories except~~ ‘
~~I have left out passages or rewritten passages~~ here
& ~~there~~ In them, as in most of the other stories
I have left out ~~passages, &~~ & rewritten
passages here & there.

In connection with this passage, it should be noted that the surviving page proofs of *The Secret Rose* (1897) cease at page 256, the end of gathering or bundle R. The next (missing) bundle would have contained, in addition to the last ten pages of 'Rosa Alchemica,' either the last pages of the book or the first pages of 'The Tables of the Law.' The missing portions of the proofs may have been removed when it was decided that 'The Tables of the Law' and 'The Adoration of the Magi' were not to be included.

H. Holograph revisions of 'The Adoration of the Magi' (National Library of Ireland)

Holograph revisions of three passages in 'The Adoration of the Magi,' in a blue exercise book also containing drafts of 'Leda and the Swan' (NLI MS 13589, folder 32); the new versions, further revised, were included in *Early Poems and Stories* (1925).

Two items of particular interest that have not been located are described in *The Library of John Quinn* (New York: Anderson Galleries, 1924):

Item 11366: Typed copies of the "Hanrahan" stories, as follows: "The Twisting of the Rope," 8 pages, quarto; "Red Hanrahan and Cathleen the Daughter of Houlihan," 4 pages, quarto; Galley Proof of "Red Hanrahan," on 4 galley sheets; "The Death of Hanrahan," one copy on 7 pages, folio, and another on 7½ pages, quarto. With corrections. In a 4to blue buckram slip case.

Item 11367: *First edition* [of *The Secret Rose* (1897)], profusely corrected in the author's autograph for a new edition [i.e., 1908]. On the title-page Yeats has deleted the printed portion reading "By W. B. Yeats, with illustrations by J. B. Yeats," and has added the words to make the title read "*The Secret Rose: and John Sherman and Doya*." The Hanrahan stories have been deleted as well as "The Binding of the Hair." On the inside front cover Yeats has written the proposed contents of the revised book.

5. Bibliography

This section identifies the various periodical publications of the stories and the volume publications and their contents. For more detailed descriptions, see Allan Wade, *A Bibliography of the Writings of W. B. Yeats,* 3d ed., revised by Russell K. Alspach (London: Rupert Hart-Davis, 1968). Wade's identification numbers for the volumes are given in square brackets. The entries for the 1914 and 1925 volumes differ from Wade's descriptions in important ways.

PERIODICAL PUBLICATIONS

1892

1. The Devil's Book (becomes 'The Book of the Great Dhoul and Hanrahan the Red' in *The Secret Rose* [1897]): *The National Observer,* November 26, pp. 39–41.
2. The Twisting of the Rope (becomes 'The Twisting of the Rope and Hanrahan the Red' in *The Secret Rose* [1897]): *The National Observer,* December 24, pp. 132–33.

1893

3. The Heart of the Spring (reprinted under the same title in *The Secret Rose* [1897]): *The National Observer,* April 15, pp. 546–47.
4. Out of the Rose (reprinted under the same title in *The Secret Rose* [1897]): *The National Observer,* May 27, pp. 41–43.
5. The Curse of the Fires and of the Shadows (reprinted under the same title in *The Secret Rose* [1897]): *The National Observer,* August 5, pp. 303–4.

1894

6. A Crucifixion (becomes 'The Crucifixion of the Outcast' in *The Secret Rose* [1897]): *The National Observer,* March 24, pp. 479–81.
7. Those Who Live in the Storm (becomes 'The Rose of Shadow' in *The Secret Rose* [1897] and is omitted from *The Collected Works in Verse and Prose* [1908] and subsequent editions): *The Speaker,* July 21, pp. 74–75.
8. Kathleen-ny-Hoolihan (becomes 'Kathleen the Daughter of Hoolihan and

Hanrahan the Red' in *The Secret Rose* [1897]): *The National Observer,* August 4, pp. 303-4.

9. The Curse of O'Sullivan the Red upon Old Age (becomes 'The Curse of Hanrahan the Red' in *The Secret Rose* [1897]): *The National Observer,* September 29, pp. 510-12.

1895

10. Wisdom (becomes 'The Wisdom of the King' in *The Secret Rose* [1897]): *The New Review,* September, pp. 285-89.

11. St. Patrick and the Pedants (becomes 'The Old Men of the Twilight' in *The Secret Rose* [1897]): *The Weekly Sun Literary Supplement,* December 1, p. 14. Also reprinted in *The Chap Book* (Chicago), June 1, 1896, pp. 50-55, where it is entitled 'S. Patrick and the Pedants.'

1896

12. The Binding of the Hair (reprinted under the same title in *The Secret Rose* [1897] and omitted from *The Collected Works in Verse and Prose* [1908] and subsequent editions): *The Savoy,* No. 1, January, pp. [135]-38.

13. Rosa Alchemica (reprinted under the same title in *The Secret Rose* [1897]): *The Savoy,* No. 2, April, pp. [56]-70.

14. The Vision of O'Sullivan the Red (becomes 'The Vision of Hanrahan the Red' in *The Secret Rose* [1897]): *The New Review,* No. 83, April, pp. 404-7; a further revised version, 'Red Hanrahan's Vision' (becomes 'Hanrahan's Vision' in *Stories of Red Hanrahan* [1904-1905]) was published in *McClure's Magazine,* March 1905, pp. 469-71.

15. Where there is Nothing, there is God: *The Sketch,* October 21, p. 548. Reprinted under the same title in *The Secret Rose* (1897); omitted from *Early Poems and Stories* (1925), but restored in the *Mythologies* page proofs (1931-32). Above the title in the *Sketch* printing is the legend 'A NOVEL IN A NUTSHELL.'

16. The Tables of the Law: *The Savoy,* No. 7, November, pp. [79]-87. Reprinted privately in book form (with 'The Adoration of the Magi') in 1897 and published in book form (1904 and 1914). Included in *Early Poems and Stories* (1925).

17. The Death of O'Sullivan the Red (becomes 'The Death of Hanrahan the Red' in *The Secret Rose* [1897]): *The New Review,* December, pp. 677-81.

18. Costello the Proud, Oona MacDermott, and the Bitter Tongue (becomes 'Of Costello the Proud, of Oona the Daughter of Dermott and of the Bitter Tongue' in *The Secret Rose* [1897]): *The Pageant,* [December], pp. 2-13.

1897

19. The Adoration of the Magi: not printed in periodical form. First printed privately in book form with 'The Tables of the Law' (1897), and published in 1904 and again in 1914. It was included in *Early Poems and Stories* (1925).

1903

20. Red Hanrahan (replaces 'The Book of the Great Dhoul and Hanrahan the Red' in *Stories of Red Hanrahan* (1904–1905): *The Independent Review*, December, pp. 478–85.

In the various publications of the stories in book form, the stories were printed in the following orders:

1897: 12, 10, 15, 6, 4, 5, 3, 18, 1, 2, 8, 9, 14, 17, 7, 11, 13.
1897T: 16, 19.
1904T: 16, 19.
1905: 20, 2, 8, 9, 14, 17.
1908 (Vol. V): 20, 2, 8, 9, 14, 17.
    (Vol. VII): 6, 4, 10, 3, 5, 11, 15, 18, 13, 16, 19.
1913: 20, 2, 8, 9, 14, 17, 6, 4, 10, 3, 5, 11, 15, 18, 13.
1914: 20, 2, 8, 9, 14, 17, 6, 4, 10, 3, 5, 11, 15, 18, 13.
1914T: 16, 19.
1925: 6, 4, 10, 3, 5, 11, 18, 20, 2, 8, 9, 14, 17, 13, 16, 19.
1927: 20, 2, 8, 9, 14, 17, 6, 4, 10, 3, 5, 11, 18.
1931–32 proofs and 1959: 6, 4, 10, 3, 5, 15, 11, 18, 20, 2, 8, 9, 14, 17, 13, 16, 19.

For more detailed information, see the following section.

VOLUME PUBLICATIONS

Volume contents other than the stories have been omitted from the following lists; for full contents, see Wade, *Bibliography*.

I. *The Secret Rose* (London: Lawrence & Bullen, Limited, 1897) [Wade 21]
    The Binding of the Hair
    The Wisdom of the King
    Where there is Nothing, there is God
    The Crucifixion of the Outcast
    Out of the Rose
    The Curse of the Fires and of the Shadows
    The Heart of the Spring
    Of Costello the Proud, of Oona the Daughter of Dermott and of the
        Bitter Tongue
    The Book of the Great Dhoul and Hanrahan the Red
    The Twisting of the Rope and Hanrahan the Red
    Kathleen the Daughter of Hoolihan and Hanrahan the Red
    The Curse of Hanrahan the Red
    The Vision of Hanrahan the Red
    The Death of Hanrahan the Red
    The Rose of Shadow

The Old Men of the Twilight
Rosa Alchemica
[There was an American edition with a new title page in 1897 (Wade 22),
and a Dublin edition of the English sheets in 1905 (Wade 23).]

II. *The Tables of the Law. / The Adoration of the Magi.* ([London: privately print-
ed], 1897) [Wade 24]
The Tables of the Law
The Adoration of the Magi

III. *The Tables of the Law and The Adoration of the Magi* (London: Elkin Math-
ews, 1904) [Wade 25]
The Tables of the Law
The Adoration of the Magi

IV. *Stories of Red Hanrahan* (Dundrum: Dun Emer Press, 1904 [actually pub-
lished 1905]) [Wade 59]
Red Hanrahan
The Twisting of the Rope
Hanrahan and Cathleen the Daughter of Hoolihan
Red Hanrahan's Curse
Hanrahan's Vision
The Death of Hanrahan

V. *The Celtic Twilight and Stories of Red Hanrahan* / Being the Fifth Volume of
the Collected Works (Stratford-on-Avon: The Shakespeare Head Press,
1908) [Wade 79]
Red Hanrahan
The Twisting of the Rope
Hanrahan and Cathleen the Daughter of Hoolihan
Red Hanrahan's Curse
Hanrahan's Vision
The Death of Hanrahan

VI. *The Secret Rose. Rosa Alchemica. The Tables of the Law. The Adoration of the
Magi. John Sherman and Dhoya* / Being the Seventh Volume of the Col-
lected Works (Stratford-on-Avon: The Shakespeare Head Press, 1908)
[Wade 81]
The Secret Rose [section title]
The Crucifixion of the Outcast
Out of the Rose
The Wisdom of the King
The Heart of the Spring
The Curse of the Fires and of the Shadows
The Old Men of the Twilight
Where there is Nothing, there is God

Of Costello the Proud, of Oona the Daughter of Dermott and of the
    Bitter Tongue
Rosa Alchemica [section title and story]
The Tables of the Law [section title and story]
The Adoration of the Magi [section title and story]

VII. *Stories of Red Hanrahan: The Secret Rose: Rosa Alchemica* (London &
      Stratford-upon-Avon: A. H. Bullen, 1913) [Wade 104]
      Stories of Red Hanrahan [section title]
        Red Hanrahan
        The Twisting of the Rope
        Hanrahan and Cathleen the Daughter of Hoolihan
        Red Hanrahan's Curse
        Hanrahan's Vision
        The Death of Hanrahan
      The Secret Rose [section title]
        The Crucifixion of the Outcast
        Out of the Rose
        The Wisdom of the King
        The Heart of the Spring
        The Curse of the Fires and of the Shadows
        The Old Men of the Twilight
        Where there is Nothing, there is God
        Of Costello the Proud, of Oona the Daughter of Dermott, and of the
            Bitter Tongue
      Rosa Alchemica [section title and story]

VIII. *The Tables of the Law; & The Adoration of the Magi* (Stratford-upon-Avon:
      The Shakespeare Head Press, 1914) [Wade 26]
        The Tables of the Law
        The Adoration of the Magi

IX.   *Stories of Red Hanrahan / The Secret Rose / Rosa Alchemica* (New York: The
      Macmillan Company, 1914) [Wade 105]
      Stories of Red Hanrahan [section title]
        Red Hanrahan
        The Twisting of the Rope
        Hanrahan and Cathleen the Daughter of Hoolihan
        Red Hanrahan's Curse
        Hanrahan's Vision
        The Death of Hanrahan
      The Secret Rose [section title]
        The Crucifixion of the Outcast
        Out of the Rose
        The Wisdom of the King
        The Heart of the Spring

    The Curse of the Fires and of the Shadows
    The Old Men of the Twilight
    Where there is Nothing, there is God
    Proud Costello, MacDermot's Daughter and the Bitter Tongue
    Rosa Alchemica [section title and story]
    [This volume was not, as Wade indicates, merely an American edition of the 1913 text, but rather a new version with numerous revisions.]

X. *Early Poems and Stories* (London: Macmillan and Co., Limited, 1925) [Wade 147]
Early Poems and Stories (New York: The Macmillan Company, 1925) [Wade 148]
[These volumes contain the same stories in the same order, but Wade's comment that 'the contents . . . are the same' may obscure the fact that the American edition does not use the same sheets and contains many readings that differ from the English edition.]
The Secret Rose (1897) [section title]
    The Crucifixion of the Outcast
    Out of the Rose
    The Wisdom of the King
    The Heart of the Spring
    The Curse of the Fires and of the Shadows
    The Old Men of the Twilight
    Proud Costello, MacDermot's Daughter and the Bitter Tongue
Stories of Red Hanrahan [section title]
    Red Hanrahan
    The Twisting of the Rope
    Hanrahan and Cathleen, the Daughter of Hoolihan
    Red Hanrahan's Curse
    Hanrahan's Vision
    The Death of Hanrahan
Rose Alchemica [section title and story]
    The Tables of the Law
    The Adoration of the Magi
[Table of Contents thus gives 'Rosa Alchemica' special status as title of a section; but the separate section title page (p. 461) in the text gives all three stories equal status.]

XI. *Stories of Red Hanrahan and The Secret Rose* (London: Macmillan and Co., Limited, 1927) [Wade 157]
Stories of Red Hanrahan [section title]
[The poem 'Sailing to Byzantium' is included in this section; for full publishing history, see *Variorum Edition of the Poems of W. B. Yeats*, ed. Allt and Alspach, p. 407.]
    Red Hanrahan
    The Twisting of the Rope

Hanrahan and Cathleen the Daughter of Hoolihan
Red Hanrahan's Curse
Hanrahan's Vision
The Death of Hanrahan
The Secret Rose [section title]
The Crucifixion of the Outcast
Out of the Rose
The Wisdom of the King
The Heart of the Spring
The Curse of the Fires and of the Shadows
The Old Men of the Twilight
Proud Costello, MacDermot's Daughter and the Bitter Tongue

XII. *Mythologies* (1931–32 page-proofs: unpublished)
Mythologies (London: Macmillan & Co Ltd, 1959) [Wade 211P]
Mythologies (New York: The Macmillan Company, 1959) [Wade 211Q]
[All three volumes contain the same stories in the same order. Variant readings between the 1932 and 1959 versions are listed in Appendix 1.]
The Secret Rose (1897) [section title]
The Crucifixion of the Outcast
Out of the Rose
The Wisdom of the King
The Heart of the Spring
The Curse of the Fires and of the Shadows
Where there is Nothing, there is God
The Old Men of the Twilight
Proud Costello, MacDermot's Daughter, and the Bitter Tongue
Stories of Red Hanrahan (1897) [section title]
Red Hanrahan
The Twisting of the Rope
Hanrahan and Cathleen, the Daughter of Houlihan
Red Hanrahan's Curse
Hanrahan's Vision
The Death of Hanrahan
Rosa Alchemica, The Tables of the Law, and The Adoration of the Magi
(1897) [section title]
Rosa Alchemica
The Tables of the Law
The Adoration of the Magi

Collation of multiple copies of the various texts revealed no variants between
copies of a given edition.

The Secret Rose, Stories
by W. B. Yeats

Designed by Richard E. Rosenbaum.
Composed by The Composing Room of Michigan, Inc.
in 10 point Baskerville V.I.P., 2 points leaded,
with display lines in Baskerville.
Printed offset by Thomson/Shore, Inc. on
Warren's Olde Style, 60 pound basis.
Bound by John H. Dekker & Sons, Inc.
in Holliston book cloth.